AN INTRODUCTION TO THE OLD TESTAMENT

An
Introduction
to the
Old Testament

By EDWARD J. YOUNG

Professor of Old Testament
Westminster Theological Seminary

WILLIAM B. EERDMANS PUBLISHING CO.
GRAND RAPIDS, MICHIGAN

ISBN 0-8028-3310-1

Revised edition, March 1960
Reprinted, June 1963
Revised edition completely reset May 1964

Sixth printing, May 1973

49-50094

TO MY MOTHER

'*His truth shall be thy shield and buckler*'–PSALM 91:4b

PHOTOLITHOPRINTED BY GRAND RAPIDS BOOK MANUFACTURERS, INC.
GRAND RAPIDS, MICHIGAN

CONTENTS

6 CONTENTS

ABBREVIATIONS

LAP	J. Finegan, *Light from the Ancient Past*
LOT	S. R. Driver, *Introduction to the Literature of the Old Testament*
OR	Oesterley and Robinson, *Introduction to the Old Testament*
OSJ	N. Glueck, *The Other Side of the Jordan*
PG	Migne, *Patrologia Graeca*
PL	Migne, *Patrologia Latina*
POT	J. Orr, *The Problem of the Old Testament*
PrG	*The Presbyterian Guardian*
PRR	*The Presbyterian and Reformed Review*
PTR	*The Princeton Theological Review*
RB	*Revue Biblique*
RJ	N. Glueck, *The River Jordan*
SAT	*Die Schriften des Alten Testaments*
SI	E. J. Young, *Studies in Isaiah*
ThR	*Theologische Rundschau*
TTP	*Tractatus Theologico-Politicus*
WThJ	*The Westminster Theological Journal*
ZAW	*Zeitschrift für die alttestamentliche Wissenschaft*
ZDMG	*Zeitschrift für die deutschen morgenländischen Gesellschaft*
AV	Authorized Version
ET	English translation
Intro.	Introduction
LXX	The Septuagint
n.d.	no date
NT	The New Testament
OT	The Old Testament
RV	Revised Version
WC	Westminster Confession of Faith

PREFACE

IT is necessary at the outset to say a word about the scope and purpose of this book. It does not profess to be a General Introduction to the Old Testament, but restricts itself to the field of Special Introduction. Nor does it even seek to deal with this field in its entirety. The subject-matter is so vast that it cannot all be adequately considered within the limits of one volume. Hence, the present treatise has confined itself to the consideration of those aspects of Special Introduction which are most fundamental to the subject. It is, therefore, the literary characteristics of the books that are emphasized in these pages. What is the nature of these books? Are they compilations of more or less heterogeneous fragments, composed at various ages and finally pieced together by later editors or redactors? Or are they, as this present volume seeks to demonstrate, literary units which exhibit an inner harmony and underlying unity?

Since the treatment of this question (the correct answer to which is of such overwhelming importance to the well-being of the Church of Jesus Christ today) forms so large a portion of the subsequent discussion, it has been necessary to omit discussion of other problems which are not immediately germane to the purpose of this volume. Thus, for example, I have said virtually nothing about chronology and archaeology. Such questions as the date of the Exodus are tempting indeed, but they do not fall directly within the purview of this work. The discoveries at Nuzu have been mentioned, for example, only because, in my opinion, they help to refute that view of the nature of Genesis advocated by Julius Wellhausen. Nor have I devoted much attention to the question of inter-pretation, unless, as in the case of Job and the Song of Solomon, such attention will aid in the understanding of the structure of the book itself. And I have said little about the problem of the identity of the Servant of the Lord in the prophecy of Isaiah.

The few brief remarks on the Canon which are contained on pp. 31ff. are included in order that the reader may clearly understand the attitude towards the Old Testament which is herein adopted. Textual remarks, however, are for the most part omitted, for it seems to me that the question of the text is of such vast importance as to require a volume

9

in itself. To discuss textual questions in a cursory way is not very helpful, hence it seemed best to omit them, otherwise the size of the book would have grown beyond all proportion. The immediate need of the Church, moreover, is for a knowledge of the *contents* of the sacred Scriptures. The judicious remarks of Keil are appropriate even today: 'And although it is true, that it is of great advantage to institute an unprejudiced and careful comparison between the text of the Hebrew and the ancient versions, and also between the contents and spirit of the historical writings of the Old Testament, and the manner in which Hebrew history was afterwards treated by both Jews and Samaritans, inasmuch as it serves to confirm both theology and the church in their belief in the integrity and authenticity of our canonical books; yet the great want of our church, at the present day, is a clear comprehension of the meaning of the Old Testament, in its fulness and purity, in order that the God of Israel may again be universally recognized as the eternal God, whose faithfulness is unchangeable, the one living and true God, who performed all that he did to Israel for our instruction and salvation, having chosen Abraham and his seed to be his people, to preserve his revelations, that from him the whole world might receive salvation, and in him all the families of the earth be blessed.'[1]

This book is the outgrowth of a series of forty articles on Old Testament Introduction which appeared during 1947–1948 in *The Southern Presbyterian Journal*. This series was the result of a suggestion made by the Rev. John R. Richardson of Atlanta, Georgia. I have used these articles freely in preparing the following pages and have often quoted from them. It is a pleasure to make public acknowledgment of my indebtedness to the *Journal*, and also to its editor, the Rev. Henry B. Dendy, for permission thus to use these articles.

The approach to the Old Testament adopted in these pages is expressed in those words of the sacred Scriptures which Wilhelm Moeller used as the motto for his *Introduction*, 'Draw not nigh hither: put off thy shoes from off thy feet, for the place whereon thou standest is holy ground' (Ex. 3:5). This verse effectively disposes of the so-called 'scientific' method, which assumes that man can approach the facts of the universe, including the Bible, with a neutral mind, and pronounce a just judgment upon them. It is time that we cease to call such a method scientific. It is not scientific, for it does not take into consideration all the facts, and the basic fact it overlooks is that of God and His relation to the world which He has created. Unless we first think rightly about God we shall be in basic error about everything else.

[1] Preface to *Joshua*, ET, pp. v, vi.

In approaching the Bible, therefore, we need to remember that it is sacred ground. We must approach it with humble hearts, ready to hear what the Lord God says. The kaleidoscopic history of negative criticism is but further evidence that unless we do approach the Bible in a receptive attitude, we shall fail to understand it. Nor need we be ashamed to acknowledge that the words of Scripture are of God. For these words are resplendent with the glory of the divine majesty. The attempt to explain them as anything less than divine is one of the greatest failures that has ever appeared in the history of human thought. What courage this fact should give us! How we should thank God day by day, that, as Warfield has so admirably said, He 'has so loved us as to give us so pure a record of His will – God-given in all its parts, even though cast in the forms of human speech – infallible in all its statements – divine even to its smallest particle! I am far from contending that without such an inspiration there could be no Christianity. Without any inspiration we could have had Christianity; yea, and men could still have heard the truth, and through it been awakened, and justified, and sanctified, and glorified. The verities of our faith would remain historically proven true to us – so bountiful has God been in His fostering care – even had we no Bible; and through those verities, salvation. But to what uncertainties and doubts would we be the prey! – to what errors, constantly begetting worse errors, exposed! – to what refuges, all of them refuges of lies, driven! Look at those who have lost the knowledge of this infallible guide: see them evincing man's most pressing need by inventing for themselves an infallible church, or even an infallible Pope. Revelation is but half revelation unless it be infallibly communicated; it is but half communicated unless it be infallibly recorded. The heathen in their blindness are our witnesses of what becomes of an unrecorded revelation. Let us bless God, then, for His inspired word! And may He grant that we may always cherish, love and venerate it, and conform all our life and thinking to it! So may we find safety for our feet, and peaceful security for our souls.'[2]

In preparing this work I have sought to give due heed to what is written in modern Introductions which are based upon a viewpoint hostile to the one herein adopted. I have tried to give sympathetic attention to what has been written by Aage Bentzen, Eissfeldt, Cornill, Sellin, Oesterley and Robinson, Driver, Pfeiffer, and others. And I must acknowledge the tremendous debt that I owe to their writings. At the same time I have consulted the earlier writers, such as Eichhorn, Michaelis, De Wette, Ewald, Hitzig, and others. And I am impressed

[2] *The Inspiration and Authority of the Bible* (1948), pp. 441–442.

with the monotonous sameness of the case against the Bible. The arguments which Eichhorn, De Wette, Bertholdt, von Lengerke, and others raised long ago are just about the same as those which appear in the most recent Introductions. This fact, for fact it is, has strengthened me in the conviction that the so-called modern school of criticism is based upon certain philosophical presuppositions which, from the Christian point of view, are negative in character and reveal an utterly inadequate conception of God and revelation.

For this reason I look with sorrow upon the increasing ascendancy of the latest phase of the modern school, commonly known as *Formgeschichte*, but more accurately designated as the 'study of the history of tradition'. This facet of criticism is also a real ally of the entire neo-orthodox movement; and neo-orthodoxy, with its low view of the Bible, is, I believe, a foe of true exegesis and biblical study.

Neo-orthodoxy offers a dualism in that it makes a distinction between the historical and the supra-historical or supra-temporal. In this latter realm it places all the great truths of Christianity. The fall of man, for example, according to neo-orthodoxy, did not actually take place upon this earth at a definite point in history. Rather, we are told, it is an idea which belongs in the supra-historical realm. These views are usually set forth in orthodox terminology, but once they are stripped of their biblical clothing and Christian language, there remains only a barren dualism. The supra-temporal world of some modern writers bears a strong resemblance to the noumenal world of Immanuel Kant. In fact they are blood relatives. It is the old area of myth and legend. The ideas of Christianity are present, but the realities are gone. This is a shadow or phantom Christianity; it is not the real thing. By its acceptance of the Scriptures as an objectively given, divine revelation, the present volume would seek to do its part in staying the progress of this latest form of criticism.

In a work of this nature it is necessary to state views in a concise manner. Oftentimes only a conclusion can be given, whereas the reasons which have produced that conclusion must be omitted. Courtesy to opposing views would at times seem to demand a more extended treatment of some subjects. However, because of the nature of the work and the need for not increasing unduly its size, conciseness has been necessary. Nevertheless, I have throughout striven to be accurate and fairly to represent those views to which I am opposed.

At the end of the discussion of each book of the Old Testament there is a section calling attention to relevant literature on the book in question. The purpose of these sections is not to give an exhaustive list of books and articles – that I am not capable of doing – but merely to present certain works which are indispensable to a serious study of that particular book, and which will guide the student in his further investigations. I make no apology for including references to so many German works. The serious student cannot afford to neglect what is written in German and it is hoped that what is here mentioned will prove of help to those who wish to study further. An asterisk after the name of a book or magazine article in the text or bibliography indicates that the work mentioned is written from the standpoint of historic orthodox Protestantism.

One who seeks to write an Introduction immediately discovers how great is the debt which he owes to others. In this work I have tried to make specific acknowledgment of such debt whenever it has been necessary. Above all, I am indebted to my former teacher, Dr. Oswald T. Allis, who has deeply influenced my views of the Old Testament. Others to whom I also owe a debt for their teaching are Dr. Joseph Reider, Gurdon Oxtoby, Allan A. MacRae, Albrecht Alt, Joachim Begrich, Karl Elliger, and the late Dr. H. H. Powell. I would also express my gratitude to the publishers, the Wm. B. Eerdmans Company, for their patience in waiting for the manuscript and for giving me complete freedom in carrying out the work. Lastly, I am deeply obligated to Miss Ruth Stahl for help in preparing the typescript and to Mrs. Meredith G. Kline for the two charts in the volume.

1 *October*, 1949   E.J.Y.

PREFACE TO THE SECOND EDITION

In this present edition an effort has been made to bring the bibliographies up to date. It is, of course, impossible to do full justice to the subject. The student who is desirous of pursuing his studies further may consult the series of commentaries mentioned on pages 404ff. In these he will find ample references to further literature.

An attempt has also been made to bring the history of Old Testament study up to date by the addition of material to chapters one and eight. The view of the Old Testament adopted in the first edition, however, remains the same. May the God of truth be pleased to use this work, imperfect as it is, to strengthen the faith of His people in the Scriptures and in their understanding of this portion of His infallible Word.

E. J. Y.

ACKNOWLEDGMENTS

Acknowledgment is here made to the following publishers for permission to quote from the works which follow their names.

The American Schools of Oriental Research (Nelson Glueck, *The Other Side of Jordan*); Harper and Brothers (R. H. Pfeiffer, *Introduction to the Old Testament*; R. D. Wilson, *A Scientific Investigation of the Old Testament*); The Presbyterian and Reformed Publishing Co. (Oswald T. Allis, *The Five Books of Moses*; Benjamin B. Warfield, *The Inspiration and Authority of the Bible*); Fleming H. Revell Co. (J. Raven, *Old Testament Introduction*; R. D. Wilson, *Studies in the Book of Daniel*, Second Series); Charles Scribner's Sons (William H. Green, *The Higher Criticism of the Pentateuch*; *Biblical and Theological Studies by the Members of the Faculty of Princeton Theological Seminary*); The University of Georgia Press (S. A. Cartledge, *A Conservative Introduction to the Old Testament*); Jos. F. Wagner, Inc. (J. Steinmueller, *A Companion to Scripture Studies*, Vol. II, *Special Introduction to the Old Testament*); Westminster Theological Seminary (*The Infallible Word*); Yale University Press (Charles C. Torrey, *Pseudo-Ezekiel and the Original Prophecy*).

CHAPTER ONE

THE STUDY OF BIBLICAL INTRODUCTION

WHAT IS BIBLICAL INTRODUCTION?

THE English word 'introduction' is derived from the Latin *introducere* (to lead in, introduce) and denotes the action bringing or leading in. It also connotes initiation into the knowledge of a subject and particularly has reference to the material which paves the way for the study of some physical subject.

In its widest sense the term 'Biblical Introduction' refers to all those studies and disciplines which are preliminary to the study of the contents of the Bible. However, the word has come to be employed in a far more restricted sense. It may be regarded as a technical term and as such is borrowed from Germany where in comparatively recent times it was introduced as a designation of certain studies which are preparatory and preliminary to the interpretation of the Bible.[1] It is in this latter sense that the word is employed in this volume. Biblical Introduction, then, is *that science or discipline which treats of certain subjects that are preliminary to the study and interpretation of the contents of the Bible.* It is sometimes designated by the word 'isagogics'.

Introduction, as a discipline, belongs to that department of theological study which may be called the Bibliological, since it has to do directly with the Holy Scripture itself.[2] It is further divided into two parts, General and Special. General Introduction is concerned with topics which relate to the Bible as a whole, such as the Canon and text. Special Introduction, on the other hand, deals with subjects which refer to the

---

[1] The corresponding German terms are *Einleitung* and *Einführung*.

[2] This term is taken from A. Kuyper, *Encyclopaedia of Sacred Theology: Its Principles** (1898), pp. 627–636. Under the department of Bibliology I should also include: (1) The languages of the Bible and their cognates; (2) Biblical Exegesis; (3) Biblical History; (4) Biblical Theology; (5) Biblical Hermeneutics; (6) Biblical Antiquities, *i.e.*, the study of ancient civilizations and of archaeological research in relation to the Bible. Kuyper divides the theological curriculum into the following departments, which proceed 'of themselves from the organic disposition of theology' (p. 628): (1) Bibliological; (2) Ecclesiological; (3) Dogmatological; (4) Diaconiological.

separate parts or individual books of the Bible and so treats of such questions as unity, authorship, date, genuineness, and literary character. With the exception of a few introductory remarks this present work will confine itself to the subject of Special Introduction.

HISTORY OF THE STUDY OF OLD
TESTAMENT INTRODUCTION

a. The early Church period
The early Church Fathers were not concerned with questions of scientific Introduction as such. Their minds were chiefly occupied with the exposition of the contents of Scripture and with the formulation of doctrine. At times, however, they were compelled to turn their attention to the consideration of Introduction. When, for example, Porphyry attacked the book of Daniel and declared it to be a forgery, Jerome was ready with a reply, but this reply was written simply in connection with his own commentary and not as a formal Introduction to Daniel.

The first approach to an Introduction is probably to be found in the writing of Augustine, *De doctrina Christiana*. This work contains valuable information upon the subject of interpretation, and Augustine himself speaks of it as *praecepta tractandarum scripturarum*. In the first two books Augustine sets forth and develops the characteristics of correct interpretation of the Bible. Of considerable interest and importance is his refutation of the Donatists and their false views upon the subject as, for example, the unduly high estimate which they placed upon the Septuagint. Among these Donatists was one Tichonius Afer who had shortly before written a work setting forth seven rules which he believed were necessary for understanding the Scriptures. Augustine's refutation of these erroneous principles is quite valuable.

Jerome, in his opposition to Rufinus, expounded some principles of interpretation. His work, entitled *Libellus de optimo interpretandi genere*, is, however, far inferior to that of Augustine.

The first known use of the term 'Introduction' appears in the *Eisagoge eis tas theias graphas* (*i.e., Introduction to the Holy Scriptures*) written by a certain Adrian, of whom little is known. Adrian first discusses the characteristics of scriptural language, such as anthropomorphisms and anthropopathisms, peculiar expressions, metaphors, *etc.*, and then considers the form of the Scriptures. He distinguishes the historical from the prophetical, and classifies the prophetical form into words, visions, and symbolical actions. Lastly, he brings forth certain observations on interpretation.

In the sixth century the African Bishop Junilius composed two books, *De partibus legis divinae,* in which he attempted to classify the language of Scripture and to inculcate a more methodical understanding of it.

Of particular interest was the work of Marcus Aurelius Cassiodorus (died about 562) who wrote two books, *De institutione divinarum scripturarum,* in which he mentioned helps for the understanding of the Bible, and gave directions for copying manuscripts. In chapters 12–15 particularly, he discusses the Canon and study of the text; otherwise his work is more or less an Introduction to theology itself.

Two other works may be mentioned, the *Prolegomena* of Isidorus Hispalensis and the preliminary remarks *de libris canonicis et non canonicis* which are to be found in the *Postilla perpetua* of Nicholas of Lyra (died 1340).

All the above works were written under the influence of, and in general agreement with, the dominating tradition of the Church. For this reason they are more or less theological in character. Possibly the work of Junilius may be regarded as somewhat of an exception, for it contains some thoughts of an independent nature, and these are due to the influence of a certain priest of the school of Nisibis, named Paul. It must not be thought, however, that these early works were not scholarly. They were indeed scholarly, but the reason why they did not deal with the questions and problems that are today found in Introductions to the Old Testament was that these problems had not yet to any great extent been raised. (See pp. 108–114 for a survey of early criticism of the Bible.)

b. The Reformation and post-Reformation years

The close of the medieval period saw far-reaching changes even in the study of Biblical Introduction. In 1536 the *Isagoge ad sacras litteras* of Santes Paginus had appeared at Lyons, France, a work quite medieval in character. Very different, however, was the *Divine Library* (*Bibliotheca sacra*) of Francis Sixtus of Sierra which was published in 1566 and which, through republication, continued to exert a wide influence. In this book there is an attempt at a history of the biblical literature and particular emphasis upon the history of interpretation.

One phase of the Hebrew text which hitherto had virtually been ignored was now brought into prominence by the appearance in 1624 of Ludwig Cappellus' *Arcanum punctationis revelatum.* Cappellus showed that the vowel points of the text were not original but were of later origin. In this stand he was assisted by J. Morinus, whereas the opposite view was upheld by the two Buxtorfs, father and son.

In 1627, Rivetus, a Protestant scholar, published an Introduction to the entire Bible. His view of inspiration was so high that he considered all discussion of the questions of Special Introduction to be without meaning. Also maintaining a high view of the inspiration of Scripture was the Lutheran General Superintendent of East Friesland, Michael Walther, who seems to be the first to have made a clear distinction between General and Special Introduction. Therefore his work (*Officina biblica noviter adaperta*, 1636) may be regarded as the first Introduction in the modern sense.

The professor of theology at Zurich, J. H. Hottinger, issued in 1649 his *Thesaurus Philologicus seu Clavis* in which he had much to say about the manuscripts of the Bible, the individual books, commentaries, and versions. Hottinger was well acquainted with Arabic and rabbinical literature, and preserved numerous extracts from these sources, given in the words of the original authors. Hence his *Thesaurus* is of great value, even at the present day.

In the following decades a former student of Buxtorf, an adherent of the Reformed faith and a professor of Hebrew at Utrecht, John Leusden, published two important books. The first of these (*Philologus Hebraeus*, 1657) deals with the Canon and text of the Old Testament, and the second (*Philologus Hebraeomixtus*, 1663) discusses for the most part various translations.

Of particular importance was the appearance in 1657 of the famous Polyglot Bible edited by the Bishop of Chester, Brian Walton. So valuable were Walton's prolegomena that they were issued separately by Heidegger (1673). They discuss with great care the text and manuscripts of the Old Testament, and serve as an excellent manual of General Introduction.

Mention must be made also of August Pfeiffer, who edited the well-known *Critica Sacra* (1680), a veritable mine of information on the text and translations of the Bible, and of Johann Heinrich Heidegger, who issued his *Enchiridion Biblicum* in 1681.

From the above brief survey it will have become apparent that the Reformation brought to the fore the importance of studying the Hebrew text itself. This was a tremendous gain. The great Reformers Luther and Calvin both studied Hebrew, and doubtless did much to encourage its study. Hence, the works on Introduction which come from this period and soon thereafter reveal a deep interest in the all-important subject of the text. In the present writer's opinion some of these works also reveal a profound insight into the problems connected with such study. As Haevernick remarks, 'Certain portions of General Introduction, such as the history of the Text, were by these theologians of the seventeenth century cultivated with the happiest results.'[3] In the providence of God the Reformation was responsible for real advance in the study of Old Testament Introduction.

c. The rise of modern criticism
After the Reformation philosophical views began to make their appearance which were, in themselves, hostile to the supernaturalism of revealed Christianity. Some of these came to expression in the *Leviathan* of Thomas Hobbes (1651), the English deist. In this work Hobbes attacked some of the traditions of the origin and date of certain Old Testament books. Based upon somewhat similar anti-supernaturalistic principles was the *Tractatus Theologico-Politicus* of Benedict Spinoza (1670).

These works were followed by the large *Histoire Critique du Vieux Testament* of Richard Simon (1678), a Roman Catholic priest. Simon was born at Dieppe in 1638, and served for some time as a professor of philosophy at Juilly.

In the first section of his *Critical History* Simon discusses the age of the various books, particularly those of the Pentateuch. He asserts that the Pentateuch, in its present form, cannot be the work of Moses, and he regards the historical books as excerpts from public annals.

The last two sections, or books, as Simon calls them, contain much valuable information, and his discussions of the expositors up to his day are important. Toward Protestant writers, Simon is sometimes unjust, although he also criticizes the Vulgate.

The work was condemned by Bossuet, Bishop of Condum, and hence destroyed. However, it was reprinted, the best edition being generally regarded as the one supervised by Simon himself (under the guise of a Protestant theologian) and issued at Rotterdam in 1685.

It was to be expected that Simon's work should meet with opposition. Some of his statements regarding the value of the Scripture text were, to put it mildly, very unguarded. For example, he asserted that the Christian religion could have maintained itself by means of tradition without any Scripture, and that it was inconsequential whether or not the scriptural text was poorly preserved, since in any case appeal could be made to it only in so far as it agreed with ecclesiastical doctrine.

Among the replies to Simon was the reply made by Ezekiel Spanheim, who expressed doubts regarding the correctness of Simon's views of the historical books. Particularly important, however, was the work of Joh.

[3] *Intro.*, ET, p. 10.

Clericus (Le Clerc), *Sentiments de quelques Théologiens de Hollande sur l'Histoire Critique du V. T. par R. Simon* (1685), in which the author, an Arminian professor at Amsterdam, attacked Simon for unfair treatment of Protestant writers. Le Clerc, however, would date the Pentateuch and historical books even later than Simon did. Simon replied with vehemence and passion.

The way had now been paved for the introduction of doubts about the trustworthiness of the Old Testament Scriptures. Hobbes and Spinoza had clearly written under the influence of non-Christian philosophy and Simon, although a Roman Catholic, nevertheless wrote from a standpoint which even Catholics recognized to be inimical to their own position.

There was still life and vigour in the Protestant Church, however, and in His good providence the Lord raised up a strong defender of the Faith. This was Johann Gottlob Carpzov, a professor of Hebrew at Leipzig, who issued two remarkable works: *Introductio ad Libros Canonicos* (1714–21), and *Critica Sacra* (1724). Carpzov's writing is apologetic and serves to expose the positions of Spinoza, Le Clerc, Simon, and others. But it also contains deep insight into the nature of Introduction, and has rightly been characterized by Haevernick[4] as a 'masterpiece of Protestant science'.

Simon's work bore fruit in the writings of J. S. Semler, professor of theology at Halle (died 1791), who carried out the principles adopted by Simon in a thoroughly negative spirit. He seems to have been in sympathy with the desire to regard the human mind as a law unto itself. But, whereas he undermined received views, he had nothing positive to offer in their stead. His work may be characterized as having a destructive tendency.

A partial rebellion from this position appeared in the work of the poet Joh. Gottfried Herder (died 1803). Herder had some appreciation of the literary beauty of the Old Testament, and this he endeavoured to convey in his writings. He was, however, far removed from the true religious spirit of Scripture. His ideas were carried out by Joh. Gottfried Eichhorn, who prepared an *Introduction to the Old Testament* (1780–83). For the most part, Eichhorn held to traditional views, although he was influenced by the advancing tide of criticism. Although he sought to call attention to the literary beauty of the Old Testament, he did not reveal a genuine understanding of its supernatural character. Hence, Eichhorn's work contributed to the result that the Scriptures came to be regarded

---

[4] *Op. cit.*, p. 12.

more and more merely as the national literature of the Hebrews, and the study of Holy Scripture as such was more neglected.

Somewhat similar was the undertaking of J. D. Michaelis (1787). However, his work was not completed – he treated only the introduction to the Pentateuch and Job. Haevernick's comments are to the point: 'In learning and depth, J. D. Michaelis was just the man to encounter Eichhorn on this field; but he was inferior to the latter in taste and culture, and he wanted a living, penetrating sense of the inner truths of Scripture.'[5]

d. The nineteeth century

In order rightly to appraise the attitude toward the science of Old Testament Introduction which appeared in the nineteenth century, it is necessary to understand somewhat the spirit of the day and the philosophical movements which were then present. The eighteenth century had witnessed the rise of an exaltation of human reason.[6] In the Reformation there had been a revolt against the arrogated authority of the Roman Catholic Church, and now men would revolt also from the authority of the Bible itself. The age was known as the Enlightenment. And Immanuel Kant had spoken of that phase of the Enlightenment known as Neology, as man's exodus from his self-encumbered minority.[7]

The term 'Enlightenment', however, when judged from the Christian point of view, is utterly erroneous. If man is the creature of God, it follows that he can be free and enlightened only when he acts in accordance with the revelation which God has given him. To reject external revelation and to regard the human mind as a law unto itself is not to become enlightened but is to fall into the grossest of deceptions. Since man is created by God, he cannot live without God. To exalt the human reason, as though it in itself were the final arbiter of all things, is in reality to substitute the creature for the Creator.

The nineteenth century suffered greatly because of the barrenness of eighteenth-century theology and philosophy. Hence many Introductions of this century were written under the assumption that the Old Testament was merely a human book and should be treated as other human books. Since we intend to discuss with considerable detail the

[5] *Op. cit.*, p. 14.
[6] For a survey of the development of thought from Wolfianism to Neology and from Neology to Rationalism the student should consult Karl Aner, *Die Theologie der Lessingzeit* (Halle, 1929).
[7] 'Ausgang des Menschen aus seiner selbstverschuldeten Unmündigkeit', in *Berliner Monatschrift* (1784). By the word *Unmündigkeit* Kant means, '*das Unvermögen, sich seines Verstandes ohne Leitung eines Anderen zu bedienen.*'

development of Pentateuchal criticism during the nineteenth century, we shall now do nothing more than call attention to a few of its outstanding authors of Introductions.

1. Wilhelm Martin Lebrecht de Wette (1780–1849) launched a vigorous attack against the traditional views of the authorship of Old Testament books. His work was written from a rationalistic standpoint, and was somewhat negative in its conclusions.

2. Heinrich Ewald (died 1875), like de Wette, rejected received views. His writings, however, were more positive in character, and he endeavoured to supply a substitute judgment. Ewald may be said to have founded a school, which is also represented to an extent in the works of Ferdinand Hitzig.

3. Ernst Wilhelm Hengstenberg, H. Ch. Haevernick, and C. F. Keil voiced protests against the 'critical' treatments of the Old Testament. These men were believing scholars who wrote with high regard for the integrity and trustworthiness of the Bible. Their writings have had great influence, particularly in England and America.

4. Friedrich Bleek (1793–1859), a former pupil of de Wette, Neander, and Schleiermacher, wrote a mediating Introduction. His work appeared in 1865, and from the second edition, 1869, an English translation was made (*An Introduction to the Old Testament*, 1869, translated by G. H. Venables). It contains much that is useful and that serves as a corrective against extreme criticism. However, even this excellent work is not completely satisfactory, for it yields too much to the negative position.

5. K. H. Graf first gave clear expression in the so-called modern school. This school, however, greatly gained in impetus and influence through the labours of Julius Wellhausen and Abraham Kuenen. Hence it is popularly referred to as the school of Graf-Kuenen-Wellhausen. In English it was represented by the lectures of William Robertson Smith, *The Old Testament in the Jewish Church* (1881). This school of thought posits an evolutionary development in the religious life of Israel. It well agrees with the liberal view of the New Testament and the Ritschlian school of theology, and rests upon the philosophical position of Hegel. It stands in clear-cut antithesis to the historic Christian religion.

6. Samuel Rolles Driver (1891) wrote one of the greatest works on Introduction. For the most part this book follows the tenets of the school of Graf-Kuenen-Wellhausen, but it is characterized by sobriety and restraint. At times it endeavours to follow a mediating course, and hence it has exercised wide influence.

7. The modern critical school found opponents even among those who

rejected the traditional Christian view of the Old Testament. Such were Eduard Riehm (*Einleitung in das Alte Testament*, 1889), and, to an extent, F. E. Koenig (*Einleitung in das Alte Testament*, 1893) and W. W. Baudissin (*Einleitung in die Bücher des Alten Testaments*, 1901).

e. The twentieth century

It is difficult to characterize the study of Introduction during the twentieth century. A reaction against certain tenets of classical Wellhausenism has appeared in the writings of Herman Gunkel (1862–1932) and Hugo Gressmann (1877–1927). These two scholars will probably always be associated as the two leading exponents of the school of source-criticism. By an endeavour to discover the situation in life which called forth individual utterances, and by a comparison of ancient mythology, Gressmann and Gunkel have in reality cast a severe blow against certain tenets of the modern critical school. Their influence has been quite widespread, and their position has received classic expression in *Die Schriften des Alten Testaments* (1911).

Of importance has been the English translation (1907) of Carl Cornill's *Introduction* (first appeared in 1891). Cornill may be regarded as a representative of the school of Wellhausen. The same viewpoint has found expression in the work of Harlan Creelman (*An Introduction to the Old Testament Chronologically Arranged*, 1917). Mention must be made also of Julius A. Bewer (*The Literature of the Old Testament*, 1912), who likewise sets forth classical Wellhausenism.

The year 1934 witnessed the appearance of three Introductions, two of which were quite similar in nature. Otto Eissfeldt (*Einleitung in das Alte Testament*) seeks to classify the literature of the Old Testament, assigning it to various categories (*Gattungen*), and endeavours to trace the development (the literary prehistory) of the various books. Eissfeldt's work shows the influence of Wellhausen very greatly and also that of the school of Gunkel-Gressmann. He seems to have no adequate conception of revelation, but rather regards the literature of the Old Testament merely as of human origin.

Somewhat similar is the volume of W. O. E. Oesterley and Theodore H. Robinson (*An Introduction to the Books of the Old Testament*). The distinguishing characteristic of this work is the attention which it pays to metrical structure in the Old Testament. It attempts, however, to account for the Scriptures merely as human literature, and follows essentially the viewpoint of the dominant critical school.

Very different is the book of Wilhelm Moeller (*Einleitung in das Alte Testament*). Moeller is a believer in the trustworthiness of Scripture, and presents cogent arguments in defence of his position. His work, while somewhat brief, nevertheless has much value.

The greatest Introduction to appear in the English language during this century is that of R. H. Pfeiffer (*Introduction to the Old Testament*, 1941). Pfeiffer's book is characterized by thoroughness and careful scholarship. Furthermore, it exhibits a candour that is most pleasing. For example, a writer who is willing to assert that three of the most influential writings in the Old Testament were technically fraudulent (p. 745) is a man who is worth listening to. However, the book is basically anti-Christian; indeed, it serves as an apologetic for an anti-theistic viewpoint.[8] Thus, for example, Pfeiffer writes, 'This traditional theory, by accepting the book [*i.e.*, Daniel] at its face value, necessarily presupposes the reality of the supernatural and the divine origin of the revelations it contains. Such miracles [as those recorded in Daniel] lie outside the realm of historical facts. . . . Historical research can deal only with authenticated facts which are within the sphere of natural possibilities and must refrain from vouching for the truth of supernatural events. The historicity of the Book of Daniel is an article of faith, not an objective scientific truth. . . . In a historical study of the Bible, convictions based on faith must be deemed irrelevant, as belonging to subjective rather than objective knowledge' (p. 755).

The author's candour in speaking thus clearly is admirable. The position itself, however, is basically anti-Christian. Yet it is probably safe to say that this viewpoint underlies most present-day study of the Old Testament.

The Danish Introduction of Aage Bentzen (1941) was translated into English in 1948, and the second edition in 1952. This able work has made available in English a historico-critical approach which pays great attention to a study of the supposed forms of the Old Testament literature.[9]

Great stress is laid upon the value of the oral tradition which supposedly underlay the Old Testament books in the Introduction of Ivan Engnell, the chief representative of the so-called Uppsala School.[10] This work has not yet been translated into English.[11]

In 1945 an Introduction written by A. F. Puukko appeared in the

---

[8] For a lengthy review of this *Introduction* by the present writer see *WThJ*, V, pp. 107–115.

[9] *Cf.* the discussion between Professor Bentzen and the present writer in *The Evangelical Quarterly*, 1951, pp. 81–89.

[10] *Gamla Testamentet, en traditions-historisk inledning*, I (1945).

[11] See p. 149 for a discussion of this viewpoint.

Finnish language.[12] It presents a literary-critical approach to the Old Testament. A second and revised edition of Arthur Weiser's *Einleitung* was published in 1949. This work, which expresses Weiser's basic viewpoint, is a study of the oral tradition and the written literature, and includes a discussion of the apocryphal and pseudepigraphical literature.

In 1950 H. H. Rowley issued a compact volume entitled *The Growth of the Old Testament* in which the reader is given a clear statement of the literary criticism of the Old Testament books. In this same year the eighth edition of Sellin's *Einleitung* appeared, distinguished particularly for its treatment of literary types.

A strong voice in defence of the supernatural origin and absolute trustworthiness of the Old Testament was raised in 1952 with the appearance of a rather thorough work, *Oud Testamentische Kanoniek*, by G. Ch. Aalders. This work is on the whole conservative, but it does manifest some tendencies, particularly in its discussion of the Pentateuch and Daniel, which, in the opinion of the present writer, tend to modify its basic conservative position.

Of particular interest and value is G. W. Anderson's *A Critical Introduction to the Old Testament* (1959). In this book the reader will find a discussion of the most recent phases of Old Testament scholarship. The same is true of *A Light to the Nations* by Norman K. Gottwald (1959). This latter work is an interpretative history of Israel and of the writings of the Old Testament, which presents the viewpoints of negative criticism.

From Roman Catholic circles several Introductions of varying merit have been issued. J. E. Steinmueller's *A Companion to Scripture Studies* (II, 1942), is written from a conservative standpoint and with full awareness of the significance of the Old Testament as a special divine revelation. Of a different nature is the *Introductio Specialis in Vetus Testamentum* by H. Höpfl (revised edn. 1946). In some instances this work rejects the conservative view of the authorship of biblical books. From Spain has come a rather popular work by A. Ulecia, *Introducciòn General a la Sagrada Biblia* (1950). A strongly conservative Introduction is *Introductio in libros sacros Veteris Testamenti* by B. Mariani (1958). With minor exceptions Mariani upholds the Mosaic authorship of the Pentateuch.

Among writers in the Eastern (Rumanian) Orthodox Church we may note the Introduction written in Rumanian by V. Prelipcean, N. Neaga, and G. Barna (1955). This is a thoroughly conservative and scholarly work.

---

[12] *Vanhan Testamentin johdanto-oppi.*

Two works from the Protestant Church represent a conservative approach to the Old Testament. Merrill Unger's *An Introductory Guide to the Old Testament* (1951) is of a popular nature, and Moeller's *Einleitung* (revised edn. 1959), written in German, is a fine statement of the conservative position.

HOW SHALL WE REGARD THE OLD TESTAMENT?

The brief survey just given, particularly with respect to the nineteenth and twentieth centuries, should make it clear that the study of Introduction has been approached from various standpoints.

There have been those who have held an extremely low view of Scripture. They have considered it as nothing more than the national literature of the Hebrews, a purely human literary production upon a level with other similar literary productions of antiquity. This position is unsatisfactory because it is in basic error. It regards the Bible as a book of only human origin, whereas, as a matter of fact, the Bible is basically a book of divine origin.

There are those who, in their study of Introduction, wish to limit themselves to the human element in the Bible. They apparently believe that it is possible to neglect entirely the question of the inspiration and divinity of the Bible, and to limit their consideration to what might be called an 'empirico-scientific method'. Let it be said with all positiveness that this cannot satisfactorily be done, and those who adopt such a method find themselves in essential agreement with those who baldly assert that the Bible is only a human production and nothing more.

For one thing, such a limitation is not scientific. A truly scientific method of investigation will take into account *all* facts, and will not limit itself in advance to a consideration of only those facts which may be known through the senses. Why should so-called facts which are discovered by the senses be regarded as alone legitimate?

A truly scientific method of study will not thus circumscribe itself. In any worthwhile study of Introduction we must consider all facts, the fact of God and His revelation as well as the so-called empirical facts. Not to consider *all* facts is to fail at the outset.

There are those who apparently think that it is possible to approach the Bible with a neutral attitude. Their position seems to be, 'Let us study Scripture as we would any other book. Let us subject it to the same tests as we do other writings. If it proves to be the Word of God, well and good, but, if not, let us accept the fact.' Essentially, this position is no different from the first two. The so-called neutral attitude towards the

Bible is in reality not neutral at all, for it begins by rejecting the lofty claims of divinity which the Bible makes and it assumes that the human mind of itself can act as judge of divine revelation. This is, in effect, to substitute the mind of man as ultimate judge and reference-point in place of God Himself.

The viewpoint adopted in this present work is that the Old Testament is the very Word of the God of truth. It is also the work of men. 'Holy men of God spake as they were moved by the Holy Ghost' (2 Pet. 1:21b). In His inscrutable wisdom God chose and prepared for the task of writing those human agents whom He desired to speak His will. Then in mysterious fashion His Spirit wrought upon them, so that what they wrote, although in a very true sense their own, was nevertheless precisely what the Spirit of God desired. The Bible, therefore, in one sense may be regarded as a human book. Basically, however, it is divine, and God Himself is its Author.

How may we know that the Bible is the Word of God? There are, of course, many reasons for believing this. The Bible itself evidences its divinity so clearly that he is without excuse who disbelieves. It bears within it the marks of this divinity. Thus, its subject-matter – its glorious doctrine of the living and true God, the Creator of heaven and earth, of man's fall into sin and of the wondrous redemption which God has wrought for man – clearly and cogently testifies to its divine origin. The same is true of all its other 'incomparable excellencies'.[13] They are without parallel in any other writing, and show most convincingly that the Bible is in a unique sense the Word of God.

That, however, which brings full persuasion and assurance that Scripture is divine is the work of God the Holy Spirit by and with the Word, bearing witness in our hearts. God testifies to us that He is the Author of the Bible. To put it simply, we believe that the Bible is from God because God has told us so.[14] It is only God who can adequately testify to that which He has spoken.

With respect to the Old Testament, particular stress should be placed upon the attitude and words of Jesus Christ. There are those who say that our Lord accommodated Himself to the thought of His day. When, for example, He said that Moses wrote of Him, He was, so we are told, merely speaking in a manner which His contemporaries would understand. Or, it is maintained, He did not intend to pronounce any judg-

---

[13] WC I; V.
[14] For an exposition of the doctrine of the inward testimony of the Holy Spirit see *IW*, pp. 40–52.

ment upon the controversial questions which now engage those who study the Old Testament.

With both these attitudes we find ourselves in hearty disagreement. Jesus Christ is the Truth, and when He spoke, He spoke words of truth. It is true that in His human nature our Lord's knowledge was limited, as may clearly be seen from a passage such as Mark 13:32. But this does not mean that He was subject to error. As man His knowledge may have been limited, but, as far as it went, it was true. Our Lord did not speak upon those subjects of which in His human nature He had no knowledge. All that He spoke was true. If our Lord was in error in questions of criticism and authorship, how do we know that He was not in error when He spoke of His saving death at Jerusalem? Admit error at one point, and we must admit it all along the line. In this present work the authority of Jesus Christ is accepted without reserve. He was, we believe, correct when He spoke of His substitutionary death, and He was correct when He spoke upon the nature of the Old Testament. What, then, did Jesus Christ actually have to say regarding the Old Testament?[15]

It must be apparent to anyone who reads the Gospels carefully that Jesus Christ, in the days of His flesh, looked upon that body of writings which is known as the Old Testament as constituting an organic whole. To Him the Scriptures were a harmonious unit which bore a unique message and witness. Nothing could be farther from the truth than to say that He thought of the Scriptures as merely a group of writings which were in conflict among themselves and which bore no particular relationship one to another. This may easily be seen by the consideration of one or two relevant passages.

When, for example, the Jews took up stones to cast at our Lord, believing Him to have been guilty of blasphemy, He opposed them by an appeal to the Old Testament (cf. Jn. 10:31-36). In this appeal He quoted Psalm 82:6, and assumed the truth of what is stated in the Psalm by asserting that 'the scripture cannot be broken'. The force of His argument is very clear, and may be paraphrased as follows: 'What is stated in this verse from the Psalms is true because this verse belongs to that body of writings known as Scripture, and the Scripture possesses an authority so absolute in character that it cannot be broken.' When Christ here employs the word 'Scripture', He has in mind, therefore, not a particular verse in the Psalms, but rather the entire group of writings of which this one verse is a part.

[15] What follows from here to the end of the chapter is quoted from an article by the author, 'The Authority of the Old Testament', in *IW*, pp. 55-70. See also J. W. Wenham, *Our Lord's View of the Old Testament* (London, 1953).

That Christ regarded the Scriptures as constituting a unit is also seen when, at the time of His betrayal, He acknowledged the need for His arrest and sufferings if the Scriptures were to be fulfilled (*cf.* Mt. 26:54). Indeed, He was concerned that the Scriptures must be fulfilled. To Him it was more important that this should take place than that He should escape from arrest. By His use of the plural, He made it abundantly clear that there existed a plurality of writings, each of which had this in common with the others: that it belonged to the category of Scripture and that, taken as a whole, it had direct reference to the sufferings which He was about to undergo. Thus, by His manner of speech, did He bear witness to the fact that the Old Testament is an organic whole and so, by implication, to the consent and harmony of all its parts.

This testimony of our Lord to the nature of the Old Testament is by no means an isolated phenomenon. Rather, not only is it made expressly clear by certain individual passages (*cf.* Mt. 21:42; 22:29; Mk. 14:49; Jn. 6:45; 15:25), but also it underlies His entire treatment of the Scriptures. In adopting such an attitude Christ placed Himself squarely in opposition to those views, so prevalent in our day, which look upon the Old Testament as merely a collection of more or less loosely related, heterogeneous material, a library rather than a book.

Not only did Jesus Christ look upon the Old Testament as forming an organic whole but He also believed that both as a unit and in its several parts it was finally and absolutely authoritative. To it appeal might be made as to the ultimate authority. Its voice was final. When the Scriptures spoke, man must obey. From them there was no appeal. When, for example, the tempter would have the Son of God command the stones to be made bread, he was silenced by the assertion, 'It is written.' This appeal to the Old Testament ended the matter. That which is written was for Christ the deciding voice.

Not only, however, was such authority attributed to the Scriptures as a unit and to particular verses or utterances, but it was also extended to include individual words and even letters. This is shown by a statement such as the following, 'It is easier for heaven and earth to pass, than for one tittle of the law to fail' (Lk. 16:17). In some instances Christ based His argument merely upon a word, as for example when, seeking to refute the Jews, He singled out the word 'gods' in Psalm 82:6. A careful reading of the Gospels will reveal the fact that the Scriptures of the Old Testament, in all their parts, were believed by Christ to be authoritative.

Is there, however, any dependable method by which one may determine precisely what books Christ regarded as belonging to the category of Scripture? Is it not possible that some books upon which He placed the stamp of His approval have been irretrievably lost, whereas others which would not have been recognized by Him are now looked upon as part of the Old Testament?

It may with confidence be said that Christ recognized as canonical the same books as those which comprise the Old Testament as we have it today. Of course, He did not leave a list of these books, nor did He expressly quote from each of them. Hence, we must look elsewhere for evidence to support our statement.

From our Lord's reference to the Old Testament it is possible to determine the extent of the Canon which He recognized. He quoted abundantly, and the nature of His quotation often lends its sanction not only to the book in which the quotation is found, but even to the entire collection itself. The force of this impresses itself upon us more and more as we notice how Christ chose from this and that book statements which would enforce and support His arguments. It appears that His earthly life was steeped in the teaching of the Old Testament. Not only were whole verses frequently upon His lips, but also His own speech was clothed with expressions from the Scriptures.

There is, however, one passage in particular in which He gives a clue as to the extent of the Old Testament of His day. After His resurrection He said to His companions, 'These are the words which I spake unto you, while I was yet with you, that all things must be fulfilled, which were written in the law of Moses, and in the prophets, and in the psalms, concerning me' (Lk. 24:44). Here He clearly recognizes that there are three divisions to the Old Testament, and that the things which were written in each of these divisions must be fulfilled. The designation 'law of Moses' refers, of course, to the first five books of the Bible; the 'prophets' includes the historical books and the works of the great writing prophets. As to the identity of these two divisions there would seem to be little doubt.

What, however, did Christ mean by 'psalms'? Did He thereby intend to refer to all the books in the third division of the Canon, or did He merely have in mind the book of Psalms itself? The latter alternative, we think, is probably correct. Christ singled out the book of Psalms, it would appear, not so much because it was the best-known and most influential book of the third division, but rather because in the Psalms there were many predictions about Himself. This was the Christological book *par excellence* of the third division of the Old Testament Canon.

Most of the books of this third division do not contain direct messianic prophecies.[16] Hence, if Christ had used a technical designation to indicate this third division, He would probably have weakened His argument to a certain extent. But by the reference to the Psalms He directs the minds of His hearers immediately to that particular book in which occur the greater number of references to Himself.

This does not necessarily mean that He did not make reference to the messianic prophecies which appear, for example, in the book of Daniel. Nor does it mean that the third division of the Canon was not yet complete. It would appear, rather, that by His language Christ set the seal of His approval upon the books of the Old Testament which were in use among the Jews of His day, and that this Old Testament consisted of three definite divisions, the Law, the Prophets and a third division which as yet had probably not received any technical designation.[17]

THE CANONIZATION OF THE SCRIPTURES

When Christ thus set the seal of His approval upon the Jewish Scriptures of His day, it meant that He considered those Scriptures to be divinely inspired. When, however, did the Jewish people who lived before Him so come to regard them? To this question many answers are given, and it is to this question that we must now direct our attention.

By the term 'canonical writings' is meant those writings which constitute the inspired rule of faith and life. Canonical books, in other words, are those books which are regarded as divinely inspired. The criterion of a book's canonicity, therefore, is its inspiration. If a book has been inspired of God, it is canonical, whether accepted by men as such or not. It is God and not man who determines whether a book is to belong to the Canon. Therefore, if a certain writing has indeed been the product of divine inspiration, it belongs in the Canon from the moment of its composition.

[16] The following books are reckoned as belonging to the Writings or *Hagiographa*: the three poetical books, Psalms, Proverbs, Job; the five *Megilloth*: Song of Solomon, Ruth, Lamentations, Ecclesiastes, Esther; and Daniel, Ezra, Nehemiah, 1 and 2 Chronicles. Apparently, however, this classification has not always been held. See R. D. Wilson, 'The Rule of Faith and Life', in *The Princeton Theological Review*, XXVI, No.3, July 1928; Solomon Zeitlin, *An Historical Study of the Canonization of the Hebrew Scriptures* (Philadelphia, 1933).

[17] There is every reason for believing that the Canon of Christ and the Canon of the Jews of His day were identical. There is no evidence whatever of any dispute between Him and the Jews as to the canonicity of any Old Testament book. What Christ opposed was not the Canon which the Pharisees accepted but the oral tradition which would make this Canon void. From statements in Josephus and the Talmud, it is possible to learn the extent of the Jewish Canon of Christ's day.

That this is so appears from the very nature of the case. If man alone were capable in his own strength of identifying accurately the Word of God, then man would be equal in knowledge with God. If God is truly God, the Creator of all things and utterly independent of all that He has created, it follows that He alone can identify what He has spoken. He alone can say, 'This is My Word, and that has not proceeded from My mouth.'

Hence, it will be seen that the word 'Canon' means far more than merely a list of books. If this low view of the meaning of the word be adopted, we by no means even begin to do justice to the various factors which are involved. The reason why many discussions of the problem of the Canon are unsatisfactory is that they proceed upon the assumption that the Canon is merely a list of books which the Jewish people itself came to regard as divine, and they neglect the theological aspect of the question almost entirely. To the Christian, however, 'Canon' has a far higher connotation; to him it constitutes the inspired rule of faith and practice. The writings of the Bible claim to be the Word of God, and their contents are in entire harmony with this claim. The Christian recognizes the Scriptures as inspired, because they are such, and bear in themselves the evidences of their divinity. Basic, therefore, to any consideration of how man comes to recognize the Bible as God's Word is the fact that it is indeed divine.

Of course, man, unaided, cannot so recognize the Scriptures, for the mind of man is affected by sin. Only God can identify for man that Word which has proceeded out of His mouth. Hence men recognize the Word of God, because God has told them what His Word is. God has spoken to them of His truth. He has identified it for them. Of great importance, therefore, for a proper understanding of the entire problem is the doctrine of the inward testimony of the Holy Spirit.

This doctrine is one which has been much abused and it is indeed a very mysterious doctrine. It does not mean that this inward testimony can be used as a criterion to determine the canonicity of a certain verse or chapter or even book. It does mean, however, that the believer possesses a conviction that the Scriptures are God's Word, and that this conviction is a conviction which has been implanted in the mind by the Third Person of the Trinity. This conviction has been the possession of God's people ever since the first portion of Scripture was committed to writing. There can be no doubt that the true Israel immediately recognized God's revelation.

There are also secondary evidences, however, which corroborate the inward testimony of the Spirit and which have led believers to accept the

Scriptures. For one thing, the fact that many devout men have together declared their belief in the Bible is in itself cogent evidence. Then, too, the character of the contents, the 'heavenly matter' contained in these writings indeed possesses evidencing value. Likewise, the 'majority of the style' and particularly the 'consent of all the parts' will impress themselves upon the believer. In addition to the 'many other incomparable excellencies, and the entire perfection' of the Bible, there remains the testimony of the Bible to itself.

These points will perhaps be more clearly understood if we examine the history of the collection of the Old Testament Scriptures. No complete history of this process has been preserved, but certain important statements are made in the Bible itself, and these statements must be taken into consideration in any discussion of the subject.

a. The Law of Moses
In the first place, therefore, we turn to the first five books of the Old Testament, which are commonly known as the Pentateuch or the Law of Moses. Traditionally, by both Jews and Christians, Moses has been regarded as the author of these books. We believe that tradition is in this point correct, and that the essential Mosaic authorship of the Pentateuch may be maintained. There may indeed be certain few minor additions, such as the account of Moses' death, which were inserted into the Pentateuch under divine inspiration by a later editor, but this by no means runs counter to the common tradition that Moses is the author of these books. When these writings had been completed they were accepted by the devout in Israel as divinely authoritative. Express provision was made for their protection and custody. 'And it came to pass, when Moses had made an end of writing the words of this law in a book, until they were finished, that Moses commanded the Levites, that bare the ark of the covenant of Jehovah, saying, Take this book of the law, and put it by the side of the ark of the covenant of Jehovah your God, that it may be there for a witness against thee' (Dt. 31:24–26). The priests were commanded to read the Law to the people: 'Thou shalt read this law before all Israel in their hearing' (Dt. 31:11). When Israel would have a king, that king was to possess a copy of the Law (Dt. 17:18, 19). Joshua was commanded to guide the people in the light of the Law. 'This book of the law shall not depart out of thy mouth, but thou shalt meditate thereon day and night, that thou mayest observe to do according to all that is written therein' (Jos. 1:8).

Throughout the history of Israel the Law was regarded as divinely authoritative. David charged Solomon to give his obedience thereto.

B

Jeroboam was denounced because of disobedience to God's commands. Some of the kings of Judah are particularly commended because of their adherence to the Law, whereas others are condemned for their lack of such adherence. The very exile itself is considered by the sacred writers to be due to infractions of the statutes and the covenant which God made with Israel's ancestors. And on the return from exile the Israelites governed themselves in accord with the Law of Moses.

It will be seen, then, that upon the testimony of the only contemporary writings of ancient Israel, the Law of Moses was regarded from the earliest times as divinely inspired and authoritative. It was final. What it commanded was to be obeyed, and what it prohibited was not to be done. Such is the picture which the Old Testament itself presents, if it be accepted as it stands.

b. The Prophetical books

Not only was the Law of Moses regarded as God's Word, but the words and writings of the prophets were also so considered. In Deuteronomy it had been said of the prophets that God would put His 'words in his [*i.e.*, the prophet's] mouth, and he shall speak unto them all that I shall command him' (Dt. 18:18). The prophets themselves believed that they spoke in the name of the Lord and that they declared His very Word to men. How frequently do they exclaim, 'The word of the Lord came unto me, saying. . . ,' 'Thus saith the Lord. . . ,' 'Hear the word of the Lord!' The message which they proclaimed, therefore, was, according to their own testimony, not a message of their own devising, but the actual Word of God.

The prophets demanded that same obedience to their words as was due to the Law of God. They had no hesitation in candidly telling Israel that her calamities and misfortunes had befallen her, not only because of her disobedience to the Law, but also because she had transgressed their words. And they frankly assert that, unless she gives heed to their message, dire distress and suffering will come upon her. The evidence to support these statements is not isolated. Rather, if one will read the prophetical writings to see what is the testimony of the prophets to their authority, he will note how frequently and consistently they assert that they are declaring the final, absolute Word of Jehovah. (*Cf.*, *e.g.*, Is. 8:5; 31:4; Je. 3:6; 13:1; Ezk. 21:1; Am. 3:1; 7:1ff.; *etc.*)

If, therefore, we are to accept the testimony of the Bible itself, we see that the words of the prophets were regarded in Israel as authoritative, decisive, and inspired. Consequently, it may easily be understood how these words in their written form would be preserved in the Church and regarded as the Word of Jehovah.

It is true that the Old Testament does not relate how the books which are commonly called the Former Prophets (*i.e.*, Joshua, Judges, 1 and 2 Samuel, 1 and 2 Kings) came to be included with the other canonical books. However, the answer to this question, it would appear, is readily at hand. The authors of these books, whoever they may have been, were men who occupied the office of prophet. In ancient Israel this was a special and unique office. The prophet was an Israelite who acted as a mediator between God and man. Just as the priest represented the people before God, so the prophet represented God before the people. In a very special sense, therefore, he was the recipient of revelation. God so implanted His words in the prophet's mouth, that the resultant delivered message was the actual Word of God.

Not all prophets wrote down their messages. As we have seen, Israel did gather and preserve the words of those prophets who committed their messages to writing. But no doubt many messages were delivered which were not recorded. However, when men of the status of prophets wrote an interpretative history of Israel, it may readily be understood why such a history would be accepted by the Israelitish Church as the Word of God. For in their interpretation of history, these authors often profess to speak as in the name of God. These writings, therefore, are historical in character, and profess to trace the hand of God in Israel's history.

Furthermore, despite the assertions of some critics, these writings are in harmony with the written prophecies. Not only are they a perfect complement to those written prophecies, but they are a necessary completion to the history contained in the Law of Moses. Upon the basis of the Law of Moses we should expect such a history of the subsequent developments in Israel. Without this interpretative history, much in the prophets would be obscure. So far as is known, none of these books has ever been disputed as to its canonicity. The Former Prophets, then, were accepted as part of the Word of God, and therefore as canonical, because they were written by men who held the high office of prophet, and who, as inspired prophets, interpreted Israel's history.

c. The Writings

How did the third division of the Old Testament, the so-called *Hagiographa*, or Writings, come to be collected and regarded as canonical? There is no direct answer given to this question in the Scriptures. The Bible does not tell us who collected these books nor at what time they were gathered. The books which belong to this third division of the Canon were written by men inspired of God who nevertheless did not occupy the office of prophet. Some of the authors, however, such as David and Daniel, did possess the prophetic gift although they did not occupy the official status of prophet. This accounts for the fact that a book such as Daniel is found not among the Prophets but among the Writings. The official status of Daniel, as a careful study of the Old Testament will reveal, was not that of prophet, but of statesman. Daniel, however, did possess the gift of prophecy.

An objection is often made to this argument. If it is true that the status of the authors of the Hagiographa was that of inspired men who did not occupy the prophetic office, then the book of Amos, it is claimed, should be included among the Hagiographa and not among the Prophets. Amos, it is asserted, distinctly maintained that he was neither a prophet nor the son of a prophet (Am. 7:14). This argument, however, is based upon a fallacious interpretation of the passage to which appeal is made. In this passage Amos is relating his prophetic call. He disclaims that he is earning his livelihood by being a prophet, since he is a shepherd and a plucker of sycamore fruit. However, God called him to be a prophet. 'Go, prophesy unto my people Israel', the Lord had said to him. These are the words by which he was inducted into the prophetic office. This objection to our argument, therefore, is without merit.

In the prologue of Ecclesiasticus (written about 130 BC) mention is made of 'the law itself, and the prophecies, and the rest of the books'. Here is witness to a third division, namely, 'the rest of the books'. The language does not tell how many or which books were considered by the author as coming under this category. However, it does imply a fixed group of books, and also implies, we think, that these books had been in existence for some time. The designation here given of the third group is as definite and explicit as are those given to the first two divisions of the Canon.

The writer of the prologue also speaks of the 'law and the prophets and the others that followed after them' and states that his grandfather, the author of Ecclesiasticus, gave himself largely to the reading of 'the law and the prophets and the other books of the fathers'. In the mind of the writer of the prologue, then, there existed three definite divisions of the Old Testament Scriptures.

We need not be alarmed because the author does not use a technical term to designate the third division. As a matter of fact, he is not consistent even in his reference to the second division. He speaks of it now as 'the prophecies' (*hai propheteai*) and now as 'the prophets' (*ton propheton*).

The technical designation 'Writings' was only applied to those books long afterward. The miscellaneous character of their contents would make it difficult to employ an adequately descriptive designation, such as was enjoyed by the Law and the Prophets. Upon the basis of what is stated in the prologue to Ecclesiasticus, there does not appear to be warrant for assuming that the third division of the Canon was still in process of collection.

In all probability these books were gathered by Ezra and those who immediately followed him. Concerning this period very little is known, but it seems to have been a time when attention was given to the Scriptures, and it may well have been that these sacred books were then collected. Nor does this necessarily mean that some inspired additions were not made to certain books at a later time. Such may very well have been the case.

To sum up, we may say that the books of the Old Testament, being immediately inspired of God, were recognized as such by His people from the time when they first appeared. That there may have been questions and minor differences of opinion about certain books does not at all detract from this fact.

It is well known that in the later Jewish schools there were certain disputes as to the canonicity of particular books, notably, Esther and Ecclesiastes. However, it is questionable whether these disputes were really more than academic. It is questionable whether they really represented the attitude of the people to any great extent.

How the books were gathered we are not told. Apparently, no religious council in ancient Israel ever drew up a list of divine books. Rather, in the singular providence of God, His people recognized His Word and honoured it from the time of its first appearance. Thus was formed the collection of inspired writings which are known as the canonical books of the Old Testament.

PART ONE

The Law of Moses

CHAPTER TWO

GENERAL OBSERVATIONS

THE first division of the sacred Canon of the Old Testament is generally designated as the Torah (*i.e.*, the Law). The noun *torah* is from a root *yarah*, 'to throw' or 'to shoot', and means 'direction', 'law', 'instruction'. As a designation of the first five books of the Bible, the word is employed in a more restricted sense to stress the legal element which forms so great a part of these books. This usage does not exclude the narrative or historical sections, but rather includes them, since they form the fitting background or framework for the legislation.

In the Old Testament, the Pentateuch is called:

1. the law: Joshua 8:34; Ezra 10:3; Nehemiah 8:2, 7, 14; 10:34, 36; 12:44; 13:3; 2 Chronicles 14:4; 31:21; 33:8.
2. the book of the law: Joshua 1:8; 8:34; 2 Kings 22:8; Nehemiah 8:3.
3. the book of the law of Moses: Joshua 8:31; 23:6; 2 Kings 14:6; Nehemiah 8:1.
4. the book of Moses: Ezra 6:18; Nehemiah 13:1; 2 Chronicles 25:4; 35:12.
5. the law of the Lord: Ezra 7:10; 1 Chronicles 16:40 ; 2 Chronicles 31:3; 35:26.
6. the law of God: Nehemiah 10:28, 29.
7. the book of the law of God: Joshua 24:26; Nehemiah 8:18.
8. the book of the law of the Lord: 2 Chronicles 17:9; 34:14.
9. the book of the law of the Lord their God: Nehemiah 9:3.
10. the law of Moses the servant of God: Daniel 9:11, *cf.* v. 13; *cf.* Malachi 4:4.

It will be noted how aptly these phrases characterize the Pentateuch. They stress its legislation, the *Law;* they indicate that it is in permanent form, the *Book;* they call attention to its human author, *Moses;* and they point to the Divine Author, the *Lord*, who is *God*.

In the New Testament the Pentateuch is called:

1. the book of the law: Galatians 3:10.
2. the book of Moses: Mark 12:26.
3. the law: Matthew 12:5; Luke 16:16; John 7:19.
4. the law of Moses: Luke 2:22; John 7:23.
5. the law of the Lord: Luke 2:23, 24.

The term 'Pentateuch' is derived from two Greek words, *pente* ('five') and *teuchos* ('volume'),[1] properly an adjective modifying *biblos* ('book'), thus, 'a five-volumed book'. Its earliest use is probably in Origen, on John 4:25 ('of the Pentateuch of Moses', *cf. PG*, XIV, col. 444). In Latin Tertullian employed it as a proper name, Pentateuchus (*Adversus Marcionem* 1:10 in *PL*, II, col. 282).

Both Philo and Josephus testify to the fivefold division of the Law. Some scholars, *e.g.*, Haevernick, believe that the division was made by the translators of the LXX. Pfeiffer thinks that it is as early as the first Hebrew edition of the work. In all probability, however, the division is natural. Genesis, Leviticus, and Deuteronomy are units in themselves. Hence we may assume that the fivefold division was the work of the original author of the Law, namely, Moses.

The Jews (*e.g.*, Jerusalem Talmud, *Sanhedrin* 10:1 [28a], Koheleth rabba on Ecclesiastes 12:11) spoke of the Pentateuch as 'the five-fifths of the Law', and each book was called a fifth part.

AUTHORSHIP

The human author of the Pentateuch was Moses, the great lawgiver of Israel. It is true that there is no superscription or introduction or express claim that the work in its entirety is from Moses (Cornill). Nevertheless, there is convincing testimony, both of an external and internal nature, to support the position that Moses wrote the Pentateuch.

a. The testimony of the Pentateuch
The following passages are of particular value for they show that important portions of the Law are said to have been written by Moses.

1. Exodus 17:14. 'And the Lord said unto Moses, Write this for a memorial in the book, and rehearse it in the ears of Joshua: for I will utterly put out the remembrance of Amalek from under heaven.' This

---

[1] The word *teuchos* properly means a tool or implement. It came to be used to designate a case for holding papyrus rolls and also for the roll itself. Hence its meaning, a volume or book.

verse shows that Moses was regarded as the proper person for writing. What he was to write probably includes the prophecy and its historical occasion, the attack of Amalek. This article, 'the' book, should probably not be stressed; although it possibly implies the existence of a definite book.

2. Exodus 24:4–8. 'And Moses wrote all the words of the Lord' (verse 4a). This refers at least to the 'book of the convenant' (Ex. 21:2–23:33), and may even include Exodus 19 and 20.

3. Exodus 34:27. 'And the Lord said unto Moses, Write these words: for in accordance with these words have I made a covenant with thee and with Israel.' This is the second command of the Lord to Moses to write. It refers to Exodus 34:10–26, the second decalogue.

4. Numbers 33:1, 2. 'And Moses wrote their goings out according to their journeys by the commandment [lit., mouth] of the Lord' (verse 2a). Here it is expressly stated that Moses wrote the list of stations from Egypt to Moab, covering the entire journey of the children of Israel. This itinerary is in reality a strong argument for the Mosaic authorship of the entire Pentateuchal narrative (see pp. 96f.). If Moses wrote this itinerary, he doubtless wrote the surrounding narrative of the wilderness wanderings.

5. Deuteronomy 31:9. 'And Moses wrote this law and gave it unto the priests the sons of Levi who bear the ark of the covenant of the Lord, and unto all the elders of Israel.' 'And it came to pass when Moses had finished writing the word of this law in a book, until they were finished' (verse 24).

Probably these words refer to the preceding books of the Pentateuch, since Deuteronomy itself recognizes a previous Mosaic legislation binding upon the people (*cf.* Dt. 4:5, 14; 29:1; *etc.*). Even, however, if the reference be restricted to portions of Deuteronomy, it witnesses to the fact that Moses wrote extended material.

6. Deuteronomy 31:22. 'And Moses wrote this song in that day, and he taught it to the children of Israel.' The reference is to Deuteronomy 32.

By way of summary we note that there are three *legislative* sections, the authorship of which is attributed to Moses, and three sections dealing with *historical* events.

In addition to the above six passages the following facts should also be noted. The authorship of Genesis is not stated, but, as will be shown later, Genesis forms an organic part of the Pentateuch (see pp. 47, 63). In the four remaining books Moses appears throughout as the principal character, the mediator of the Law. It is Moses to whom God utters the Ten Commandments, and who was the central figure in that aweful transaction at Sinai. It is Moses to whom the Lord reveals, by personal communication, the instructions for building the Tabernacle (Ex. 25–31). Throughout the account of the erection of the Tabernacle, we constantly meet the phrase 'as the Lord commanded Moses'. In the book of Leviticus we often find such phrases as 'the Lord spake unto Moses saying', and this is true also of Numbers.

The book of Deuteronomy begins: 'These are the words which Moses spake unto all Israel,' etc. (verse 1). In verse 5 we read, 'On this side Jordan, in the land of Moab, began Moses to declare this law, saying.' 'Deuteronomy is largely made up of elaborate discourses declared to have been delivered by Moses, the primary aim of which is to rehearse the laws already given and apply them to the new conditions under which Israel will shortly live, and to exhort the people to loyalty and obedience' (*FB*, p. 6).

b. The testimony of the remainder of the Old Testament
Of particular importance is the book of Joshua, which is filled with references to Moses. Joshua should not be regarded as Moses' successor for, because of his exalted position, Moses had but one successor, even Christ. Joshua, however, derived his authority from Moses. The Law of Moses was to be his guide and standard. Hence we frequently find Joshua acting 'as the Lord commanded Moses' (*e.g.*, 11:15, 20; 14:2; 21:2; *etc.*). But there are several explicit references to the written Law itself as the work of Moses; note 'this book of the law' (1:7, 8); 'written in the book of the law of Moses' (8:31; *cf.* also verses 32, 34; 23:6); 'the word of the Lord by the hand of Moses' (22:9; *cf.* also verse 5).

In Judges 3:4 we read '. . . to know whether they would keep the commandments of the Lord which he commanded their fathers through the hand of Moses.' References to Moses are found in Kings, Ezra, Nehemiah, and Chronicles. We find such expressions as 'the law of Moses' (1 Ki. 2:3); 'the book of the law of Moses' (2 Ki. 14:6); '. . . the law that my servant Moses commanded them' (2 Ki. 21:8); 'the book of Moses' (Ezr. 6:18; Ne. 13:1). (*Cf.* also 1 Ki. 8:9, 53–56; 2 Ki. 23:25; 22:8 with 2 Ch. 34:14; 2 Ch. 23:18; 25:4; 35:12; Ezr. 3:2; Ne. 8:1–8).

The references in the prophets to Moses are rather infrequent. For the most part, the prophets speak merely of the law as, *e.g.*, in Isaiah 1:10. The precise connotation of the word 'law' in each instance of its occurrence may be somewhat difficult to determine. However, the only authoritative law recognized in the Old Testament is the Law of Moses, and it is to this Law that the prophets are referring. Note that Daniel speaks explicitly of 'the oath that is written in the law of Moses the servant of God' (9:11–13), and Malachi warns, 'Remember ye the law of Moses my servant, which I commanded unto him in Horeb for all Israel, with the statutes and judgments' (4:4).

The presupposition of the Old Testament witness is that there is in existence a written book known as the Law, and that the contents of this Law were given to Moses by the Lord. On the question of the authorship of the Law, the Pentateuch and the remainder of the Old Testament know of only one human author, and that author is Moses.

c. The testimony of the New Testament

The New Testament bears clear testimony to the Mosaic authorship of the Pentateuch. On this question our Lord and the Jews seem to have had no quarrel. He objected rather to their misinterpretation of the Law. Christ quotes passages of the Law as from Moses, e.g., 'Moses because of the hardness of your hearts suffered you to put away your wives' (Mt. 19:8; Mk. 10:5). (Cf. also Mt. 8:4; Mk. 1:44; 7:10; 12:26; Lk. 5:14; 20:37; 16:31. Note particularly Lk. 24:27, 44; Jn. 5:47; 7:19.)

The remainder of the New Testament is in harmony with the witness of our Lord. (Cf. Acts 3:22; 13:39; 15:5–21; 26:22; 28:23; Rom. 10:5, 19; 1 Cor. 9:9; 2 Cor. 3:15; Rev. 15:3.)

Like the Old, the New Testament bears witness to a writing known as the Law, and regards Moses as its author. In fact, in the New Testament the words 'Moses' and 'law' are equivalent.[2]

WHAT IS MEANT BY MOSAIC AUTHORSHIP?

When we affirm that Moses wrote, or that he was the author of, the Pentateuch, we do not mean that he himself necessarily wrote every word. To insist upon this would be unreasonable. Hammurabi was the author of his famous code, but he certainly did not engrave it himself upon the stele. Our Lord was the author of the Sermon upon the Mount, but He did not write it Himself. Milton was the author of Paradise Lost, but he did not write it all out by hand.

The witness of sacred Scripture leads us to believe that Moses was the fundamental or real author of the Pentateuch. In composing it, he may indeed, as Astruc suggested, have employed parts of previously existing written documents. Also, under divine inspiration, there may have been later minor additions and even revisions. Substantially and essentially, however, it is the product of Moses. The position for which conservatives

---

[2] The internal evidence for Mosaic authorship will be discussed in connection with the individual books.

contend has been well expressed by Wilson: 'That the Pentateuch as it stands is historical and from the time of Moses; and that Moses was its real author, though it may have been revised and edited by later redactors, the additions being just as much inspired and as true as the rest.'[3]

[3] *A Scientific Investigation of the Old Testament* (1929), p. 11.

CHAPTER THREE

GENESIS

NAME

THE Jews designated the book according to its first word, *B'reshith* ('In the Beginning'). In Talmudic times it was also called 'Book of the Creation of the World'. The title 'Genesis' is from the LXX rendering of 2:4a, 'This is the book of the *geneseos* of heaven and earth', and of the subsequent headings, 5:1; 6:9; 10:1; 11:10; 11:27; 25:12; 25:19; 36:1; 36:9; 37:2. The word means 'origin', 'source', 'generation', and has been adopted by most translations as the title of the book.

PURPOSE

The purpose of the first book of the Pentateuch is to give a brief survey of the history of divine revelation from the beginning until the Israelites are brought into Egypt, ready to be formed into the theocratic nation. It relates the creation of the world, of man, God's covenant with man, the fall into sin, the covenant of grace, and the lives of the patriarchs.

Broadly speaking we may say that the book comprises two parts. The first of these deals with the period from the creation to the call of Abraham (Gn. 1–12), and the second with the call or preparation of the patriarchs. The first section is somewhat negative, showing the need for the segregation from the world of a peculiar people, and the remaining section serves the positive end of relating the segregation of that people.

Genesis 1–12 is again divided into two parts by the narrative of the flood. It will be noted that at the beginning of the antediluvian period God entered into covenant with Adam (Gn. 2:16, 17), and at the beginning of the postdiluvian section He made a covenant with Noah (Gn. 9:8ff.). These two covenants, universal in extent, failed to preserve among men the true religion and hence provided the need for the more limited covenant made with Abraham, the head of the chosen race. Since man broke the universal covenants, the Lord segregated the chosen people from the remainder of the world, so that the true religion might grow and flourish and finally, in the open stage of the world, contend with and overcome the forces of evil. Thus, the two preliminary periods serve the purpose of making clear the insufficiency of the first two universal covenants and the necessity of selecting a particular people to be the Lord's chosen race.

a. 1:1–2:3. The creation of the heaven and the earth

This section is introduced by a general, comprehensive statement of the creation (1:1), which states the fact that all things had their beginning through a creative act of God.

The details of bringing the earth from its original, unformed condition to its present, well-ordered state are given in verses 2–31. Verse 2 contains three nominal or circumstantial clauses, which state the conditions in existence at the time when God said, 'Let there be light' (verse 3). This threefold condition had existed from the point of absolute creation until the first creative word was spoken (verse 3). How long this was, we are not told.

Genesis 1 places its stress upon God's absolute monergism. The word God (*Elohim*) occurs in this chapter 32 times, and nearly always as subject. Thus, God 'created' (3 times), 'said' (10 times), 'saw' (7 times), 'divided' (once), 'called' (3 times), 'made' (3 times), 'set' (once), 'blessed' (twice). Note also, 'the Spirit of God moved' (verse 2), 'he called' (verse 5), 'called he' (verse 10), 'created he' (verse 27, twice).

The chapter also emphasizes the divine complacency in the creation. Seven times we are told that God saw 'that it was good', and in verse 31 this is particularly stressed. Furthermore, the creation account is told in terms of fiat and fulfilment. There are eight of these fiats, *e.g.*, 'let there be light' (verse 3). Seven times the fulfilment is stated, *e.g.*, 'and there was light' (verse 3); and six times the phrase 'and it was so' is employed, thus stressing that the purpose of God had been fully carried out.

The work of creation is comprised in a hexameron, or period of six days, coming to a majestic climax in the resting of the Creator on the seventh day. The length of these days is not stated but a certain correspondence between some of them may be observed. Thus:

1. Light	4. Luminaries
2. Firmament, division of waters	5. Birds, fishes
3. Dry land, vegetation	6. Animals, man

The name *Elohim* is particularly appropriate for this chapter, since the chapter exalts God as the mighty Creator. The distinctive vocabulary indicates not a particular author, but is chosen because of the peculiar contents of the chapter. It would be difficult to write in Hebrew upon these subjects without employing this particular vocabulary.

Genesis 1 is monumental in character, and exhibits a stately cadence of grandeur as it reveals the sovereign Creator uttering His will, and that will coming to immediate fulfilment. So the narrative proceeds until it reaches its mighty climax. The Lord beholds the finished world and pronounces it very good.

We are not to regard the chapter as the reworking by the Priestly School of a myth that was common to ancient tradition. Rather, the chapter is sober history. Although Genesis does not purport to be a textbook of science, nevertheless, when it touches upon scientific subjects, it is accurate. Science has never discovered any facts which are in conflict with the statements of Genesis 1. The chapter stresses this particular earth for religious reasons – it was on this earth that man sinned and man's redemption occurred. But Genesis does not teach that the earth is the centre of the universe or solar system. It is geocentric only in a religious sense; not for an instant can its accurate statements be regarded as out of harmony with true science.

b. 2:4–4:26. The generations of the heavens and the earth

The introductory statement, 'These are the generations', *etc.*, is extremely important for a correct understanding of the framework of Genesis. It occurs eleven times in Genesis and always as the heading of the section which follows. The word 'generations' in this phrase signifies that which is begotten or generated. The parallel uses of the phrase make this clear. Thus, *e.g.*, 'the generations of Noah' (6:9) heads the section which deals with the descendants or offspring of Noah. It is true, as Driver remarks[1] that some account of the person named in the phrase is also given, but since this account is usually of such a minor or secondary character, it in no sense detracts from what has been said above.

This phrase in 2:4, therefore, introduces the account not of the creation of heaven and earth, but rather of the offspring of heaven and earth, namely, man.[2] Man's body is from the earth, and his soul is of heavenly origin, breathed into him by God. Thus, from this key phrase, we learn

[1] *LOT*, p. 7.
[2] It has been suggested that this phrase may originally have stood as a heading to chapter 1 and that it was moved to its present position by a redactor. But if this were so, the present section (2:5–4:26) would have no heading, and the first section (*i.e.*, 1:2–2:3) would have two headings, namely 2:4a and 1:1. Furthermore, violence would be done to the meaning of the title by forcing it to serve as heading of a section dealing with the creation of heaven and earth, whereas the content of the title shows that it should introduce an account of the 'offspring' or 'generations' of the heaven and earth.

that 2:4ff. does not profess to present an account of creation. There are not, therefore, as some critics maintain, duplicate accounts of the creation in Genesis. Rather, the grand theme of 2:4–4:26 is the formation of man and the first state of human history.

That this section is not a duplicate history of creation is also evident from its contents: (1) the words of 2:4b, 'in the day that the Lord God made the earth and the heavens', rather than introducing an account of creation, serve to point out that the creation has already taken place; (2) the entire description in chapter 2 prepares the way for the planting of the garden of Eden (2:8, 9); (3) that which is fundamental in a creation account is missing in chapter 2, *e.g.*, formation of the earth, sea, dry land, firmament, sun, moon, stars, vegetation and earth, *etc.* In 3:18, man is to eat the herb of the field, but the only previous mention of this is in chapter 1, not in chapter 2.

In relating the planting of Eden, chapter 2 is not chronological but topical in its method of treatment. It serves as an introduction to the narrative of the fall (chapter 3). Thus it explains the nature of man, his body formed from the dust and his life inbreathed by God. This is to enable the reader to understand how, on the one hand, the possibility of elevation to a higher immortality could be offered man and, on the other, how the sentence of dust returning to dust could be imposed. It also sets forth Eden, which was to be the scene of the temptation, and introduces the reader to Adam and Eve, the actors in the temptation. In addition, the chapter calls attention to the two trees and to the covenant of works which God in grace made with Adam. It thus sets the stage for the tragic action of chapter 3.

When the purpose of chapter 2 is thus clearly recognized, it will be apparent that any contrasts made between the two upon the assumption that each is an independent account of creation are beside the point. There are different emphases in the two chapters, as we have seen, but the reason for these is obvious. Chapter 1 continues the narrative of creation until the climax, namely, man made in the image and likeness of God. To prepare the way for the account of the fall, chapter 2 gives certain added details about man's original condition, which would have been incongruous and out of place in the grand, declarative march of chapter 1.

It should be noted that there are no contradictions between chapters 1 and 2. The principal alleged contradictions concern the order of creation and the conception of God.

According to chapter 2 the order of creation is said to be man (verse 7), vegetation (verse 9), animals (verse 19), woman (verse 21f.). But in answer to this it should be noted that the order of statement is not chronological. Can we seriously think that the writer intended us to understand that God formed man (verse 7) before there was any place to put him? To insist upon a chronological order in chapter 2 is to place a construction upon the writer's words that was never intended. In reality, chapter 2 declares nothing regarding the relative priority of man and vegetation.

Nor does chapter 2 teach the creation of man before the animals. Here again, the chronological order is not stressed. The chapter has described the formation of Eden and the placing of man in the garden. It now speaks more particularly of man's condition, showing his need of a help meet for himself, and that such a help meet was not found among the animals. Verse 19 may rightly be paraphrased, 'and the LORD GOD having formed out of the ground every beast of the field, and every fowl of heaven, brought them unto the man'.

In chapter 2 an anthropomorphic conception of God is said to appear. God 'fashions', 'breathes', 'plants', 'places', 'takes', 'sets', 'brings', 'closes up', 'builds', 'walks', *etc.* But this objection is superficial. An anthropomorphic conception of God also appears in chapter 1. Indeed, it is impossible for the finite mind to speak of God without using anthropomorphic language. Chapter 1 asserts that God 'called', 'saw', 'blessed', 'deliberated' (verse 26 'let us make'), God distributed His work over a period of six days, He 'rested'.

Chapter 1 lays stress upon the divine complacency. This stress is to prepare the way for the fall related in chapter 3. We should, therefore, regard chapter 1 as introductory and basic for the proper understanding of chapter 2. Chapter 2 assumes the creation of heaven and earth, sun, moon, stars, *etc.* In reality, chapter 2 cannot be understood without chapter 1.

Chapter 3 is to be considered not as legend, but as history, which it purports to be. The same characters, Adam and Eve, appear as in chapter 2. The whole is related as straightforward narrative. The tragic results of the fall are apparent in human life, just as chapter 3 asserts. Man is naked, that is, he is inwardly polluted by sin so that he needs covering. He is also guilty, because of sin, and cannot stand in the presence of the holy God.

The speaking serpent is unusual and striking. In a fable or legend we are accustomed to animals speaking, but not so here. Adam has just named the creatures (2:19), *i.e.*, he has exercised his God-given intelligence, he has demonstrated that he was created in the image of God, he has shown his superiority over the lower creation by recognizing the proper function and characteristics of each beast. He has shown that he himself is the crown of creation and superior to the beasts. In chapter 3, however, a serpent speaks. It breaks the bounds imposed upon it by God. It would rise above man, whereas it should be subservient to man. None of this bears the characteristic of mere legend. Rather, it is related as history. The serpent, as appears from the curse later inflicted upon it, was the mouthpiece or instrument of Satan. The speaking serpent, therefore, cannot be regarded as a mark of legend. The historicity of the account is proved by 2 Corinthians 11:3 (*cf.* also Jn. 8:44). If we consider the account of the fall, which purports to be history, as mere symbolical legend, would not consistency require that we also regard the account of our redemption as mere symbolical legend?

The purpose of chapter 4 is to show the rapid growth and increase of sin from Abel's murder to Lamech's song of hate. The chapter also reveals how the arts and sciences were cultivated by the descendants of Cain. The often-heard objection[3] that Cain could not have been the son of the first man, or that he could not have found a wife, is hardly worthy of serious consideration. In the nature of the case, since the Bible teaches that mankind has come from an original pair, Cain must have married a sister.

Nor are there two accounts of Cain in chapter 4, one condemning him to be a 'fugitive and a vagabond', the other setting him forth as 'the proud ancestor of the line of tent-dwellers who introduced the refinements of civilization (4:17–22)'.[4] If these accounts were in such conflict, why would the supposed redactor, presumably an intelligent man, have thus pieced them together? Also, the city which Cain built may have been a merely a nomadic encampment (*cf.* Nu. 13:19). The reference of Lamech (verse 24) to Cain's being avenged, proves beyond question the unity of this section.

c. 5:1–6:8. The book of the generations of Adam

The insertion of the line of Cain in 4:17ff. has introduced an important characteristic of the framework of Genesis. It is the custom of Moses, in his relation of the genealogical history from Adam to Jacob, to interrupt the narrative at the proper point and to insert the genealogy of a divergent line (here the Cainites) before reverting to the history of the chosen people. (*Cf.* 25:12–19, which gives the genealogy of Ishmael, followed by the genealogy of Isaac, 25:19ff.; and 36:1 and 36:9, which

---

[3] *Cf. IOT*, pp. 162, 163.
[4] *IOT*, p. 163.

give the generations of Esau, followed in 37:2 by the generations of Jacob.)

There is similarity in the names of the genealogies of chapters 4 and 5. The two, however, should not be regarded as mere variants of one genealogy, for the following reasons: although there is some similarity in the names, there is also great diversity; the Scriptures profess to record different genealogies; and those with similar names are described as being different people. Thus, Enoch (chapter 4) is the son of Cain and begets Irad. Enoch (chapter 5) was begotten of Jared, many generations after Seth. The Enoch who begat Methuselah was noted for his piety and was translated. Lamech (chapter 4) was begotten of Methusael and is portrayed as particularly self-trusting and vengeful. The Lamech of chapter 5, on the other hand, is begotten of Methuselah and is set forth as a man of faith, who sees in the birth of his son Noah a fulfilment of God's promise.

The genealogy of chapter 5 is not intended to furnish a chronology. Rather, Moses selected ten representative names in order to show the unrestrained, universal reign of death over man. Of each except Enoch it is said, 'And he died'. The omission of these words after Enoch's name only serves to bring out the universal presence of death. The words immediately call to mind the serpent's lie, 'Ye shall not die.' (Gn. 3:4 is generally attributed to J or S, *i.e.*, the Seir source of R. H. Pfeiffer;[5] yet chapter 5 is attributed to P.)

Since chapter 5 cannot be used to compute a chronology, we should probably interpret phrases such as 5:15 to mean that Mahalaleel begat the line which culminated in Jared. This would not be the case, however, in verses 3 and 28.[6]

The short section, 6:1-8, is introduced to show both the wickedness of man which made the flood necessary, and the righteousness of Noah. It thus connects chapter 5 with the following. The 'sons of God' are not angels, but the chosen race. Through intermarriage between the chosen line and the seed of the world great wickedness appeared.

d. 6:9–9:17. *The generations of Noah*

Allis has done remarkable service in calling attention to the unity of this section.[7] He points out that (1) the cause of the flood is the sinfulness of man (*cf.* 6:5, 11–13); the Lord announces His repentance at having

---

[5] See p. 148.

[6] See *Bibliotheca Sacra*,* April 1890, and B. B. Warfield, 'On the Antiquity and the Unity of the Human Race' in *Studies in Theology*,* 1932, pp. 235–258.

[7] *FB*, pp. 95–99.

made man (6:6, 7); (2) the purpose of the flood is to destroy mankind (*cf.* 6:7, 13, 17; 7:4, 21–23; 8:21); (3) the text lays emphasis upon the saving of a thoroughly representative remnant (*cf.* 6:8, 18–20 [the animals]; 7:1–3, 7–9, 13–16; 8:16–19).

Moses begins this section with a statement as to the upright character of Noah (6:9) in order to contrast Noah with the general wickedness of mankind (6:11–13), and also to explain the remark in 6:8. He then recapitulates, mentioning Noah's three sons (6:10), and mankind's corruption (6:11–13), thus to prepare the way for the instructions regarding the building of the ark (6:14–21). The chapter closes with a statement of Noah's obedience (6:22).

The Lord now gives the command to enter the ark and to take clean beasts by sevens and unclean beasts by twos (7:14). This command is obeyed.

On the seventeenth day of the second month (7:11, 12) Noah entered the ark as God had commanded him. The rain fell upon the earth forty days and forty nights. There is no contradiction as to the number of beasts which entered the ark. At the first announcement of the flood and the command to build the ark (6:14–21) Noah was to bring in male and female (*i.e.,* two) of each kind of animals and birds. At the command to enter the ark (7:1–4) it is specified that of clean beasts Noah was to bring in by sevens, but of unclean beasts by twos. The second command is more specific than the first; there is no contradiction. The distinction between clean and unclean is not an evidence of the post-Mosaic age, but is a distinction evidently known from the beginning.

The rains continued for forty days, until the waters prevailed fifteen cubits above the heights of the mountains (7:17). Note that four successive stages are mentioned: the waters increased and bare up the ark, and it was lifted up above the earth (7:17b); the waters prevailed, and were increased greatly upon the earth (7:18a); the waters covered the high hills (7:19); the waters covered the mountains (7:20). And three emphatic statements of the power of the waters are made: all flesh died (7:21); 'all in whose nostrils was the breath of life, of all that was in the dry land, died' (7:22); universal and particular terms are now combined (7:23).

The waters prevailed upon the earth for a total of 150 days, *i.e.,* for 110 days after the rain had stopped (7:24). There are seven stages in the decline of the water: a wind passes over the earth to cause the waters to assuage (8:1); the sources of the flood cease to such an extent that the ark can rest on Ararat (8:2–4), on the seventeenth day of the month, *i.e.,* 150 days after the beginning of the flood; the tops of the mountains appear (8:5), in the tenth month, first day, *i.e.*, about seventy-three days after the ark rested on Ararat; after forty days, a raven is sent forth, and also a dove, but the waters are still too high for the dove to find a resting-place (8:6–9); after seven days, the tops of the trees emerge (8:10, 11); after seven days, the dove is sent forth again, but returns no more (8:12); the flood ends on the first day of the first month of Noah's 601st year (8:13). On the twenty-seventh day of the second month, *i.e.*, exactly one year and ten days after the rains began to fall, the earth is dry (8:14).

The account of the flood is told in terms of universality. This does not necessarily mean that the flood covered the entire face of the globe. Rather, it was universal in that it destroyed all flesh. If the habitations of mankind were limited to the Euphrates valley, it is quite possible that the flood was also limited.

Genesis 6:9–9:17 closes with an account of Noah's building an altar (the first altar mentioned in the Bible) and sacrificing. The offering is accepted by the Lord, who declares that He will not again curse the earth (8:20–22). God blesses Noah, grants him permission to eat meat (9:1–4), and establishes His covenant with Noah (9:9–17). As a result of the sin of Ham, Canaan is cursed, and Noah prophesies blessing for the world through Shem (9:25–27).

e. 10:1–11:9. The generations of the sons of Noah
This brief section records the dispersion of mankind over the earth. It contains a table of nations which is inserted for the purpose of showing the relation of these peoples to the chosen race, all of whom have come from the same ancestry and will ultimately share in the blessing of Abraham (12:1–3). Particular attention is devoted to the Canaanitish tribes (10:15–19).

This section bears an intimate relation with what precedes and follows: 10:1 connects it with the preceding account of the flood, 11:1–9 recounts the building of the tower of Babel and the dispersion of mankind. Some think that this section is from a different author than chapter 10, but passages such as 10:10 and 10:25 show that the contents of 11:1–9 were in the mind of the writer of chapter 10.

f. 11:10–26. The generations of Shem
The section has certain similarities with chapter 5, which also gave the genealogy of the chosen line. It does not present a mere list of names, as does chapter 10 but, like chapter 5, states the age of the father at the birth of the son, and the length of his life after the birth of the son, and it mentions his begetting other sons and daughters. Both chapter 5 and this

section close with mention of a father who has three sons (5:32 and 11:26). This section obviously continues the genealogy of chapter 5, yet is inexplicable without the intervening sections.

g. 11:27–25:11. The generations of Terah

The principal theme of this section is the life of Abraham, the patriarch. Abraham was called from his land in answer to a three-fold promise, and with respect to each element of this promise was severely tested.

1. The promise of a land: 12:7; 13:15, 17; 15:7, 18; 17:2; 24:7; 28:4, 14. The testing:

    (i) Abraham was a sojourner in the land (12:10;17:8;20:1;21:23, 24; 23:4).

    (ii) The land was occupied by others (12:6; 13:7; 15:18–21).
    (iii) He was twice driven out by famine (12:10ff.; 20:1ff.).
    (iv) His descendants were to be sojourners in a foreign land.
    (v) The land was invaded by distant rulers (14:1ff.).
    (vi) Abraham had to buy a burial place (23:1ff.).

2. The promise of a numerous seed: 12:2; 13:15; 15:5; 17:2, 4, 16; 18:18; 22:17; 26:4; 28:4; 32:12. The testing: 11:30; 15:2, 3; 16:1; 17:17; 22:12.

3. The promise of universal blessing: 12:3; 18:18; 22:18. The testing:

    (i) Twice Abraham is the source of trouble (chapters 12 and 20).
    (ii) Abram and Lot must separate (13:5ff.).
    (iii) Foreign kings fight against him (chapter 14).
    (iv) He must protest to Abimelech (21:22ff.).

The life of Abraham has been variously interpreted. According to Philo of Alexandria, the life of Abraham is an allegory which illustrates certain truths, namely, the perfection of a wise man by instruction. Julius Wellhausen refuses to regard Abraham as a historical personage; he suggests that he might be a free creation of the writer's imagination. Theodor Noeldeke urges that Abraham was a deity, who had fallen to the plane of a mere human, and thus appears in Genesis. Hugo Winckler regards Abraham, because of his connection with Harran, as identified with Sin, the moon god. Hermann Gunkel regards the 'sagas' of Genesis as similar to those of other peoples of antiquity. These 'sagas', he thinks, gradually formed an Abraham cycle. Albrecht Alt[8] regards Abraham as

---

[8] Der Gott der Väter (1929).

a historical personage, and believes that it is possible to know something of Abraham's religion.[9]

It is necessary to regard the account of Abraham in Genesis as historically accurate. The narrative purports to be straightforward history, and this is substantiated by the testimony of the New Testament (Mt. 1:1; 8:11; 22:32; Mk. 12:26; Lk. 3:23-34; 13:28; 16:22-30; 20:37; Jn. 8:37, 39, 40, 52, 53, 56, 58; Acts 3:13, 25; 7; Rom. 4; 2 Cor. 11:22; Gal. 3; Heb. 2:16; 6:13; 7:1-9; 11:8, 17; Jas. 2:21, 23; 1 Pet. 3:6). Furthermore, the science of archaeology has more and more been substantiating the biblical record of patriarchal times. The following points may be noted:

1. Some critics have asserted that the art of writing was unknown before the end of the second millennium BC. Wellhausen and Graf thought that Israel had no written documents before the time of the Kings. The texts from Ras Shamra (fifteenth and early fourteenth centuries BC), discovered in 1929, prove that writing was known to the Canaanites by the middle of the second millennium BC.

2. During the patriarchal period, as archaeology has shown, the hill country was but sparsely settled, whereas the coastal plains contained the sedentary population. This well agrees with the representation of Genesis that the patriarchs wandered in the hill country. Furthermore, the cities mentioned in Genesis were in existence at this time: Bethel, Ai, Jerusalem (Salem), Shechem, Gerar, Dothan, Beersheba.[10]

3. In 1935 there were discovered at Mari on the Euphrates (Tell Hariri) over 20,000 tablets, most of which belong to the early part of the second millennium BC. These discoveries confirm the biblical picture that Israel's ancestors came from the region of Harran. The city of Nahor (Gn. 24:10) appears in these texts as Nakhur. At the time of Hammurabi (eighteenth century BC) the place seems to have been ruled by an Amorite prince. Serug and Terah also appear as names of towns near Harran.[11]

4. Glueck[12] points out the accuracy of Lot's description (Gn. 13:10). Archaeology has shown that the Jordan Valley has always been occupied, and that it is one of the richest parts of ancient Palestine.

5. Concerning the account of the invasion of Chedorlaomer (Gn. 14), Glueck writes, 'The archaeological facts agree completely with this

[9] Cf. the present writer's article 'The God of the Fathers' in WThJ, Nov. 1940, pp. 5-40.
[10] See Albright, The Archaeology of Palestine and the Bible, pp. 132, 133.
[11] Cf. FSAC, pp. 179, 180.
[12] RJ, p. 73.

literary tradition. There was about 1900 BC such a thoroughgoing destruction visited upon all the great fortresses and settlements of the land, within the limits we have examined, that the particular civilization they represented never again recovered. The blow it received was so crushing as to be utterly destructive.'[13] Glueck also points out why he believes the figure 318 (Gn. 14:14) to be correct.[14]

6. Genesis 14:6 mentions the Horites, whose historicity has long been denied. They are now known as the Hurrians, a people who played a most important role in the second millennium BC.

7. An important Hurrian centre was Nuzu (Yorgan Tepa) about a dozen miles south-west of modern Kirkuk. The tablets discovered here (1925–1931) have cast much light upon the background of Genesis.

(i) It was a custom at Nuzu for those without children to adopt a son, who would serve them and bury and mourn for them. In return he would be designated heir. If, however, a son should be born, the adopted son must forfeit his rights to the real son. (*Cf.* Gn. 15:1–4.)

(ii) If the wife was barren she might provide a slave to bear children for her husband. (*Cf.* Gn. 16:2.)

(iii) Should the slave bear children, the legitimate wife was forbidden to send her away. Hence Abraham's apprehension at Sarah's conduct. (*Cf.* Gn. 21:11–12.)

8. According to archaeology, occupation of the district in which Sodom and Gomorrah were situated ceased about the beginning of the second millennium. This supports the biblical representation of the destruction of the Cities of the Plain.[15]

In the light of these facts, the view of Wellhausen that the patriarchal narratives are merely the free creation of a later age must be decisively rejected.

In 12:6b and 13:7b there is an alleged *post-Mosaicum*, 'the Canaanite was then in the land'. It is thought that the word 'then' indicates that the words were written at a time when the Canaanites were no longer in Palestine. But the phrase is simply used to emphasize the greatness of God's promise. The land was promised to Abram, but the presence of the Canaanites made the promise seem unbelievable. Despite their presence, however, Abram believed.

In 13:7b the statement simply makes it clear that there was not room for both Abram's and Lot's cattle. If any contrast is intended by the

13 *The Other Side of the Jordan* (1940), p. 114.
14 *RJ*, p. 74.
15 *Cf. BA*, V, No. 2, and VI, No. 3.

word 'then', it is with an earlier period when the Canaanite was not in the land.

The mention of Dan (Gn. 14:14) is no argument against Mosaic authorship. It may not be the Dan of Judges 18:29, or, if it is, is it not possible that in the course of repeated copying the later, more familiar name may have been inserted? Also, the phrase, 'In the mount of the Lord he shall be seen' (Gn. 22:14) does not refer to the Lord's manifestation in the Temple which was later built on the mount, but to the Lord's appearance to Abraham at the time of his testing.[16]

The phrases 'which is in Hebron' (Gn. 13:18) and 'the same is Hebron in the land of Canaan' (Gn. 23:19b) are to be regarded as explanatory remarks probably added by Moses. In Abraham's day, Hebron as a city seems not to have been in existence. This is but another evidence of the accuracy of Genesis.

h. 25:12–18. The generations of Ishmael

i. 25:19–35:29. The generations of Isaac

The life of Abraham repeats itself in that of his son Isaac. However, the accounts of Isaac's life are not mere duplicates of Abraham's. Isaac was a real character, although of a passive nature.

Archaeology has cast interesting light upon the background of this section:

1. One of the tablets from Nuzu speaks of a certain Tupkitilla, who for three sheep transfers his rights of inheritance to a grove to his brother Kurpazah.[17] This reminds us of Esau's selling his birthright (Gn. 25:29–34).

2. One text records the lawsuit of a certain Tarmiya against his two brothers who had contested his right to marry a certain woman. He won his case because he had received his father's blessing. Like the patriarchal blessings, this one was oral, possessed legal validity, and was made by a dying father to his son.[18]

3. Of particular interest is a tablet from Nuzu which speaks of the relationship between a certain Nashwi and his adopted son Wullu. Nashwi gives his daughter to Wullu and, upon his death, Wullu is to be the heir. Should Nashwi beget a son, however, Wullu must share his inheritance with the son, and the son will receive Nashwi's gods. The possession of the gods apparently implied headship in the family. Hence

---

[16] See Hengstenberg, *DGP*, II, pp. 146–282; Green, *HCP*, pp. 47–52.

[17] *Cf. BA*, III, No. 1, p. 5.

[18] *Cf.* Gn. 27, and *BA*, III, No. 1, p. 8.

we may understand Rachel's zeal in stealing the teraphim and also the seriousness of her action (Gn. 31:19–35).[19]

4. The proper name Jacob has appeared as a place-name in Palestine in the fifteenth century BC, and also in tablets from northern Mesopotamia in the eighteenth century BC. Apparently it stands for 'May God [El] protect'.[20]

j. 36:1–37:1. The generations of Esau

An alleged anachronism appears in this section: 'And these are the kings that reigned in the land of Edom, before there reigned any king over the children of Israel' (Gn. 36:31). It has been asserted that these words must have been written after the establishment of the monarchy in Israel. Hence, some conservative scholars have thought that this statement was written under divine inspiration at a time later than Moses. However, it is not necessary to make such an assumption. In the first place, there is no evidence that any of these Edomite kings was later than Moses' time.[21] Furthermore, kings had been promised (cf. Gn. 17:6; 35:11). Since the kingship had been prophesied (cf. also Nu. 24:7; Dt. 17:14ff.), it is perfectly possible that Moses could have written this verse.

k. 37:2–50:26. The generations of Jacob

There is no reason why chapter 49 may not have been uttered by Jacob. Driver believes that it was incorporated by J from an independent source, and that it reflects the background of the time of the Judges, Samuel, and David. Pfeiffer thinks that it was the work of a poet living about 960 BC, who probably used early tribal traditions.

But Jacob is here set forth in the rôle of a prophet who beholds the future condition of his sons as grown into tribes. This is the essence of the prophetic character of the blessing, rather than the prediction of particular historical events. There is no utterance in the poem which announces the capture of the promised land, or which points specifically to the time of Joshua.

Furthermore, the poem does not fit any one particular historical period. Genesis 49:10 might be regarded as fulfilled in David's time, but if so, what is said about Levi (49:5–7) does not apply to that time. Nor can the poem be regarded as a mere collection of detached oracles (Kuenen); for it bears unmistakable signs of unity.[22] What is said about Levi must be pre-Mosaic. (Cf. Dt. 33:8–11, which is quite different.)

[19] See Sidney Smith, 'What were the Teraphim?' in JTS, XXXIII, pp. 33–36.
[20] See FSAC, pp. 325, 326.
[21] See Green, The Unity of the Book of Genesis,* pp. 425–428.
[22] See IOT, p. 277.

SPECIAL LITERATURE ON GENESIS

G. Ch. Aalders, *De Goddelijke Openbaring in de Eerste Drie Hoofstukken van Genesis** (Kampen, 1932); Arthur Algeier, *Ueber Doppelberichte in der Genesis* (Freiburg i. B., 1911); Albrecht Alt, *Der Gott der Väter* (Stuttgart, 1929; reprinted in *Kleine Schriften*, I, Munich, 1953, pp. 1–78); Benjamin Wisner Bacon, *The Genesis of Genesis* (Hartford, 1892); F. M. Th. Bohl, *Das Zeitalter Abrahams* (Leipzig, 1930); Karl Budde, *Die biblische Urgeschichte* (Giessen, 1883); *Die biblische Paradiesgeschichte* (Giessen, 1932); J. Chaine, *La Livre de la Genèse* (Paris, 1948); Walther Eichrodt, *Die Quellen der Genesis* (Giessen, 1916); O. Eissfeldt, *Die Genesis der Genesis* (Tübingen, 1958); A. H. Finn, *The Creation, Fall, and Deluge** (n.d.); Alex R. Gordon, *The Early Traditions of Genesis* (Edinburgh, 1907); William Henry Green, *The Unity of the Book of Genesis** (New York, 1910); Richard Kraemer, *Die biblische Urgeschichte* (Wernigerode, 1931); Sigmund Mowinckel, *The Two Sources of the Predeuteronomic Primeval History (JE) in Gen. 1:11* (Oslo, 1937); William Turnbull Pilter, *The Pentateuch: A Historical Record** (London, 1928 – deals largely with Gn. 14); Israel Rabin, *Studien zur vormosäischen Gottesvorstellung* (Breslau, 1929); J. Ridderbos, *Abraham de Vriend Gods** (Kampen, 1928); K. Robast, *Die Genesis** (Berlin, 1951); H. E. Ryle, *The Early Narratives of Genesis* (London, 1892); Hans Schmidt, *Die Erzählung von Paradies und Sündenfall* (Tübingen, 1931); E. J. Young, *Studies in Genesis One** (Philadelphia, 1964).

CHAPTER FOUR

EXODUS

NAME

THE book of Exodus was called by the Jews after its opening words, *we'elleh shemoth* ('And these are the names'), or simply *shemoth* ('names'). The LXX designated it, according to its central theme, *Exodos* (the word appears in Ex. 19:1), and the Vulgate, *Exodus*.

PURPOSE

The second book of the Pentateuch serves as a connecting link between the preparatory history contained in Genesis and the remaining books of the Law. It begins with a brief statement of the rapid growth of the Israelites. Following this, it sets forth the preparations for the exodus itself. These were both of a negative and positive kind. Negatively, the people were prepared for deliverance by the hard bondage which was imposed upon them, causing them to long for freedom. Positively, they were prepared by the mighty miracles which God performed on their behalf, thus convincing them that He was indeed the Lord, their covenant-redeemer God, and the God of all power. Following the narration of this double preparation, the book recounts the actual exodus from Egypt, through the Red Sea to Mt. Sinai (1–19).

This marks the first great division in the Pentateuch. Up to this point the Law was distinguished primarily by narrative; from here on it is characterized by legislation. The people are now ready to be organized as the theocratic nation, and hence must receive the legislation necessary for such organization. This legislation consists of three parts: that given at Mt. Sinai (Exodus, Leviticus), that given in the wilderness wanderings (Numbers), and that delivered in the plains of Moab (Deuteronomy).

The remainder of Exodus (*i.e.*, 20–40) concerns that legislation given by God to Israel at Mt. Sinai. First, the basic moral law is proclaimed, and this is followed by certain ordinances which are the foundation of the covenant that is ratified. Then come directions for the erection of the Tabernacle, the dwelling-place of the holy God. Because of the transgression of the covenant in connection with the sin of the golden calf, the directions were not carried out for a time. Finally, however, the Tabernacle was built, and God took up His dwelling therein.

ANALYSIS

a. 1:1–7. Introduction

The introductory word 'And' connects Exodus with the preceding narrative of Genesis, and the statement of verse 1 presupposes likewise the account of the entry into Egypt given in Genesis 46. The list of Jacob's sons (verses 2–5) is a summary of the more detailed account in Genesis 46:8–37, yet the order of names is more like that of Genesis 35:23–26. These facts establish the connection of this section with Genesis; at the same time they prepare the way for the account of the affliction which follows.

The section is a unit, and verse 6 should not be separated and given to J as some critics do. But even though verse 6 partially (but note that it contains additional information; it is by no means a mere repetition) repeats the contents of Genesis 50:26, it should not be omitted, for it prepares the way for the understanding of verse 8. If we omit verse 6, verse 8 becomes almost meaningless.

The statement in verse 7 of the immense increase of the Israelites stands in marked contrast to their small number upon entering Egypt and is necessary for the understanding of the king's concern (verses 9, 10) and the severe affliction that followed (verses 11ff.). Verse 7 is a remarkable endeavour adequately to express the great increase of the people. We may translate, 'And the children of Israel were fruitful, and they teemed, and they multiplied, and they became powerful exceedingly, and the land was filled with them.'

b. 1:8–7:7. The bondage of Israel in Egypt

Verses 9 and 20 allude to verse 7 and thus the unity of chapter 1 is shown. A new king had arisen who did not acknowledge the merits of Joseph in relation to Egypt, and who was alarmed at the great growth of the Israelites. Hence, by four measures he sought to oppress them. One, taskmasters were appointed (verse 11). Two, this was not successful, and so the bondage was intensified and the people made to serve with rigour (verses 13,14). Three, command to the midwives was issued to destroy the male children (verses 15, 16). And four, then the entire people were commanded to destroy the male children (verse 22). The measures adopted form a continuous series which progresses in severity, and this argues for the unity of the section. It also prepares the way for chapter 2 which is inexplicable without this background.

Chapter 2 first narrates the birth and preparation of Moses. This is necessary for the account of his later actions (verses 11ff.). It is incorrect to assign verses 1–10 to one document, and verses 11–23a to another. For verse 11 speaks of 'when Moses was grown', and this is inexplicable without the preceding. Chapter 2 relates how Moses came to be in the wilderness, and thus prepares us for the events recorded in chapter 3.

The preparation of Moses is continued in chapter 3, which recounts God's appearance to him at Horeb. The chapter obviously presupposes the preceding history. Verse 6 implies knowledge of the patriarchal history of Genesis. Verse 7 connects the chapter with 1:11–14. Verses 8 and 17 remind us of Genesis 15:18. There is a unity in the account of Moses' hesitation. He first appears as humble (3:11), he then complains that the people will not hear (4:1) and that he is not eloquent (4:10), and finally he refuses to go (4:13).

As a result of the mighty revelation at Sinai and God's gracious signs (4:2–12) Moses sets out for Egypt, and first convinces the people (4:30, 31). Next, he and Aaron appear before Pharaoh, who refuses to hearken to them (5:2) and increases the hardships of the people (5:6ff.). The officers of the people complain to Moses and Aaron (15:20–23).

The Lord then renews His promise (note that 6:3, 4 presupposes knowledge of Genesis) and introduces Himself in the character of Jehovah, the mighty covenant-redeemer God. The people still refuse to hearken to Moses, who returns to the Lord.

At this point (i.e., 6:14ff.) a genealogical table is inserted into the narrative, and obviously this is the proper place for such an insertion. Moses has received his final commission to Pharaoh. He is now shown as the leader of Israel and is ready for the great conflict with the oppressor. What better place could there be for the account of the line of Moses and Aaron than at precisely this point? A final statement of the Lord's intentions is then made in 7:1–7, which closes with a remark as to the age of Moses and Aaron.

By way of summary it may be said that this entire section indicates a remarkable unity. Each part is necessary for the proper understanding of the rest, and the book of Genesis is also a requisite for the correct understanding of this section. Further, the subsequent portions of Exodus are inexplicable without this preliminary part. The people of Israel appear here in complete bondage. From this bondage no human deliverer can set free, but only God.

c. 7:8–13:16. The Lord's wonders in Egypt
The purpose of this section is to demonstrate the superiority of the true

God over the false religions of Egypt. Pharaoh, the enemy oppressor, must be convinced that the God of Israel is the Sovereign of heaven and earth. The Israelites, too, must be convinced. Hence, in connection with the exodus, we have the first great period of biblical miracles. These miracles were necessary as accompaniments to the mighty act of deliverance which God would perform in bringing forth the people from Egypt and establishing them in Canaan. A miracle is a direct act of God's special revelation, performed by God in the external world, contrary to the ordinary course of nature, and designed to be an attestation or sign. Such were these wonders. The Scripture intends us to regard them as true miracles.

The plagues described in this section form a symmetrical scheme, and the first nine of them may be subdivided into groups of three each.

1. Blood (7:14–25)   4. Flies (8:20–32)   7. Hail (9:13–35)
2. Frogs (8:1–15)   5. Murrain (9:1–7)   8. Locusts (10:1–20)
3. Lice (8:16–19)   6. Boils (9:8–12)   9. Darkness (10:21–27)

It should be noted that the first and second plague of each series is announced to Pharaoh beforehand. The following command (with slight variations) regularly recurs in the first of each series: 'And the Lord said unto Moses, Rise up early in the morning, and stand before Pharaoh, and say unto him, Thus saith the Lord God of the Hebrews, Let my people go that they may serve me' (cf. 7:15, 16; 8:16; 9:13). The second of each series is introduced as follows: 'And the Lord said unto Moses, Go unto Pharaoh, and thou shalt say unto him, Thus saith the Lord, Send my people that they may serve me' (cf. 8:1; 9:1; and 10:1, where only the first words of the command are given). The first in each series is announced in the morning by the riverside, and the second in the king's palace, but each of the third is given without previous warning (cf. 8:16; 9:8; 10:21).

This arrangement reveals the unity of the section. The series of three times three leads up to a climax in the tenth plague. It should be noted that within the plagues there is an increase in severity and intensity, and the last three seem designed to take away from man the staff of life. In the first three the Egyptian magicians vie with Moses. They imitate the first two plagues, and Pharaoh cried out for deliverance from the second plague. At the third, the magicians acknowledge the hand of God to be present. 'This is the finger of God' (8:19). From this point on, the magicians are out of the contest.

With the second series a distinction between Israelites and Egyptians is introduced (8:23). Whereas the first series had affected the entire land, from the fourth plague on only the Egyptians are affected; and in all but the sixth and eighth plagues attention is called to the protection of Israel.

At the second and fourth and in the entire third series Pharaoh sends to Moses and Aaron with particular urgency to secure their intervention. There is an increase in the intensity of his urgency:

1. 'Intreat the Lord ... and I will let the people go' (8:8).
2. 'Go ye, sacrifice to your God .... I will let you go' (8:25,28).
3. 'I have sinned .... Intreat the Lord' (9:27–28).
4. 'I have sinned .... Forgive ... intreat' (10:16, 17).
5. 'Go ye, serve the Lord' (10:24).

The first series is wrought with the rod of Aaron; in the second no rod is mentioned; in the third the hand or rod of Moses appears.

The unity and symmetry of this section clearly show that we are not to regard it as compiled by a redactor from various previously existing documents, but rather as the work of one author. The nine plagues would be sufficient to establish the supremacy of the God of the Hebrews and to prepare for the tenth. The number ten probably indicates completeness, *i.e.*, by these plagues the Lord has exhibited the greatness of His power, so that no longer could the Egyptians claim excuse.

The account of the Passover (chapter 12) is to be regarded as historical and as a literary unit. The introductory words (12:1) show that this is a historical occurrence. The words 'in Egypt' are important as serving to point out that the first observance of the Passover had peculiar significance. The ceremony was to be conducted in private homes in a manner that clearly reveals that there was as yet no central sanctuary or priesthood. At the same time these introductory words are in accordance with the general Pentateuchal custom of indicating the place where God revealed His laws (*cf.* Lv. 7:38; 25:1; 26:46; 27:34, Nu. 35:1; 36:13).

Of the three annual feasts the Passover alone is said to have been instituted in Egypt. Why should this be unless, as a matter of actual fact, the Passover was instituted in Egypt? The words 'in Egypt' are in reality an indication of genuineness. Furthermore, the later laws relating to the feasts also connect the Passover and the Feast of Unleavened Bread with Egypt (*cf.* Ex. 23:15; 34:18 – note that both these sections are said to have been written by Moses [Ex. 24:4 and 34:27] – Nu. 9:1ff.; Dt. 16:1–8).

We must, therefore, reject the view that Exodus 12 is a late composition, intended to explain the origin of a festival that had long been observed in Israel. In other words, the idea that the Passover gave rise to the story of the supposed events of the Exodus is incorrect.

d. 13:17–18:27. The exodus from Egypt

This section begins (13:17–19) with a general statement of the departure and of the reasons why the people went through the wilderness of the Red Sea. The first stages of the journey are then stated (verse 20), and the guidance of God is related (verses 21, 22). The entire section is a compact unit.

Chapter 14:1–14 relates a command of the Lord to Moses, explaining the detailed line of march to be pursued in leaving Egypt, and hence in no way conflicts with 13:17–19. In 14:5–9 we are told of Pharaoh's reaction when he learned that the people had left, a reaction which is consistent with his attitude expressed in verse 3 when he learns that the people are hemmed in.

The crossing of the Red Sea is also told in a compact, unified narrative. Moses first announces the Lord's salvation (14:13, 14), and this is followed by the command of God (verses 16–18). Moses then obeys God's command, and the Israelites cross safely. The Egyptians, however, are drowned. The result is that Israel believes the Lord (verse 31).

The Sea of Reeds (*yam suf*) is probably to be located near modern Qantarah.[1] The deliverance is to be regarded as supernatural, and the events as a miracle. Attempts to account for the event as it is described in Exodus, merely upon the basis of natural phenomena, fail. The Lord here intervened in a special, miraculous way.

The song of Moses (chapter 15) with its stress upon the miraculous (verses 8, 10) confirms the prose account of chapter 14. Verses 13–17 do not presuppose the existence of the people in Canaan (Driver, Bentzen), but rather very clearly look forward to an introduction into the land. Verse 17 contains no specific reference to Jerusalem, but simply anticipates the permanent dwelling of the Lord in the land which He had chosen for His people. There is no warrant for regarding 15:1–19 as the work of a late psalmist.[2]

The brief song of Miriam, the antiquity of which even Pfeiffer acknowledges, was inserted by Moses after his own song. Miriam was the prophetess, and it was fitting that she should thus lead the women. There is no warrant for denying the authenticity of this song.

The account of the journey to Sinai is told with straightforward simplicity. As the present writer has stated elsewhere, 'It is perhaps understandable that those who have never been in the desert of Sinai would scoff at the historicity of the narratives in the Book of Exodus. But one who has been in this region knows that the narratives bear the air of

[1] See Albright, *BASOR*, No. 109, p. 16.
[2] *IOT*, p. 274.

reality. It is almost impossible to think that they were written by anyone who did not know the desert.'[3] There is no objective evidence to support the assumption that this section could not have been written by Moses.[4]

e. 19:1–24:18. The covenant at Mt. Sinai

In the third month of the departure from Egypt the Israelities arrived at Sinai. As soon as the people were encamped before the mount, Moses ascended, and God gave him the necessary instructions for preparing the covenant arrangements. Moses is first told of God's purpose to make of Israel a peculiar nation (verses 4–9), and he is then commanded to prepare the people for the revelation (verses 10–15). 'The promise precedes the demand; for the grace of God always anticipates the wants of man, and does not demand before it has given' (Keil). The people's preparation was to consist in their sanctification (verse 15), and the setting of bounds about them (verse 12). Moses obeyed the Lord, and on the morning of the third day the Lord came down upon the mount (verse 20), which was in smoke and quaked. Then Moses (verse 25) went down to the people. This awesome scene sets the background for the promulgation of God's holy law.

The Ten Commandments are repeated with a few alterations in Deuteronomy 5:6–21. According to many critics, the Decalogue of Exodus is E, and some even maintain that it is not an original part of E, but a later insertion. It is thought to be later than the Decalogue in Deuteronomy and even to have been worked over in the style of Deuteronomy. It contains Deuteronomic language, style, and idioms, and therefore it cannot be attributed to Moses.

But this view is incorrect. Exodus 20 is not only earlier than Deuteronomy, but there is no reason whatsoever why it may not be attributed to Moses. The Decalogue of Deuteronomy is exactly what might be expected in a free reproduction given by Moses in a popular address. (1) Deuteronomy contains back references, e.g., 5:12, 15, 16 (cf. 'as the Lord thy God hath commanded thee'). This would be without meaning if Deuteronomy were original. (2) Deuteronomy contains rhetorical amplifications, e.g., verse 14, 'thine ox, nor thine ass, nor of any of thy cattle'. (Cf. also verse 21, 'his field'; verse 16, 'that it may go well with thee'; verse 18, 'desire'.) (3) The Deuteronomic Decalogue, as might be expected, contains characteristics of Deuteronomy, e.g., verse 14, regard for the oppressed; verse 15, a motive taken from the deliverance from Egypt; verse 21, the wife is placed before the house, the particular here

---

[3] PrG, April 10, 1944, p. 110.
[4] See pp. 73f. for special bibliography.

being stated before the general, possibly a hortatory device to emphasize the value of the wife as most precious (*cf*. Pr. 12:4; 31:10).

Not only is Exodus 20 the original from which Deuteronomy 5 was derived, but Exodus 20 is also to be regarded as Mosaic. (1) The presence of Deuteronomic characteristics does not 'preclude the attribution of the Ten Commandments to Moses' (Pfeiffer). This argument holds good only if it can be proven – and it cannot – that no part of Deuteronomy could have come from Moses. If Deuteronomy is essentially Mosaic, and Exodus 20 is also Mosaic, we might well expect that the same characteristics would be present in both. (2) It is said that there is no trace of animus against idols before Isaiah's time, and hence the first commandment could not be from Moses. [5] This statement, however, is based upon a false evolutionary conception of Israel's history (*cf*. Dt. 8:11, 17, 19). (3) It is further argued that observance of the Sabbath would be inconceivable among nomads in the desert, and also that the Sabbath is said to be a Canaanitish institution. But the origin of the Sabbath is found in a divine action (Gn. 2:2, 3). (*Cf*. also Ex. 16:23–29, which shows that the Sabbath was observed in the desert. Ho. 2:11 does not support the position that the Sabbath was a Canaanitish institution.)

The brief section formed by 20:22–23:33 is of Mosaic origin (*cf*. 20:22; 21:1). It refers to the general form of worship in Israel; to the rights of the Israelites in civil and in ceremonial matters; and to the Lord's attitude towards His people. [6]

1. The general form of worship in Israel (20:22–26). The Israelites were to construct an altar of earth or unhewn stones at the place where God would reveal Himself. This altar could not be erected wherever Israel chose, but only where God made a revelation of Himself.

2. Civil legislation (21:1–23:13). This section consists of judgments (*mishpatim*), *i.e*., the rights which would secure the political order and form the civil state. Many of these laws are based upon the following form: Protasis ('if' [*ki*, like the *shum-ma* of Hammurabi's Code] and the imperfect); Apodosis (the imperfect). The Protasis is often expanded by specific, explanatory, conditional clauses, introduced by 'if' (*'im*).

It is true that the form of these laws is similar to that of other ancient codes; nevertheless, these particular laws were drawn up by Moses under divine inspiration for the specific use of Israel. It is obvious that they were never intended for observance in the desert, but are anticipatory, pointing forward to the time when Israel should dwell in the land (*e.g*.,

[5] Pfeiffer has elaborated this argument in his article, 'The Polemic against Idolatry in the Old Testament' in *JBL*, 43, pp. 229–240.
[6] See p. 74 for special bibliography.

20:22; 21:1; 23:9, 15, 20–23, 27–33). It is this fact which explains their agricultural background.

The section 21:1–23:13 deals with the rights of slaves (21:2–6); the daughter sold as a maid-servant (21:7–11); the principle of retribution, *lex talionis* (21:12–32); death (verses 12–14); maltreatment of parents, kidnapping, cursing (verses 15–17); bodily injuries (verses 18–32), property (21:33–36), theft (22:1–4), injury to another's fields (22:5–6), dishonesty (22:7–15), seduction (22:16, 17), sundry laws (22:18–31), in which laws the introductory 'if' (*ki*) is often omitted 'inasmuch as they make demands upon Israel on the grounds of its election to be the holy nation of Jehovah, which go beyond the sphere of natural right, not only prohibiting every inversion of the natural order of things, but requiring the manifestation of love to the infirm and needy out of regard to Jehovah' (Kiel) and, finally, protection of rights (23:1–13).

3. Ceremonial legislation (23:14–19). This consisted of the three annual festivals – unleavened bread (verse 15), harvest, and ingathering (verse 16).

4. The Lord's attitude towards His people (23:20–33). The ratification of the covenant is related in 24:1–18.

f. 25:1–31:18. The sanctuary and priesthood

This section naturally follows the Book of the Covenant. In order that an external manifestation of the covenant might be made, the Lord commands the erection of a Tabernacle in which He may take His dwelling. The pattern and arrangements were revealed to Moses by God in the mount. The section may be analysed as follows: introduction, in which the people are commanded to bring gifts for the sanctuary (25:1–9); a description of the ark, the throne of the Lord in the sanctuary (verses 10–22); the table of shew-bread and golden candlestick (verses 23–40); the manner of constructing the Tabernacle (chapter 26); the altar of burnt offering and the outer court (27:1–10); the candlestick (verses 20, 21); the institution of the priesthood and the service of consecration (chapters 28, 29); the altar of incense and its use (30:1–10); sundry laws respecting the service. Moses receives the two tables of the law (30:11–31:18).

g. 32:1–35:3. The covenant broken and renewed

The unity of this section is particularly apparent, although some critics have sought to deny it.

1. It is incorrect to say (*e.g.*, Driver) that 32:34–33:6 contains traces of a double narrative; *i.e.*, 33:3b, 4, repeated in 33:5, 6. To say this is to

misunderstand the emphasis of the passage. When the people heard that the Lord would not go in their midst, they mourned because they had incurred His displeasure, and, as a sign of mourning, did not put on (*lo' shathu*) their ornaments. In order that this beginning of repentance might lead to a permanent change of heart, the Lord repeated His description (verse 5, 'And the Lord said' – *wayyo'mer*) of the people and issued a new command, 'Throw away [*horedh*] thy ornaments from upon thee, that I may know what I should do to thee.'

2. It is gratuitous to assume that 33:7–11 was preceded by an account of the construction of the Tent of Meeting and to affirm that the ornaments of verses 4–6 were offered for the use of the Tent. The ornaments were not worn, as an expression of mourning upon the part of the people. Further, the tenses of these verses (they have a frequentative force) merely describe habitual practice during the time of this provisional sanctuary. The name of this provisional sanctuary (*'ohel mo'edh* – tent of the assembly) was taken from the instructions already given concerning the future sanctuary (*e.g.*, 21:21; 28:43; *etc.*). It temporarily represented the thought which would find permanent embodiment in the future structure, that the Lord dwelt in the midst of His people. Although the sin of the people had been great, the Lord had not abandoned them. Nevertheless, this temporary sanctuary was outside the camp, as the Lord would not yet dwell within the sinful nation.

3. In 34:1 it is said that the Lord will write upon the tables of the Law, but in 34:28 it is Moses who writes thereupon. This, according to Driver, is 'the great difficulty' in 34:1–28. Verse 28, however, does not state that Moses wrote. To make Moses the subject of 'and he wrote' (verse 28) is to confuse the 'ten words' (verses 1, 28) with that which Moses actually did write, namely, the contents of the preceding verses (verse 27 – 'these words' refers to the preceding context, not to the ten commandments of verse 28). The subject of 'and he wrote' (verse 28) is the Lord. There is no contradiction here.

The only refutation of the higher critical analysis of this section is to work carefully through the text, allowing it to speak for itself. When this is done, the clear unity and harmony of the section become apparent. Even Driver confesses that, although 32–34 'displays plain marks of composition, it fails to supply the criteria requisite for distributing it with every detail between the different narrators'.[7] May not the reason for this be that the section is after all a unified whole, the product of one writer?

[7] *IOT*,[8] p. 39.

h. 35:4–40:38. The preparation and erection of the Tabernacle
This section is repeated for the most part almost word for word from
25–31, except that the past is employed instead of the future, *e.g.*, 'And
thou shalt make a vail of blue, and purple and scarlet, and fine twined linen
of cunning work: with cherubims shall it be made' (26:31); 'And *he made*
a vail of blue, and purple, and scarlet, and fine twined linen: with
cherubim made he it of cunning work' (36:35).

This repetition of the exact phraseology of the instructions given to
Moses in chapters 25–31 serves to impress upon the mind of the reader the
fact that these instructions were obyed in detail.[8] The principal omissions
are the Urim and Thummim (28:30), the consecration of the priests
(29:1–37), the oil for the lamps (27:20ff.), and the daily burnt offering
(29:38–42). But the reason for these omissions is that these subjects are
discussed later (Urim, Lv. 8:8; oil, Lv. 24:2; daily offering, Nu. 28:3;
priests, Lv. 8).

The completion of the Tabernacle is an external pledge of the
permanence of the covenant of grace. The God of deliverance (the Lord)
has taken up His abode in the midst of His people. Yet, they are excluded
from immediate access into His presence by the veil which shut off the
most holy place to all but the high priest and to him also, except on the
Day of Atonement. Through endeavour to obey the Sinaitic legislation
the people would be taught their need of a mediator, a mediator who
would combine the prophetic office of Moses and the priestly office of
Aaron. Thus, the arrangements of the Tabernacle were typical, preparatory for the one Sacrifice that has taken away the sins of the world.

ALLEGED POST-MOSAICA IN EXODUS

1. Exodus 6:26, 27. 'These are that Aaron and Moses.' It has been
suggested that one would only write thus of individuals who had lived in
the past. But it should be noted that these words follow a genealogy, and
have the force of 'This is the genealogy of Moses and Aaron to whom
God spoke' (verse 13). Thus, when verse 26 is compared with verse 14 it
has the same force as verse 27 when compared with verse 13.

'The words are repeated at the end of verse 27, in order to mark
precisely the close of the genealogy and the resumption of the history.
They here perform the same service as the phrases of transition in more
connected historical writings. At the beginning the genealogical
reference predominates, and Aaron stands as the elder, – at the end, the
historical point of view is taken, and Moses is named first as the most

---

[8] *FB*, p. 61.

important personage; just as in ver. 13, Moses is first, where the author passes from the history to genealogy.'⁹

2. Exodus 16:33–35. It is the phrase 'before the testimony' (verse 34) which causes the difficulty. How, it is asked, could this reference to the tables of the Law have been written by Moses before the Law was actually given? But, since this is the principal passage concerning the manna, why may not Moses have written it at a later time and inserted it here? Verse 35 is also said to point to a time beyond Moses. But this verse merely states that the Israelites ate manna until they came to an inhabited land. It says nothing about the termination of eating manna or about their practice after they entered an inhabited land. Hence, it is perfectly possible that Moses, while reviewing the Pentateuch in the plains of Moab, may have inserted this verse.

3. Exodus 16:36. The explanation of the value of an omer is said to indicate a time of composition when the value of the omer was no longer known. But the word 'omer' is used throughout this passage (verses 16, 18, 22, 23) and nowhere else in the Scriptures. The omer, however, was not a measure but a small cup, and it is perfectly understandable that Moses might have remarked upon the size of this cup when it was used to gather the manna.

SPECIAL LITERATURE ON EXODUS

Andreas Eberharter, *Der Dekalog* (Münster i. W., 1929); Wilhelm Engelkemper, *Heiligtum und Opferstätten in den Gesetzen des Pentateuchs* (Paderborn, 1908); Hugo Gressman, *Mose und seine Zeit* (Göttingen, 1913); B. Jacob, *The Decalogue* (Philadelphia, 1923); Melvin Grove Kyle, *Moses and the Monuments** (Oberlin, 1920); A. Lucas, *The Route of the Exodus of the Israelites from Egypt* (London, 1938); Sigmund Mowinckel, *Le Décalogue* (Paris, 1927); Martin Noth, *Die Gesetze im Pentateuch* (Halle, 1940); W. M. Flinders Petrie, *Egypt and Israel* (London, 1911); E. C. Richardson, 'The Documents of the Exodus, Contemporary, Original, and Written',* in *PTR*, 10, pp. 581–605; A. Sanda, *Moses und der Pentateuch* (Münster i. W., 1924); Ernst Sellin, *Mose und seine Bedeutung für die israelitisch-jüdische Religionsgeschichte* (Leipzig, 1922); Olaf A. Toffteen, *The Historic Exodus* (Chicago, 1909); David Volter, *Aegypten und die Bibel* (Leiden, 1909); *Mose und die aegyptische Mythologie* (Leiden, 1912); Paul Volz, *Mose und sein Werk* (Tübingen, 1932); Harold M. Wiener, *The Altars of the Old Testament* (Leipzig, 1927); R. D. Wilson, 'Critical Note on Exodus 6:3',* in *PTR*, 22, pp. 108–119; C. de Wit, *The Date and Route of the Exodus** (London, 1959).

SPECIAL LITERATURE ON THE JOURNEY TO SINAI

Franklin E. Hoskins, *From the Nile to Nebo** (Philadelphia, 1912); Ditlef Nielsen, *The Site of the Biblical Mount Sinai* (Leipzig, 1928); Edward Robinson, *Biblical Researches in Palestine, Mount Sinai and Arabia Petraea* (Boston, I, 1841; II, 1856, the relevant section

⁹ Hengstenberg, *DGP*, II, p. 168.

being in I, pp. 49–254); Ludwig D. Schneller, *Durch die Wüste zum Sinai* (Leipzig, 1910);
Arthur Penrhyn Stanley, *Sinai and Palestine* (New York, 1857, pp. 1–108 discuss Sinai).

SPECIAL LITERATURE ON THE BOOK OF THE COVENANT

Albrecht Alt, *Die Ursprünge des israelitischen Rechts* (Leipzig, 1934); Alfred Jepsen,
Untersuchungen zum Bundesbuch (Stuttgart, 1927); James A. Kelso, 'The Code of Ham-
murabi and the Book of the Covenant',* *PTR*, 3, pp. 399–412; Abraham Menes, *Die
vorexilischen Gesetze Israels* (Giessen, 1928); Julian Morgenstern, 'The Book of the
Covenant', in *HUCA*, V, pp. 1–151; VII, pp. 19–258; VIII–IX, pp. 1–150; J. W.
Rothstein, *Mose und das Gesetz* (Berlin, 1911).

CHAPTER FIVE

LEVITICUS

NAME

LEVITICUS, the third book of Moses, opens with the words 'And he called' (*way yiqra'*), and is so designated by the Jews. In Talmudic times it was also called Law of the Priests (*torath kohanim*). In the LXX it bears the title *Levitikon* ('Levitical', an adjective modifying the word *biblion*, 'book', which is to be understood). The Vulgate designates it simply *Leviticus*.

PURPOSE

The book of Leviticus contains the laws which are to govern the organized people of God in their religious and civil life. At Mt. Sinai the Israelites had been formally organized into the theocratic nation. The basic law had been given, the covenant had been ratified, and the Tabernacle had been erected. Thus, the Lord had taken up His abode in the midst of His people. Before the people could continue their journey to the promised land, however, it was necessary that they should know the laws which were to guide them in their worship of the Lord at the Tabernacle. These laws are contained in Leviticus. Hence, it is apparent that, although Leviticus is a self-contained unit, it is in its proper place and presupposes for its correct understanding the narratives of Exodus.

ANALYSIS

There is in the book a deep, underlying unity of plan and thought which expresses itself in a twofold way. First, Leviticus deals with the removal of that defilement which separates man from God and, secondly, with the restoration of the lost fellowship between man and God.

I. THE REMOVAL OF THAT DEFILEMENT WHICH SEPARATES MAN
FROM GOD (CHAPTERS 1–16)

a. 1:1–7:38. The law of sacrifice
From the Tabernacle, God's dwelling-place, the Lord spoke to Moses,

even as He had promised in Exodus 25:22, revealing His holy will concerning the sacrifices whereby the defilement of the sinful people might be removed and they might draw near to Him in humble faith.

1. Chapter 1. The burnt offering. The general term for offering is *korban*, which is applied to various types of offerings. It is that which is 'brought near' to the Lord.

2. Chapter 2. The meal offering (*minhah*). Note in verses 4–16 the tender, individualizing second person singular, as in Deuteronomy. It is not an indication that the chapter was combined from different sources.

3. Chapter 3. The peace offering (*zevah shelamim*).

4. Chapter 4:1–5:13. The sin offering (*hatta'th*).

5. Chapter 5:14–26. The guilt offering (*'asham*).

6. Chapter 6:8–13. Burnt offerings; 6:14–23, meal offerings; 6:24–30, sin offerings.

7. Chapter 7. Various sacrifices.

The fuller statements in chapter 44 regarding the sin offering (in comparison with Ex. 29:12; Lv. 8:15; 9:9, 15) do not indicate an advanced stage in the growth of the sacrificial system. Rather, the purpose is, since this passage contains the specific law of the sin offering as it is to be observed by various classes of people, to present the law in its fullness.

It should be noted that the laws in chapters 1–5 are addressed to all Israel, those in chapters 6, 7 to Aaron and his sons. The laws in these two latter chapters also, in some respects, exhibit a slightly different point of view from those in 1–5. This does not imply, however, diversity of authorship. This is seen in that both sections mention the same kinds of sacrifice and there are obvious references from one section to the other. (*Cf.* 6:17 with chapter 4; 3:5 with 6:22; 6:30 must be understood in the light of 4:22–27.)

b. 8:1–10:20. The consecration of the priests

According to the instructions in Exodus 29:1–36 and 40:12–15, Moses proceeds now to anoint Aaron and his sons.

1. 8:1–5. The Lord's command; preparation for the anointment.

2. 8:6–13. The washing, clothing and anointing of the priests.

3. 8:14–32. The ceremony of sacrifice in connection with the consecration.

4. 9:1–7. Moses instructs Aaron as to his entry into office.

5. 9:8–21. Aaron and his sons enter upon their office.

6. 9:22–24. Aaron blesses the people, and the Lord's glory is manifested.

7. 10:1–3. The strange fire of Nadab and Abihu.

8. 10:4–7. Nadab and Abihu are carried from the camp.

9. 10:8–11. Abstinence from wine in the Tabernacle is enjoined upon the priests.

10. 10:12–20. Concerning the eating of the holy things.

There is no conflict between the practice of 9:11, 15 and 10:16–20, and it is incorrect to say that 10:16–20 is a correction (Driver) of 9:15b. The law was (*cf.* 4:1–21) that there could be *burnt* only the flesh of the sin offering whose blood *had been brought within* the Tabernacle and applied to the altar of incense. But 9:8ff. is dealing with a special case, the induction of the priests into office. Since the purpose is not to make expiation for some particular sin of Aaron's but rather to remove whatever sin might make him unfit for service in his priestly office, the blood *on this occasion* was not taken into the Tabernacle but was applied to the horns of the altar of burnt offering where the congregation communed with the Lord.

c. 11:1–15:33. The clean and unclean; purification

1. Chapter 11. Clean and unclean animals. The chapter serves as an introduction to the laws of purification. It is the penetration of sin into the material creation that produces in man's mind a horror or disgust of certain kinds of animals for food.

Verses 2b–23 are repeated essentially in Deuteronomy 14:6–20. Both accounts are not to be regarded as derived from an earlier common source, nor is Deuteronomy earlier than Leviticus. Rather, Leviticus is the earlier account and Deuteronomy is a later account, and serves as a summary. Deuteronomy presents the gist of the law and is what one might expect in a popular summary made by Moses such as Deuteronomy claims to be.

2. Chapter 12. Purification of a woman after childbirth.

3. Chapters 13, 14. The laws of leprosy. A fourfold division appears here. (i) 13:1–44, leprosy in man; (ii) 13:47–59, leprosy in garments; (iii) 14:1–32, purifications; (iv) 14:33–35, leprosy in houses. Of the above (ii), (iii) and (iv) are each divided into four subdivisions.

4. Chapter 15. Purification after certain secretions. Verses 1–15, a running issue from man; verses 16–18, the issue of seed; verses 19–24, the issues of woman; verses 25–33, diseased issue of woman.

d. 16:1–34. The Day of Atonement

The chapter contains laws for the general expiation of the sins of the people for the year (verses 1–28), and directions for the annual celebration of the festival (verses 29–34). These two subjects are not imperfectly connected (Driver), but rather verse 29 leads naturally from one to the other. 'And it shall become to you an eternal statute.' The words obviously refer to what has just been related and also introduce the following section. Hence, there is no warrant for the assumption of composite authorship.

II. THE RESTORATION OF THE LOST FELLOWSHIP BETWEEN MAN AND GOD (CHAPTERS 17–26)

e. 17:1–16. The blood of sacrifice

Chapters 17–26 are thought by many critics to distinguish themselves by certain characteristics from the main body of the so-called P document. They have been generally designated as the Law of Holiness or H, a title first given (das Heiligkeitsgesetz) by A. Klostermann in 1877.

These laws, although they present striking resemblances in some respects to Ezekiel, nevertheless form an integral part of the Mosaic legislation, and are not to be regarded as an independent body of legislation. It is true that they stress the subject of holiness, and it is this fact which gives them their particular complexion. There is present a hortatory form, somewhat similar to that of Deuteronomy, and this is surely natural in a section the purpose of which is to enjoin holiness of life.

It is obvious that chapter 17 forms a connecting link with what precedes. Note, e.g., the following expressions, all of which presuppose the preceding narrative and legislation of Exodus and Leviticus: verse 2, 'unto Aaron, and unto his sons'; verse 3, 'the camp'; verses 4, 9, 'the door of the tabernacle of the congregation'; verse 5, 'unto the priests, and offer them for peace offerings'; verse 6, 'priest shall sprinkle the blood upon the altar of the Lord . . . burn the fat'; verse 8, 'strangers which sojourn'; verse 9, 'shall be cut off from among his people'; verse 11, 'atonement'. It will not do to say that these phrases have been added or inserted to bring the chapter into conformity with P, for when these phrases are omitted very little remains.

It should be noted that verses 3, 4 are intended to be a temporary law, to be observed in the wilderness before the entry into the land of promise. Hence, this chapter is to be regarded as earlier than Deuteronomy.

f. 18:1–20:27. Religious and ethical laws and punishments

1. Chapters 18, 19. Religious and ethical laws. (i) 18:1–5. Introductory. The words 'I am the Lord' both here and throughout the chapter (cf. verses 2, 4, 5, 6, 21, 30) serve to emphasize the necessity for holiness which the Lord requires. (ii) 18:6–18. Laws against incest. (iii) 18:19–23.

Prohibition of other sexual sins. (iv) 18:24–30. Sundry warnings. The standpoint in verses 24–30 does not change, nor is the conquest looked back upon as already having occurred (Driver). Rather, the passage must be understood in the light of the participle *meshalleach* in verse 24, which verse I would translate, 'Ye shall not defile yourselves in all these, for in all these have the nations which I am about to send away from before you defiled themselves.' (v) 19:18. The Lord's purpose that His people should be holy. (Note again the recurrence of the phrase 'I am the Lord', verses 3, 4, 10, 12, 14, 16, 18, 25, 28, 30, 31, 32, 34, 37.) (vi) 19:9–18. Laws of conduct towards one's neighbour. (vii) 19:19–32. Sundry statutes.

2. Chapter 20. Punishments. The punishments here prescribed are so closely related to the crimes mentioned in chapters 18 and 19 that it is obvious the three chapters come from one author. The fact that four of the cases mentioned in chapter 18 are not referred to in chapter 20 and the fact of slight variation in grouping is but evidence of genuineness. A redactor would have taken pains to insure perfect correspondence.

g. 21:1–22:33. The holiness of the priests
This section falls into two principal parts. (1) 21:1–22:16. The sanctity of the priests. (i) verses 1–6. The priests must not incur defilement by touching the dead. (ii) Verses 7–15. The marriage of priests. (iii) Verses 16–24. Priests with bodily weaknesses. (iv) 22:1–16. Reverence for those things that are sanctified. (2) 22:17–33. Sacred oblations.

It is true that this section exhibits a unique character, but this is because of the subject-matter. Phrases which are said to exhibit the ideas of P are supposed by some to have been added by a redactor. But these phrases simply show that the chapters constitute an integral part of Leviticus.

h. 23:1–24:23. The consecration of seasons
1. Chapter 23. A list of the times at which holy convocations were to be held. (i) Verses 1–3. The Sabbath. (ii) Verse 4. The annual feasts. Passover, verses 5–8. First-fruits, verses 9–14. The Feast of Harvest, verses 15–22. (iii) Verses 23–25. Pentecost. (iv) Verses 26–32. The Day of Atonement. (v) Verses 33–43. The Feast of Tabernacles.

It is obvious that this chapter presents a difficulty to the critical analysis. Nearly everything herein mentioned has already been set forth in the so-called P document. In fact, the chapter presupposes both Exodus and chapters 1–16 of Leviticus. Driver seeks to escape the difficulty by saying that the chapter consists of excerpts taken from two sources in such a manner that they mutually supplement one another. He divides the chapter as follows:

H	9–20	22		39b	40–43	
P	1–8		21	23–38, 39a	39c	44

However, it is obvious that even the verses attributed to H contain elements which belong to the so-called P document, *e.g.*, verse 10, first-fruits (*cf.* Ex. 22:29); verse 11, wave offering (*cf.* Ex. 29:24; Lv. 14:12, 24; *cf.* also Lv. 7:30; the terms *wehenif, tenuphah* belong decidedly to P); verse 39b, the feast of seven days (*cf.* Nu. 29:12). Verse 43b certainly presupposes knowledge of the account of the exodus. These phenomena simply prove that the chapter is a unit and that it bears an integral relation to the entire book of Leviticus.

2. Chapter 24. (i) Verses 1–4. The sacred candlestick. (ii) Verses 5–9. The shewbread. (iii) Verses 10–23. The account of one who had blasphemed. This account serves to illustrate the administration of the divine law and also provides the reason for certain of the laws.

i. 25:1–55. The sabbatical and Jubilee years

Many critics believe that this chapter is composed of elements belonging both to H and P. According to Driver the marks of H are most prominent in verses 1–7; 14f.; 17–22; 35–32; 42, 43, 55, and are least prominent in verses 29–34. However, there is a unity in this chapter which really precludes hair-splitting analysis into 'documents'. (1) Verse 1. Introductory heading. Note the words 'Moses' and 'Sinai' which point back to Exodus 34:32. (2) Verses 2–7. The sabbatical year. (3) Verses 8–55. The year of Jubilee. Section 3 is further divided as follows: (i) Verses 8–12. The observance of the year of Jubilee. (ii) Verses 13–34. The effects of the Jubilee observance upon the possession of property and upon (iii) verses 35–55, the personal freedom of the Israelite.

j. 26:1–46. Promises and threats

As the Book of the Covenant had concluded with promises and threats (Ex. 23:20–33), so also does the entire Sinaitic legislation. (1) Verses 1, 2. Introduction; the essence of the whole law is summed up in these two commandments, the prohibition of idolatry and the injunction to true worship. (2) Verses 3–13. The blessing which comes from faithfulness to the Law. (3) Verses 14–33. The curse which comes from disobedience to the Law. This section falls into four sub-sections: (i) Verses 18–20. Resistance to the punishments of verses 14–17. (ii) Verses 21, 22. Actual rebellion. (iii) Verses 23–26. Persistence in rebellion. (iv) Verses 27–33. Continued apostasy. (4) Verses 34–45. The purpose of God's judgment. (5) Verse 46. Concluding statements regarding the entire Sinaitic legislation.

According to many critics, Leviticus 17–26 consists of elements belonging to P which have been combined with excerpts from an earlier, independent body of law (H), supposed to be characterized by peculiar phraseology and principles. But against this must be argued the remarkable unity of structure which these chapters exhibit, and secondly, their integral relationship with the earlier chapters of Leviticus. Note, further, and this cannot lightly be dismissed, the claim is made seventeen times in these chapters that the Lord spoke unto Moses the laws which follow. Further, the entire section begins with the statement, 'And the Lord spake unto Moses, saying' (17:1), and closes with the summary, 'These are the statutes and the judgments and the laws which the Lord gave [*nathan*] between Himself and the children of Israel in Mount Sinai by the hand of Moses' (26:46).

k. 27:1–34. An appendix
Since vows were not an essential part of the laws of the Sinaitic covenant, but rather were an expression of willing devotion, the directions for making vows are given after the formal conclusion of the covenant (26:46). The chapter falls into seven parts: (1) 1–8. The vows of persons. (2) 9–13. Animals. (3) 14–15. A house. (4) 16–25. Land. (5) 26–27. Firstlings. (6) 28–29. Devoted things. (7) 30–34. The tenth of the land.

THE LEVITICAL SACRIFICES

The people of Israel were formally constituted as the theocracy in whose midst the holy God took His abode. But the 'kingdom of priests and holy nation' was also a sinful people. How might it draw nigh unto God? In order to make possible the access of the sinner to God, the sacrificial system was instituted.

Sacrifices serve a two-fold end, that of expiation and that of consecration. It will be seen, therefore, that sacrifice, particularly as it serves the end of expiation, has to do with sin. In the Bible, sacrifices are regarded as offerings, *i.e.*, that which is brought near to the Lord, gifts of holiness. These holy gifts are brought to the altar where the Lord dwells, and the Lord directly consumes the sacrifices. This, of course, must be understood symbolically and not in any crass, naturalistic sense.

All that might be brought unto the Lord as an offering had to be ceremonially clean. From the animal kingdom, oxen, sheep, goats and pigeons might be sacrificed; and from the vegetable kingdom, corn, wine, and oils. Thus, the sacrifice came from that which sustained the life of the offerer (the animal kingdom), and from that which the offerer produced by the toil of his life(the vegetable kingdom). Hence it may be said that in sacrifice the entirety of the offerer's life was consecrated to the Lord.

The sacrifice was also a substitute, offered in the stead of the sinner. In itself, of course, it did not have power to put away sin, but was typical of the one great sacrifice of Christ, and to Him it pointed forward.

How, then, should the contrite sinner bring his offering to the Lord? There were several steps in the process. The animal chosen had to be a perfect specimen, free from blemish or defect, for to the holy God only the best must be brought. When the animal was brought into the sanctuary, the offerer was to lay his hands upon it, or, as the phrase literally says, was to lean his hands upon it. This act symbolized the transfer of sin from the offerer to the offering. Thus the offering was regarded as the substitute for the offerer. Sin with its death-bringing penalty had rested upon the offerer. But by laying his hands upon the offering there was symbolized the fact that the penalty of death now rested upon the offering and no longer upon the offerer.

After the offerer's hands had lain upon the offering there followed the next step, the slaying of the offering upon the place of slaying (the altar). The offering was to be slain by the hands of the one who brought it, and by the priests its blood was to be applied to the altar. Thus, for example, we read, 'And he [the offerer] shall kill the bullock before the Lord: and the priests, Aaron's sons, shall bring the blood, and sprinkle the blood about the altar that is by the door of the tabernacle of the congregation' (Lv. 1:5). The sacrifice, therefore, was slain, its blood poured out and, as the symbol of life, brought before God by being applied to the altar.

The blood was said to make a covering for the soul. 'For the life of the flesh is in the blood; and I have given it to you upon the altar to make covering for your souls: for it is the blood that makes covering by reason of the life' (Lv. 17:11). The thought seems to be that the blood which was shed and applied to the altar blotted out or obliterated sin from the sight of God by being smeared over the altar. Man and his sin is that which needs covering, and this covering is procured by God, not by man. Thus, at this important point, we are reminded again that the salvation of the sinner is by grace. It is of God and not of man. 'The priest [as the representative of God] shall cover him on account of his sin' (Lv. 4:35). Such is the divine interpretation.

Next followed the burning of certain parts of the animal upon the altar. This burning was to offer a sweet-smelling odour to the Lord. Thus it was symbolical of that substitutionary consecration which was offered to God by the victims. We are reminded of the words of Paul, 'Christ also loved us and gave himself up for us, an offering and a sacrifice to God for an odour of a sweet smell' (Eph. 5:2). Lastly, and peculiar to the peace offerings, there was the sacrificial meal, prepared by the Lord Himself. Thus was symbolized the blessed fact that sin had been expiated, and the barrier between God and man removed. It also included a state of positive favour and blessedness.[1]

SPECIAL LITERATURE ON LEVITICUS

Patrick Fairbairn, *The Typology of Scripture*,* II (Edinburgh, 1864), pp. 317–460; George Buchanan Gray, *Sacrifice in the Old Testament* (Oxford, 1925); Sven Herner, *Die Opfermahle nach dem Priesterkodex* (Lund, 1911); Walter Stephen Moule, *The Offerings Made Like Unto the Son of God** (London, 1915); W. O. E. Oesterley, *Sacrifices in Ancient Israel* (London, 1937); P. Dionys Schoetz, *Schuld und Sündopfer im Alten Testament* (Breslau, 1930); Alex. Stewart, *The Mosaic Sacrifices** (Edinburgh, 1883); Adolf Wendel, *Das Opfer in der altisraelitischen Religion* (Leipzig, 1927).

SPECIAL LITERATURE ON THE LAW OF HOLINESS

Bruno Baentsch, *Das Heiligeits-Gesetz* (1893); *CH*, pp. 269–283; A. Klostermann, *Der Pentateuch* (1893), pp. 368ff.; *POT*, pp. 308–315; *IOT*, pp. 239–250; Riehm, *Einleitung*, I (1889), pp. 177–201; W. Kornfeld, *Studien zum Heiligkeitsgesetz* (1952); R. Rendtorff, *Die Gesetze in der Priesterschrift. Eine gattungsgeschichtliche Untersuchung* (1954).

[1] See Geerhardus Vos, *Biblical Theology** (1948), pp. 172–190.

CHAPTER SIX

NUMBERS

NAME

B Y the Jews this book is called 'In the wilderness' (*bemidhbar* – the word is construct) or 'And he spake' (*wayedhabber*). The LXX gave it the title 'Numbers' (*arithmoi*), and this is followed by the Vulgate.

PURPOSE

The book of Numbers follows naturally the legislation of Leviticus. The priestly laws have been revealed, and the nation is now ready to continue its march to the land of promise. Hence, Numbers first relates the preparations which were made for the departure from Sinai. It then narrates the departure of the Israelites from Sinai until finally they come to the plains of Moab, and then closes with the recital of certain events which occurred there, together with instructions for the conquest and division of the land.

ANALYSIS

The book falls into three principal divisions: (*a*) 1:1–10:10. Preparations for the departure from Sinai. (*b*) 10:11–21:35. The journey from Sinai to the plains of Moab. (*c*) 22:1–36:13. Events in the plains of Moab.

a. 1:1–10:10. Preparation for the departure from Sinai
The period herein described occupied nineteen days, from the 1st to the 20th of the second month of the second year after the exodus from Egypt.
  1. Chapters 1–4. The numbering and arrangement of the people. The census recorded in 1:1–54 was taken exactly one month after the erection of the Tabernacle (Ex. 40:17). It included the sum of the congregation, according to their families, by the house of their fathers, and it included only those who could serve in military service, twenty years of age and upward (1:2, 3). The total thus obtained was 603,550. (1:46). The census in chapter 2 gives the order of the tribes in their camps, each by its standard (*degel*) in relation to the Tent of Meeting. It is

obvious that chapters 1–4 presuppose a condition when the people were not settled in the land.

Three objections to these chapters have been made. (i) If the number of fighting men was about 600,000, the total population, it is claimed, would then be about 2½ million, and it would have been impossible for the seventy families which came into Egypt to have multiplied thus rapidly during the time of their oppression. But while this rapid multiplication might be unusual, it certainly was not impossible, and we should note that the Bible stresses the extraordinary fruitfulness of the Hebrews (Ex. 1:7). (ii) The wilderness of Sinai, it is claimed, could not have sustained so great a group of people. But if the people were encamped in the plain of Er-Rahah before Jebel es-Safsaf, they were in a plain about four miles in length and quite wide, with which several wide, lateral valleys join. Further, the sustenance of the people was not the natural produce of Sinai but the miraculous gift of manna. (iii) The order of march is said to be impossible, as described in chapter 2 and 10:14–20. But if the account is so impossible, surely no writer would have devised such an impossible scheme. The very difficulty involved is but an indication of historicity. Since so little is said about the details of the march, we are in no position to question the historicity and accuracy of the statements made.

In chapter 3 there is given the roll of the tribe of Levi. This tribe was chosen in place of the first-born of all the tribes in order to aid the priests in the performance of the duties of the sanctuary.

Chapter 4 relates the mustering of the three families of the Levites. (i) Verses 1–20. The Kohathites. (ii) Verses 21–28. The Gershonites. (iii) Verses 29–33. The Merarites. (iv) Verses 34–49. Summary of the mustering of the Levites: 2,750 Kohathites; 2,630 Gershonites; 3,200 Merarites; *i.e.*, 8,580 Levites from the total of 22,000 (3:39) who were qualified to serve.

2. Chapters 5, 6. Cleansing and blessing of the congregation.

3. Chapters 7:1–9:14. The last events at Sinai. (i) Chapter 7. Offering of gifts from the tribes. (ii) Chapter 8. The consecration of the Levites. (iii) Chapter 9:1–14. The Passover at Sinai.

4. Chapters 9:15–10:10. The cloud and trumpets for the march.

The first section of Numbers obviously forms a literary unit. This fact is recognized even by negative criticism which assigns the entire section to the so-called P document.

b. 10:11–21:35. The journey from Sinai to the Plains of Moab

1. Chapters 10:11–14:45. The journey from Sinai to Kadesh-barnea.

This section describes the removal from Sinai (10:11–36), the complaining of the people at Taberah and their lusting at Kibroth-hattaavah (chapter 11). Then follows an account of the presumptuous conduct of Miriam and Aaron against Moses (chapter 12), the sending forth of the spies, and the murmuring and subsequent punishment of the people.

It has been claimed that 12:3 must be post-Mosaic, for Moses would not write of himself in the third person nor would he speak of himself in the terms herein employed. But Moses speaks of himself elsewhere in the third person (*e.g.*, Ex. 6:27; 7:1, 20; *etc.*). There is nothing unusual in this use of the third person (*cf.*, *e.g.*, Caesar's Commentaries).

Nor can it be maintained that Moses would not have written of himself as in 12:3. It was because of his exalted position in the divine economy that Moses was the meekest of men and therefore would not stoop to defend himself against such an attack. Hence the Lord spake suddenly, coming to his defence. If verse 3 be not original, the action of the Lord (verse 4) is inexplicable.

Chapters 13 and 14 are said to contain a double narrative, and are partitioned as follows by Driver:

P 13:1–17a	21	25–26a to 'Paran'		32a	
JE	17b–20	22–24		26b–31	32b–33

P 14:1–2 (in the main)		5–7	10	26–30	34–38	
JE	3–4	8–9	11–25	31–33		39–45

The reasons for making such a partition are said to be that certain verses repeat or parallel what is said in other verses, and that there are differences of representation. Apparently the first to conduct the critical attack on these chapters was Vater, who noticed that whereas in 14:6, 30, 38 both Joshua and Caleb are mentioned, in 13:30 and 14:24 Caleb alone appears. Hence he concluded that 14:1–10, *etc.* was a separate document.

But the first really thorough analysis was undertaken by Knobel and his results have in the main been adopted by the critics. There is in these chapters, however, a certain unified progression which no critical analysis can destroy. Thus:

(i) 13:1–25 relates the mission of the spies. It is claimed, however, that there were two different starting-points. According to P, the spies started from the wilderness of Paran; according to JE, from Kadesh, which is in the wilderness of Zin (*e.g.*, Nu. 20:1; 27:14). But it should be noted, and Driver acknowledges this, that *nowhere* is it explicitly stated that the spies started from Kadesh. The word 'Kadesh' comes from verse 26, where it is identified as being in Paran. Verse 26 should be translated,

'And they went and came back . . . unto the wilderness of Paran, to Kadesh.' Even if the critical partition were correct, it should be noted that the redactor wished to associate Kadesh and Paran. Since Kadesh was on the border of Paran and Zin, it might be said to be in either. We conclude, therefore, that the only starting-point mentioned is Paran. It is further asserted that according to JE the spies went only to Hebron (13:22-25), whereas according to P (13:21) they even went to Rehob in the far north (*cf.* Jdg. 18:28). But even JE does not restrict the spies to Hebron and Eshcol. They are commanded to go up not only southward (verse 17), but also up into the mountain, *i.e.*, the land proper (*cf.* Jos. 11:3), and they are commanded to find out about the land and its cities. And this is precisely what they present in their report (verses 27-31, JE). We conclude, therefore, that the spies did as Moses commanded, they went through the whole land. Such a conclusion is based on what is said in verse 21 (P) and what is said in the verses attributed to JE. (An incidental evidence of Mosaic authorship is verse 22b, with its implication that Zoan was better known than Hebron.)

(ii) 13:26-33. The evil report of the spies which Caleb opposes in vain. This section is supposed to contain at least two discrepancies. (*a*) According to JE (*i.e.*, verses 27-31), the land is represented as being fertile and unconquerable, whereas according to P (verse 32), it is impoverished. To support this interpretation of verse 32, appeal is sometimes made to Leviticus 26:38 and Ezekiel 36:13. But it is questionable whether Leviticus 26:38 will bear this interpretation. At any rate, what Numbers 13:32 means is not that the land is impoverished, but rather that there were powerful foes who would devour the people. Nowhere is there any intimation that the people feared the unhealthiness of the region, rather they feared the mighty people of the land (*cf.* verse 32b). We conclude, therefore, that this alleged contradiction is imaginary. (*b*) According to JE (verse 30), Caleb acts alone, and later he alone is exempted from the sentence of exclusion from Palestine (14:24, JE). In P, however, Joshua is included with Caleb among the spies (14:6, 30, 38). Here again the contradiction is imaginary. But, we may ask, are we to believe that there was actually an Israelitish tradition to the effect that Joshua could not enter the promised land and that an editor would insert such a tradition (JE) into the very book which relates his appointment to be Moses' successor to bring about the conquest and division of the land? The answer to the alleged discrepancy must be found in a careful exposition of the text. To that we must now devote our attention. 13:26-33 relates the unfavourable report which the spies brought back. Against this report Caleb, for some reason – possibly since he was of the tribe of

Judah, the leading tribe, Joshua allowed him to take the initiative and kept himself in the background – stood out in opposition.

(iii) 14:1–10. These verses *continue* the narrative of 13:26–33 and in no sense are to be regarded as parallel or as presenting a variant account. On hearing the spies' report the people break out in rebellion, and to quell this rebellion Joshua and Caleb act. The fallacy of negative criticism is to make 14:6 a parallel to 13:30, an utterly unwarranted procedure. When the text is allowed to speak for itself, the alleged discrepancy disappears.

(iv) 14:11–25 recounts the Lord's anger against the rebellious people. Moses intercedes, and the Lord replies that the people shall not enter the land. Caleb, however, since he opposed the report of the spies, will enter the land. The reason why Caleb is mentioned is that he had stood out in opposition to the spies. It is absurd to assume that Joshua was excluded. As far as the report of the spies is concerned Joshua is in the background and Caleb takes the lead. The entire account is perfectly harmonious and unified.

(v) 14:26–45. Moses announces that only Caleb and Joshua will enter the promised land.

2. Chapters 15:1–19:22. Events during the thirty-seven years of wandering. (i) Chapter 15 contains various laws of sacrifice; the punishment of one who has broken the Sabbath; the law of tassels upon the clothes. (ii) Chapters 16–17:13. The rebellion of Korah. (iii) Chapter 18. Service of the priests and Levites. (iv) Chapter 19. The law of purification.

The section 16–17:13 also has been cut up in most unwarrantable fashion. Thus, Driver partitions the verses as follows:

P	16:1a		2b–7a (7b–11)		(16,17) 18–24		27a 32b 35 (36–40) 41–50
JE		1b–2a		12–15		25–26 27b–34	– chap. 17

Apparently the first to attempt to partition this section was Staehelin,[1] who sought to sunder the account of the rebellion of Korah from that of Dathan and Abiram. Others have followed in the attempt, and the above analysis of Driver is probably representative.

The principal alleged grounds for the partition are, first, according to JE, we have the account of a rebellion of laymen against Moses and the civil authority which he claimed; secondly, P is said to contain two strata. In the first, Korah, representing the people at large, complains against Moses and other tribes, not Aaron and other Levites. In the

[1] *Kritische Untersuchungen* (1843).

second, an enlargement of the narrative, Korah the Levite opposes to Aaron and his exclusive rights.

The best way to oppose this strange construction is simply to read the text carefully and allow it to speak for itself. We may then note three objections. First, there is absolutely no objective warrant for dividing 16:1 and partitioning it between P and JE. Note that the two parts of the verse are connected by 'and' (must we call in the redactor here?) and both are constructed similarly. Thus:

P Korah, the son of Izhar, the son of Kohath, the son of Levi

JE and Dathan and Abiram, the son of Eliab and On, the son of Peleg, sons of Reuben.

This presents all the malcontents acting in concert with Korah as leader. Why may not men with slightly different grievances act together? Secondly, the entire group is represented as protesting to Moses (16:2), to Moses and Aaron (16:3). Moses answers Korah, the leader (16:8–11). Moses next deals with Dathan and Abiram (16:12–15). Korah, Dathan, and Abiram are again united in 16:24, 27. Thirdly, the people are warned to leave the dwelling-place of Korah, Dathan, and Abiram. Dathan and Abiram (verses 25, 27) were in their tents, but not Korah (verses 16–19). Evidently Korah, in defiance of the warning, had later gone to his tent. Hence, he and his men were swallowed up. His children, however (26:9–11), from which the later singers were descended, were not swallowed up. This is an incidental evidence of genuineness. One would not invent such a story about the ancestor of so prominent a family.

3. Chapters 20, 21. The journey from Kadesh to Moab. This section also is partitioned between P and JE. Thus, according to Driver:

P	20:1a (to 'month')	2	3b–4	6–13		22–29		21:4a (to 'Hor')	
JE			1b–3a	5	14–21		21:1–3		4b–9

P	21:10–11		22:1
JE		12–35	

Here, again, the critical partition is without merit. The grounds for partition are purely arbitrary, for the narrative, as it stands, is a straightforward unit. Miriam's death at Kadesh is recorded (20:1). The people murmur because of lack of water (20:2–6). Moses smites the rock and brings forth water (20:7–13). These verses form such a unit that it is practically impossible to separate them without an absolute disintegration of the whole section. In 20:14–21 we are told of Moses' negotiations with Edom and of Edom's refusal to allow Israel passage through its land. Hence the Israelites journeyed to Mt. Hor, where Aaron died (20:22–29). Chapter 21 relates the threat of Arad (21:1–3), the journey from Mt. Hor, the murmuring of the people, and the fiery serpents (21:4–9). The remainder of the chapter continues the narrative of the journey, and the battle with Sihon and Og (21:10–35). The song (verses 14ff.) has the simplicity of the desert and is an incidental evidence of genuineness. It was evidently taken from the 'Book of the Wars of the Lord' (*sefer milhamoth yehowah*).

c. 22:1–36:13. Events in the Plains of Moab

1. Chapters 22–24. Balaam and his prophecies. The historicity of Balaam is proven by 2 Peter 2:15; Jude 2; Revelation 2:14. The section 22:22–35 is often sundered from the context, but the verbal similarity of verse 35 with verses 20, 21 shows that it should not thus be separated. In 22:12 God forbids Balaam to go, for he must not curse the people. In 22:20 Balaam is permitted, not commanded, to go (*tha'aseh*), but if he goes he must be subject to God's lead. Balaam goes, not to obey God, but to curse the people (20:20, 21). Hence the displeasure of the Lord is manifested in sending the angel to reiterate that Balaam must be subject to God's lead. Thus the entire account is a unit.

2. Chapter 25. The idolatry of Israel and the zeal of Phinehas.

3. Chapter 26. The second census of Israel. The variants between chapters 2 and 3 are not to be explained upon the assumption that the original census belonged to the time of the united monarchy and these chapters represent different recensions.[2] Note that 26:4 contains an explicit reference to the preceding census. Thus the verse links the present situation with the previous one. Further, both censuses are attributed to Moses. Nor is there anything in the censuses – not even the large numbers – which is incongruous with the Mosaic age.[3]

4. Chapter 27. Zelophehad's daughters and their claim.

5. Chapters 28, 29. The order of offerings.

6. Chapter 30. The law of vows.

7. Chapter 31. The war of vengeance against Midian.

8. Chapter 32. The inheritance on the east side of Jordan. Driver partitions this chapter as follows:

P	18, 19	24–32 (33)
JE 32:1–17 (in the main)		20–27 (in the main) 34–42

---

[2] See *FSAC*, p. 192.

[3] For a convincing recent discussion of the problem, see *FB*, pp. 241–243.

But this can be done only with difficulty. Verse 1 speaks of Reuben and Gad, whereas in the remainder of the chapter the order is reversed. Since Reuben was the elder, however, is it not natural that he should be named first? Then, since the Gadites were more active, is it not to be expected that they should subsequently be named first? Surely this mere change of order does not require difference of author. It is obvious (verse 2) that the Gadites did take the lead. The chapter is a unit, and in order to carry through its partition the critics are in frequent need of the redactor.[4]

9. Chapter 33:1–49. The list of Israel's encampments. This list of camping-places is of particular interest. It indicates the route of march which is marked out, not in P alone, nor in JE alone, but in their supposed combination, *i.e.*, in the Pentateuch as we now have it. But this does not mean that the list is later than the Pentateuch for it contains some names which do not occur in the Pentateuchal narrative. Since the presence of these names is an indication of genuineness – for why should anyone add them? – we may assume that we are dealing with a record which is indeed Mosaic, as it purports to be (verse 2). But if this record is Mosaic, then we have a strong argument for the Mosaic authorship of the other Pentateuchal narratives of the journeys.

10. Chapters 33:50–36:13. (i) The allotment of Israel's territory west of Jordan. (ii) Appointment of the levitical cities and the cities of refuge. (iii) The marriage of heiresses.

ALLEGED POST-MOSAICA IN NUMBERS

1. Numbers 4:3 gives the age of the Levites upon entering service as thirty years, but Numbers 8:24 says that that which belongs to the Levites is from twenty-five years old and upwards. How could Moses have written something thus contradictory? it is asked. The contradiction, however, is imaginary, not real. Chapter 4 relates to service at the Tabernacle of the congregation, until the time when it would be established in a permanent place. Thus 4:3, 'to do the work at the tent of meeting [*beohel moʻedh*]'. Note that only *one* duty of the Levites is mentioned. So also in 4:4: 'the service', 'at the tent of meetings'. Verses 5–14 give directions for packing the Tabernacle and its parts. Note also verse 15, 'at the tabernacle', and verse 19. So throughout the chapter. The concluding verses 47–49 give the ages in connection with this specific service.

---

[4] For a thorough defence of the unity of the chapter, see Green, 'The Pentateuchal Question' in *Hebraica*, 8, pp. 231–237.

On the other hand, chapter 8 deals with the regular service of the Levites *in* the tabernacle, *e.g.*, 8:24, 'for the service in the work of the tent of meeting' (*litseva' tsava' ba'avodhath*). Hence there is no contradiction between the two. In later times (see 1 Ch. 23:25, 26; 2 Ch. 31:17; Ezr. 3:8) the regular service of the Levites began at the age of twenty. If the modern view of the Pentateuch were correct, would not the law have been patterned after existing practice? Also, what would be the point at a late date of the detailed instructions for carrying the Tabernacle? Chapter 4 is in reality an evidence of genuineness.

2. Numbers 13:16, it is said, records the giving to Joshua of his name, although this name had already belonged to him in Exodus 17:9; 24:13; and Numbers 11:28. But this does not invalidate Mosaic authorship. If there really were an anachronism here, would not the final redactor of the Pentateuch have noticed it? The verse may be translated, however, 'These are the names [*i.e.*, the original names] of the men whom Moses sent to spy out the land, and then [after having previously been called Hoshea] Moses called Hoshea the son of Nun, Joshua.' This does not mean that the change of name was made at this particular time; in fact, it does not state when the name was changed. Joshua is the name employed when the man was engaged in particular service; here, however, he is called Hoshea, because, as a spy, he is engaged merely in a civil task.

3. Numbers 21:14. The reference in this verse to the 'book of the wars of the Lord' has long been singled out as a phrase that Moses could not have written. However, it is not necessary to regard the reference as a later gloss. The purpose of the quotation is not to verify a geographical notice but to call the attention of the people to what God has done for them. Thus, the force of verse 14 is, 'wherefore [since by God's help Israel took the land by the Arnon] it is said in the book of the wars of the Lord [verse 15] Vaheb [he took] in a storm,' *etc.* 'Wars' (*milhamoth*) refers not only to actual battles, but to all the manifold victories which God had obtained for His people (*cf.* Ex. 14:14, 25; 15:3; 12:41, 51; Nu. 33:1). Hence there was abundant material to form the subject of such a book. The critical objection assumes that the book refers only to physical battles.

4. Numbers 24:7. The mention of Agag in this verse is said to be an anachronism, since Agag reigned in the days of Samuel (*cf.* 1 Sa. 15:8). It is quite possible, however, that Agag was not a proper name, but a general designation of the Amalekite kings, as Pharaoh was of the Egyptians. Such would certainly be in keeping with the ideal emphasis of Balaam's prophecies generally.

SPECIAL LITERATURE ON NUMBERS

W. A. Albright, 'The Oracles of Balaam', in *JBL*, LXIII, 1944, pp. 207–233; Samuel Cox, *Balaam* (London, 1884); E. W. Hengstenberg, *Die Geschichte Bileams und seine Weissagungen** (1842); J. J. Knap, *Bileam: Toepasselijke Verklaring Zijner Profetieën** (Kampen, 1929).

CHAPTER SEVEN

DEUTERONOMY

NAME

THE fifth book of Moses bears the name 'These are the words' (*'elleh haddevarim*, or simply *devarim*). It came also to be designated by the Jews as 'Repetition of the law' (*mishneh hattorah*, or simply *mishneh*), from the words in 17:18. It has also been called 'The book of admonitions' (*sefer tochahoth*). The LXX has rendered 17:18 'this second law' (*to deuteronomion touto*), and the Vulgate, 'Deuteronomium', which is really an incorrect rendering of the passage.

PURPOSE

Deuteronomy contains the last addresses of Moses to the people, delivered in the plains of Moab. It is not to be regarded as merely a recapitulation of the three previous books but, rather, as Keil has so admirably stated, 'a hortatory description, explanation, and enforcement of the most essential contents of the covenant revelation and the covenant laws, with emphatic prominence given to the spiritual principle of the law and its fulfilment, and with a further development of the ecclesiastical, judicial, political, and civil organization, which was intended as a permanent foundation for the life and well-being of the people in the land of Canaan'.[1] The laws of Deuteronomy are spoken by Moses to the people (1:5) and are clothed in a hortatory form. In no sense is its legislation to be regarded as a new or second law, differing essentially from that of the previous books of the Pentateuch.

ANALYSIS

a. 1:1–4:43. The first discourse
1. 1:1–5. Heading and introduction. The introductory words connect the book with what precedes, and also identify the content of what follows as Mosaic. This content well agrees with the introductory statement of Mosaic authorship. The geographical references in 1:1, 2

[1] *The Pentateuch*, ET, III, p. 270.

do present difficulties, but there is not sufficient reason to assume the text to be corrupt. It may be that the message was spoken twice, first between Horeb and Kadesh, and secondly in the plains of Moab. At any rate, the verses present a wide geographical background for the book.

2. 1:6–46. A review of the Lord's guidance from Horeb to Kadesh. The change between singular and plural (*e.g.*, *cf.* verses 20, 21), is not an indication of confusion (Welch), nor of divergent authors. The singular has a particular, tender, individualizing force, and is used in phrases such as 'the Lord thy God'. It is what might be expected in a parenthetic discourse such as this.

3. 2:1–3:29. A further review of God's guidance, from Kadesh to the borders of the Amorites; the conquest of Sihon and Og. Welch believes that 2:4–7, with its command to pass through Edom, is a later addition, intended to correct the statement of verse 8 that the people avoided Edom.[2] Hence he finds a conflicting account at this point. But the contradiction is only apparent, not real. The divine command (verse 4) has to do with passing over (not passing directly through) the eastern boundary of the Edomites. This has no relation to Numbers 20:14–21, which belonged to an earlier stage of the narrative, not noticed in Deuteronomy. Hence, in accordance with this command, Israel passed by from the vicinity of (*me'eth*) Edom (verse 8). A redactor who wished to correct the supposedly false impression created by verse 8 would simply omit verse 8. To add verses 4–7 and to leave verse 8 would be merely to create confusion. Welch's assumption, on the face of it, is unnatural.

Welch further regards 2:26–30 as not original because of the phrase 'as this day' (verse 30), and the representation of Moses sending envoys immediately after having received a divine revelation that Sihon had been delivered into the hands of Israel. But would not the redactor clear up these supposed anachronisms? Further, the phrase 'as this day' could easily have been employed by Moses. In fact, it is just what might be expected in a summary of past events such as Moses here gives. Nor is there any conflict between verses 24 and 26ff. In verse 24 the Lord announces the final defeat of Sihon. Moses, however, is sincere in his desire to pass peaceably through the land. Hence, he sends envoys, and thus it is made clear to Sihon that his own stubbornness brings about the downfall of his kingdom.

Chapter 3:14–17 is considered by some as a later addition to harmonize the text with Numbers. But the insertion of the verses may well have been by Moses himself. There are, however, difficulties in the text.

[2] *DFC*, p. 169.

4. 4:1–43. An exhortation to obedience to the law. The introductory section forms an essential unit. It is true that there are difficulties, but there does not seem to be sufficient warrant for the assumption that there are many interpolations. Moses does shift between the singular and plural in his use of the second persons, but on the whole the chapters present what might be expected in a hortatory, popular summary.

b. 4:44–26:19. The second address of Moses

1. 4:44–49. These verses serve to announce the address of Moses upon the law and also to call attention to the place and time of its deliverance.

2. 5:1–11:33. An extended exposition of the Ten Commandments, the foundation law of the theocracy.

(i) Chapter 5. Exposition of the moral law. In verses 1–5 Moses solemnly summons the people to hear the statutes and judgments of the Lord in which the covenant was contained. The ten covenant words are then repeated from Exodus 20 with slight variations (verses 6–21); and Moses then (verses 22–23) explains more fully the nature of the events which had occurred at Sinai after the deliverance of the Decalogue.

(ii) Chapter 6. The following commands are announced, together with the purpose of observing them (verses 1–3). Beginning with verse 4 Moses proceeds to expound the covenant law, the heart of which has already been set forth in the Ten Commandments.

(iii) Chapter 7. For the proper observance of the law, it will be necessary to abolish all idolatry. Hence, the people were commanded to exterminate the Canaanites. This command would be without meaning if the people had long been in the land and there were no more Canaanites, but it is full of meaning if spoken by Moses to a people about to enter a land which was inhabited by Canaanites.

(iv) Chapter 8. A reminder of God's dealings with the people in order to warn them against forgetting the Lord.

(v) 9:1–10:11. Moses rehearses the various sins and rebellions of the people and thus warns them against self-righteousness.

(vi) Chapter 10:12–11:33. Exhortation to obedience. Obedience to the law will bring blessing, but disobedience a curse. The choice of blessing or curse is thus set before the people.

3. 12:1–26:19. An exposition of the principal laws. This section consists of statutes and ordinances, part of which are repetitions of the Sinaitic legislation and part of which have regard to circumstances not considered by that legislation. The purpose is to regulate the entire life of Israel, the holy nation of God, when she comes into the land of Canaan. The laws herein enjoined are of a triple character: religious,

political, or civil; and sundry laws designed to promote the general well-being of the people.

(i) Chapter 12. The law of the one place for worshipping God. This law is in essential agreement with Exodus 20:21, which taught that an altar might be built only where the Lord recorded His name. It should be noted that nowhere in Deuteronomy is Jerusalem specified as the only legitimate sanctuary. There were other places also, which had served as a central sanctuary, e.g., Shiloh (cf. also the erection of the altar on Mt. Ebal, 27:5ff.). It has long been maintained that this law in Deuteronomy was aimed at producing the reformation under Josiah. But it should be noted that that reformation produced not a centralized sanctuary, but rather an abolition of idolatry. This fact, it seems to me, is decisive against the widely held view that Deuteronomy was a product of the seventh century BC.

Chapter 12:10ff. teaches that the sanctuary is to be erected not immediately, but only after the Lord has given rest to the people from their enemies. Surely this is a strange command to place in a book the purpose of which would be to bring about *immediate* centralization of worship under Josiah.

Welch divides 12:1–28 broadly into two sections: verses 1–12, which use the second plural; and verses 13–28, which use the second singular. This, however, is certainly no criterion for distinguishing different authors, since it characterizes Deuteronomy and also other parts of the Old Testament. If this principle were carried through consistently, it would chop up the Scripture into fragments that were almost without meaning.

Note that in verse 5 'the place' does not refer to Jerusalem, but to the place of revelation. The similar language of verse 21 argues for the unity of the chapter and is against Welch's hypothesis.

Verses 15–16 have been thought to conflict with Leviticus 17:1ff., which teaches that the slaughtered animal must be presented at the sanctuary. But there is no real conflict. The levitical law evidently applied to the period of the wilderness, when it could be practicably obeyed; the law of Deuteronomy is intended for the settled life in Palestine, when it would be no longer practicable to carry out the injunction of Leviticus 17:1ff.

(ii) Chapter 13. The punishment of idolators and of those who tempt to idolatry. Verse 1 is similar to 4:2 in thought. Three cases are mentioned: (a) verses 2–6. A prophet who leads the people into idolatry. The terms 'prophet' and 'dreamer of dreams' correspond to the two media of revelation mentioned in Numbers 12:6. (b) Verses 7–12.

Temptation to idolatry which has come from close blood-relatives and friends. (c) Verses 13–19. A city has been led into idolatry.

Welch would cut out verses 4b, 5 because of their use of the second plural, and because these verses contain theology, not law. This latter argument is subjective. Deuteronomy is not a dry legal code, but a parenetic exposition of the law. These verses are clearly Deuteronomic in character, and form an integral part of the section.

(iii) Chapter 14. The Israelites are to avoid the customs of the Canaanites and unclean food. The tithe of fruits.

a. Verses 1, 2. This heathenish rite was earlier prohibited in Leviticus 19:28. Apparently it was a custom widespread in Palestine (cf. Is. 3:24; Je. 16:6; Am. 8:10; etc.).

b. Verses 3–21. This section deals with clean and unclean animals, and agrees essentially with Leviticus 11:2–20. Deuteronomy, however, is later than Leviticus. It is, in reality, a summary of the law in Leviticus adaptable to the people as they are ready to enter the promised land. Verses 4b and 5 do not appear in Leviticus. It is probable that the mention of these edible animals in verses 4b, 5 is a strong evidence of Mosaic authorship, since several of these apparently were not known either in Palestine or the Nile region, but are desert inhabitants. Hence there would be no reason for enumerating them in the earlier Leviticus, but now the people would be familiar with them.

c. Verse 21b is a repetition of Exodus 23:19b; 34:26b. This law was possibly a prohibition of a magical milk charm practiced among the Canaanites, for on one of the texts from Ras Shamra there is the command 'Make to seethe a kid in the milk', tb [h g] d bhlb.[3]

d. Verses 22–29 deal with the bringing of tithes. This section does not conflict with Numbers 18:21ff. In the earlier legislation (i.e., Lv. 27:30; Nu. 18:21ff.) when the people were yet in the nomadic stage, the tithes were given to the priests and Levites who would probably be most in need of them. Now, however, when the people are ready to enter Palestine and begin a settled life, a wider use of the tithe is enjoined.

(iv) Chapter 15. Laws for the benefit of slaves and the poor.

a. Verses 1–11. The year of release. Cf. also Exodus 23:10ff.; Leviticus 25:1–7. The Deuteronomic law is an expansion of these. The more specific character of the provisions in Exodus and Leviticus is due to the fact that they were intended for a nomadic people, whereas the more general character of the Deuteronomic provisions is intended for a people about ready to enter a state of settled life.

b. Verses 12–18. The manumission of Hebrew slaves. This law

[3] Cf. Syria, XIV, 2, p. 130, line 14.

is based on Exodus 21:2–6 and is here repeated for the purpose of explaining how it should be fulfilled. Love for the slave should make provision for his prosperity after he has been set at liberty. In Leviticus 25:39–46 it is taught that slaves are to be freed in the year of Jubilee, really a humanitarian law, which would evidently provide that, should the Jubilee year arrive before the slave had served seven years, he could be freed. Verse 17 is not in conflict with Exodus 21:6, but is repeated to guard against any application of the law not motivated by love. It does not repeat some of the details of Exodus, namely, the public declaration before the judges, but the important thing is the piercing of the ear, which doubtless occurred in private in both instances.

c. Verses 19:23. The first-born of cattle (*cf.* also Ex. 13:2, 12; Lv. 27:26ff.; Nu. 18:15ff.).

(v) Chapter 16:1–17. The three annual feasts (*cf.* Ex. 12; Lv. 23; Nu. 28, 29). Moses repeats the laws concerning the sacrificial meals to be held at the feasts at the central sanctuary. The appointed seasons are omitted, although this does not mean that they were unknown to Deuteronomy.

a. Verses 1–8. The Passover. Apparently the term 'Passover' (*pesah*) includes not only the paschal lamb but all the sacrifices slain during the seven days of Mazzoth, as seems to be indicated from the words of verse 2, 'of the flock and the herd', and the reference to eating unleavened bread (verse 2, note the word 'therewith', *'alau*).

b. Verses 9–12. The Feast of Weeks (*cf.* Ex. 23:16; 34:22; Lv. 23:15ff.; Nu. 28:26ff.).

c. Verses 13–15. The Feast of Tabernacles (*cf.* Ex. 23:16; 34:22; Lv. 23:33ff.; Nu. 29:12ff.).

(vi) 16:18 – 17:20. The administration of justice and choice of a king.

a. Verses 18–20. The appointment of judges.

b. Verses 21–22. Prohibition of sacred trees and pillars.

c. Chapter 17:1–7. The punishment of idolatry.

d. Verses 8–13. The higher court of appeal.

e. Verses 14–20. Choosing a king. The law is optional, but the requirements for the king are quite strict. The king must be an Israelite (verse 15); he must not multiply horses (verse 16) *i.e.*, seek to become opulent, lest the people by his action be led back to Egypt, whence the horses would come (*cf.* 1 Ki. 10:28); he must not take many wives, lest his heart be turned from God; he must not multiply for himself silver and gold (verse 17). Rather, he must have for himself a copy of the law, and this is to be his guide.

The existence of a human king does not conflict with the ideal of the theocracy. For the king herein portrayed was to be not a despotic, selfish dictator, but a man who would walk in the light of the Lord, and by his wise and just administration would bring blessing to his kingdom and glory to the name of the covenant God. He should be a true type of the King of kings.

Samuel's attitude (1 Sa. 8:6–17) in no sense conflicts with this ideal. When the people asked for a king, they were perfectly within their rights. That to which Samuel objected was the untheocratic spirit in which the request was made. The people did not ask for a king out of concern for the good of the divine theocracy. They wanted a king in order that they might be like the nations round about, and the distinctive feature of the theocracy was that Israel should be unlike the nations round about.

Hence, it is incorrect to appeal to the incident in 1 Samuel as evidence that the Deuteronomic law was not yet in existence. Such appeal really betrays a lack of understanding of the passage in Samuel. Furthermore, if Deuteronomy were later than Samuel, we should expect to find in it some of the characteristic features of the latter, *e.g.*, 1 Samuel 8:11ff.

(vii) Chapter 18. The priest, Levites, and prophets.

a. Verses 1–8. The rights of the priests and Levites. In verse 1 the phrase 'the priests the Levites' distinguishes between priests and Levites. This is shown by the following words 'the whole tribe of Levi' and by the distinction between priests (verses 3–5) and 'a Levite' (verses 6–8). It is not correct to say that Deuteronomy knows no distinction between the priests and the Levites. In the middle books of the Pentateuch, when Aaron and his sons actually occupied the priestly office, it was natural that the priests should be designated as the sons of Aaron. In Deuteronomy, on the other hand, a book of more general and prophetic character, generic designations are used.

b. Verses 9–22. The law of the prophet. When Israel should come into the land there would be need for further divine revelation which would be based upon and in agreement with the foundational Sinaitic legislation. To supply this need, the Lord would raise up the prophetical institution. The section is a unit, and may be analysed as follows: (1) verses 9–13. The nine abominations of the Canaanites, which Israel is not to learn. (2) Verses 14, 15. Because of these abominations the Canaanites are to be dispossessed of their land. For Israel the prophetic institution is to be established. Its divine origin is stressed (verse 15, *yakim leka yehowah*), and thus it is to be distinguished from all superficially similar religious practices of antiquity. The prophet is to be (i) an Israelite; (ii) like Moses in that he, too, will be a mediator between

God and man. (3) Verses 16–18. The prophetic institution is to be established in response to Israel's plea at Horeb for a mediator. (4) Verses 19–22. Certain criteria for distinguishing between true and false prophets.

(viii) Chapter 19. Certain criminal laws. Verses 1–13 deal with the cities of refuge, and like Numbers 35:9–34 constitute an elaboration of the law first revealed in Exodus 21:12–14. Verse 14 treats of the removal of a neighbour's landmark, namely, that boundaries which former persons (*ri'shonim*) have set should not be removed by later persons. Verses 15–21 treat of laws concerning witnesses.

(ix) Chapter 20. Laws concerning future wars. Verses 1–9 have to do with military service. Verses 10–20 concern sieges. Only after an offer of peace has been rejected should an attack on an enemy's town be made. During such a siege the fruit-trees should be spared.

(x) Chapter 21. Sundry laws. Verses 1–9 deal with the expiation of a murder committed by an unknown person. This practice was ancient (*cf.* Code of Hammurabi, no. 24). Verses 10–14 concern marriage with a woman who has been captured in war; verses 15–17, the rights of the first-born; verses 18–21, the punishment of a refractory son. Verses 22, 23 enjoin the burial of the criminal who has been hanged.

(xi) Chapter 22. Sundry laws, continued. Verses 1–12 explain the proper attitude of an Israelite towards a neighbour and also towards the natural order of life. Verses 13–29 present various laws concerning unchastity, adultery, intercourse with a betrothed virgin and an unbetrothed virgin.

(xii) Chapter 23. The rights of citizenship in the congregation. Verse 1 should more properly be reckoned as verse 30 of the previous chapter. Verses 2–9 mention those that are to be excluded. Verses 10–15 concern purity of the camp in time of war. Verses 15–19 maintain that an escaped bondman is not to be returned to his master; religious prostitution is not to be tolerated. Verses 20–26 deal with various rights of citizenship.

(xiii) Chapter 24. On divorce. Verses 1–4 prohibit remarriage in a specific case of divorce; verse 5 exempts those newly wed from service in war; verses 6–9 list various prohibitions; verses 10–15 give warnings against oppression of the poor; verses 16–22 give warnings against injustice, and laws concerning gleaning which exhibit generosity towards the helpless.

(xiv) Chapter 25. Laws concerning corporal punishment. Verses 1–3 prohibit extreme severity in corporal punishment; verse 4 is humanitarian – the threshing ox is not to be muzzled; verses 5–10 discuss levirate marriages; verses 11–16 give sundry laws; verses 17–19 order the Amalekites to be exterminated.

(xv) Chapter 26. Thanksgiving at the presentation of the first-fruits and tithes. It should be noted that the Book of the Covenant also closed with the law of the firstfruits (Ex. 23:19).

c. 27:1–30:29. *The renewal of the covenant*

1. Chapter 27. Ratification of the law. Verses 1–8 teach that the Israelites, when they have crossed the Jordan, are to set up on Mt. Ebal great stones, covered with lime, and to write the law upon these stones. They also are to build an altar for offering their burnt and slain offerings. This section in reality supports the claim of Mosaic authorship. It should be noted that the occupation of Palestine is clearly represented as future (*e.g.*, verse 3). Furthermore, the method of writing also points to ancient times. Evidently the writing was to be with a stylus upon a prepared surface, as was the custom in Egypt. The practice of engraving laws upon stones was in itself a rather widespread one (*cf.*, *e.g.*, the famous Code of Hammurabi). Verses 9–10 unite the two sections of the chapter by the divine injunction to obedience of the law. Verses 11–26 proclaim blessing and cursing, as already suggested in 11:29. Upon Mt. Gerizim the people themselves were to give expression to blessing, and upon Mt. Ebal to curse.

2. Chapter 28. Blessing and curse. Verses 1–14 set forth the blessings for obedience, and verses 15–68 the curses for disobedience. This section contains a sixfold repetition of the word 'cursed'.

3. Chapters 29, 30. Conclusion of the covenant. This is really a renewed declaration of the covenant made at Horeb.

d. 31:1–34:12. *Moses' last words and his death*

1. Chapter 31. Final arrangements. Verses 1–8, the appointment of Joshua; verses 9–13, the law to be recited every seven years; verses 14–23, the commission of Joshua, and the command to write the song; verses 24–30, the law to be placed beside the ark of the covenant.

2. Chapter 32. The song of Moses. The purpose of this beautiful psalm is to contrast the faithful dealings of the Lord with the faithlessness of the nation. Verses 1–3, introduction; verses 4–6, theme of the poem, the faithfulness of the Rock, who is God; verses 7–14, a survey of God's dealings with Israel; verses 15–18, the apostasy of Israel; verses 19–33, the Lord will bring severe visitation upon His rebellious people; verses 34–43, mercy will be shown to the nation, and vengeance upon its enemies; verses 44–52, epilogue.

The poem is a prophetic anticipation of the future, when the nation will dwell in the land. It presents an ideal picture and is didactic in nature. There is no valid reason for denying the Mosaic authorship; the vocabulary contains archaic forms, and the language is pure. There is nothing that would betray a late date. Furthermore, the song follows naturally after 31:19ff. (note particularly verse 30).

Driver maintains that verses 7–12 present the exodus and occupation of Canaan as in the distant past. He also maintains that Israel is settled in Palestine, and because of her idolatry is on the verge of ruin, verses 13–30; only deliverance lies in the future, verse 34ff. The maturity of the thought and style of composition are also believed to be evidences of a date later than Moses. Internal evidence shows that the song is by a different author from the remainder of Deuteronomy. There are said to be two introductions to the song, 31:16–22 and 31:24–30. Driver is not dogmatic as to the date of composition. He favours a time somewhat earlier than the compilation of JE, but admits the possibility that since its theological standpoint presents great affinities with the prophets of the Chaldean age, it may be assigned to the time of Jeremiah and Ezekiel.

But Driver's arguments are not cogent. Verses 7–12 do not look back upon the exodus and conquest of Canaan as in the distant past. Verses 7, 8 may refer to patriarchal times. At any rate, the exodus is not set forth as belonging to remote antiquity. Nor is it true that verses 13–30 present Israel as on the verge of exile. These verses rather present a theme that recurs in Scripture. No particular historical incidents are presupposed; rather the verses teach the common theme that pride and prosperity lead often to punishment. Nor are there two introductions to the song, each by a different author. Chapter 31:16–22 simply records the Lord's command to write the song, and verse 22 states that Moses obeyed the command. It is a general statement of the fact that Moses wrote out the song and taught it to the people; verse 30 on the other hand serves as a specific introduction to the song itself.

With regard to the content of the poem, there is absolutely nothing incompatible with Mosaic authorship. The ideas and vocabulary fit in well with the time of Moses. Compare verse 7, *dor wador*, 'generation to generation', with *dr dr* of the Ras Shamra texts; the 'eagle' of 32:11 should be compared with Exodus 14:4. God as a Rock points back to Genesis 49:24. The word 'Jeshurun' occurs only in Deuteronomy 33:5, 26 (in Is. 44:2 it is taken from these passages). The word *godhel* (verse 3) is a Pentateuchal word when denoting God's greatness (*cf.* Dt. 3:24; 11:2; Nu. 14:19). The plural 'days', *yemoth* (verse 7), occurs again only in the Mosaic prayer (Ps. 90:15).

Pfeiffer teaches that the thought and language of the poem point to the first half of the fifth century BC as the time of composition. It is, he thinks, an 'illuminating historical document for the religion' between the time of Zechariah and Nehemiah, and exhibits an intense religious and nationalistic spirit such as characterized early Judaism. However, the arguments which apply against Driver's theory hold good here also.

3. Chapter 33. The blessing of Moses. This blessing falls into three general parts: verses 1–5, the heading and introduction; verses 6–25, the blessings pronounced upon the various tribes; verses 26–29, the conclusion.

Although this blessing was actually pronounced by Moses himself, it was evidently not written down by him, as may be seen from 33:1, in which Moses seems to be distinguished from the writer. The words of the blessing, however, are to be regarded as Moses' own. The entire passage is a prophetic glimpse of the future, set forth in an ideal manner. There is no reference to any historical circumstances of a post-Mosaic age, and this fact is a strong argument for the authenticity of the poem.

Negative criticism is by no means unanimous in discovering a date for the blessing, but the principal reasons for denying it to Moses are the following: first, the poem says nothing about Simeon, and this is taken to indicate a time when Simeon had become absorbed into Judah; secondly, the conquest of Palestine, verses 27ff., appears as an accomplished fact; and thirdly, verse 4 cannot likely have come from Moses. In answer to the above, however, it may be said: first, the omission of Simeon is due to the prophetic character of the poem. In Genesis 49:7 Simeon was to be scattered abroad in Israel and to lose his distinctive individuality as a tribe. This was later fulfilled (cf. Jos. 19:2–9). The Simeonites had not sought to undo the evil which Jacob had cursed, and hence were not entitled to a special blessing as was Reuben. However, they are probably included in the general blessing of verses 1 and 29 and in the blessing upon Judah. Secondly, verses 27ff. are also to be regarded as presenting an ideal picture. They do not represent the conquest as a historically accomplished fact, but rather set forth the Lord as the sure dwelling-place of the people. And finally, verse 4 evidently personifies the nation and identifies Moses with his people.

Driver remarks, and the remark is worthy of serious consideration, that internal evidence is indecisive, and 'conclusive criteria fail us'. The following views have been held as to the date: the reign of Jeroboam I (Driver, Dillmann); the reign of Jeroboam II (Kuenen, Cornill, Pfeiffer [in part]; and the period of the Judges (Kleinert).

4. Chapter 34. The death and burial of Moses. Both Philo and

Josephus[4] believed that Moses wrote this account of his own death. In *Baba Bathra* 14b, these words are assigned to Joshua, 'Moses wrote his own book and the section concerning Balaam [*i.e.*, Nu. 22:2–25:9], and Job. Joshua wrote his own book and eight verses of the Law [*i.e.*, Dt. 34:5–12].' Ibn Ezra also taught that this chapter was written by Joshua. It is perfectly legitimate to regard this brief account of Moses' death as having been written by a later hand under divine inspiration and then appended to the book of Deuteronomy.

ALLEGED POST-MOSAICA IN DEUTERONOMY

1. Deuteronomy 1:1 employs the expression 'beyond the Jordan' (*'ebher hayyarden*), and this is said to indicate the standpoint of one who was in Palestine. The objection is an old one, having been raised by Ibn Ezra and later by Spinoza. It is true that the phrase means 'beyond the Jordan', but evidently it had somewhat of a technical sense, exactly like the modern equivalent 'Transjordania'. It is perfectly possible for a person who lives east of the Jordan today to speak of himself as being in Transjordania. Or one may think of the Roman distinction of Gallia *citerior* and *ulterior*. On the other hand, passages such as Deuteronomy 3:20, 25; 11:30; Joshua 5:1; 9:1; 12:7; 1 Kings 5:4; *etc.* apparently use the phrase in a non-technical sense as referring to Palestine.[5]

2. Deuteronomy 10:6, 7 has long been regarded as a source of difficulty. It is said that these verses teach that Aaron died at Moserah, and from Moserah the Israelites journeyed to Gudgod and from Gudgod to Jotbah. But according to Numbers 20:22ff. Aaron's death occurred long after the sojourn at Mt. Horeb. It is difficult, then, to see why it was introduced at this point. Furthermore, the order of stations in Numbers 33:31–33 was Moseroth, Bene-jaakan, Hor-haggidgad, Jotbathah. Lastly, according to Numbers 20:22ff.; 33:38, Aaron died at Mt. Hor, not at Jotbah.

In answer to these objections, however, it may be said: (i) This passage in Deuteronomy does not correspond to Numbers 33:31–33 but rather to Numbers 33:37, *i.e.*, with the last journey of Israel from Kadesh to the south. Since Numbers 33:1–35 deals with the earlier journeys of Israel and details their encampments, it is not to be expected that the camps should be enumerated on the last journey (*i.e.*, verses 37ff.). Hence, there is no contradiction between Numbers and Deuteronomy as far as the order of stations is concerned. (ii) It is quite possible that Moserah (pl. Moseroth) was the name of the general locality in

---

[4] *Antiquities* iv. 8. 48.
[5] For a full discussion, see Hengstenberg, *DGP*, II, pp. 256–264.

which Mt. Hor was situated. At any rate Deuteronomy also teaches that Aaron died at Mt. Hor (*cf.* Dt. 32:50). It is inconceivable that, if there really had been an error here, the 'redactor' would not have noticed it.

SPECIAL LITERATURE ON DEUTERONOMY

Aage Bentzen, *Die josianische Reform* (Kopenhagen, 1926); Herbert Breit, *Die Predigt des Deuteronomisten* (München, 1933); Karl Budde, *Das Lied Moses. Deut. 32* (Tübingen, 1920); *Der Segen Moses. Deut. 33* (Tübingen, 1922); George G. Cameron, 'The Laws Peculiar to Deuteronomy',* in *PTR*, 1, 1903, pp. 434–456; A. R. Hulst, *Het Karakter van de Cultus in Deuteronomium* (Wageningen, 1938); M. G. Kline, *Covenant of the Great King** (Grand Rapids, 1963); G. T. Manley, *The Book of the Law** (London, 1957); Gerhard von Rad, *Das Gottesvolk im Deuteronomium* (Stuttgart, 1929); Arthur-Robert Siebens, *L'Origine du Code Deuteronomique* (Paris, 1929); Georg Sternberg, *Die Ethik des Deuteronomiums* (Berlin, 1908); Adam C. Welch, *The Code of Deuteronomy* (London, 1924); *Deuteronomy: The Framework to the Code* (London, 1932); Harold M. Wiener, *Das Hauptproblem des Deuteronomiums* (Guetersloh, 1924); 'The Laws of Deuteronomy and the Arguments from Silence', and 'Deuteronomy and the Argument from Style', in *PTR*, 5, 1907, pp. 188–209 and 605–630 respectively; Adolf Zahn, *Das Deuteronomium** (Guetersloh, 1890).

SPECIAL LITERATURE ON THE PRIESTS AND LEVITES

Samuel Ives Curtiss, Jr., *The Levitical Priests** (Edinburgh, 1877).

CHAPTER EIGHT

THE LITERARY CRITICISM OF
THE PENTATEUCH

'THE authority of the holy scripture, for which it ought to be believed and obeyed, dependeth not upon the testimony of any man or church, but wholly upon God (who is truth itself), the author thereof; and therefore it is to be received, because it is the word of God' (WC, I:IV).[1] That these words set forth a high view of the authority of the Scriptures, and therefore of the Old Testament, is a fact which cannot be denied. The Scripture, according to this viewpoint, possesses an authority which is of so great a nature that it ought to be believed and also obeyed. This authority it derives, not from man or even from the Church, but only from God, who is its author.

This high view has been commonly held by the historic Christian Church, and is embodied in her official creeds. The early fathers appealed to the Bible as authoritative Scripture, and throughout her history the Church has followed suit.[2] Nevertheless, there have been those both within and without the pale of the Church who have dissented from this high and noble view of the Bible.

It is difficult to discover precisely when hostile criticism of the Bible first made its appearance. Of course, all sin is a criticism of the Word of God, a manifestation of the desire to be wise above that which God has commanded. But conscious dissatisfaction with the Old Testament probably made its first appearance in the Egyptian city of Alexandria. Alexandria had become a centre of Greek philosophy and culture, and it was to be expected that in such a city serious attention would also be devoted to the Bible. Such study, furthermore, might be expected to be conducted under the influence of Grecian philosophy. Clement of Alexandria (*Stromata* i. 15, *etc.*) mentions a certain Aristobulus, a peripatetic, who taught that the Jewish philosophy was older than that

---

[1] See B. B. Warfield, 'The Westminster Doctrine of Holy Scripture', in *The Westminster Assembly and Its Work* (New York, 1931), pp.155–257.

[2] *Cf.* the official creeds of the historic Church, and the statements therein made concerning the authority of Scripture. See Philip Schaff, *The Creeds of Christendom*, 3 vols. (New York, 1881–82).

of Greeks and that Plato had derived his ideas from the Mosaic Law. Apparently there was in Alexandria quite a biblical school, and evidently even before the time of the LXX the Old Testament had been translated into Greek (*Stromata* xi. 93.3). Clement further mentions a certain Demetrius who had composed a book on the kings in Judaea and who, in his list, differed from Philo.

Mention may also be made of a certain Dositheus, the Samaritan, who rejected the prophets upon the ground that they had not spoken under the inspiration of the Holy Spirit ('*qui primus ausus est prophetas quasi non in spiritu sancto locutos repudiare*').[3] In the *Indiculus de Haeresibus*,[4] mention is made of the group called Meristae, who are said to divide the Scriptures and not to believe all the prophets.

THE FIRST TWO CENTURIES

a. The Gnostic sects[5]

The second century beheld the Christian Church struggling with a formidable foe, the phenomenon known as Gnosticism, a philosophical system which for a time seriously threatened the Church's progress.

The Gnostic system was hostile to the Old Testament and manifested a strong antipathy towards Judaism. According to Gnosticism, spirit and matter were opposed to one another. The world owed its ultimate existence to spirit or to the spiritual world. Its immediate cause, however, was the Demiurge, an emanation from the Supreme God. This Demiurge was considered to be an inferior being, the God of the Jews, and in this thought is to be seen the underlying cause for much of Gnosticism's hostile criticism of the Old Testament.

1. Simon Magus. In Acts 8:10 we read of Simon whom the Samaritans regarded as 'that power of God which is called Great'. According to Epiphanius[6] there was a certain Simon – whether it was the Simon of Acts 8:10 is a disputed question – who held that neither the Law nor the Prophets were from the good God. The *Clementine Homilies*[7] represent Simon as criticizing certain Old Testament anthropomorphisms. Thus, he thought that such passages as Genesis 3:22; 18:21 show that God is

---

[3] *Against all Heresies*, in Oehler, *Corporis Haereseologici*, I, pp. 271–279; *cf.* also Jerome in *PL*, 23, col. 187; *Clementine Homilies*, *PG*, 2, cols. 92, 96.

[4] Ed. Oehler, p. 283.

[5] In the following three sections I have drawn largely upon material in my unpublished doctoral thesis, *Biblical Criticism to the End of the Second Christian Century*.

[6] *Against Heresies*, *PG*, 41, col. 292.

[7] *PG*, 2, col. 436.

ignorant; Genesis 3:22 that God is envious; and Genesis 22:1 that He is both wicked and ignorant.

2. The Ophites. This cult was evidently of pre-Christian origin and a precursor of the principal Gnostic schools. According to the Ophites (*ophis*, 'serpent') it was the serpent who gave man the knowledge of good and evil. The fall, therefore, was a fall upwards. The serpent was to be exalted, and the God of the Old Testament despised.[8]

3. The Cainites. This group glorified Cain, Esau, Korah, the Sodomites, and the like as their ancestors. They considered Cain to be a martyr to the wrath of the Demiurge. Their perversion of the Old Testament was doubtless due to their philosophy.[9]

4. The Syrian School; Satornilus and Tatian. (i) In accordance with the underlying Gnostic dualism, Satornilus of Antioch, a contemporary of Ignatius, taught that some prophecies had been spoken by the angels who created the world and some by Satan.[10] (ii) Tatian, best known for his *Diatessaron*, or *Harmony of the Gospels*, regarded the Old Testament as the work of an inferior God, and denied salvation to Adam.[11]

5. The Egyptian School. Educated at Alexandria, Valentinus later journeyed to Rome and there attained to the height of his influence and power. Apparently he approved of some parts of the Law and disapproved of others, and also emended or altered the sacred text for the sake of improving it. Also he is said to have transposed passages and to have disregarded the order and continuity of the text. Such action, according to Irenaeus, is to be attributed to deceit. But Valentinus' attitude towards the Scriptures must be judged in the light of his philosophical background.[12]

6. The Italian School: *The Epistle of Ptolemy to Flora.* Of Ptolemy himself practically nothing is known apart from the fact that he was the author of a letter to a certain Christian lady named Flora, in which letter he sought to convert her to Gnosticism and appealed to Scripture in support of his arguments. Some would date Ptolemy's activity between AD 145 and 180, and this date is quite possibly correct. Ptolemy's letter has been preserved by Epiphanius.[13]

In brief, Ptolemy's argument is as follows. The Law, according to

[8] *Cf. Catalog of Philaster*, ed. Oehler, i. 5; *PG*, 41, cols. 641ff.; *PG*, 7, cols. 694–704; Lipsius, 'Ueber das ophitische System' in *Zeitschrift für wissenschaftliche Theologie*, 1863–64).

[9] *Cf. PG*, 41, col. 656.

[10] *Cf.* Irenaeus, *PG*, 7, cols. 675ff.

[11] *Cf. PG*, 6, col. 848; 41, cols. 831ff.

[12] *Cf. PG*, 7, col. 523.

[13] *PG*, 41, cols. 557–568.

some, was established by God the Father. But others ascribe it to the devil, whom they also believe to have founded the world. Since, however, the Law is imperfect, it cannot have come from the perfect God, and since it enjoins justice, it cannot have come from the adversary, for he is unjust.

The Law which is embraced in the five books of Moses was not given by one author. Parts have come from God, others from Moses, and still others from the elders among the people. For example, God united man and woman and forbade divorce. Moses, however, permitted it, and so acted contrary to the decrees of God. Ptolemy adduces other examples and concludes that the Law is of a threefold authorship, containing ordinances from the elders, from Moses, and from God.

That part of the Law which is from God is further divided into three parts: the Law proper, containing genuine precepts, free from admixture with evil; such are the Ten Commandments; the part which Christ did away with, such as the law of retaliation; typical and symbolical laws, which Christ employed in a spiritual manner. The God who was the author of this law was the Demiurge.

It must not be thought that Ptolemy denied the Mosaic authorship of the Pentateuch. The Pentateuch was composed by Moses but not all the laws which it contained were the work of Moses as a lawgiver. All the laws, however, were placed in the five books of Moses. Moses may be regarded as the compiler, although not the author of these laws.

b. Marcion and the Old Testament

A native of Pontus and son of a Christian bishop, Marcion came to Rome about AD 138 and there united with the church. At Rome he came under the influence of the Gnostic Cerdo who proclaimed that the God of the Old Testament and that of the New were different Beings.

Marcion came to teach that there were two gods, one austere, a corrupt tree bringing forth corrupt fruit, the producer of moral evil; the other the good and benevolent God of the New Testament. Marcion also separated the law and the gospel, and he became known in Tertullian's eyes as 'the author of the breach of peace between the Gospel and the Law'.[14]

Since, according to Marcion, the Creator was corrupt, it would also follow that His work, the Law, was corrupt. The corruptions and imperfections which Marcion thought he found in the Old Testament were set forth in his work, *The Antithesis*. Since, however, this work is lost, we

---

[14] *Contra Marcionem*, i. 19.

are dependent largely upon Tertullian for information as to what it contained.

Since man has fallen into sin, reasoned Marcion, it must be concluded that God was neither good nor powerful, nor did He possess fore-knowledge. Again, God's ignorance and weakness are thought to appear from the question addressed to Cain, 'Where art thou?' Also, why would God ask Adam if he had eaten of the forbidden fruit unless He were in doubt?

In the account of the golden calf, Moses is thought to appear greater than God. The *lex talionis* gave permission for mutual injury, and the sacrifices and ceremonies were thought to be burdensome and trouble-some and probably needed by God Himself. Furthermore, in taking gold and silver from the Egyptians, the Israelites acted dishonestly, and for this God was responsible. God should also be blamed for having hardened the heart of Pharaoh.

The God of the Old Testament was, according to Marcion, fickle, and not true to His own commandments. He forbade work on the seventh day, yet at the siege of Jericho ordered the ark to be carried around the city for eight days, which naturally involved labour upon the Sabbath. God was also unjust and lacking in foresight in His dealings with men.

Marcion rejected allegory in his interpretation of scriptural pro-phecies, believing that the prophecies either had already been fulfilled in history or that they would be fulfilled in the future at the time when Antichrist should come. At any rate, the Scripture was to be interpreted literally, not allegorically.

Most of the Old Testament saints were regarded in a poor light by Marcion, and to some of them even salvation was denied. This was but in keeping with the low view which Marcion held of the Jewish people.

Marcion's criticism of the Old Testament can in no sense be regarded as scientific. It proceeded from a prejudiced philosophical background. His strictures and also his exegesis oftentimes appear to have been superficial, and they were apparently offered at times without serious consideration of the text and its background. His approach to the Scripture was not that of an impartial student but that of one who employs the Scripture to suit his purpose.[15]

c. Non-Gnostic sects of the first two centuries

1. The Nazarites. This group apparently consisted of Christians of Jewish birth who practised the Jewish manner of life. According to John

[15] *Cf.* Tertullian, *Contra Marcionem*, PL, 2, cols. 263ff.; Harnack, *Marcion, das Evangelium vom fremden Gott* (1924).

of Damascus they denied – and this seems to be the first recorded denial – the Mosaic authorship of the Pentateuch.[16]

2. The Ebionites. This group, sometimes known as Pharisaic Ebionites, is said by Epiphanius[17] to have detested the prophets, receiving none of them. Also they rejected certain words of the Pentateuch as not having come from Moses.

3. The Clementine Homilies.[18] These Homilies present a form of Ebionism, with some similarities to Gnosticism. In them it is maintained that Moses delivered the Law to seventy chosen men, but later certain falsehoods were added to the Scriptures by the wicked one. Thus the Scriptures are said to misrepresent God in many ways. For example, they set forth God as ignorant and thus are false, the work of a man. They also misrepresent godly men. Adam was really not a transgressor, Noah the righteous one was never drunken, Abraham never lived with three wives at once, Jacob never associated with four, nor was Moses a murderer.

The account of Moses' death was not written by Moses, for how could he write that he had died? About five hundred years after Moses' time the Law was found in the Temple, and five hundred years later at the time of Nebuchadnezzar it was burned and destroyed.

The hypothesis employed in the Homilies for explaining difficult passages in the Bible is in reality that of interpolations made by the devil himself. And the criterion for deciding what is and what is not a diabolical interpretation is whether the given passage is thought to be in harmony with the creation. The judge of this, of course, is the human mind, and thus the criticism of the Clementine Homilies is really a form of philosophical rationalism.

Some of these same views appear in the *Epistle of Peter to James*,[19] wherein it is asserted that the countrymen of Moses corrected the incongruities of the Bible, so that no-one should be confounded at the various utterances of the prophets.

Certain minor sects, *e.g.*, the Ossenoi, rejected some of the Prophets, and the Valesii rejected both the Law and the Prophets. No doubt there were other sects also, of which no information is extant, that likewise adopted a hostile attitude towards the Old Testament.

[16] *Cf. PG*, 94, cols. 688–9; Epiphanius, *Adversus Haereses, PG*, 41, col. 257; Harnack, *Lehrbuch der Dogmengeschichte*[5] (1931), I, pp. 310–334.

[17] *PG*, 41, col. 436.

[18] Although the Homilies in their present form are evidently later than the second century, nevertheless the viewpoint which they present was doubtless very early, and for that reason they are discussed at this point.

[19] *PG*, 2, col. 25.

d. Celsus[20]

One of the strongest attacks which the nascent Christian Church had to sustain came from a man named Celsus. A certain convert of Origen, Ambrose by name, sent to him Celsus' treatise, *The True Word*, and urged him to prepare a reply. Origen was somewhat loath to undertake the task, believing that the best refutation of such false charges was to be found in silence. More mature reflection, however, compelled him to take up the pen in defence of the Faith.

Almost nothing is known about the identity of Celsus. In fact, Origen himself was not sure of his opponent's identity. Whoever Celsus was, he was a man of great learning and ability, who realized that he was facing in Christianity a powerful movement, and he was determined to check its growth as much as possible. Hence, in Celsus we find a representative of the Graeco-Roman world, a world which sees itself in peril.

Celsus' objections to the Old Testament are not based upon patient research and investigation, but rather reflect the attitude of a prejudiced mind. Origen's great apologetic, *Contra Celsum*, was probably written about AD 248–249, some seventy years after Celsus had made his attacks.

Celsus shows a very sketchy knowledge of Old Testament history. The Hebrew nation, he thought, commenced in a revolt from the Egyptians, for the Jews were descended from the Egyptians. He tended to disparage the Jews as a people who had never done anything remarkable and 'were never held in repute or account'. The doctrine of creation taught in Genesis is dismissed as being 'very silly', and the rite of circumcision is said to have been adopted from the Egyptians. Particularly did Celsus criticize anthropomorphic statements in the Bible. God is regarded as a tired, over-worked Being, as a result of the six-day creation. Of such nature were Celsus' objections.

One point, however, should be stressed. Celsus did not deny the Mosaic authorship of the Pentateuch, as has sometimes been affirmed.

Summary of the first two centuries

During the first two centuries of the Christian era there is no recorded instance of criticism that is hostile to the Bible among the Church Fathers or in the orthodox Church itself. The Apostolic Fathers and the subsequent Ante-Nicene Fathers, in so far as they expressed themselves on the subject, believed Moses to be the author of the Pentateuch, and the Old Testament to be a divine book.

[20] For special literature on the subject, see *Contra Celsum* in *PG*, XI, ET in *The Ante-Nicene Fathers*, IX; Edward J. Young, 'Celsus and the Old Testament' in *WThJ*, VI, pp. 168–197.

Such instances of hostile criticism as are extant from this period come either from groups that were considered to be heretical, or from the external pagan world. Furthermore, this criticism reflected certain philosophical presuppositions and is of a decidedly biased and un-scientific character. As far as available evidence is concerned, it may be said that the Church itself looked upon the Old Testament as the authoritative Word of God.

THE THIRD CENTURY TO THE REFORMATION

1. Concerning Ezra, the restorer of the Law, we read the following tradition in 4 Esdras 14:21, 22 (*c.* AD 90): 'For thy law is burnt, therefore no man knoweth the things that are done of thee, or the works that shall begin. But if I have found grace before thee, send the Holy Ghost into me, and I shall write all that hath been done in the law, that men may find thy path, and that they which will live in the latter days may live.' This Jewish opinion, namely, that Ezra restored the books of the Old Testament which had been lost or destroyed in the downfall of Jerusalem, had been adopted by many of the early Christian Fathers, *e.g.*, Irenaeus, Tertullian, Clement of Alexandria, Jerome, Basil the Great. The language of these Fathers is not always as cautious as could be desired, and a superficial study of this language might leave the impression that they believe that Ezra under divine inspiration completely rewrote the books that had been lost. Quite possibly, however, what the Fathers meant was that Ezra edited or reproduced from various sources the books of Scripture. At any rate, whatever the precise meaning, they do not employ this belief to deny the Mosaic authorship of the Law.

2. Porphyry, the noted antagonist of Christianity was probably born in AD 232 or 233 in Tyre. He studied at Athens under Longinus and later at Rome under the neo-Platonist, Plotinus. At about forty years of age, while in Sicily, he wrote his magnum opus, *Against the Christians*. The twelfth book was devoted to an attack upon Daniel, in which he asserted that the book was written not by Daniel but by an unknown writer of the second century BC. Porphyry candidly states that this must be so because Daniel himself could not so accurately have depicted the future.

In all probability Porphyry denied the Mosaic authorship of the Pentateuch.[21]

3. Julian the Apostate, nephew of Constantine, was born in AD 331 and educated under the Arian Bishop Eusebius of Nicomedia. He

[21] See Edward J. Young, 'Porphyry and His Criticism of Daniel' in *CD*, 1949, pp. 317ff.

renounced Christianity and spoke with great contempt of the Old Testament, ranking Moses and Solomon far below the pagan philosophers and lawgivers. He considered the Mosaic history of the creation to be defective, and maintained that Moses taught both monotheism and polytheism.

4. Jerome (died 420), discussing the words 'unto this day' of Genesis 35:4 and Deuteronomy 34:5, 6, remarks, 'We must certainly understand by "this day" the time of the composition [contesta est] of the history, whether you prefer the view that Moses was the author of the Pentateuch or that Ezra re-edited it. In either case I do not object [sive Moysen dicere volueris auctorem Pentateuchi, sive Ezram eiusdem instauratorem operis, non recuso].[22] Some have apparently understood this remark to involve a denial of Mosaic authorship, but such is not the case. Jerome is merely not pronouncing upon the question at this point. His concern is simply whether the words 'unto this day' refer to the time of 'publishing or writing the books'. There is evidence available to show that Jerome probably did believe that Moses was the author of the Pentateuch.[23] Jerome did state that Deuteronomy was found in the Temple during the twelfth year of Josiah's reign ('quando inventus est liber Deuteronomii in templo Dei').[24] But this does not show that Jerome denied the Mosaic authorship of Deuteronomy.

5. Theodore of Mopsuestia (died c. 428) was a theologian of the school of Antioch and an adherent of the principle of grammatico-historical exegesis. After his death his works were condemned by the Second Council of Constantinople, 553. Apparently Theodore maintained that parts of Job could not have been written by a righteous man, and that the Song of Solomon was an uninteresting epithalamium written by Solomon in honour of his marriage to an Egyptian princess. Theodore also rejected the titles of the Psalms ('tas te epigraphas ton hierotaton hymnon kai psalmon kai odon pante ekbalon'), attributing their authorship to the period of Zerubbabel and Hezekiah. He also apparently was the first to place the authorship of some of the Psalms in the time of the Maccabees.[25]

6. Anastasius the Sinaite, patriarch of Antioch towards the close of the seventh century, wrote a work, Hodegos, i.e., Guide, in which he set forth certain difficulties that had been presented to him by those who

---

[22] De Perpetua Virginitate, PL, 23, col. 199.
[23] Cf. Adversus Jovinianus, PL, 23, col. 226.
[24] Commentary on Ezekiel, i. 1, PL, 25, col. 17; Against Jovinianus, PL, 23, col. 227.
[25] See Robert Devreesse, Le Commentaire de Théodore de Mopsueste sur les Psaumes (1939); H. Kihn, Theodor von Mopsuesta und Junilius Africanus als Exegeten (1880).

had left the Church. Some of these involved the Mosaic authorship of Genesis, the alleged discrepancies in Genesis, *etc.*[26]

7. Hiwi al Balkhi was a Jewish rationalist of the ninth century who lived in Balkh, Persia. He wrote a polemic against the Scriptures in which he set forth some two hundred difficulties. He sought to show that God was unjust, for example, in that He accepted the gift of Abel but rejected that of Cain, God was ignorant, not omnipotent, and He changed His mind. He further sought to show that polytheism was taught in the Bible, and that the Old Testament contained contradictions.[27]

8. Ibn Hazm of Cordoba, Spain (994–1064), in defending Islam as the true faith sought to show that the Bible was not the Word of God. He complained of the anthropomorphic representations of God, and maintained that the Bible taught polytheism. Further, he thought that he found erroneous statements and errors in chronology, and he attributed the authorship of many statements in the Pentateuch to Ezra.[28]

9. Abu Ibrahim Isaac ibn Yashush, commonly spoken of as Isaac ben Jasos (982–1057/8), was a Spanish grammarian and probably also a physician. From references in the writings of Ibn Ezra it appears that Isaac regarded Genesis 36 as having been written not earlier than Jehoshaphat's time. He identified the Hadad of Genesis 36:35 with the Hadad of 1 Kings 11:14, and his work was denounced by Ibn Ezra as one that should be burned, since its author was babbling vanities (*mahbil*).

10. Abraham ben Meir ibn Ezra, commonly referred to as Ibn Ezra (1092/3–1167), was a Spanish exegete, who wrote many valuable commentaries on the Old Testament. There is no question that Ibn Ezra maintained the Mosaic authorship of the Pentateuch, yet he evidently believed that certain verses were later additions. For example, with regard to the words, 'the Canaanite was then in the land' (Gn. 12:6) he thought that the verse had a secret and the prudent man would be silent. He also referred to such passages as Genesis 22:14; Deuteronomy 1:1; 3:11, and evidently questioned them. He also spoke in such a way as to suggest a late origin for Isaiah 40–66.

11. Andreas Bodenstein, usually called Carlstadt after his native

[26] See *PG*, 89, cols. 284, 285.

[27] See Judah Rosenthal, 'Hiwi al Balkhi' in *JQR*, 38, pp. 317–342; 419–430; 39, pp. 79–94.

[28] For a brief summary, see A. Guillaume, *Prophecy and Divination* (1938), pp. 415–420, and a translation into Spanish, Miguel Asin, *Abenhazam de Cordoba*, II (1928).

place, was a contemporary of Luther (1480–1541). Apparently he regarded Luther as a rival, and for a time, when the course of the Reformation was in his hands, it came close to shipwreck. Carlstadt denied the Mosaic authorship of the Pentateuch, but his reasons for doing so were indeed strange. Unless a man were demented, he argued, he would not maintain that Moses had written the account of his death (*'nisi plane dementissimus Mosi velut auctori tribuet'*). The style, however, of this section which records Moses' death is the same as that of the Pentateuch generally, hence Moses was not the author of that either. Further, Carlstadt thought that there were many things in Deuteronomy which Moses would not have written.

THE REFORMATION TO THE NINETEENTH CENTURY

1. Andreas Masius, a Roman Catholic lawyer of Belgium (died 1573) wrote a commentary on Joshua (published in 1574 under the title *Josuae Imperatoris Historia*) in which he set forth the view that Ezra and possibly those associated with him, under divine inspiration, may have made certain interpolations in the books of Moses. A somewhat similar position was also advanced by a Flemish scholar of the Jesuit order, Jacques Bonfrère. He believed that certain words and phrases could not be attributed to Moses speaking in the role of a prophet, but rather were the insertions of a later hand. Essentially similar opinions were entertained by the Spanish Jesuit, Benedict Pereira (*c.* 1535–1610). While holding to the Mosaic authorship of much of the Pentateuch, he nevertheless believed that there was considerable later addition.

2. Thomas Hobbes did not deny the Mosaic authorship of those passages which were expressly attributed to Moses, but as for the rest, he thought that it was written more concerning Moses than by him (*'videtur Pentateuch pontius de Mose quam a Mose scriptus'*).[29]

3. Isaac Peyrerius (died 1676) was a French clergyman of the Reformed persuasion who later went over to the Roman Catholic Church. He wrote the *Systema Theologicum ex prae-Adamitorium Hypothesi* (1665), in which he sought to demonstrate that Adam was the head only of Israel and not of the entire human race. As to the Pentateuch he thought that Moses had kept a diary or account of the principal events, and had prefaced this with an account of the history of the world. These documents, however, were lost, and the present Pentateuch consists of abstracts derived from these. It is, therefore, not the work of Moses, but of a later time. Peyrerius later retracted these views.

[29] See p. 19.

4. Benedict Spinoza (1632–1677) was born in Amsterdam of a prominent Holland-Jewish family. He received a general Jewish education, studied Latin, mathematics and medicine, and later became a student of Descartes. In 1670 he published his *Tractatus Theologico Politicus*, in which he set forth certain criticisms of the Scriptures. The purpose of his book was to show that philosophy and organized religion should occupy different spheres.

Spinoza makes reference to Ibn Ezra and discusses some of the passages upon which he had commented. He thinks that Ibn Ezra himself was not convinced of the Mosaic authorship of the Pentateuch (in this, however, he was probably mistaken), and Spinoza himself denies Mosaic authorship by endeavouring to adduce further evidence. Thus, he argues, Moses is spoken of in the third person, he is described as the meekest of men (Nu. 12:3), and the last chapter of Deuteronomy clearly shows that Moses was not the author. On the other hand, certain passages were written by Moses. On the whole the Pentateuch may be regarded, thought Spinoza, as the work of a late compiler, possibly Ezra.

5. Simon and Le Clerc (see pp. 19, 20).

6. Episcopius, the Remonstrant theologian, in his *Institutiones Theologicae* (1650) asserted that there were many post-Mosaica in the Pentateuch. He seems to have objected particularly to Numbers 12:3: 'Who can believe that Moses could write this of himself?' Joshua, also, he thought, was compiled into one book by Ezra.

7. Campegius Vitringa, in discussing Genesis 2 (*Observationes Sacrae*, 1689), suggested that Moses used ancient scrolls of the patriarchs together with his own descriptions and derived some of his information from these ancient scrolls. It was this idea, that Moses employed previously existing documents in compiling his writings, that was later developed by Astruc.

8. Anthony van Dale (1696) also suggested that Ezra was the restorer of the Pentateuch and had inserted the so-called post-Mosaica which had troubled men like Spinoza and Simon.

9. H. B. Witter asserted (*Jura Israelitarum in Palaestina*, 1711) that there were two parallel accounts of creation, namely, Genesis 1:1–2:4 and 2:5–3:24, and that these two accounts were distinguished by the use of different divine names. Witter is, therefore, as far as is known, the first to suggest the divine names as criteria for distinguishing documents.

10. Jean Astruc was born 19 March 1684, at Sauve, Languedoc, in France. His father had been a Protestant pastor but, with the revocation of the edict of Nantes, had entered the Romanist Church. Astruc studied at Montpelier, a centre of medicine, becoming an M.A. in 1700 and a

doctor of medicine in 1703. He continued to lecture at Montpelier and Toulouse until 1729, when he moved to Paris and devoted himself to the great literary work of his life, *De morbis venereis*. He remained in Paris until his death.

In 1753 there appeared Astruc's work on Genesis with the title, *Conjectures sur les mémoires originaux dont il paroit que Moyse s'est servi pour composer le Livre de la Genèse. Avec des Remarques, qui appuient ou qui eclaircissent ces Conjectures.* In the preface Astruc explained that he had hesitated to issue his work lest some would abuse it to lessen the authority of the Pentateuch. However, a friend, who is described as very zealous for religion ('*tres zèle pour la Religion*'), told him that the idea that Moses had used memoirs had already been advanced by well-approved authors – Les Abbez Fleury and le François. Hence, Astruc was emboldened to publish, although he did so anonymously.

Moses, he argues, refers to events which took place over two thousand years before his time. This information Moses must have received either by direct revelation, or from the reports of those who had themselves been witnesses of the events. But since in Genesis Moses speaks as a simple historian, it is obvious that he received his knowledge from his ancestors. This knowledge could have been transmitted either by oral tradition or by written tradition, *i.e.*, by memorials which had been left in writing. According to Astruc, the latter was the case.

Moses actually possessed certain old memoirs which contained the history of his ancestors from the creation of the world. In order not to lose any of these he divided them by pieces ('*par morceaux*') according to their contents. These pieces he assembled, one following another, and from this assemblage the book of Genesis was formed.

There are four principal reasons why Astruc advances this thesis: (i) Genesis contains striking repetitions of the same events, *e.g.*, the creation, the flood. (ii) God is designated by two different names, Elohim (*Dieu*), which indicates that He is the supreme Being, and Jehovah (*l'Eternel*), the name which expresses His essence. (iii) This distinction appears only in Genesis and the first two chapters of Exodus. Hence, Astruc limits his discussion accordingly to this part of the Pentateuch. (iv) Certain events are related in Genesis before others although they took place later.

These considerations, thinks Astruc, make it natural to want to analyse (*décomposer*) Genesis. Nor is the undertaking as difficult as one would think. One need only join together all the places where God is constantly called Elohim. These Astruc placed in a column which he designated A, and this he regarded as the original document. Side by side with this Astruc placed all the passages that employ the name Jehovah, and this column he called B.

However, Astruc soon found it necessary to discover other documents, and these were as follows:

C, repetitions, *e.g.*, the flood

D, events extraneous to the history of the Hebrew people

E, the wars of the five kings, Genesis 14

F, Genesis 19:29ff., a 'manifest interpolation'

G, Genesis 22:20–24

H, Genesis 25:12–19, the genealogy of Ishmael

I, Genesis 34, a chapter similar in character to chapter 14

K, Genesis 26:34ff.

L, Genesis 28:6–10

M, Genesis 36:20–31

N, Genesis 39, interpolation.

Astruc remarked that his success was more happy than he had dared hope for. Certain points in Astruc's work must be stressed:

(i) Astruc did not deny the Mosaic authorship of Genesis. In fact, he went to some length to defend it.

(ii) Astruc recognized that the divine names could not be used as criteria for analysing the entire Pentateuch.

(iii) Astruc's own work shows that the divine names are not sufficient criteria for analysing Genesis into documents. He is compelled to carry out his analysis upon the basis of secondary criteria. Furthermore, his own work shows that certain passages, notably Genesis 14, do not fit into a documentary analysis.

(iv) Since the divine names and even certain secondary criteria are not sufficient for analysing Genesis, Astruc is compelled to discover the presence of 'interpolations'.

(v) In asserting that Moses may have used written memoirs in compiling Genesis, Astruc doubtless hit upon the truth. His basic mistake was in going a step farther and claiming that it was possible for us today to discover the extent of these documents. The subsequent course of criticism has shown that the process of recognizing the extent of these documents is by no means the easy thing that Astruc thought it to be.

Astruc's work seems to have passed entirely unnoticed, although it was reviewed with disfavour by Michaelis. Ten years after its appearance, Voltaire, in the article 'Genesis' in his *Philosophical Dictionary*, says, 'It is principally this verse [Gn. 36:31] that determined Astruc to give up the inspired authority of the whole Book of Genesis, and suppose the author had derived his materials from existing memoirs and records. His work is ingenious and accurate, but it is rash, not to say audacious. Even a council would scarcely have ventured on such an enterprise. And to what purpose has it served Astruc's thankless and dangerous labour – to double the darkness he wished to enlighten? Here is the fruit of the tree of knowledge of which we are all so desirous of eating. Why must it be, that the fruit of the tree of ignorance should be more nourishing and more digestible?'[30]

11. Johann Gottfried Eichhorn asserted his independence of Astruc, but performed essentially the same work, although far more thoroughly. In his *Einleitung* (1780–83) he analysed Genesis and Exodus 1–2 into sources, which he called J and E, after the divine names. These sources, he thought, probably rested upon written traditions, and were pieced together by Moses. Later, however, he gave up the theory of a Mosaic redaction, and asserted that the sources were pieced together by an unknown redactor.

12. Karl David Ilgen was the successor of Eichhorn in the chair of Oriental languages at Jena. In 1798 he published a work with the pre-possessing title, *Die Urkunden des jerusalemischen Tempelarchivs in ihrer Urgestalt als Beitrag zur Berichtigung der Geschichte der Religion und Politik* (i.e., *The Documents of the Archives of the Temple of Jerusalem in their Original Form, as a Contribution to the Corroboration of the History of Religion and Politics*). In order to write the history of the Israelites Ilgen desired to make available their literary documents. To do this, however, he sought to free them from the accretions which he believed had grown up around them. The original archives of the Temple, he thought, had become torn, and mixed up.

Ilgen came to the conclusion that in the book of Genesis there were seventeen different individual documents, and these he assigned to three different authors, two Elohists and one Jehovist. Thus: (i) the first Elohist (E^1), ten sections; (ii) the second Elohist (E^2), five sections; (iii) the first Jehovist (*sefer eliyah hari-'shon*), two sections. The first Jehovist began with the twelfth chapter. Passages which Astruc had regarded as Jehovistic were assigned to the second Elohist.

The following remarks may be made: First, in mentioning a first Jehovist, Ilgen allowed for the possibility of a second; thus, it would seem, suggesting that even the Jehovistic sections were not a unity. Second, in assigning Astruc's Jehovistic passages in Genesis 1–11 to his second Elohist Ilgen again showed the insufficiency of the divine names

---

[30] ET (1901), 5, p. 187. For special literature on Astruc, see Adolphe Lods, *Jean Astruc et la critique biblique au XVIIIe siècle* (Strassburg-Paris); Howard Osgood, 'Jean Astruc'* in *PRR*, III, 1892, pp. 83–102.

as criteria for carrying on the critical analysis. Third, in dividing the content of Genesis between two Elohists, Ilgen anticipated the position of Hupfeld (1853).

Soon after the publication of his work on Genesis, Ilgen became rector of the Pforta School and apparently gave up specialized study of the Old Testament.

Summary

For a time after the Reformation, certain scholars were troubled by the presence in the Pentateuch of passages which, they believed, could not have been written by Moses. Hence, it was asserted by some that Moses could not have been the author of the entire Pentateuch. But this was the exception. By the great majority of scholars, Mosaic authorship was accepted and even defended.

Vitringa, an orthodox theologian, merely suggested that Moses might have employed ancient memoirs of the patriarchs. Witter is probably to be regarded as the father of the documentary theory, since he called attention to the divine names and also to alleged parallel accounts. However, this was only in germ form.

Astruc stoutly maintained the Mosaic authorship of the Pentateuch. He merely thought that Moses had used previously existing documents and that the divine names furnished the clue for identifying these documents. This was essentially the position of Eichhorn. These men, together with Ilgen, may be regarded as representatives of the earlier documentary hypothesis.[31]

[31] Quite possibly other scholars also might be classified as representatives in one way or another of this hypothesis. Thus, J. G. Hase (1785) declared that the Pentateuch was compiled in the time of the exile from old documents which were partly Mosaic but which were enlarged and changed. In 1805 he retracted this position, declaring that the Pentateuch was the work of Moses, but that it contained certain interpolations, and that Ezra had been the last to work on it. Friedrich Karl Fulda, a pastor, taught (1791–95) that certain laws, songs, and sections had come from Moses, but that these were present only in fragments. In David's time the laws were collected, and from this collection and from historical books our present Pentateuch was finally compiled in Ezra's time. H. Corrodi maintained (1792) that the Pentateuch consisted of various parts and was at least as old as the Davidic Psalms. J. C. Nachtigall (1794) asserted that the entire Pentateuch was gathered and arranged before the schism. Later, he attributed very little to Moses, maintaining that the Mosaic part was written on stones and in hiero- glyphs, and that much was handed down by word of mouth. From the time of Samuel these traditions were written down and collected, and the present Pentateuch was probably compiled by Jeremiah during the exile. J. K. R. Eckermann sought to show, in opposition to Nachtigall, that unless the Pentateuch had been in existence before the schism, the Samaritans could not have received a copy. Hence, it must have been written during the days either of Samuel or David.

THE NINETEENTH CENTURY

a. The fragmentary hypothesis

In the writings of the earliest advocates of the documentary hypothesis, the weaknesses of this hypothesis clearly appear. The divine names, which to Astruc seemed such satisfactory guides for the analysis of documents, proved after all to be very unsatisfactory. Astruc was elated over what he thought was success, but Ilgen actually applies some of Astruc's Jehovistic passages to an Elohistic writer. Further, Ilgen had to find two Elohistic writers. Why should two such competent men come to opposite conclusions? Is it not possible that the whole process of partitioning writings into various documents is very subjective? The subjective character of the process becomes clearer as we trace its history further.

1. Alexander Geddes was a Scottish Roman Catholic priest, who in 1792 issued a translation of the Bible up to and including Joshua and in 1800 his *Critical Remarks*. In these works Geddes asserted that the Pentateuch, in its present form, was not the work of Moses, but was probably compiled during the reign of Solomon in Jerusalem. Although taking its present form during the reign of Solomon, the Pentateuch was compiled from ancient documents, some of which 'were coeval with Moses, and some even anterior to Moses'. These documents amounted to a mass of fragments, large and small, which were independent of one another and were pieced together by a redactor. There were, thought Geddes, two series of fragments, and this phenomenon was due to the presence of the divine names.

On the other hand, Geddes definitely rejected the two-document theory of Astruc and Eichhorn as 'a work of *fancy*'. He further united the book of Joshua to the Pentateuch, 'both because I conceive it to have been compiled by the same author and because it is a necessary appendix to the history contained in the former books'. Thus, Geddes anticipates the modern view of a Hexateuch, rather than a Pentateuch.

Although Geddes claimed to be true to religion, and even said, 'I willingly profess myself a sincere, though unworthy, disciple of Christ; Christian is my name, and Catholic my surname', nevertheless he appealed to reason, and, as his words reveal, autonomous human reason, as the 'only solid pillar of faith'. Geddes' position, therefore, was at bottom rationalistic and hostile to supernatural Christianity. Christianity and reason, of course, are not enemies, for Christianity is the only *reasonable* explanation of life, and true reason, which is derived from God, is both humble and receptive. To regard the unaided reason of man, however, as autonomous, and the final court of judgment, is to set up man as the judge of God's revelation. It is rationalism of a very bold type. Geddes, therefore, whether he wished it or not, was attacking the Christian religion, and it is no wonder that the authority of his church opposed him.

2. Johann Severin Vater in his *Commentar über den Pentateuch* (1802–5) developed more fully the fragmentary hypothesis of Geddes. He sought to demonstrate the gradual growth of the Pentateuch from individual fragments, of which he found about thirty-eight. Some of these were from the time of Moses, but the Pentateuch in its present form belongs to the age of the exile.

It should be noted that up to this time documentary analysis had for the most part been confined to Genesis. Vater, however, continued it throughout the remainder of the Pentateuch. Indeed, he regarded the kernel of the Pentateuch as a book of law, and taught that Deuteronomy went back to the time of David or Solomon.

3. Anton Theodor Hartmann in his *Historisch-kritische Forschungen über die Bildung, das Zeitalter und den Plan der fünf Bücher Mosis* (1831) carried this theory still further. He thought it questionable whether the art of writing was known in Moses' days, but believed that it came to be known among the Hebrews only in the days of the Judges. Most of the portions of the Pentateuch, according to Hartmann, took their rise sometime between the age of Solomon and the exile and, in its present form, the Pentateuch is the product of the time of the exile. Holding to such a view of the historical origin of the books, Hartmann naturally came to believe that the narratives of the Pentateuch were myths and distorted traditions.

4. Wilhelm Martin Lebrecht De Wette must also be named among the adherents of the fragmentary hypothesis. In his *Beiträge zur Einleitung ins AT* (1806–7), he taught that the oldest parts of the Pentateuch belonged to David's time. Originally there were individual, independent fragments, which were pieced together by different compilers; thus, the compiler of Leviticus was a different person from the compiler of Exodus, *etc.* Deuteronomy was composed under Josiah, and, since it is presupposed in the other Pentateuchal books, they must be later. This view had received particular expression in De Wette's dissertation, *Dissertatio qua Deuteronomium a prioribus Pentateuchi libris diversum alius cuiusdam recentioris auctoris opus esse demonstratur* (1805). This view of Deuteronomy became pivotal in later discussions.

With respect to Genesis, De Wette returned to the documentary hypothesis and maintained that the author of Genesis had an Elohim-document which extended at least to Exodus 6, and this he supplemented with excerpts from one or possibly more Jehovistic sources. De Wette rejected very pronouncedly the historical character of the Mosaic history and regarded Genesis as containing a type of epic poem. He may be regarded, then, as holding the fragmentary hypothesis only in a limited way.

We may at this point add some general remarks on the weaknesses of the fragmentary hypothesis.

1. The fragmentary hypothesis is a *reductio ad absurdum* of the principles and methods of the earlier two-document hypothesis. As Green remarks, 'Admit the legitimacy of this disintegrating process, and there is no limit to which it may not be carried at the pleasure of the operator; and it might be added, there is no work to which it might not be applied.'[32] The reader should consult E. D. McRealsham (C. M. Meade): *Romans Dissected. A New Critical Analysis of the Epistle to the Romans.* *

2. It is almost inconceivable that a work bearing the manifest inner unity and harmony of the Pentateuch could have been compiled from a congeries of conflicting and independent fragments.

3. The allusions of one part of the Pentateuch to other parts clearly show that the fragmentary hypothesis is incorrect.

4. Advocates of the fragmentary hypothesis have not only denied the Mosaic authorship of the Pentateuch, but also its essential historicity. The rationalism of Geddes influenced Vater, and Vater in turn influenced De Wette. The spirit of Geddes prevailed among the advocates of this hypothesis, whether they were conscious of the fact or not.

5. In view of the New Testament witness to the historicity of Pentateuchal events, the fragmentary hypothesis, in so far as it denies such historicity, must be rejected.

The hypothesis of fragments by no means commanded universal assent. It is necessary, therefore, to consider some who either wrote directly against it or who advocated their own views. We shall first consider those who set forth individual views.

1. Concerning particular opposition to the writings of Vater and De Wette, there were those who sought to maintain the essential Mosaic authorship of the Pentateuch. Among them may be mentioned Kelle (1811), Fritzsche (1814), Jahn, and to a certain extent, Rosenmueller (1821).

2. L. Bertholdt in his Biblical Introduction (1813) asserted that the

[32] *HCP*, p. 72.

Pentateuch was essentially Mosaic, although compiled in its present form at some time between Saul and the end of Solomon's reign.

3. Count Volney, in his *Recherches nouvelles sur l'histoire ancienne* (1814), maintained that our present Pentateuch was compiled by Hilkiah (2 Ki. 22) out of genuine Mosaic records and some later additions.

4. J. G. Herbst, a professor at Tübingen, held that the Pentateuch was edited in the time of David, and that it consisted of the genuine writings of Moses with some additions.

5. In 1832 Eichhorn modified somewhat his earlier belief in the Mosaic authorship of the Pentateuch.

6. Heinrich Ewald gave what might be called a death blow to the fragment hypothesis. In his work on Genesis, *Die Komposition der Genesis kritisch untersucht* (1823), Ewald presented a strong defence of the book's unity. He sought to turn aside from what he called the *Hypothesenstrudel*, and to discover what the narrator in Genesis really wishes to say. He did not maintain that Moses was the author, but he did hold that Genesis was a remarkable book, coming from a very early time ('*der grauen Vorzeit*'). Genesis, he thought, appeared to be a unit, designed to exhibit the history of God's people from their origin until they were brought down to Egypt. Certain idioms and expressions, he thought, betrayed the unity of the book. Certain characteristics of Genesis also appear in Arabic literature where, for example, one may find repetitions and particular headings within a larger book. These, therefore, are no indication of diversity of authorship. Ewald concludes that we should no longer look for different narrators, where there is the greatest harmony, nor should we seek to divide into individual pieces that which is so strongly bound together ('*in einzelne Stücke trennen, was tausendfache Bände aufs genaueste an- und ineinander verknüpfen*').

In the present writer's opinion Ewald made a real contribution to the problem of the unity of Genesis by his appeal to Arabic literature.[33]

7. C. P. W. Gramberg in 1829 sought to trace the development of various Israelitish institutions such as the feasts, priesthood, sacrifice, sanctuaries, *etc.* Genesis and Exodus, he thought, were from old sources, both oral and written, and were compiled sometime between David and Hezekiah. Leviticus and Numbers belong to the beginning of the exile, and Deuteronomy, compiled from post-Josian sources, belongs to the end of the exile. Gramberg taught that the redactor, in combining the Elohist and Jehovist, made some changes and additions of his own

[33] See Robert Dick Wilson, 'The Use of "God" and "Lord" in the Koran'* in *PTR* Oct. 1919, pp. 2–8.

Gramberg, therefore, may legitimately be regarded as a forerunner of the development hypothesis of Wellhausen.

8. Wilhelm Vatke asserted that the Mosaic state was not historical, and the Law, rather than being the foundation, was the product of a state which already existed. The lawbook which was discovered during Josiah's reign was essentially parts of the code in Exodus. Deuteronomy, on the other hand, arose after the Josianic reform, and the last portions of the law came from the exile. Even more markedly than Gramberg, therefore, Vatke was a forerunner of Wellhausen. Vatke expressed his opinions in his work *Die Religion des ATs nach den kanonischen Büchern entwickelt* (Berlin, 1835).

9. J. F. L. George, in *Die älteren jüdischen Feste mit einer Kritik der Gesetzgebung des Pentateuchs* (Berlin, 1835), divided Israel's history into three periods. To the earliest he attributed the historical portions of the Pentateuch, namely, Genesis, parts of Exodus, and Numbers. To the second belonged the Judges and Prophets. Deuteronomy appeared towards the close of this period. The third period was that of the hierarchy, and at this time the latest books of the Old Testament, including portions of the Pentateuch, were produced. This reconstruction of Israel's history was influenced by the Hegelian philosophy.

10. E. Bertheau (1840) regarded the three middle books of the Pentateuch as containing a large collection of genuine Mosaic laws, consisting of seven groups, each of which in turn had seven series, and of these each had ten precepts. The remainder of the legal matter and the historical portion was added later.

b. The supplement hypothesis

In his treatment of Genesis, De Wette had maintained that the author had before him a document (E) which he supplemented with bits from other sources. Thus, he held essentially to an hypothesis of supplements. This view tended in the opposite direction from the fragmentary hypothesis. In reality it tended towards maintaining the unity of the biblical books, and hence, as far as it went, was a step in the right direction.

1. Heinrich Ewald, in a review of *Kritische Untersuchungen über die Genesis* (1830) by J. J. Staehelin, expressed the opinion that at the basis of the first six books of the Bible lay an Elohistic writing in which the author had used older sections, such as the Ten Commandments. Later, a parallel writing arose, and this employed the name Jehovah. A later hand took excerpts from this J document and inserted them into the basic document E, and at times his work is visible.

2. P. von Bohlen advanced a somewhat similar position (1835) in a study on Genesis. He assumed the existence of an original writing which had been taken over by an Israelitish author and adopted for his purposes. Von Bohlen also considered Deuteronomy the earliest portion of the Pentateuch, dating it about the time of Josiah. The remainder he considered not to have been completed until the exile.

3. Friedrich Bleek advocated a form of the supplement hypothesis in his work on Genesis, *De libri Geneseos origine atque indole historica observationes quaedam contra Bohlenum* (1836), which, as its title shows, was directed against von Bohlen. The redactor who supplemented the Elohistic source was, he asserted, the Jehovist himself. However, Bleek also thought that many passages in the Pentateuch were originally Mosaic, and that with these books we are standing on historical ground. Deuteronomy differs from the previous books in that it is not a collection, but a unit, and related to Jeremiah. There were, according to Bleek, two principal redactions of the whole Pentateuch. One occurred during the period of the yet undivided monarchy, and was made by the compiler of Genesis. The second was made by the compiler of Deuteronomy, sometime near the end of the Judaean state, and this also included Joshua. The whole work, thus redacted, was discovered in the eighteenth year of the reign of Josiah. Many of the above ideas were set forth in Bleek's earlier works (1822, 1831). In the fifth and sixth editions of his *Introduction* (1840, 1845), De Wette maintained that there had been a threefold redaction of the Hexateuch: the Elohistic, the Jehovistic, and the Deuteronomic. The Jehovist had supplemented the Elohistic document, a work of the time of Jeroboam I. Thus, de Wette now supported the supplement hypothesis.

A mature expression of Bleek's views may be studied in the English translation of his *Introduction* (1869), a very valuable work, which is characterized by sobriety and moderation. Bleek was an evangelical Christian, and although some of his views appear to be untenable and out of harmony with the evangelical Christian position, nevertheless, Bleek, because his desire was to be constructive, is even today worthy of serious study.

4. In 1843 Staehelin published his *Critical Investigations*, in which he maintained that the Pentateuch (and Joshua) was redacted in the time of Saul, possibly by Samuel. At the basis of this, however, lay another work, which contained much of Genesis, most of the middle books, and the geographical part of Joshua. This was composed soon after the conquest of Palestine.

5. Caesar von Lengerke (1844) assumed a threefold redaction of the

Hexateuch. The basic writing, he thought, was Elohistic, composed in the early part of Solomon's reign. The redactor was the Jehovist, whose work contained most of the Pentateuch. This work was written about the time of Hezekiah, whereas most of Deuteronomy and Joshua came from about the time of Josiah.

6. Franz Delitzsch, in his commentary on Genesis (1852), held that all the portions of the Pentateuch attributed to Moses (Deuteronomy and Exodus 19–24) were actually written by him. The remaining laws were Mosaic, but were codified by the priests after the conquest of Canaan. After the conquest the Elohistic document was written, possibly by Eliezer, and in this the Book of the Covenant was incorporated. Someone else then supplemented this work, also including Deuteronomy.

7. Friedrich Tuch in his commentary on Genesis (1858) gave classic expression to the supplement hypothesis. Tuch held that in the Pentateuch there were two documents, which could be distinguished by their use of the divine names. Of these, the Elohistic is basic, embracing the entire Mosaic period, and even continuing into the book of Joshua. The supplementer (*Ergänzer*) is the Jehovistic author, who inserted material to his own into the E document. According to Tuch, the Elohist belonged of the time of Saul, and the Jehovist to the age of Solomon.

The supplement hypothesis breaks down, however, before one very clear fact. Since the supplementer was generally regarded as 'J', it is perfectly clear why the J passages would contain allusions to the E passages. But why do the E passages, supposedly written before the supplementer 'J' began his work, contain allusions to or presuppose the contents of the J sections? Here the theory fails. There are other difficulties also, but this is the chief one. This theory was subjected to a thorough refutation in 1844 by J. H. Kurtz in a discussion of Genesis 1–4. Two years later, 1846, appeared his work on the unity of Genesis, *Die Einheit der Genesis*, which continued the refutation. Unfortunately Kurtz later gave up his position.

c. The crystallization hypothesis

1. Heinrich Ewald was yet to change his mind again. As he had helped in establishing, so he aided also in destroying the supplement hypothesis. In his *History of the People of Israel* (1840–1845) he asserted that in the Pentateuch there were fragments which did not go back either to E, J, or to Deuteronomy. To Moses, Ewald assigned the Decalogue and a few laws. The list of stations in Numbers 33, Genesis 14, *etc.*, he considered also to be very old. In addition he found a work, the Book of Covenants, which he thought was probably written by a Judaean, during the time

E

of the Judges. Further, there was the Book of Origins, written by a Levite in the early years of Solomon's reign. This about approximated the Elohist of the supplement hypothesis. In addition there was also a third narrator, probably a contemporary of Elijah who, with the help of the first historical work, narrated the Mosaic history. A fourth – prophetic – narrator is also to be found, and a fifth – a Judaean of the time of Uzziah or Jotham.

This fifth narrator constantly used the divine name Jehovah, and was the editor. From this work our Hexateuch is derived, and in the final redaction three hands were active. About 600 BC Leviticus 26:3–45 was inserted. In the first edition of his work Ewald maintained that Deuteronomy was added during the latter half of Manasseh's reign, but in subsequent editions he taught that it was originally an independent work added about 500 BC by the final editor.

2. August Knobel (1861) taught a simpler form of this crystallization hypothesis. He held to a basic document, E, from the period of Saul, hence he is sometimes classified as an adherent of the supplement hypothesis. Side by side with this was another document of later origin, a Book of Rights. In addition there was the J document, the Book of Wars, and the author of this was also the supplementer. Lastly came Deuteronomy, which was contemporary with Jeremiah.

3. Eberhard Schraeder (1869) while really presenting a form of the crystallization hypothesis, sought to unite the various hypotheses. He taught that the Pentateuch consisted of two original documents, E, and the theocratic narrator, a second E. These two were worked into one by the Jehovist, and Deuteronomy was the work of another author.

d. The modified documentary hypothesis

The crystallization hypothesis was an attempt to remove the difficulties of the supplement hypothesis by means of the introduction of additional supplements. Exactly one hundred years after the appearance of Astruc's work, Hermann Hupfeld undertook to remove the difficulty in an entirely different manner. In his important work, *Die Quellen der Genesis und die Art ihrer Zusammensetzung von neuem untersucht* (1853), Hupfeld sought to show that:

1. The J sections in Genesis were not mere disconnected supplements to an earlier Elohistic basis, but themselves formed a continuous document.

2. On the other hand, the Elohistic sections were not a continuous document, but rather were composite, consisting of two documents. This idea had already been advanced by Ilgen, De Wette, and, to an extent,

by Knobel. There were thus a first Elohist and a second Elohist. Strangely enough, Hupfeld maintained the second Elohist, although employing the divine name Elohim, nevertheless in his language and other characteristics was closer to the Jehovist than to the first Elohist.

3. These three documents were put together into their present form by a redactor. Hupfeld laid much stress upon the redactor, and allowed him great freedom in his work. In fact, many of the 'difficulties' in the Pentateuch may be ascribed to this redactor.

The chronological arrangement of the documents by Hupfeld, therefore, was as follows:

> First Elohist (*die Urschrift*)
> Second Elohist
> Jehovist
> Deuteronomy

With respect to Hupfeld's partition of Genesis, certain remarks should be made. In the first place, Hupfeld begins his second E at Genesis 20, whereas his first E virtually concludes at this point. This looks like the breaking in two of a document that was continuous, especially since the second E seems to presuppose some of the first E. At least, the continuity and completeness of the first E are destroyed. Another point of importance is that the content of first E is largely genealogical, statistical data and extraordinary events, such as the creation, flood, *etc*. Such material is not the property of any one writer, but is due to the subject-matter itself. Again, Hupfeld's insistence that the second E was closer to J than to the first E is really clear evidence of the unsatisfactory character of the divine names as criteria for distinguishing documents. Lastly, without the lavish use of the redactor which Hupfeld made, the whole theory falls to the ground.

Nevertheless, Hupfeld's views gained ground, and it is probably correct to speak of him as the real founder of the modern documentary hypothesis; that is, the hypothesis that the Pentateuch consists of four principal documents. In its essentials, this theory was accepted by Edward Boehmer (1860), who was the first to publish the text of the various documents in various types of print; Theodor Noeldeke (1869), who also attacked the supplement hypothesis; August Dillmann (1886), who used the letters A, B, C, D, to distinguish the documents; and Franz Delitzsch (1880).

We move now to some more general remarks and arguments against the documentary hypothesis. The four documents which Hupfeld thought he had discovered came to be variously designated. The designation which had prevailed to the present is the following:

P (Priestly) — Hupfeld's first Elohist
E   —   second Elohist
J   —   Jehovist
D   —   Deuteronomy

It is not our intention to engage in a long refutation of this hypothesis. This has been amply done many times. The principal arguments against the documentary theory are the following:[34]

1. Positive claims are made in various portions of Scripture that the Pentateuch is Mosaic.

2. The theory is unnatural. It is too much of a strain upon one's credulity to be asked to believe that a work, which exhibits the inner unity and harmony of purpose found in the Pentateuch, should have had its origin in the manner postulated by this hypothesis. The phenomenon is unparalleled in the history of literature.

3. The divine names are not adequately distributed in Genesis to form the basis for analysis into documents. The following facts should be noted:

(i) The name Jehovah (*yehowah*) does not appear in the following chapters, Genesis 1, 23, 33, 34, 35, 36, 37, 40, 41, 42, 43, 44, 45, 46, 47, 48, 50, nor in Exodus 1, 2. In the last eleven chapters of Genesis it occurs but once, *i.e.*, Genesis 49:18. In the last twenty chapters it appears fifteen times, three of these appearances being in chapter 38, and 8 in chapter 39. Despite this fact, portions of J are thought to be found in each of these twenty chapters.[35]

(ii) The name Elohim is not found in Genesis 10–16, 18, 29, 34, 36, 37, 38, 47, 49.

(iii) The Deity is not mentioned as such in Genesis 23, 24, 36, 37, and 47. Nevertheless, according to Carpenter and Harford, these chapters are distributed as follows:

J	P	E
34:2b–3ac, 5, 7, 11,	23:1–20	37:5–11, 13b–14a, 15–
19, 26, 29b–31.	34:1–2a, 3b, 4, 6, 8–	17a, 17b–18a, 19,

---

[34] These brief remarks apply to the hypothesis as such, as it has generally been held since Hupfeld's time.

[35] See, *e.g.*, Carpenter and Harford, *The Composition of the Hexateuch* (1902), pp. 511–514.

36:32–39.	10, 12–18, 20–25,	22–25a, 28a, 28c–
37:2b, 2d–4, 12–13a,	27–29a.	31, 32b–33a, 34, 36.
14b, 18b, 21, 25b–	36:1ab–5a,5b–8, 9–28,	
27, 28b, 32a, 33b,	29.	
35.	37:1–2ac.	
47:1–4, 6b, 12–27a,	47:5–6a, 7–11, 27b–28.	
29–31.		

A careful study of this table and of the above facts will make it clear that the analysis really depends upon criteria other than the divine names.

(iv) The distribution of the divine names is most pronounced in the early portions of Genesis, particularly in chapters 1–3. In 1–2:3 Elohim appears thirty-five times, and in 2:4–3:24 Jehovah Elohim occurs twenty times. This is a phrase which occurs only once in the remainder of the Hexateuch (Ex. 9:30), and comparatively rarely in the remainder of the Old Testament.

(v) The variations in the divine names, particularly in the early chapters of Genesis, are due to theological reasons. For example, when in Genesis 3:2 the serpent speaks of God as Elohim, it is quite understandable that the covenant name, Jehovah, would not appear in the serpent's mouth.[36] It should also be noted that in certain cases the use of the names may be explained as a desire to avoid needless repetition. In this connection we may note also that the usage of the LXX does not correspond throughout with that of the Hebrew text. The usage, in certain instances, may be due to other reasons; in no case does it really indicate a different author.

(vi) The name Jehovah occurs in passages which are attributed to P, and Elohim appears in so-called J passages. Thus, *e.g.*,

J	E	P
Gn. 7:9, 'as Elohim had commanded Noah'	Gn. 20:18, 'For Jehovah', *etc.*	Gn. 7:16b, 'and Jehovah shut him in'

This phenomenon, only one example of which is here given, occurs several times. It is but another evidence of the fact that, as the Pentateuch stands, the analysis cannot be carried through upon the basis of the divine names.

(vii) The characteristics of the usage of the divine names in the

[36] This thought has been given classic expression by Hengstenberg in his *DGP*, I, pp. 213–393.

Pentateuch may be paralleled in the Koran, which is generally attributed to one man, Mohammed, as its author.

4. Since the analysis cannot be carried on with the aid of the divine names alone, it is necessary to call in a supposed redactor whenever the analysis breaks down. A few glaring examples will show what a weak procedure this is.[37] The italicized words are those which are generally attributed to a redactor.

Genesis 2:4b (J) 'in the day that Jehovah *Elohim* made', *etc.* (so throughout this section).

Genesis 7:16 (P), 'as God had commanded him, and *Jehovah* shut him in'.

Genesis 14:22 (?) 'unto *Jehovah*', God [*El*] most high'.

Genesis 20:18 (E), 'for *Jehovah*', *etc.*

Genesis 21:1b (P), 'and *Jehovah* did', *etc.*

5. The analysis destroys the unity of otherwise continuous documents. A few examples will make this clear:

(i) Genesis 5 (P) speaks of the widespread reign of death over mankind, but Genesis 1:31 (P) said that all was very good. If, then, God created everything good, why should death reign over all? P does not explain this. The explanation is given in JE (Gn. 3). As P stands, therefore, it is incomplete.

(ii) Exodus 3:4 reads, 'And when *Jehovah* saw that he turned aside to see, *Elohim* called unto him', *etc.* Hence, 4a is given to J and 4b to E.

(iii) Genesis 19:29 is given to P, and refers to the destruction of Sodom and Gomorrah. Yet, the account of the destruction itself is found not in P but in J.

(iv) The document has a particularly fragmentary character. The similarity of its style, however, is to be accounted for because of the sameness of its contents, not because it is the work of a different author.

6. After Exodus 6:3 the divine names cannot be used to distinguish documents. This verse, generally attributed to P, is supposed to teach that the name Jehovah had not previously been revealed. According to this passage, the name which the patriarchs knew was El Shaddai, and not Jehovah. Hence, previous occurrences of the name Jehovah are attributed by critics of the documentary school to J. Those occurrences which are found in P, such as Genesis 17:1, are given to a redactor.

However, this is a mistaken interpretation. The verse does not mean that the name Jehovah, as a vocable, was not known before this time. In the Bible the name of a person represents his character or being. This

[37] See E. S. Brightman, *The Sources of the Hexateuch* (New York, 1918) to discover how frequently the redactor is employed.

verse, therefore, teaches that in His character of Jehovah, *i.e.*, covenant-redeemer God, God was not known to the patriarchs, a statement which is perfectly true.

7. A careful study of the alleged doublets and parallel passages in Genesis will reveal that in reality they are not doublets at all. (*Cf.*, *e.g.*, the discussion of the relationship between Genesis 1 and 2, pp. 50, 51.)

e. Hengstenberg and his school

It must not be thought that the various divisive hypotheses were universally accepted. Such was not the case. Under the spiritual impetus of Ernst Wilhelm Hengstenberg, there grew up a school of reverent, believing scholarship. This school was not reactionary. It represented, rather, an endeavour to pay full deference to the authority of Holy Scripture, and at the same time to take full cognizance of the results of the latest scholarship.

The undisputed leader of this movement was Hengstenberg, whom B. B. Warfield has called 'one of the most searching expounders of the Scripture that God has as yet given His Church'.[38] Born in 1802, Hengstenberg early distinguished himself in scholarly work. Before the age of twenty he had finished a translation of Aristotle's *Metaphysics*, and he early issued a Latin translation of the *Moallakah* of Amr'ilkeis. While a student at Basel he was converted, and at once plunged himself into the study and defence of the Old Testament. He wrote many commentaries, as well as the masterful *Christology of the Old Testament*. It is, however, with his work on the Pentateuch that we are now principally concerned. This has been made available in English under the title, *Dissertations on the Genuineness of the Pentateuch* (1847). This work should be carefully read by every serious student of the Old Testament. Hengstenberg answers in most thorough fashion, once for all, the multifarious arguments which have been raised against the genuineness and integrity of the five books of Moses.

Among those who may be classified as having come under Hengstenberg's influence are M. Drechsler,[39] H. Ch. Haevernick and Karl Friedrich Keil. Although the writings of these men belong to the last century, they are nevertheless valuable even today. Had their words been heeded, the subsequent course of criticism would have been quite different. The spirit of the times, however, was against them, and their work could not stem the advancing tide of divisive criticism. Truth, however, must not be measured by majorities, and the student of the Old

[38] 'The Divine Messiah in the Old Testament' in *Christology and Criticism* (1929), p. 5.
[39] *Die Einheit und Echtheit der Genesis* (1838).

Testament, if he is really desirous of maintaining the truth, must pay serious heed to the work of these believing scholars.

f. The development hypothesis[40]

In a lecture given during the summer semester of 1834, Eduard Reuss had expressed the opinion that the basic Elohistic document, rather than being the earliest, was in reality the latest. In 1850 he again gave expression to this thought, but, at the time, it found little reception.

During the years 1862–1879 the Bishop of Natal, John William Colenso, produced a work, *The Pentateuch and Joshua Critically Examined*, in which he attacked the basic document of the supplement hypothesis as being unhistorical and late.

1. Karl Heinrich Graf's work on the historical books of the Old Testament (1866) marked a turning-point in Pentateuchal criticism. George and Vatke had already suggested that the levitical legislation was later than Deuteronomy and that it could not have arisen earlier than the time of the exile. In 1862, a Rabbi, Dr. J. Popper, had ascribed Exodus 35–40 and Leviticus 8–10 to the scribes who lived after Ezra's time. Graf's work had somewhat the effect of a climax to these earlier views. He took his starting-point not from Genesis, but from the legislation. Deuteronomy, he thought, was composed under the reign of Josiah, and it presupposed only the Jehovistic legislation of the Book of the Covenant. The levitical laws, on the other hand, belonged to the time of Ezra. It is of note that Graf ascribed Leviticus 18–26 to Ezekiel. As to the remainder of the Pentateuch, Graf held to the supplementary hypothesis, maintaining that the basic document had been supplemented by the Jehovist, and that the resultant work had been edited and redacted by the Deuteronomist.

Graf's work was attacked by Riehm and Noeldeke at two principal points. They insisted that the Jehovist was not the supplementer but the composer of an independent document, and further that the levitical legislation could not be divorced from the basic document.

Graf was influenced by these criticisms, and modified his original position to the extent of asserting that the basic writing was not the earliest portion of the Pentateuch, but the latest. It will be noted that this involved a complete reversal in the dating of the basic document. The former order, P E J D, had now become E J D P or J E D P.

2. Graf's theory was strengthened, and impetus given to its propagation, by the appearance of Abraham Kuenen's *De Godsdienst van*

---

[40] In tracing the history of the development hypothesis, I have in large measure been guided by Riehm.

Israel (1869–70). Kuenen had worked independently of Graf, at least in part.

3. Essentially the same view was expressed in 1874 by August Kayser (*Das vorexilische Buch der Urgeschichte Israels*). He maintained that the basis of the Pentateuch was the Jehovistic document, into which parts of an Elohistic document had been incorporated. Deuteronomy came from Josiah's time and was bound up with the Jehovistic document. Next came Ezekiel's legislation, including Leviticus 17–26. The Elohim document (P) probably was from Ezra. Finally came the incorporation of all into one whole. This viewpoint Kayser presented largely upon the basis of literary-critical considerations.

4. It was Julius Wellhausen (*Die Komposition des Hexateuchs*, 1876–7) who brought this hypothesis to the position of dominance. According to Wellhausen, the earliest parts of the Pentateuch came from two originally independent documents, the Jehovist and the Elohist. From these two the Jehovist compiled a work that was principally narrative. In Josiah's time came Deuteronomy, and the Deuteronomist incorporated this in the Jehovistic work and revised the whole, principally Joshua. The priestly legislation of the Elohim document was largely the work of Ezra. A later redactor then worked over the whole. Leviticus 17–26, while coming from Ezekiel's time, was nevertheless not the work of Ezekiel.

Wellhausen combined his dating of the various alleged documents with a particular evolutionary reconstruction of Israel's history, a reconstruction which was based upon the Hegelian philosophy. The early religion of Israel, thought Wellhausen, was but the spontaneous expression of natural religious impulse. The historical character of the patriarchal narratives in Genesis was denied, and Moses himself became more or less a nebulous figure. Before the Deuteronomic reform, sacrifices were offered at all places in the land; there was no central sanctuary. To show that this plurality of sanctuaries existed, Wellhausen appealed to Exodus 20:24–26. This state of affairs, however, was brought to an end by the Deuteronomic reform under Josiah (622 BC). The levitical legislation was far later. Thus, on this scheme, there is a development of the religious institutions of Israel and there is also a development in Israel's idea of God.

5. This scheme of Wellhausen found wide acceptance. It was embraced in Germany by Kautzsch, Smend, Giesebrecht, Budde, Stade, Cornill, and others. In Great Britain it was principally introduced by a Presbyterian minister, William Robertson Smith, in his lectures which were published under the title, *The Old Testament in the Jewish Church* (1881). It was also set forth by S. R. Driver in his *Introduction*. In America

it was accepted by Benjamin Wisner Bacon of Yale in *The Genesis of Genesis* (1893) and *The Triple Tradition of the Exodus* (1894).[41]

This reconstruction, popularized by Wellhausen, is generally spoken of as the Graf-Kuenen-Wellhausen hypothesis. In order to distinguish it from the documentary hypothesis, which indeed forms its basis and without which it could not stand, we prefer to speak of it as the development hypothesis. It has by no means died out even today. In England it has been set forth by Oesterley and Robinson in *Hebrew Religion: Its Origin and Development*[2] (1937)[42] and in America by R. H. Pfeiffer in his *Introduction* (1941).

The opposition to the development hypothesis was varied.

1. The older German scholars held off from it. Dillmann placed P earlier than D, thus: E, 900–850; J, 800–750; P, 800–700; D, 650–623. W. W. Graf Baudissin asserted that the essential basis of P was earlier than Deuteronomy, and so also did Rudolf Kittel. Eduard Riehm wrote most convincingly (1872) against the position that the priestly document is the latest part of the Pentateuch, and Franz Delitzsch (1877) attacked this idea strongly. Nor did Noeldeke accept the theory.

2. Reactions among Jewish scholars were interesting. C. G. Montefiore, in the Hibbert Lectures of 1892,[43] embraced in its essentials the development hypothesis. On the other hand, David Hoffman wrote against Wellhausen on the basis of a study of the *Halachach* (*i.e.*, the legal part of Jewish tradition) and sought to prove that P could not be late.[44]

3. In 1892 A. Klostermann attacked the whole theory of four documents, and substituted what amounted to a new form of the crystallization hypothesis. The original Mosaic law was constantly being expanded, he alleged, because it was read in worship. Especially under Solomon did it receive many additions, namely, the laws regarding the Tabernacle. Again, under Josiah it was further expanded by the incorporation of Deuteronomy.

The strongest attacks upon the development hypothesis, however,

---

[41] A most thorough study of the entire problem is given in H. Holzinger's *Einleitung in den Hexateuch* (1893). The student who cannot read German, however, should study J. E. Carpenter and G. Harford Battersby, *The Hexateuch* (2 vols., 1900); J. E. Carpenter, *The Composition of the Hexateuch* (1902); C. A. Briggs, *The Higher Criticism of the Hexateuch* (1893).

[42] See review by the present writer in *WThJ*, I, 1938, pp. 59–64.

[43] *Lectures on the Origin and Growth of Religion as Illustrated by the Religion of the Ancient Hebrews.*

[44] *Die Neueste Hypothese über den Pentateuchischen Priesterkodex* (1879–1880).

were made by those who were determined to be true to the supernatural character of the Old Testament and who rightly saw in this new hypothesis a most dangerous enemy to the historic Christian religion.

4. In 1885 Edwin Cone Bissell issued *The Pentateuch: Its Origin and Structure*, in which he clearly set forth the weaknesses of Wellhausen's theory. Wilhelm Moeller, in 1889, began a series of publications, in which he cogently refuted the development hypothesis.[45] And in 1886 Geerhardus Vos issued *The Mosaic Origin of the Pentateuchal Codes*, another convincing refutation of Wellhausen's views.

5. The really strong man, however, was found in W. H. Green, Professor of Oriental and Old Testament Literature in Princeton Theological Seminary. A spiritual descendant of men like Hengstenberg, Haevernick, and Keil, Green had been a chosen associate of Joseph Addison Alexander, and was well equipped to carry on the old Princeton tradition of intelligent loyalty to the Bible. Green had early demonstrated his ability in *The Pentateuch Vindicated from the Aspersions of Bishop Colenso* (1863). In 1883 there appeared his *Moses and the Prophets*, which was a direct reply to Kuenen and William Robertson Smith. This was followed by the Newton lectures for 1885, entitled, *The Hebrew Feasts*, a work which attacked the development hypothesis at its heart. In 1888 an amicable debate on 'The Pentateuchal Question' was begun between Green and William Rainey Harper in the pages of *Hebraica*. The material offered in these articles is extremely valuable. As a result of this debate, Green published in 1895 his masterpiece, *The Unity of the Book of Genesis*, and in this year there also appeared his volume, *The Higher Criticism of the Pentateuch*. Green's learned works, without doubt, constitute the most thorough and convincing refutation of the development hypothesis. The Church of God may ever be grateful that He has given to her such an apologete!

6. In 1906 appeared the work of James Orr, *The Problem of the Old Testament*, which is also a very thorough discussion of the documentary theory and quite valuable.

The development hypothesis, as propounded by the school of Wellhausen, is untenable, and it is so for the following reasons:

1. It is a theory that is essentially anti-supernaturalistic in character. It posits a development in Israel's religious life and institutions which is naturalistic. Upon this view the Israelites began, apparently, as did other people; yet, upon the basis of qualities resident within themselves,

45 *Historisch-Kritische Bedenken gegen die Graf-Wellhausensche Hypothese von einem früheren Anhänger.*

supposedly developed the glorious conceptions of God which are contained in the prophets. If this is so, why did Israel alone develop such sublime doctrines? There were deep thinkers elsewhere, and philosophers of ability also, but no other nation produced conceptions of God such as those which are contained in the Old Testament. For this phenomenon the Christian Church, of course, has a ready answer. It is that God intervened in a special way in Israel's history. This is also the plain teaching of the Bible itself. But the Wellhausen school seeks to get along without this special intervention of God. It endeavours to explain a supernatural revelation upon the basis of naturalistic principles. It must, therefore, be rejected.

2. If the development hypothesis is correct, then two of the legal documents of the Pentateuch are fraudulent. Both Deuteronomy and the so-called priestly legislation, the Scriptures declare, were spoken and delivered by Moses. Such, however, we are told, was not actually the case. Rather, this ascription to Moses was merely a device employed to gain a hearing for the law. It is difficult to believe that works produced in such a manner could bring about obedience of heart. And the shocking nature of this assumption becomes particularly clear when we remember that it was none other than the Lord of truth who repelled the temptation of the evil one by quoting from the book of Deuteronomy.

3. The statement that Exodus 20:24 legalized worship at any sanctuary indiscriminately is based upon a false exegesis of the passage in question. The passage simply teaches that 'in every place' or 'in all the places' where God records His name (i.e., where there is divine revelation), an altar may be built. This does not violate the unity of the sanctuary, for the same Book of the Covenant (Ex. 23:14–19) requires the appearance of the males three times a year before the Lord, i.e., at a central sanctuary.

It should be noted further that the erection of the memorial altar (Jos. 22:10–19) was at first regarded as a rival sanctuary and was so resented by the nine and one-half tribes that they were ready to go to war. They clearly regarded (verse 19) the Tabernacle as the central sanctuary.

Deuteronomy is in perfect agreement with the Book of the Covenant upon this point, for it, too, looks forward to the time when, after the conquest of the land, the Lord would choose a place out of all the tribes to put His name there, and that at this place the people should worship Him.

4. The unity of the altar was apparently the law of Israel's life from the beginning. Rivalry of sanctuaries had never been permitted and was not found even in patriarchal times. Jeremiah, the contemporary of

Josiah, looked upon Shiloh as the place where the Lord had set His name at the first (*cf.* Je. 7:12, 14; 26:6, 9).[46]

5. When Hilkiah found the Book of the Law, he said, 'I have found *the* book of the law.' The phrase appears to be definite, as though the high priest were referring to a well-known law book. Too much stress, however, should not be placed upon this.

6. The reform of Josiah was primarily directed against idolatry and the abolishing of heathenism. This is particularly strange when one remembers that, according to the development hypothesis, Deuteronomy was produced in order to bring about centralization of worship. Nevertheless, such was the case. Deuteronomy did not accomplish what it was supposed to have accomplished, for in Josiah's reformation, centralization of worship occupied a very secondary place (*cf.* 2 Ki. 23:8, 9), and the major emphasis was placed upon the extirpation of idolatrous practices.

7. Jeremiah was a contemporary of Josiah, and yet he apparently knows nothing of centralization of the sanctuary as the aim of the covenant (*cf.* Je. 7:10ff.).

8. It should further be noted that Deuteronomy looks for a central sanctuary only after the Lord has given the people rest from all their enemies round about (Dt. 12).

9. Under Hezekiah (2 Ki. 18:22) there was a reform in the interests of unity and sanctuary. However, the importance of this passage has sometimes been minimized by advocates of the development hypothesis.

10. Deuteronomy clearly presupposes the existence of portions of the so-called priestly code. A few examples will suffice. Leviticus 11 is earlier than Deuteronomy 14:3–21, and not *vice versa* (*cf.* comments on Lv. 11); Deuteronomy 22:9–11 shows knowledge of Leviticus 19:19; Deuteronomy 24:14 of Leviticus 19:13; Deuteronomy 25:13–16 of Leviticus 19:35; Deuteronomy 28 of Leviticus 26; Deuteronomy 12 of Leviticus 17; *etc.*

WELLHAUSEN TO THE FIRST WORLD WAR

1. It is difficult to characterize the period of literary criticism which followed Wellhausen. For one thing, advocates of Wellhausen's position became more and more microscopic and 'atomistic' in their partition of documents. Instead of speaking merely of J, E, D, and P, scholars began to refer to J, J¹, J², J³; E, E¹, E², E³; P, P¹, P², P³; *etc.* Kuenen himself had begun to point out enlargements in the so-called E source. In 1906

---

[46] Some valuable comments upon this point are made by John D. Davis in 'The Sanctuary of Israel at Shiloh',* *PTR*, 16, pp. 204–220.

Otto Procksch gave further impetus to splitting up the text by carrying out this idea further (*Das nordhebräische Sagenbuch. Die Elohim-Quelle*). Some scholars sought for an earlier dating of the documents. Thus Eduard Koenig, one of the most profound Hebraists of this century and also a firm believer in the supernatural, dated the documents as follows: E, 1200; J, 1000; D, 700–650; P, 500.

2. B. D. Eerdmans in 1908 began a series of studies (*Alttestamentliche Studien* I–IV, 1908–14), in which he presented a solution of the Pentateuchal problem quite different from that of the regnant hypotheses. Eerdmans was a professor at Leyden, and a strong opponent of the orthodox views of Abraham Kuyper. He rejected the idea that the divine names could be used as criteria for distinguishing documents. Rather, he maintained, the material belonged to four different stages of development, of which the earliest is polytheistic, the latest monotheistic. At the basis of all was a polytheistic Book of Adam (beginning at Gn. 5:1) which originated sometime before 700 BC. Later there was united with this another polytheistic work, a so-called 'Israel' recension. After the discovery of Deuteronomy, however, the earlier writings were re-edited in a monotheistic sense, and this entire work was further expanded after the exile.

These four books of Eerdmans were written in conscious opposition to the documentary analysis, and also to the idea that the Prophets preceded the Law. Eerdmans' ideas, however, have not found widespread acceptance.

3. Harold M. Wiener, an English lawyer, in 1909 issued the first of several works dealing with the question of the Pentateuch. Wiener attacked the documentary hypothesis by appeal to the LXX in which the divine names differ somewhat from the Massoretic text. He held that there are some post-Mosaic elements in the Pentateuch but argued for its essential Mosaicity. He endeavoured to harmonize alleged discrepancies, particularly between the laws, and was often quite successful. On the whole he is at his best in the refutation of the Wellhausen position rather than in the presentation of a positive reconstruction.

4. Ernst Sellin in his *Introduction* (1910) added an emphasis to the development hypothesis which heretofore had generally been lacking. The Pentateuch, he thought, grew up from a Jehovistic source. However, a problem appeared to Sellin, namely, how was it that when a later source appeared, it never succeeded in carrying out the intentions of its author to supplant the already existing sources? The answer, thought Sellin, is to be found in the fact that the sources were used in liturgical service.

5. Of particular importance was the work of J. Dahse (climaxing in his *Textkritische Materialen zur Hexateuchfrage*, 1912) in which he made a thorough study of the use of the divine names in the LXX, pointing out wherein they differed from the Hebrew. Dahse also demonstrated how untenable were the names Jacob and Israel as indications of different literary sources. Dahse's book is unquestionably a strong blow against the documentary hypothesis. Wellhausen himself acknowledged that it touched the weak spot.

6. Rudolph Smend, an adherent of the school of Wellhausen in 1912 issued his work on the narrative of the Hexateuch (*Die Erzählung des Hexateuchs auf ihre Quellen untersucht*). In this book he advocated a documentary hypothesis of his own. Since, however, this view has gained adherents, we shall speak of it as the *new documentary hypothesis*. The essence of the theory, namely, that there are two Jehovists, had already been hinted at by Ilgen, and was set forth in 1885 by Charles Bruston. Smend designated these two Jehovists as J^1 and J^2, and regarded them as two parallel authors, whose works continued throughout the Hexateuch. At the same time he insisted upon the unity of the E source and denied that E consisted of many additions. P and D, on the other hand, he thought, were characterized by many additions or supplements.

7. Powerful onslaughts against the divisive analysis were made by Wilhelm Moeller. In 1912 there appeared one of his most cogent works, *Wider den Bann der Quellenscheidung*. In this book Moeller reviews the arguments for the documentary hypothesis and shows clearly their weaknesses. He argues for the unity of the Pentateuch, and does so in a particularly compelling manner.

THE FIRST WORLD WAR TO THE PRESENT DAY

a. The school of form-criticism

In 1901 there was issued a book which contained within it the seeds of a viewpoint which would in reality strike a heavy blow at the Graf-Kuenen-Wellhausen theory. This was Hermann Gunkel's *Die Sagen der Genesis*, which was an introduction to his large commentary on Genesis. According to Gunkel, the narratives or sagas (to use his word) of Genesis were the stories which were told among the ancient Israelites. For generation after generation, indeed, century after century, they were told, until finally they took on a crystallized form. Then they were written down. Not all of these stories were written down in Genesis, but only some of them. At first these stories had no relation one to another, but in time they came to be attached to some favourite figure, such as Abraham or Jacob. Some time before the prophets, these stories were gathered into small collections, as, for example, those which centred about Abram. At a later time, they were collected into a larger group, the documents which are known as J, E, *etc*. Then finally they were united together. The unit of investigation, therefore, is the individual saga. But this consideration, as a matter of fact, obliterates the peculiar characteristics of the alleged documents.

The sagas of Genesis, according to Gunkel, are not necessarily true. They are simply folk-lore, like the folk-lore to be found in other nations. Hence, it would be a great mistake to regard them as allegories; they are not that. They are stories, and the task of the investigator is to determine their original form.

There is a certain superficial resemblance between Gunkel's theory and the old fragment hypothesis of the last century. The fragment hypothesis failed, as we have seen, largely because of the presence of cross references. But that objection would not apply to Gunkel's theory, since, according to him, the documents are not the products of *authors* but are mere collections of sagas.

It will be noted, therefore, that a high antiquity is claimed for the original form of these stories, and this is quite at variance with the Wellhausen scheme. Furthermore, since these sagas are supposed to be similar in nature to those of other nations, they can really be understood only with the help of archaeology, comparative religion, *etc*. Hence, we may speak of Gunkel's method as the school of comparative religion. For this reason, there is much valuable information in Gunkel's writings, and also many true exegetical insights.

Gunkel continued to write, applying his principles to other books of the Old Testament. Hugo Gressmann made a thorough study of Exodus along similar lines. Quite a number of scholars have associated themselves with this school of thought, among whom may be mentioned Hans Schmidt, Max Haller and Sigmund Mowinckel.[47]

b. The new documentary hypothesis

By his argument that there were two Jehovistic authors, Smend re-opened the entire question of the documentary analysis and his thesis gained adherents.

1. Walther Eichrodt in 1916 issued a work (*Die Quellen der Genesis*, the first part of which had appeared a year previously, as his doctoral thesis) in which he sought to accomplish two purposes. On the one hand, he

[47] For an examination of this position the student should consult *Die Schriften des Alten Testaments* (3 vols., 1921–1925).

tried to refute Eerdmans, and on the other, he sought to ground more securely Smend's hypothesis, namely, the existence of two Jehovistic writers. This he thought to accomplish by a study of the patriarchal narratives. Essentially the same thing was attempted in 1921 by J. Meinhold.[48]

2. In 1922 Otto Eissfeldt gave this theory (it is really a five-document theory) its classic expression. In his *Hexateuch-Synopse*, Otto Eissfeldt identified the J^1 of Smend as the *Laienquelle* (the laity source), since he regarded it as the most secular. The second J of Smend he designated merely as J. Thus, Eissfeldt identified L J E D P. In his *Synopsis* Eissfeldt passed over Leviticus entirely and also the first thirty chapters of Deuteronomy. He based his argument principally upon duplicate accounts, and from the presence of these he sought to find his four documents. He thought to find about fifty passages in which these fourfold elements appear, and hence concluded that the fourfold thread in the narrative was proved ('*so darf die Annahme eines vierfachen Erzählungs-Fadens als erwiesen betrachtet werden*', p. 6).

c. Studies in the 'priestly code'

1. In 1924 Max Loehr began a re-investigation of the problem of the Hexateuch in which he virtually denied the existence of the 'priestly code'. The existence of an independent document P in Genesis, he thought, was an assumption that rested upon error. Instead, Ezra had introduced into our Hexateuch a writing which contained literary units of medium size. This about amounted to a revival of the fragment hypothesis. Volz also attacked the unity of the so-called P in Genesis.

2. Of particular importance was the study of Gerhard von Rad, *Die Priesterschrift im Hexateuch* (1934). He sought to destroy the unity of the so-called P document by alleging that there were two parallel, individual writings, Pa and Pb. These two stand, according to von Rad, in a definite relationship to one another. One of them maintains a certain priestly-clerical character, and exhibits greater precision in naming dates and persons. Hence, it represents a more advanced stage of development.

d. Studies in Deuteronomy

If any result of negative criticism seemed to be sure, it was that Deuteronomy was a product of Josiah's time, and the reformation of Josiah was a Deuteronomic reform. In fact, Deuteronomy was regarded as so important that some had spoken of it as the Achilles' heel of Pentateuchal

[48] 'Die jahwistische Berichte in Gen. 12–50', in *ZAW*, 39, pp. 42–57.

criticism. The Wellhausen position with respect to Deuteronomy, however, was by no means secure.

1. Johannes Hempel in 1914 expressed the view that a priest who introduced the thought of centralization of worship had edited Deuteronomy, incorporating an ancient rule of the Temple from Solomon's time and also a legal and military document. In 1920 Harold Wiener again took up his pen[49] and attacked the Wellhausen position. This position was also attacked by G. R. Berry in an article (1920) in which he maintained that the code found in the Temple was not Deuteronomy but the Law of Holiness. In the same year R. H. Kennett[50] asserted that Deuteronomy was a product of the exile, composed in Palestine at the time when the sons of Aaron were supposed to have taken the place of the Zadokite priests in the Temple. Others also have adopted substantially this view.

2. Gustav Hoelscher[51] found laws and ideals in Deuteronomy which approach the utopian, and argued that therefore they could not have originated while the Judaean state was still in existence. Rather, they belonged to a time when the state no longer existed and the Jews were no longer an independent people. Furthermore, according to Hoelscher, the prophecy of Jeremiah and also of Ezekiel set forth abuses which were forbidden in Deuteronomy, and would have been corrected, had Deuteronomy really been the book that occasioned Josiah's reform. Hence, Hoelscher would assign an exilic or post-exilic date to Deuteronomy. T. Oestreicher, on the other hand[52] would place the code of Deuteronomy long before the age of Josiah. In 1924 W. Staerk asserted that Deuteronomy 12 did not refer to centralization of worship in Jerusalem.

3. A. C. Welch[53] argued in a very convincing fashion for an earlier date for Deuteronomy. He contended that only in one passage in the code itself was the demand for centralization of the sanctuary unequivocally expressed. The conflict in the book is not between one and many sanctuaries, but between Jahvism and Baalism. The laws come from the early monarchy or even earlier and from northern Israel.

4. Wilhelm Moeller in 1925 came forward again with a cogent defence of the Mosaic authorship of Deuteronomy. As the title of his work implies (*Rückbeziehungen des 5. Buches Mosis auf die vier ersten Bücher*)

[49] *The Main Problem of Deuteronomy* (Oberlin).
[50] *Deuteronomy and the Decalogue.*
[51] 'Komposition und Ursprung des Deuteronomiums' in *ZAW*, 40, 1923, pp. 161–255.
[52] *Das Deuteronomische Grundgesetz* (1923).
[53] *The Code of Deuteronomy* (1924); and *Deuteronomy: the Framework to the Code* (1932).

Moeller sought to show that Deuteronomy contained references to and reflections upon the four earlier books.

5. Gerhard von Rad, in his licentiate's dissertation of 1929, also broke with the idea that Deuteronomy must be presupposed as the basis of Josiah's reform. In another study,[54] he attributed Deuteronomy to levitical circles that wished to restore the tradition of the Old Shechemite amphictyony.

What direction future studies of Deuteronomy will take, no-one, of course, can tell. But Achilles' heel has been wounded. Wellhausen's view no longer has the advocates that it had thirty years ago.

e. Other recent developments

1. We have seen that Smend and his school divided the so-called J into two; von Rad did the same with P, and Deuteronomy has been shifted to both pre- and post-Josianic dates. The alleged E document, too, has not escaped attack. In their book, *Der Elohist als Erzähler ein Irrweg der Pentateuchkritik?* (1933), Paul Volz and Wilhelm Rudolph have presented an interesting thesis, although one that has not gained wide acceptance. In this work the authors have limited their discussions to Genesis, Volz writing on Genesis 15–36, and Rudolph on the stories of Joseph. According to these writers, E is not an independent document; it is simply a later edition of J, and possibly a product of the Deuteronomic school.

In a later work[55] Rudolph applied his thesis to the remainder of the Hexateuch. J becomes the prominent narrative, and to it Rudolph ascribes the continuous sections which usually had been attributed to E.

2. Edward Koenig and Edward Naville both in 1914 criticized the Wellhausen position. Koenig[56] wrote chiefly in opposition to the position which Dahse had advanced. Naville wrote a series of learned books and articles in favour of the Mosaic authorship of the Pentateuch. Moses, he thought, wrote the Pentateuch in the cuneiform Accadian language. Ezra translated it into Aramaic, and just before the Christian era it was translated into Hebrew.

3. D. Hoffmann and B. Jacob, two Jewish scholars, should also be mentioned. Hoffmann wrote a powerful attack upon the position of Wellhausen,[57] and Jacob[58] set forth arguments against the documentary theory in general.

---

[54] *Deuteronomium Studies* (1947); ET, *Studien in Deuteronomy* (1953).
[55] *Der Elohist von Exodus bis Joshua* (1938).
[56] *Die Moderne Pentateuchkritik und ihre neueste Bekämpfung.*
[57] *Die wichtigste Instanzen gegen die Graf-Wellhausensche Hypothese* (1916).
[58] *Quellenscheidung und Exegese im Pentateuch* (1916).

4. Edgar Sheffield Brightman in 1918 in *The Sources of the Hexateuch* published the texts of the various alleged documents. This work enables the reader at a glance to see how the Pentateuch has commonly been partitioned. It is a most useful handbook.

5. Martin Kegel, beginning in 1919, produced several articles, the most famous of which is his *Away from Wellhausen!* in which he attacked several of the basic tenets of the development hypothesis.

6. A. Sanda, a Roman Catholic scholar, in 1924 produced a positive interpretation of the Pentateuchal problem. Genesis, he claimed, was written by Moses himself; the remainder was written by Joshua either from Moses' diary or from dictation, and after the discovery of Deuteronomy in Josiah's day, all were united to form the Pentateuch.

7. D. C. Simpson in his *Pentateuchal Criticism* (1924) wrote in defence of the development hypothesis and principally in opposition to Dahse and Wiener.

8. Wilhelm Moeller in *Die Einheit und Echtheit der fünf Bücher Mosis* in 1931 came forth again in defence of the Mosaic authorship of the Pentateuch.

9. U. Cassuto in 1934 alleged that Genesis was an organic unity composed towards the close of David's reign.

10. J. Morgenstern[59] asserted that there was a source, additional to J, E, D, and P, namely K (Kenite) which was present in a fragmentary condition. This K document was supposed to have been made the basis of Asa's reform (1 Ki. 15:9–15).

11. J. H. Hertz in 1935 defended the Mosaic authorship of Deuteronomy in his work, *The Pentateuch and Haftorahs: Deuteronomy.*

12. Sigmund Mowinckel in 1936, in a study of Genesis 1–11, found two strands apart from P. One of these is E, which he attributed to the redactor (R^{JE}).

13. R. H. Pfeiffer in his large *Introduction* (1941) gave expression to a view that he had earlier presented. He found a fourth source in Genesis, namely S (South or Seir). This S source, thinks Pfeiffer, is divided into two parts. It is found in Genesis 1–11, omitting P, and in parts of Genesis 14–38.

14. Oswald T. Allis in 1943 in *The Five Books of Moses* wrote a powerful refutation of both the documentary and development hypothesis and entered a strong plea for acceptance of the Mosaic authorship of the first five books of the Old Testament.

15. Martin Noth in his *Ueberlieferungsgeschichte des Pentateuchs* (1948) gave a rather significant turn to the course of criticism. Noth maintained

---

[59] *The Oldest Document of the Hexateuch* (1927).

that the 'deuteronomic' history began in Deuteronomy itself and continued down to the exile.

16. Ivan Engnell[60] adopts Noth's identification of the 'Deuteronomistic' work. From this he separates the first four books, which he calls the 'tetrateuch'. This work – a complex of literary traditions which are for the most part quite old – was edited rather late. Engnell makes a distinction between narratives and laws and so between Genesis on the one hand and Exodus-Numbers on the other. He does not discover 'documents' in the sense of the older criticism but rather is interested in discovering the traditions and small units. The narratives supposedly existed for years in the form of oral traditions and finally were written down and edited, the last tradent probably having been the editor of P. The last redaction of the Tetrateuch took place probably in post-exilic times. Whether it is older (as tradition) than the Deuteronomic work, we cannot determine.

17. In his first study of Hebrew historical writing[61] Gustav Hoelscher discussed the so-called J document and traced it to 1 Kings 12:19. In later studies,[62] he discussed the so-called E source. He assigned E, as well as other early material usually assigned to P, to J[2], and maintained that the E source continues the history down to 2 Kings 25:30.

18. R. Brinker, in his study on *The Influence of Sanctuaries in Early Israel* (1946), maintained that the origin of the priestly document is to be found in the *torah* of the old Canaanitish sanctuary at Gibeon, whereas Samuel and others compiled D for the united nation.

19. An attempt to identify and delimit J, J[2], and E was made in thorough fashion by Cuthbert A. Simpson.[63] Simpson's views were exposed to thorough examination and criticism by Otto Eissfeldt.[64]

20. Another emphasis appeared when Edward Robertson maintained that for a clearer understanding of the period of the Judges more attention should be devoted to the Samaritan sources.[65] In *The Old Testament Problem* (1950), Robertson placed Deuteronomy in the time of Samuel and again emphasized the importance of the Samaritan tradition.

[60] *Gamla Testamentet, en traditionshistorisk inledning,* I (1945).

[61] *Die Anfänge der hebräischen Geschichtsschreibung* (1942).

[62] *Geschichtsschreibung in Israel. Untersuchungen zum Jahvisten und Elohisten* (1952).

[63] *The Early Traditions of Israel, a Critical Analysis of the Pre-Deuteronomic Narrative of the Hexateuch* (1948).

[64] *Die ältesten Traditionen Israels: ein kritischer Bericht über C. A. Simpson's The Early Traditions of Israel* (1950).

[65] *Investigations into the Old Testament Problem: The Results* (1949).

21. F. V. Winnett, in a study of *The Mosaic Tradition* (1949), held that Exodus and Numbers have a continuous tradition that came from northern Israel. This tradition was revised in the south after the fall of Samaria, and thus the Deuteronomic account arose. The tradition was revised again after the exile.

22. In his notes on the Hexateuchal problem the Roman Catholic scholar A. Van Hoonacker virtually accepted both Mosaic authorship and documentary analysis. These notes were collected and edited by J. Coppens.[66]

23. J. Coppens himself made a valuable survey of recent study of the Hexateuchal problem in his *Chronique d'Ancien Testament, Le Problème de l'Hexateuque* (1953). He showed that in the different sources of the Hexateuch, the greatness of Moses appears in his strong personality and influence.

24. Umberto Cassuto has vigorously opposed the documentary analysis. In 1941 he gave eight lectures in Hebrew on the documentary hypothesis, and then published a commentary in Hebrew on Genesis 1:1–6:8 (1944). In 1951 appeared a commentary on Exodus. A new edition of this work appeared in 1953. There is much that is valuable in Cassuto, but a stronger defence against documentary analysis can be made.

25. J. Steinmann, a Roman Catholic scholar, wrote a Pentateuchal study that attributed to Moses a large part in the tradition and even in the collecting of material for the Pentateuch.[67]

26. In his study of *The Growth of the Pentateuch* (1955), I. Lewy offered a substitute for the documentary theory of Wellhausen. The substitute is of such a nature, however, that it has not gained many adherents.

27. W. J. Martin, writing in defence of the trustworthiness of Scripture, offered some cogent considerations on the question of style and analysis in the Pentateuch.[68]

Conclusion

More than two hundred years have passed since Jean Astruc made the first serious attempt to partition Genesis into documents. He was jubilant over what he thought to be success. Subsequent scholarship however, has not been able to agree. And the history of the documentary

---

[66] *De Compositione Literaria et de Origine Mosaica Hexateuchi Disquisitio Historico-Critic* (1949).

[67] *Les plus anciennes Traditions du Pentateuque* (1954).

[68] *Stylistic Criteria and the Analysis of the Pentateuch* (1955).

analysis shows that scholarship has not succeeded in satisfactorily analysing the Pentateuch into documents.

It is probably true that most scholars of today who reject the Mosaic authorship of the Pentateuch hold to some form of the four-document theory in the order J E D and P. But even these seem to be pushing the dates of J and E earlier. The full effect of the writings of Volz and Rudolph, Eissfeldt, Welch, and von Rad cannot yet be seen; they are too recent. But they are harbingers of a different day to come. They are evidences of the fact that the standard J E D P of the Wellhausen school is gradually giving way.

Although the documentary hypothesis is rather generally held by those who reject the Mosaic authorship, it is a kaleidoscopic hypothesis; it continues to change its form. It would not be surprising at all if the 'conventional' J E D P arrangement should in the future undergo considerable shuffling. The writings of Eissfeldt, von Rad, and others seem to point this way (*cf.* the chart on next page).

At any rate, from the brief survey of the history of Pentateuchal criticism, we venture to make certain observations:

1. Objections to the genuineness of any portion of the Pentateuch which are based upon a theory of the evolutionary development of Israel's religious institutions must be rejected. It is becoming abundantly clear that the reconstruction of Israel's history which is associated with the name of Wellhausen is based upon the Hegelian philosophy. (Wellhausen himself acknowledged his indebtedness to Vatke and Hegel.) To give to such a philosophy of history a priority over the express claims of sacred Scripture is not to be scientific. Hence, since the development hypothesis, as it has generally been presented, rejects the special, supernatural intervention of God in the history of Israel, it must be rejected as unscientific and as incapable of correctly explaining the facts.

2. Any theory which relies upon the divine names as criteria for documentary analysis is bound to fail, since these names do not constitute valid criteria for such analysis. The usage of divine names in the Ras Shamra texts is evidence that the names cannot serve as such criteria.

3. The strongest argument for the analysis of documents appears to be the presence of alleged doublets and parallel passages. But this is in reality a question of exegesis. Are these really doublets and parallel passages? We insist that a careful exegetical study of such passages will show that they are not doublets. We protest against the constant reiteration that, for example, there are duplicate accounts of the creation in Genesis. *If exegesis be permitted to remain upon the throne, the documentary analysis will go by the board.*

Hypothesis	Chief Exponents
	Eighteenth Century
EARLIER DOCUMENTARY (Two documents in Genesis)	Astruc (1753)[1] Eichhorn (1780–83 J E) Ilgen (1798; E^1 E^2 J)
	Nineteenth Century
FRAGMENTARY (Covering the entire Pentateuch)	Geddes (1800) Vater (1802–5) De Wette (1806–7) Hartmann (1831)
SUPPLEMENT (Basic document E supplemented from other sources)	Ewald (1830; Hexateuch) von Bohlen (1835; Genesis) Bleek (1836; Genesis) Staehelin, von Lengerke, Delitzsch, Tuch (1843–58)
CRYSTALLIZATION	Ewald (1840–45; five narrators, three final redactors) Knobel (1861; E, Book of Rights, J D) Schraeder (1869; E^1 E^2 – worked over by J – D)
MODIFIED DOCUMENTARY (P – Hupfeld's E^1 – E J D)	Hupfeld (1853; E^1 E^2 J D)
DEVELOPMENT (The basic Elohistic document is the latest, not the earliest document)	Graf (1866; E J P D or J E D P) Kuenen (1869–70) Kayser (1874) Wellhausen (1876–77)
	Twentieth Century
NEW DOCUMENTARY (Two Jehovists – Smend)	Eichrodt (1916) Eissfeldt (1922; L – Smend's J^1 – J E D P)
'Priestly Code' Studies Studies in Deuteronomy	von Rad (1934; J E D P^1 P^2) Hoelscher (1923; post-Josianic) Oestreicher (1923; pre-Josianic) Welch (1924, '32; pre-Josianic) Moeller (1925; Mosaic) von Rad (1929; post-Josianic)
The E document	Volz, Rudolph (1933; J D P)

[1] Dates given here are dates of publication of principal writings; see text for titles.

4. There are, of course, difficulties in the position that Moses himself wrote the Pentateuch. But these seem to be almost trifling when compared with the tremendous difficulties that emerge upon any alternate theory of composition. There are, however, certain factors which have not received sufficient consideration.

(i) For one thing, it is perfectly possible that in the compilation of the Pentateuch Moses may have made excerpts from previously existing written documents. If he did so, this fact may account for some of the alleged difficulties that appear. For example, it might *in certain cases* explain the use of the divine names in Genesis.

(ii) On the other hand we must remember that the Bible, when considered in its human aspect, is an Oriental book. Now, parallels from antiquity show that the Oriental mind did not always present his material in the so-called logical order of the Occidental. The fact that the Pentateuch is, considered from the human side, a product of the Orient, may to some extent account for its form. One thing at least is clear. The elaborate 'scissors-and-paste' method which the documentary analysis postulates is without parallel anywhere in the ancient Oriental world.

(iii) Furthermore, we may ask, who in Israel's history was better prepared than Moses to write the Pentateuch? He had the time and also the training and learning to do so. Also, as human founder of the theocracy, he had the information that was requisite. The Pentateuch exhibits an inner plan and structure that betray a great mind. Who, better than Moses, could have produced such a work?

More than two hundred years of exhaustive study have been unable to produce a satisfactory substitute for the time-honoured biblical view that Moses himself was the human author of the Law. Hence, we cannot do better than to regard the Pentateuch as the product of the great lawgiver of Israel.

SPECIAL LITERATURE ON THE LITERARY CRITICISM
OF THE PENTATEUCH

For a general survey of the field up to 1885, the student should consult Edwin Cone Bissell, *The Pentateuch: Its Origin and Structure: An Examination of Recent Theories** (New York, 1910), where he will find a bibliography of more than 2000 titles, pp. 410–475.

Recent surveys of Pentateuchal studies are by George A. Barton, 'The Present State of Old Testament Studies' in *The Haverford Symposium on Archaeology and the Bible* (New Haven, 1938), pp. 47–78; Otto Eissfeldt, 'Modern Criticism', in *Record and Revelation* (Oxford, 1938), pp. 74–109; Augustine Bea, 'Der heutige Stand der Pentateuchfrage', in *Biblica*, 16, 1935, pp. 175–200. More specialized surveys are by P. Humbert, 'Die neuere Genesis-Forschung', in *ThR*, 1934, pp. 147–160, 207–228; L. Kohler, 'Der Dekalog', in *ThR*, 1929, pp. 161–184; W. Baumgartner, 'Der Kampf um das Deuteronomium', *ThR*, 1929, pp. 7–25; and J. A. Bewer, L. B. Paton, G. Dahl, 'The Problem of Deuteronomy. A Symposium', in *JBL*, 47, pp. 305–379.

A collection of essays directed against the Graf-Wellhausen hypothesis is found in the 'Aftermath Series',* edited by Bishop H. M. DuBose (Nashville, 1923–1924). *Cf.* also T. K. Cheyne, *Founders of Old Testament Criticism* (New York, 1893); E. M. Grav, *Old Testament Criticism. Its Rise and Progress* (New York, 1923); Cuthbert Aikman Simpson, *The Early Traditions of Israel* (Oxford, 1948); Hans Joachim Kraus, *Geschichte der Historischkritischen Erforschung des Alten Testaments von der Reformation bis zur Gegenwart* (1956); Emil Kraeling, *The Old Testament since the Reformation* (1955).

See also Umberto Cassuto, *The Documentary Hypothesis* (Jerusalem, 1961); W. J. Martin, *Stylistic Criteria and the Analysis of the Pentateuch** (London, 1955); G. E. Mendenhall, *Law and Covenant in Israel and the Ancient Near East* (Pittsburgh, 1955); J. A. Motyer, *The Revelation of the Divine Name** (London, 1955).

PART TWO
The Prophets

CHAPTER NINE

THE PROPHETS

THE second division of the Old Testament canon is called *The Prophets*, not primarily because of the prophetical contents of the books, but because the authors occupied the prophetical office. The first part of this section bears the title *Former Prophets*, and comprises Joshua, Judges, 1 and 2 Samuel and 1 and 2 Kings. In the Hebrew arrangment 1 and 2 Samuel and 1 and 2 Kings are counted as one book each.

The four Former Prophets are anonymous. Their writings are an interpretative history of God's dealings with the theocratic nation from the time of the entrance into Canaan until the dissolution of the theocracy in the exile. This history serves to complement and to furnish the necessary background for the correct understanding of the *Latter Prophets*. Without this interpretative history, much in the Latter Prophets would be obscure.

Not only, however, do we have here a complement to the later prophetical books, but we also have a necessary completion to the history contained in the Pentateuch. This history of Israel is herein interpreted in agreement with Israel's foundational Law. The great constitutional foundation of the nation has been given and now the nation's history is to be presented in the light of that constitution, and hence the importance of the Former Prophets.

The second division of the Prophets is known as the Latter or Writing Prophets. The term 'latter' evidently does not have reference to historical chronology but rather to the fact that this section is preceded by the Former Prophets. These prophets are also referred to as the Writing Prophets since they are the authors of the remarkable literary productions which comprise the content of this section. These prophecies were written down (Is. 8:1ff.; 30:8; Hab. 2:2ff.) in order that they might be preserved in permanent form (*cf.* also Je. 30:2; 36:1ff.). Perhaps passages such as Jeremiah 36:4; Isaiah 8:16; *etc.* cast some light upon the method in which they were written down. In some cases the prophet, under the protecting inspiration of the Spirit of God, may have written down long sections of his message shortly after having delivered them orally. On the other hand, it may be that some of the prophecies were never delivered orally, but were purely literary products.

Objection is taken to this view by the 'History of Tradition' school. This school, following the pioneer work of Hermann Gunkel, maintains that the original form of the prophetic message is the spoken word. The prophets, thinks Gunkel, were not writers but orators. If in reading the prophecies we think of ink and paper we are wrong at the outset. Furthermore, the original utterance of the prophet was short and detached. It is our task to unravel the husks of tradition, both written and oral, until we arrive at the original independent utterance which in ecstatic enthusiasm the prophet spoke.

According to this school, there gathered about each of the great prophets a group of disciples who handed down the prophet's poems and oracles. At first this was done orally, and later these pieces were committed to writing. It is important to note the conception of 'corporate personality' which, according to this school, existed between the prophet and his disciples, who were regarded as standing in the relationship of head and body. There is, therefore, difference of opinion among the scholars who advocate these views as to whether the actual words of the prophets can be recovered. Engnell says no, Bentzen says it is difficult but not impossible, and Mowinckel says yes.

In the opinion of the present writer the method of the 'History of Tradition' school must be rejected completely. It is basically a form of scepticism and is also intensely subjective. It really denies and destroys the beautiful unity and harmony that appear in the prophetical books.[1]

The books of the Latter Prophets are Isaiah, Jeremiah, Ezekiel, and the twelve minor prophets. These latter were regarded by the Jews as forming a single book. This is the general order in the Hebrew manuscripts, and also in the LXX. In *Baba Bathra* 14b, however, is the following statement, 'Our rabbis taught: The order of the Prophets is, Joshua, and Judges, Samuel, and Kings, Jeremiah and Ezekiel, Isaiah and the Twelve.'

But this arrangement is based upon theological reasons. An explanation appears in *Baba Bathra* itself: 'But indeed! Isaiah is previous to Jeremiah and Ezekiel; Isaiah should be placed at the head. Answer:

---

[1] For an introduction to the position of this school – also called form-criticism, *Gattungsforschung*, enquiry into types, *etc.* – see Sigmund Mowinckel, *Prophecy and Tradition: The Prophetic Books in the Light of the Study of the Growth and History of the Tradition* (1946), and my review of this book in *WThJ*, XI, pp. 80–85. Gunkel's statement of this position as applied to the prophetical books appeared in *SAT*, II, 2, 1923, pp. IX–LXX. I have discussed Schmidt's application of this method to Is. 7:10–16 in *SI*, pp. 73–81.

The Book of Kings ends with desolations, and Jeremiah throughout [speaks of] desolations, and as for Ezekiel, it begins with desolations and it concludes with consolations, and Isaiah throughout speaks of consolations. We place together desolation with desolation and consolation with consolation.' This order has been preserved also in some German and French manuscripts. But there is no reason for departing from the traditional Massoretic order: Isaiah, Jeremiah, Ezekiel, the Twelve.

CHAPTER TEN

JOSHUA

NAME

THE first book of the Former Prophets is named after its principal character, Joshua. In the Hebrew the word has four forms: *yehoshu'a* (Dt. 3:21), *yeshoshu'a* (*e.g.*, Jos. 1:1 and generally); *hoshe'a* (Dt. 32:44) and *yeshu'a* (Ne. 8:17). In the LXX, the name appears as *Iesous Naus, i.e.,* Joshua the son of Nun, and the Vulgate has *Liber Josue.*

POSITION IN THE CANON

In the Syriac version the book of Job usually comes between the Pentateuch and Joshua. This is due to the belief that Moses was the author of Job. But in the Hebrew Canon, Joshua follows the Pentateuch and introduces the second division of the Old Testament Canon, and this is its proper place.

It is true that in the ancient Church we hear sometimes of an Octateuch and a Heptateuch. Certain Greek lists counted Genesis to Ruth as *Oktateuchos*, and Latin lists regarded Genesis to Judges as *Heptateuchus.* Ambrose also, in writing on Psalm 119 says, '*Inveni Heptateuchum, inveni regnorum libros, inveni prophetarum scripta*', etc.[1] However, these expressions may simply have been terms of convenience. The great distinction between the Law on the one hand and the subsequent books on the other seems never really to have been broken down in the Church. And the reason for this is clear, since Christ Himself had made this distinction (*e.g.*, Lk. 24:27, 44).

Alexander Geddes, it will be remembered, included Joshua with the Pentateuch as a unit, and, apparently, he was the first to have done so. At any rate, since his time many scholars have spoken of a Hexateuch rather than a Pentateuch.[2] The question to be faced is, does Joshua belong with the Pentateuch as a unit or is the time-honoured and Christ-approved distinction between Moses and the Prophets correct? Does the

---

[1] *PL*, XV, col. 1584.
[2] See 'The Alleged Secondary Deuteronomic Elements in the Book of Joshua', by the present writer in *The Evangelical Quarterly*, Oct. 1953, pp. 142-157.

Old Testament, in other words, begin with a Pentateuch or a Hexateuch? That the term Hexateuch is incorrect may be seen from the following considerations:

1. There is no evidence that historically Joshua was ever regarded as forming a unit with the Pentateuch. On the other hand, the Law is always separated from the subsequent books. Ecclesiasticus distinguishes between the Law and the Prophets (48:22–49:12). Josephus (*Contra Apionem* i. 7ff.) referred to the five books of Moses and clearly distinguished them from what followed. This view also was held by Christ, and this fact is determinative. The Massoretic note at the close of the Pentateuch speaks of the totality of the verses of the Law, and says that 'the five-fifths of the Law are completed'. Further, it should be noted that in the annual and triennial systems of reading the Law, Joshua was not included. When the *Haphtaroth* (*i.e.*, reading selections from the Prophets) were added to the reading of the Law, selections from Joshua were included among them.

2. The Samaritans took over only the Pentateuch, but not Joshua. This is inexplicable, if there was in existence a Hexateuch. It is particularly inexplicable when we remember how the book of Joshua seems to favour the Samaritans (*cf.* 24:1, 32). Is not this conclusive evidence that the Samaritans did not look upon Joshua as an integral part of the Law?

3. There are linguistic peculiarities in the Pentateuch which do not appear in Joshua. Thus, the pronoun *hu'* is used for both genders; *ha'el* for *ha'elleh*, and, strangely enough, the name Jericho is spelled *yereho* instead of *yeriho*. On the other hand, the phrase 'Jehovah, the God of Israel', which occurs fourteen times in Joshua, is very rare in the Pentateuch. These arguments, of course, are not conclusive, but they have their place.

4. The idea of a Hexateuch in reality causes embarrassment to the documentary hypothesis. In the Pentateuch, P is the foundational document, but in Joshua P appears only in chapters 13–21.[3] If the alleged sources of the Pentateuch are continuous, and run through Joshua, why was this sharp division made between the two? How and when was it made? These are questions for which there is no answer. According to Holzinger (p. 501) Joshua was separated from JED by the redactor, and the separation from Pg was even earlier. But this is more subjective speculation. If the alleged sources did really regard the conquest as a proper sequel to the Mosaic age, why was the break made? The inability of negative criticism to answer this question exhibits a weak point in the documentary analysis.

[3] See Holzinger, *Einleitung in den Hexateuch* (1893) for tables.

5. Chapman[4] remarks, 'The Ideal Israel has the Hexateuch for its Bible', and appeals to *Nedarim* 22b: 'If Israel had not sinned, they would be reading only the five books of the Law and the book of Joshua.' But Chapman's interpretation of this passage is erroneous. The words are of Adda son of Hanina, who expressly distinguishes between the Pentateuch on the one hand, and the book of Joshua on the other. The reason why he mentions Joshua is that 'it records the disposition of Palestine' (among the tribes). Hence, Adda's point is that the only book *in addition to* the Pentateuch which Israel would have needed, had she not sinned, was Joshua, and this is quite a different thing from the modern idea of a Hexateuch.

We conclude therefore that the Hexateuch is a phantom. Joshua does not belong with the Law as its completion, but rightly belongs with the Former Prophets.

AUTHOR

According to the position of the dominant negative criticism the book of Joshua is not a literary unit, composed by a single author. Rather, the alleged sources of the Pentateuch are said to be present here also. The two primary sources are thought to be J (*c.* 950–850) and E (*c.* 750). These were re-edited in JE (*c.* 650), most of J being discarded. This editor is supposed to have introduced harmonistic statements. JE was thoroughly revised (*c.* 550) by the Deuteronomic school, which provided the introduction (chapter 1) and conclusion. This revision continued until about 400. At the end of the fifth century P was added by a priestly redactor (Rp). Further additions also were made as late as the third and even second centuries.

Joshua, therefore, is regarded as essentially a Deuteronomic book, whereas the Pentateuch, is supposed to have a priestly framework. Incidentally, this is a strong argument against the whole idea of a Hexateuch.

For our part we cannot accept the documentary analysis as applied to Joshua. We are too greatly impressed with the internal unity of the book to give credence to such analysis. Furthermore, there is truth in the remark of Steinmueller: 'The literary arguments of the critics are based fundamentally upon a false religious preconception of the evolutionary development of the religion of the Hebrews, which cannot be sustained.'[5]

Certain parts of the book are said to have been written by Joshua

---

[4] *An Introduction to the Pentateuch* (1911), p. 7.
[5] *A Companion to Scripture Studies*, II (1942), p. 73.

himself (24:26). Some parts seem to be the work of an eyewitness (*e.g.*, 5:1, 'until we had passed over', though some manuscripts read 'they'; 5:6; 16:4; and the detailed descriptions of chapters 7–8). From this we may conclude that there was a basis written by Joshua.

In its present form, however, the book cannot have been written by Joshua, for it records events which did not take place until after his death. Among these are the conquest of Hebron by Caleb, of Debir by Othniel and of Leshem by the Danites. And the accounts of the death of Joshua and of Eleazar show that the book is later than Joshua's time. (A Jewish tradition alleges that Eleazar added the account of Joshua's death, and that Phinehas added the account of Eleazar's death.)

Although the book in its present form is not from the hand of Joshua, it is nevertheless very ancient. In all probability it was written under divine inspiration by someone, possibly an elder (Kiel), who had been an eyewitness to most of the events recorded in the book.

PURPOSE

The purpose of the book is to show how God brought the theocratic nation from the wilderness into the promised land. It serves thus to continue the history contained in the Pentateuch and to trace the history of the theocracy under Joshua. It also serves to show how Joshua faithfully performed the work which had been entrusted to him by God, and how God, in fulfilment of His promises, gave the promised land to His people.

ANALYSIS

a. 1:1–12:24. The conquest of Canaan

1. 1:1–9. Introduction to the entire book. Joshua receives directions to proceed with the people across the Jordan and is assured that, if he is faithful to the Law, he will be successful. Verse 1 connects the thought with the Pentateuch, upon the foundation of which the author of Joshua wrote. The language of the section closely approximates Deuteronomy 11:22–25 (*cf.* 1:9 with Dt. 3:21f.; 31:6–8, 23). This does not indicate a secondary D redaction (D²). It merely shows that the author meditated deeply in the Word of God. Psalm 1:2 is evidently based upon Joshua 1:8.

2. 1:10–2:24. The preparations for crossing the Jordan. Joshua makes immediate preparations for his work. He reminds Reuben, Gad, and the half-tribe of Manasseh that they, too, are to help in the conquest, and

this they promise to do. Two spies are sent to Jericho, and they return. The description of Rahab's house as being upon the town wall (2:15) seems to be an evidence of antiquity. Excavation has shown that houses were built upon the walls.[6]

Although this section constitutes a straightforward unity, it is nevertheless divided into documents by some critics. Thus *OR* analyse: E, 1:10, 11a; 2:1–9 (also to J); 2:12–16; 22–24. J, 2:1–9 (also to E); 2:17–21. D, 1:11b–18; 2:10–11.

3. 3:1–4:25. The crossing of the Jordan. Preparations for the crossing are made, 3:1–6; the crossing is commenced, 3:7–17; description of the actual crossing, 4:1–14; conclusion, 4:15–24.

According to S. R. Driver there are superfluous repetitions and actual contradictions in this section. He advances three arguments which may be briefly considered.

(i) In 3:17 the people have crossed the Jordan, but 4:4, 5, 10b implies that they have not yet crossed. In fact, 4:11 is thought to leave us where we were at 3:17. In reply it may be said that if this is an actual contradiction, the final redactor has bungled badly. But is there really a contradiction? Not at all. 3:17 relates in summary form the crossing of the people and the fact that the priests remained in the midst of the river until the people had crossed. After the people had crossed, Joshua issued directions for the erection of the memorial stones (4:1–10). During this time the priests were still standing in the river. 4:10 serves as a summary of all that has occurred, and adds the information that the people had passed over quickly. 4:11 connects with 4:10 (not with 3:17) and completes the narrative by stating that *finally* (*i.e.*, after the people had crossed) the priests and the ark passed over the river.

(ii) 4:8 and 9 are said to speak of two different ceremonies. Verse 8 is said to be the sequel of verse 3, whereas verse 9 is thought to go with verses 4–7. But Driver's argument is without force. Verse 3 gives the command to erect the stones (at Gilgal). Verses 4–7 give an explanation of the meaning of the act. Verse 8 records the fulfilment of the command. Verse 9 relates to an action of Joshua's distinct from that given in verses 3–8. We may safely assume that Joshua was acting under divine command, even though the express command is not mentioned.

(iii) 3:12 is said to be superfluous, if it belongs to the same narrative as 4:2. But this by no means follows. 3:12 gives a preview of what is about to happen. After the crossing the command is repeated, for the time has come when it is to be obeyed. To accomplish this, Joshua repeats the exact words of the command, which is far more effective than a mere

[6] See *JJ*, p. 132.

allusion, such as 4:4 ('the twelve men, whom he had prepared'). The fact that no fulfilment of the command is given in 3:13–17 is strong evidence of the unity of the entire passage.

4. 5:1–12. The incidents at Gilgal. The narrative is a unit. Verse 2 ('at that time') connects with verse 1, and verses 3–9 obviously reflect upon verse 2. Verse 10 continues the narrative, and relates the observance of the Passover. Verse 11 connects with verse 10 (after the Passover), and verse 12 connects with verse 11 ('old corn'). Nevertheless, this beautiful unity is denied by some critics. Thus *e.g.*, *OR* assign to E, 5:2–3, 8–9; D, 5:1; P, 5:4–7, 10–12.

5. 5:13–6:27. The capture of Jericho. The Angel of the Lord encourages Joshua. The city is encompassed for six days, and then taken. Rahab is saved. The historicity of the event is proved by Hebrews 11:30–31.[7] See also 6:26 with 1 Kings 16:34.

Pfeiffer thinks there are two entirely different accounts of the fall of Jericho. One is in 6:3b, 4, 6; the other in 6:3, 5, 7, 10, 16b, 17. But for seven days the warriors were to march around the city. For six days they were to do this once a day, but on the seventh they were to do it seven times. It is obvious *e.g.*, that 3b refers to 3a. (*Koh* here refers to what precedes, as in Gn. 15:5.) Verse 5 also clearly belongs with verse 4, 'when they make a blast' (*bimeshok*). Unless this refers to the 'priests' of verse 4, it makes no sense.

6. 7:1–26. Achan's theft. As at Jericho God had shown Himself merciful to Israel, so now at Ai, because of Achan's sin, He manifests His justice. The interchange between singular and plural in verses 25, 26 is simply to show the prominence of Achan in the punishment. To appeal to this as an evidence of confusion is beside the point.

7. 8:1–35. The destruction of Ai, verses 1–29; erection of the altar upon Mt. Ebal, verses 30–35. Many writers stress the difficulty occasioned by the mention of 30,000 men in verse 3 and 5,000 in verse 12. Joshua, it is charged, is represented as stationing 30,000 men in ambush in the evening, and on the next morning dispatching 5,000 men to the same place for the same purpose. But the order of events seems rather to have been the following. When Joshua received divine assurance of success, he chose 30,000 men (verse 3) and sent them away (verse 9). He also relates what he himself did (verse 9b). In verses 10, 11, Joshua begins a detailed account. He reviewed the troops, and as they approached Ai, he separated 5,000 to go into ambush. In other words, verse 9 is a general summary statement of the execution of the command, the details of

---

[7] The fallen walls excavated by Garstang (see *JJ*, pp. 145–147) are now known to belong to a period much earlier than that of Joshua.

which begin in verse 10. This would seem to explain the text, but I grant that it is extremely difficult. At any rate, difficult as it is, we are not justified upon the basis of such a passage in concluding that this section is a compilation from separate sources.

Nor is 8:30–35 misplaced. It is true that Ebal is some distance from Ai-Bethel. But, after all, the distance was only some twenty miles, and there is no reason why the reliability of the text should be questioned. Further, these verses are in the style of the remainder. They do not have the characteristics of an interpolation.

8. 9:1–27. The deceit of the Gibeonites. Verses 1, 2 serve to introduce chapters 9–11. The Gibeonites, obtaining by craft a league with Israel, are condemned to perpetual servitude. Verse 27 shows the antiquity of the passage, for the site of the Temple has not yet been determined.

9. 10:1–43. The conquest of southern Canaan. Joshua first defeats the five kings at Bethhoron, and then gains possession of the southern cities. Keil would regard verse 12 as containing a mere poetic statement, and for this he makes out a good case. But the verses seem rather to teach that a real miracle had occurred. What the precise nature of the miracle was, however, is difficult to say. Evidently, the day was prolonged.[8]

Verses 12–14 are parenthetical, an extract introduced by the author of Joshua from the book of Jasher, except, of course, the question in the middle of verse 13. This was an ancient, poetical book (*cf.* also 2 Sa. 1: 18).

10. 11:1–15. The conquest of northern Canaan. At the waters of Merom, Joshua defeats the confederacy headed by Jabin, and captures his towns. The Jabin of Judges 4:2 is evidently a successor of the one named here.

11. 11:16–12:24. Completion of the conquests, and list of the defeated kings. 11:16–23 gives a review of the entire conquest. 12:1–6 summarizes Moses' defeat of the kings on the east of Jordan, and 12:7–24 summarizes Joshua's defeat of the kings in Palestine. Since this chapter includes information not previously given, it serves as a necessary appendix to 1–11, which is indispensable to the completeness of the history.

b. 13:1–24:33. The distribution of the territory

1. 13:1–7. The cities not yet taken, and the command to divide the land among the nine and a half tribes. Note that in verses 4–6 Sidon

---

[8] As an introduction to the subject, the reader should consult E. W. Maunder, 'Joshua's Long Day',* in *Journal of Transactions of Victoria Institute*, LIII, 1921, pp. 120–148; R. D. Wilson, 'What Does "The Sun Stood Still" Mean?',* *PTR*, 16, 1918, pp. 46–54.

seems to be the chief Phoenician city, whereas later (even by Solomon's time) Tyre became most important. This is an evidence of antiquity.

2. 13:8–21. The territories of the eastern tribes.

3. 14:1–19:51. The territories of the western tribes. The territories to be distributed by lot, 14:1–5; the approach of Caleb, verses 6–12; Joshua gives Hebron to Caleb, verses 13–15; Judah's inheritance, chapter 15; Joseph's inheritance, chapters 16, 17; the Tabernacle erected at Shiloh, 18:1; preparation for second distribution, 18:2–10; inheritance of Benjamin, 18:11–28; Simeon, 19:1–9; Zebulun, verses 10–16; Issachar, verses 17–23; Asher, verses 24–31; Naphtali, verses 32–39; Dan, verses 40–48; Joshua receives Timnath Serah, verses 49–51.

Certain marks of antiquity appear in this section. In chapter 15 the towns of Canaan are called by their old names: verse 9, Baalah, later Kirjath-jearim; verse 49, Kirjath-sannah, later Debir; verse 54, Kirjath-arba, later Hebron. In 16:10 the Canaanites are in Gezer, but in Solomon's time (1 Ki. 9:16) they were destroyed by Pharaoh. In 18:16, 28 it is evident that Jerusalem is not yet the capital of the Israelites.

Certain objections to this section have been made. Betharabah is said to be ascribed to Judah (15:6), then to Benjamin (18:22). But evidently this desert place (15:61) stood on the border. Hence, it might have belonged to both (in 18:18 it is called merely Arabah), or else it was first assigned to Judah, and later given to Benjamin. As to Bethshemesh (Irshemesh in 19:41), it was on the border of Judah, and was given not to Dan but to the Levites (21:16). Certain cities, e.g., Tappuah, within the territory of Manasseh, were assigned to Ephraim. There are various reasons why this might have been; certainly this is no evidence of contradiction or of conflicting traditions.

Further, it is alleged that in some passages the portion of Joseph's two sons is said to be *one* (16:1; 17:14–18), but in others it is *twofold* (16:5, 8; 17:1a). This objection is without weight. In order that Mannasseh might not be separated from Ephraim, Joseph's descendants drew *one* lot. Their inheritance, however, was immediately divided (16:6–8). There is no conflicting tradition here. See the older commentaries (Calvin, Keil, and others). After describing the southern border of Joseph (16:1–3), the narrative is said to start afresh (16:4), and to repeat the description (16:5–8). However, this is not correct. Verse 4 is a summary statement of verses 1–3. It serves as a conclusion. Verse 5 then begins to specify the border of Ephraim. This description (difficult as it is) should nevertheless be distinguished from that of verses 1–3.

4. 20:1–9. The cities of refuge.

5. 21:1–45. The cities for the priests and Levites.

6. 22:1–34. The two and one half tribes. These return to their land and erect an altar by the Jordan.

7. 23:1–24:33. Conclusion. Introduction to Joshua's first discourse, 23:1, 2. He reminds the people of God's gracious acts, verses 3–13, and then summarizes his thoughts, verses 14–16. Chapter 24: 1–28 describes the renewal of the covenant at Shechem, and verses 29–33 mention the death of Joshua and of Eleazar.

SPECIAL LITERATURE ON JOSHUA

Wm. F. Albright, 'The Israelite Conquest of Canaan in the Light of Archaeology', in *BASOR*, No. 74, 1939, pp. 11–23; Albrecht Alt, 'Das System der Stammesgrenzen im Buche Josua', in *Sellin-Festschrift* (1927), pp. 13–24; A. Fernandez, 'Critica Historico-Literaria de Jos. 3:1–5:1', in *Biblica*, 12, 1931, pp. 93–98; 'El limite Septentrional de Benjamin', *Biblica*, 13, 1932, pp. 49–60; John Garstang, *The Foundations of Bible History; Joshua, Judges* (London, 1931); Beatrice L. Goff, 'The Lost Jahwistic Account of the Conquest of Canaan', *JBL*, 53, 1934, pp. 241–249; Martin Noth, *Das System der zwölf Stämme Israels* (Stuttgart, 1930).

CHAPTER ELEVEN

JUDGES

NAME

THE book receives its name from the rulers 'judges' (*shophetim*), who ruled over Israel during the period between Joshua and Samuel. The same name appears also in the LXX (*Kritai*), and in the Vulgate.

AUTHOR

Divisive criticism does not regard the book of Judges as a literary unit, but considers it a compilation of different sources. It is thought to be essentially a Deuteronomistic book, coming from about 550. There are supposed to be two independent sources, J and E, although these symbols do not necessarily indicate a continuation of the previous J and E. In fact, by some scholars they are thought to be more closely connected with the alleged 'sources' in the book of Samuel. These two sources were united about 650–600 (JE). The redactor (RJE) also made some additions of his own, most of them supposed to be harmonistic. After the destruction of Jerusalem, a Deuteronomic edition of the book is supposed to have been prepared to convince the exile that punishment had come because of their violation of the Deuteronomic code. Some further redactions were also made, until the book reached its present form.

According to the Talmud (*Baba Bathra* 14b), 'Samuel wrote the book which bears his name and the Book of Judges and Ruth.' But how trustworthy is this tradition? There is evidence that Judges is a very ancient book. According to 1:21, the Jebusites were still in Jerusalem when the book was written. Hence, the book must have been edited before the events recorded in 2 Samuel 5:6ff. (David's capture of the city). It is said in 1:29 that the Canaanites dwelt in Gezer, which points to a time before Pharaoh gave the city to Solomon (1 Ki. 9:16). In 3:3 Sidon rather than Tyre is the chief Phoenician city. This points to a time before the twelfth century. Isaiah 9 refers to Judges 4, 5, 6, and passages such as 17:6; 18:1; and 21:25 seem to imply a time in the early monarchy when its blessings were fresh in mind. (The reading of 18:30 is not certain, and some would emend it to read, 'until the day of the captivity of the ark,' *i.e.*, by the Philistines [*ha'aron* instead of *ha'aretz*].)

All of this leads to the conclusion that the book was compiled during the early days of the monarchy, either during the reign of Saul or the early days of David. It is quite possible that this author made use of sources, both oral and written, but the remarkable unity of the book's structure precludes any such scheme of compilation as that proposed by the divisive criticism.

PURPOSE

The book of Judges serves to show that the theocratic people need a righteous king. Without a king who reigns under the special authority of God, confusion follows. 'Every man did that which is right in his own eyes.' The book thus has a negative purpose. When the people are without a ruler, there must be awakened within them longings and aspirations after a true king. Thus, by the period of the Judges, they gradually were brought to see their need of a king.

During this period the rulers of the people were termed judges. These were not, however, merely civil magistrates who administered justice and adjudicated disputes. Primarily, they were deliverers (lit. 'saviours', *moshe'im*), endued with the power of the Spirit of God, who were called upon to deliver and to govern the people in times of declension and oppression.

The book of Judges carries on the history of the people from the time of the death of Joshua to the rise of Samuel as a prophet of the Lord. During this time the people were to take possession of the land which had been allotted to them, by driving out and exterminating the remaining Canaanites, and to build up and establish the theocratic nation. They soon, however, grew weary of their tasks, and often adopted friendly terms with the Canaanites and sometimes took over their gods. Hence, by way of punishment, they were given over to their enemies. When, however, they repented, the Lord raised up judges, who were saviours and deliverers, upon whom He sent His Spirit, and who delivered the people and the land from oppression. But no sooner was a judge dead than the people fell back into apostasy. We see, therefore, in the book of Judges, a period of constant alternation between apostasy and its consequent oppression upon the part of foes, followed by deliverance under a judge. This tragic state of affairs paved the way for the institution of prophecy as such under Samuel.

ANALYSIS

a. 1:1–2:5. *The Introduction*

1. 1:1. Introduction to the entire book. This verse is an offence to some critics of the negative school, for it is thought that this section (*i.e.*, 1:1–2:23) contains an account not subsequent to Joshua's death, but at least parallel to the narrative of Joshua. The verse is therefore regarded as an editorial addition. This, however, is subjective, and is done in the interests of a certain theory. There is no objective evidence which demands such a view of this verse. Note that the verse begins as does Joshua 1:1. It clearly places the events *after* the death of Joshua (not Moses, as Kittel suggests). These events are therefore to be regarded as subsequent, not parallel to the narratives of Joshua.

2. 1:2–36. A summary of the existing political conditions. This summary has a nationalistic emphasis. It does not, however, conflict with the representation of Joshua. That book presents Joshua as the great leader; this section places its emphasis upon the work of the tribes. There is no real conflict.

In 1:10 Judah is said to be substituted for Caleb (Jos. 15:13–19). But there is no conflict. Caleb received a part in Judah. Why may not he have taken the lead against Hebron? Thus, Judah in the person of Caleb would fight against Hebron. In 1:21 Benjamin is said to be substituted for Judah (Jos. 15:63). Again there is no conflict. Doubtless both tribes had warred against Jerusalem, and at that time could not drive out the Jebusites. Later, however, the city was divided between Judah and Benjamin. In 1:8 Judah is said to have taken Jerusalem, and this is asserted to be incorrect (contrast with 1:21) since Jerusalem was first taken later by David. However, this statement (1:8) is made in connection with the account of Adoni-bezek. Evidently Judah at this time had attacked Jerusalem and burned it. However, they could not hold it permanently. As 1:21 shows, they did not drive out the Jebusites, but 1:8 was evidently an attempt along this line. We simply do not know enough about the situation to declare 1:8 unhistorical. Again 1:18 and 19 are said to be in conflict. But if they are, the redactor must have been sleeping to put them so close together. However, there is no conflict. 1:18 relates a capture of the Philistine territory. This was doubtless temporary. At any rate, even though the territory was taken, the inhabitants could not be driven out ('dispossessed', *lehorish*). Judah might take by storm, but she could not dispossess the inhabitants. Chapter 1 evinces evidences of literary unity with later parts of the book. Thus: (i) To deliver into one's hand (*nathan beyadh*) occurs in 1:2; (J) 2:14, 23; (E²) 6:1; 7:7; 13:1;

15:12; 18:10; 20:28. (ii) To set on fire (*shillehu va'esh*) occurs in 1:8 and
20:48. (iii) To smite with the edge of the sword (*hikkah lephi herev*) occurs
in 1:8, 25; 20:48. (iv) Unto this day (*adh hayyom hazzeh*) occurs in 1:21;
6:24; 10:4; 15:19; 19:30. (v) Would dwell (*yo'el lasheveth*), 1:27, 35;
17:11; 19:6. Chapter 1:1-2 should be compared with 20:18, 23, 27, and
1:16 with 4:11.

3. 2:1-5. The Angel of the Lord. The people are reproached for
breaking the covenant with the Lord.

b. 2:6-16:31. The judges of Israel

1. 2:6-3:6. Israel's relations with the Lord. A new generation had arisen
(2:10) which knew not the Lord, and which forsook Him in order to
worship the gods of Canaan (2:11, 12). As a result of this apostasy, the
Lord delivered the people into the hands of spoilers (*shosim*, 'plunderers'),
who despoiled them (2:14). The grace of God then manifested itself in
the raising up of judges who delivered the people from the spoilers
(2:16). This would be followed by a relapse into apostasy (2:19), and the
Lord, therefore, determined to leave in the land the nations which
Joshua had not taken in order thereby to test the people (2:22). These
nations are then listed (3:1-6).

We have to do here not with idealized, but with actual, history.
Nevertheless, this section has been severely criticized. Thus, it is argued,
2:23 cannot be the original sequel of 2:20-22, since the Lord's not
delivering the nations into the hand of Joshua (2:23) cannot be a
consequence of what took place *after Joshua's death* (verse 21). This objection
is not without weight. In reply we would say:

(i) The word 'Joshua' (2:23 – this is the word which occasions the
difficulty) may be an error and should possibly be emended to 'Israel'
(Kittel). However, this is without objective textual support.

(ii) Since it is difficult to account for the deliberate introduction of
this difficult reading, unless we attribute it to the thoughtlessness of a
scribe, we may allow the reading to stand (*lectio difficilior praestat*) and
assume that the word 'Joshua' simply stands for the people as such. It
would be then merely an equivalent for Israel.

Further, the reasons why the nations were not driven out are said to be
inconsistent. In 3:1-3 the reason given is that Israel might learn the art
of war, but in 2:22 and 3:4 it is that Israel might be tested morally. But
there surely is no conflict here. 'To learn war' here means, as the previous
context would seem to show, 'to learn to depend upon the Lord for help
in fighting against Canaan'. Hence, this is really but one of the means
whereby Israel was to be morally tested.

Lastly, the list of nations in 3:3 is said to be not consistent with that in 3:5, since the former refers to those occupying certain districts, and the latter represents the entire population. But 3:3 must be understood in the light of Joshua 13:2–6. Chapter 3:5 then serves as a general statement that the Israelites dwelt in the midst of the Canaanites (six groups being enumerated) thus to explain Israel's apostasy.[1]

2. 3:7–11. The judgeship of Othniel. Othniel, the son of Kenaz, delivers Israel from Chushan-Rishathaim, king of Mesopotamia. He secured rest for Israel for forty years.

3. 3:12–30. The victory of Ehud over the Moabites. Ehud was a Benjamite and left-handed. The oppression under Eglon, king of the Moabites, had lasted eighteen years (3:14). After the deliverance, however, Israel had peace for eighty years (3:30). Under Othniel and Ehud all Israel, apparently, rose up against its oppressors. The phrase 'to draw the sword' (*shalaph herev*) of 3:22 occurs also in 8:10, 20; 9:54; 20:2, 15, 17, 25, 35, 46.

4. 3:31. Shamgar, the son of Anath, slew six hundred Philistines with an ox-goad. He is not called a judge, nor is the period of his labours reckoned in the chronology. He apparently wrought no permanent victory. Evidently he acted out of deep concern, seizing the first weapon that came to hand.

5. 4:1–5:31. The oppression of Jabin, and the deliverance under Deborah and Barak. This victory and the defeat of Jabin's general, Sisera, are described in a poetic ode, chapter 5, which is regarded by all schools of thought as being very ancient, some having gone so far as to say that it is the earliest piece of writing in the Bible. This, of course, is incorrect. It evidently is, however, contemporary, the work of Deborah herself, and was included by the author of the entire book, who also wrote the fourth chapter. It should be noted that in this battle not all Israel was engaged. Reuben and Gilead, Dan and Asher took no part in the conflict.

Chapter 4 is said to differ from chapter 5 in important details:

(i) Two, not six tribes engage in battle (*cf.* 4:10 with 5:14, 15, 18). But these are not mutually exclusive accounts. 4:10 simply states Barak's initial act. Chapter 5, being poetic, naturally mentions the other tribes. Note that 4:23, 24 does not limit the victory to two tribes but gives it to the children of Israel.

(ii) Sisera, while sleeping, is pierced by Jael (4:21); but in chapter 5

---

[1] For a fair representation of the view of negative criticism, see A. B. Davidson, 'The Prophetess Deborah' in *The Expositor*, 5, 1887, pp. 38–55.

he is hit on the head 'while drinking sour milk outside the tent'.[2] However, the two statements are supplementary. A mere reading of them will show that there is absolutely no contradiction. The poetical account (chapter 5) does not seek to give all the details, but lays its stress upon the death of Sisera (*e.g.*, 5:27, which is obviously poetic).

(iii) Chapter 4 speaks of Jabin, the king, whereas 5:19 mentions the 'kings' of Canaan with Sisera, not Jabin, as head (Driver). But again, 5:19 is poetic, and the word 'kings' may simply refer to leaders under Jabin. But chapter 5 does not say that Sisera is the head of the kings. As Jabin's general, he doubtless took a leading part, and hence the prominence ascribed to him in both chapters 4 and 5.

(iv) Some have denied that Deborah was a historical personage, and assert that the words 'a mother in Israel' (5:7) indicate a metropolis, not a person. However, in Genesis 35:8 the word 'Deborah' obviously refers to a historical person. Chapter 4 supplies certain details which are lacking in chapter 5, and are necessary for a proper understanding of the song.[3]

Chapters 2 to 5 present the first stage in the attitude of the Lord towards the rebelling people. At Bochim the people are threatened by the Angel of the Lord (2:1–5). Thus it is said, 'The Canaanites shall be as thorns in your sides, and their gods shall be a snare unto you' (2:3). The oppressions of this stage were from without and lasted a rather long time. Between each oppression there were long intervals of peace. Othniel and Ehud were stirred up by the Spirit of God; Barak was summoned to war by the prophetess Deborah.

6. 6:1–8:35. The work of Gideon. The oppressing Midianites are defeated by Gideon, whose history is related with some fullness since it manifests so clearly the gracious working of the faithful covenant God in the deliverance of His people. This account is distinguished by certain literary peculiarities. Some think that two (or three) sources are employed, and that there were two accounts of Gideon. This is based upon such considerations as the fact that Gideon is sometimes called by the name Jerubbaal. However, the account is a unity, and attempts to parcel it into documents must be pronounced a failure.

7. 9:1–57. The episode of Abimelech. In this section appears the remarkable parable of the trees.

---

[2] Pfeiffer, *IOT*, p. 329.

[3] For a splendid defence of the genuineness and historicity of the song, see the article by Burton L. Goddard, 'The Critic and Deborah's Song',* *WThJ*, III, 1941, pp. 93–112.

8. 10:1–5. Tola and Jair serve as judges, ruling twenty-three and twenty-two years respectively.

The structure of chapters 6 through 10:5 may be represented as follows:

The Lord again threatens His people, this time through the medium of a prophet (6:7–10). It is said, 'I delivered you out of the hand of the Egyptians, and out of the hand of all that oppressed you; I said unto you, I am the LORD your God; fear not the gods of the Amorites; but ye have not hearkened to my voice' (6:8–10). The oppression of the Midianites lasts seven years, and is followed by forty years of rest under Gideon (8:1–3), and under Tola and Jair there are apparently forty-five years of peace (10:2, 3). This period is characterized by the fact that serious internal disruption and disorganization appears. Ephraim becomes exceedingly jealous of Gideon and the victorious tribes; Succoth and Peniel refuse assistance (8:4–9, 14–17). Not only does all Israel not fight against the foe, but not even the entire army of Gideon is permitted to fight. The Lord brings victory by the hand of only three hundred men, that the people might not vaunt themselves against Him.

9. 10:6–12:7. Deliverance by Jephthah. Jephthah, the son of a harlot, was invited by the leaders of Gilead to become their leader, but assented only on condition that in case of victory he should so continue. He vowed that if victorious, he would sacrifice to the Lord the first one who came from the doors of his house to meet him. This proved to be his daughter. In fulfilment of the vow, he probably devoted her to perpetual virginity, but of this one cannot be certain.

E (11:34) is said to represent Jephthah as a respected house owner in Mizpeh, whereas J (11:1–3) represents him as the son of a harlot who became a bandit. But if these statements were contradictions why would a redactor place them in the same chapter? Is it not obvious that Jephthah while in exile gathered a force and possessions so that he did actually become a man to be reckoned with?

10. 12:8–15. Three judges, Ibzan, Elon and Abdon, ruled for seven, ten and eight years respectively.

11. 13:1–16:31. The history of Samson. For the historicity of Samson, see Hebrews 11:32. The divine power displayed in the Judges was culminated in Samson, who possessed this power by virtue of being a Nazarite. In his natural character, however, he was an extremely weak man.

The structure of chapters 10:6 through 16:31 is as follows: The people are again threatened by the Lord: 'Ye have forsaken me and served other gods: wherefore I will deliver you no more; go and cry unto the gods which ye have chosen; let them deliver you in the time of your tribulation' (10:13, 14). Internal decay becomes more and more apparent. Jephthah is called by the elders of Gilead, and Samson is set apart from his mother's womb.

c. 17:1–21:25. Two appendices

1. 17:1–18:31. The episode of Micah the Ephraimite and the Levite who is consecrated priest in his house. The unity of this narrative is obvious. Even negative criticism regards these two appendices as belonging to the earliest stratum of the book. These episodes make abundantly clear the need for a king at this time. Pfeiffer, following Arnold, would analyse these accounts, not into sources, but into a narrative, with which a late commentary and some glosses have been incorporated.

2. 19:1–21:25. The crime at Gibeah in Benjamin and its punishment.

SPECIAL LITERATURE ON JUDGES

Otto Eissfeldt, *Die Quellen des Richterbuches* (Leipzig, 1925); Andres Ferdandez, 'El Atentado de Gabaa', in *Biblica*, 12, pp. 297–315; H. Haensler, 'Der historische Hintergrund von Richter 3, 8–10', in *Biblica*, 11, pp. 391–418; 12, pp. 3–26, 271–296, 395–410; Siegfried Sprank and Kurt Wiese, *Studien zu Ezechiel und dem Buch der Richter* (Stuttgart, 1926); Harold M. Wiener, *The Composition of Judges 2:11 to 1 Kings 2:46* (Leipzig, 1929); C. A. Simpson, *Composition of the Book of Judges* (1957).

CHAPTER TWELVE

THE BOOKS OF SAMUEL

NAME

THESE two books are named after Samuel, not only because he was the principal character in the first part, but also because he anointed the other two principal characters, Saul and David. Originally these books were regarded as one.[1] The LXX divided the books into two, and this division was followed in the Old Itala and Vulgate. The translators of the LXX called the two books, The First and Second Books of Kingdoms (*bibloi basileon*), and the two books of Kings were called the Third and Fourth Books of Kingdoms. The Vulgate, however, changed the title to Books of Kings. The division into two books seems first to have been introduced into the first edition of Daniel Bomberg's printed Hebrew Bible (Venice, 1516–1517). The designation 'Samuel', found in the Hebrew manuscripts, has been retained in the English translation, although the Authorized Version adds to the title 'Otherwise Called the First (Second) Book of the Kings'.

AUTHOR

According to *Baba Bathra* 14b, 'Samuel wrote the book which bears his name and the Book of Judges and Ruth.' However, in 15a we read, 'Samuel wrote his book [*sifro*]. But is it not written in it, Now Samuel was dead?' Hence, while Jewish tradition may have maintained that Samuel wrote the book, objection to this position was raised at an early time.

It is obvious that Samuel cannot have been the author of the entire book, since his death is recorded in 1 Samuel 25:1; 28:3, and events are mentioned which took place long after Samuel's death. We do not know who the author was. In the light of 1 Samuel 27:6 ('Ziklag pertaineth unto the kings of Judah until this day'), it seems obvious that the books were not completed in their present form until sometime after the division of the kingdom. Whoever the author was, he made use of

---

[1] See *Baba Bathra* 14b; Jerome, *Prologus galeatus*; Eusebius, *Ecclesiastical History*, vii. 25. 2.

previously existing written documents, and these most likely 'in the chronicles ['al divre] of Samuel the seer, and in the chronicles of Nathan the prophet and in the chronicles of Gad the seer [hozeh]' (1 Ch. 29:29). What the precise content of these written documents was is not known. We may conclude, then, that the books of Samuel were composed under divine inspiration by a prophet, probably of Judaea, who lived shortly after the schism and who incorporated into his work earlier written material.

Those who espouse the documentary hypothesis with respect to the Pentateuch have generally maintained that the principal contents of the books of Samuel were preserved in two more or less parallel but independent sources, which are similar to J and E. The earlier account is said to have come from about the time of Solomon, and the later one from the eighth century. About a century later they were united.

For an early expression of this theory the student should consult H. P. Smith, *Samuel*, in *ICC* (1902).[2] The earlier document begins at 4:1b, and is the continuation of Judges 13–16. It gives an account of the events from the first encounter between Israel and the Philistines to the accession of Solomon. According to Pfeiffer, it is 'the outstanding prose writing and historical masterpiece of the Old Testament'[3] and, when freed from later additions, a well-organized literary unit. The author was probably Ahimaaz, as first suggested by Klostermann,[4] and this Ahimaaz, or whoever the author was, is thought by Pfeiffer to be 'the father of history' in a far truer sense than Herodotus, and his style is unsurpassed in Hebrew prose.

Whereas Saul and David are the principal characters of the early source, Samuel is said to be the protagonist of the secondary or late source. This source is confined to parts of 1 Samuel 1–24, and is supposed to be 'clouded with legends and distorted by theories'[5] and is of multiple authorship. Chapter 1 may be dated about 750 BC, and the original form of 17 and 18 about a century later. The rest, thinks Pfeiffer, comes from between 650 and 550 BC.

This late source is a correction of the earlier and is based upon two theories which dominate its viewpoint: the monarchy is an apostasy from the Lord, and 'good or bad fortune among mortals is an exact divine retribution for human conduct'.[6] 'The mist of legend and the compelling

---

[2] It is found later in R. H. Pfeiffer, *IOT*, pp. 341ff., and in 'Midrash in the Books of Samuel' in *Quantulacumque*, pp. 303–316.

[3] *IOT*, p. 356.

[4] *Die Bücher Samuelis und der Könige* (1887), pp. xxxii ff.

[5] *IOT*, p. 362.

[6] *IOT*, p. 362.

authority of dogmas conspire to produce in the late source an atmosphere of make-believe and the illusions of a *mirage*.'[7]

How the two sources were joined together is not perfectly clear, and no effort was made to harmonize divergencies as was the case with 'RJᴱ'. The late source was probably not an independent document but rather the addition of corrections and improvements to the original history.

Because of the character of the so-called late source, the Deuteronomist edition was more or less perfunctory. But principally was this so because the fundamental Deuteronomic doctrine, namely, that national disaster was due to failure to worship Jehovah exclusively and correctly, was not applicable to the first two kings of Israel. Certain parts of Samuel, however, were probably suppressed by the Deuteronomists.

1 Samuel 2:27–36 and 2 Samuel 7 are thought by Pfeiffer to be the two most elaborate instances of late midrashic additions which are historically worthless.

Pfeiffer has presented the 'two-source' theory with some elaborateness. According to Otto Eissfeldt[8] there are three basic sources in Samuel, not two. He regards the books of Samuel, therefore, as composed of three parallel sources, which are probably the continuations of the three sources of the Heptateuch, L, J, and E. In 1 Samuel these sources are more or less interwoven, but in 2 Samuel they are thought to be consecutive. We are compelled to reject both theories as being out of harmony with the unified character of the books.

PURPOSE

The purpose of the books of Samuel is to relate the account of the establishment of the monarchy, and of Samuel's part therein. Samuel was both a judge (1 Sa. 7:6, 15–17) and a prophet (1 Sa. 3:20). He serves, therefore, to connect the period of the Judges with the early monarchy.

There was a twofold preparation for the kingdom. During the period of the judges confusion prevailed, and thus the Israelites came to see their need of a centralized government. In the second place, the king must be a good king, not a selfish autocrat, but a man who was after God's heart, who in his faithful and just reign would point forward to the Great King to come. Under the reign of Saul, a self-willed autocrat, the lesson was taught that the king must be one who would reign in righteousness.

Not only do the books of Samuel recount the establishment of the

[7] *IOT*, p. 363.
[8] *Einleitung*, pp. 306–317; *Die Komposition der Samuelisbücher* (1931).

monarchy, but they serve to point out that this great institution was of divine origin.

a. 1 Samuel 1:1–7:17. Samuel as judge
1. 1:1–2:10. The birth of Samuel and the song of Hannah. While Eli was high priest, a devout Israelitish woman, Hannah, prayed for a son. Her prayer was answered, and she bore a son, Samuel, and dedicated him to life-long service to the Lord. She then praised the Lord (2:1–10) in a beautiful song of prophetic character.

The song of Hannah is assumed by some critics to belong to a time later than Hannah. The following reasons are offered: verse 10 is said to assume the establishment of the monarchy; the theme is one of national victory rather than of personal thanksgiving (verses 4, 7, 10); and the language and style are said to be similar to those of late psalms.

In answer, however, it should be noted, that (i) the king of whom Hannah speaks is the *ideal* king. To speak thus does not necessarily presuppose an actual king. For the monarchy had been promised from a very early time (Gn. 17:6; Dt. 17:14–20; Jdg. 8:22), and was in the thoughts of the people. And who would be so worthy thus to anticipate the future monarchy as the mother of him who should guide the nation through the critical period of the establishment of the Davidic kingdom? (ii) The theme is prophetic. In her own experience Hannah discerned the general laws of the divine economy. 'The experience which she bowed down and oppressed as she was, had had of the gracious government of the omniscient and holy covenant God, was a pledge to her of the gracious way in which the nation itself was led by God, and a sign by which she discerned how God not only delivered at all times the poor and wretched who trusted in Him out of their poverty and distress, and set them up, but would also lift up and glorify His whole nation, which was at that time so deeply bowed down and oppressed by its foe' (Keil). Further, there is no mention whatever of national victory in this poem, the only possible allusion to war being in verse 4, where the purpose, apparently, is to contrast the warrior with the weak man, rather than to allude to the defeat of an *enemy* warrior. If the theme is really so far removed from Hannah's circumstances, why should any late compiler think of attributing it to Hannah? (iii) The language proves nothing as to the date. God is called a Rock, verse 2 (*cf.* Dt. 32:4, 15, *etc.*). Reduplication (verse 3, *gevohah gevohah*) also occurs in Deuteronomy 2:27. This song of Hannah is the prototype of the Magnificat (Lk. 1:46–55) and of

Zacharias' prophecy (Lk. 1:68–79), which show how the song was understood by the devout in Israel.

2. 2:11–3:21. Samuel's childhood and vision. 2:27–36 is dated by some as very late (possibly after 400, Pfeiffer). But there is no warrant for regarding this section as a late midrash, since it bears the characteristics of genuine prophecy.

3. 4:1–22. The death of Eli. It is argued that chapters 1–3 lead us to expect great emphasis upon the fall of Eli's house in the sequel, but since chapters 4–7 do not have this stress chapters 1–3 are said to be the work of a later hand. This objection, however, fails to understand the purpose of these chapters. Chapters 1–3 provide the necessary background with respect to Samuel. Included in this is the statement of the low condition of the priesthood and the announcement that Eli's house will fall. The writer then proceeds to relate the low condition of the country itself, and this is done by portraying how the ark is taken, the glory is departed. Thus the stage is set for the work of Samuel.

4. 5:1–6:21. The ark in Philistine territory.

5. 7:1–17. The ark returned.

The representation of Samuel as judge (7:15) is no evidence of a later viewpoint. It is only after Samuel assumes the government of all the nation that his judgeship begins.

Verse 13 does not conflict with accounts of later Philistine invasions. It means that the Philistines no longer returned to invade with lasting success. The hand of the Lord was against them so that they were repulsed with severe loss, even though they were not completely driven out, nor was Israel entirely free from paying tribute to them.

c. 1 Samuel 8:1–31:13. The reign of Saul

1. 8:1–22. Israel expresses desire for a king. Since Samuel's sons as judges had perverted justice, the elders of Israel entreated Samuel to appoint a king. The request, however, was made in an untheocratic spirit, and Samuel pronounced it tantamount to a rejection of Jehovah. Nevertheless, Jehovah commanded Samuel to fulfil the people's desires, and to warn the people by relating to them the prerogatives of the king. Samuel then promised the king.

2. 9:1–10:27. Saul is anointed king. The Lord brings the man whom He has chosen as king before Samuel (9:1–14), Samuel reveals to Saul God's purpose, anoints him and dismisses him, declaring that three signs will confirm his choice by God. Thus is it emphasized that the choice of Saul was by God, not by either Saul or Samuel. Having secretly anointed Saul, Samuel now summons the people to Mizpeh and instructs the

tribes to choose a king by lot. Thus Saul's election is confirmed. The
account is straightforward and unified. Attempts to discover two
divergent viewpoints concerning the monarchy must be pronounced
failures.

Eissfeldt, *e.g.*, thinks to discover three sources with respect to the kingship (i) 10:21b–27; 11:1; (ii) 9:1–10, 16; (iii) 8; 10:17–21a. Those who
apply the two-document theory also find divergent accounts. Thus
9:1–10:16 and 10:27b–11:11, 15 represent Jehovah as having ordered
Samuel to anoint Saul, whereas 7:2–8:22; 10:17–27a; 11:12–14 and
chapter 12 regard the monarchy as an apostasy from Jehovah. But it
should be noted that both these viewpoints are expressed in 12:12, 13ff.
and that this chapter is generally regarded as a unit. As a matter of fact
there are no conflicting viewpoints about the monarchy. It had early
been prophesied that Israel would have a king, yet the people asked for a
king in a wrong spirit. Let the student read carefully the order of events
under point 2 above. He should also compare the material under
Purpose, above, and the notes on Deuteronomy 17.

3. 11:1–15. Saul's victory over Ammon. Before entering upon the
duties of government, Saul proves his worth, and the opportunity to do
this is given by the enmity of Nahash the Ammonite. Saul is made king at
Gilgal.

4. 12:1–25. Samuel's address. Samuel now lays down his office as
judge, but as prophet he continues to advise the king.

5. 13:1–15:35. The early reign and rejection of Saul. Saul proves to
be disobedient to Samuel's orders, and the Lord removes His Spirit from
the disobedient king. Saul's rejection, however, is not followed by his
immediate deposition.

A duplicate account is said to be found in the fact that Saul is twice
deposed (13:14 and 15:26–29) but continues to rule until his death. But
this objection is not correct. In 13:14 Saul himself was not rejected; it is
merely stated that because of his foolish deed, his sovereignty would not
continue for ever, *i.e.*, by being transmitted to his posterity. At his second
transgression (15:26–29) Saul himself is rejected, and he continues in
office without the presence of the Spirit of God.

6. 16:1–23. David chosen to be king. At first sight it might appear that
the Lord (16:2) commands Samuel to tell a lie as to his purpose in going
to Bethlehem. But Samuel was as a matter of fact going to Bethlehem to
sacrifice. There was no need to tell the entire truth upon this occasion.
If Samuel had been asked, 'Are you going to Bethlehem in order to
anoint David as king?', and in answer had said to Saul, 'I am going only
to sacrifice', then Samuel would have been guilty of dissimulation, and so

also would the Lord. Such, however, was not the case. There is a vast difference between dissimulation, or acting under false pretences, and not telling the entire truth. There was no point in Samuel's revealing at this time the principal object of his mission. 'There was no dissimulation or falsehood in this, since God really wished his prophet to find safety under the pretext of the sacrifice. A sacrifice was therefore really offered, and the prophet was protected thereby, so that he was not exposed to any danger until the time of full revelation arrived' (Calvin). Once we admit, as we are compelled to, the genuineness of the Lord's intention for Samuel to sacrifice, the difficulty disappears.

7. 17:1–31:13. The last days and downfall of Saul. The unity and purpose of this section may best be seen by working carefully through the text with the aid of a sympathetic commentary such as that of Keil. The school of negative criticism believes that it can discover several evidences of composite authorship in this section.

(i) David is said to have been introduced to Saul twice (16:14–23 and 17:55–58). If Saul had known David as well as appears from chapter 16 (e.g., 16:23) it is objected, why, after the battle with Goliath, does he ask whose son David is? Some have supposed that Saul pretended not to recognize David, or that his malady had so affected him that he failed to make recognition. But these assumptions are unnecessary. When Saul asked whose son David was, he obviously was endeavouring to ascertain more than the mere names of David and his father. These he knew already. What Saul desired to discover was 'what kind of man the father of a youth who possessed the courage to accomplish so marvellous a heroic deed really was: and the question was put not merely in order that he might grant him an exemption of his house from taxes as the reward promised for the conquest of Goliath (verse 25), but also in all probability that he might attach such a man to his court, since he inferred from the courage and bravery of the son the existence of similar qualities in the father' (Keil). It was, therefore, the social condition of David and his father which Saul desired to ascertain. 18:1 shows clearly that a *lengthy* conversation had ensued. Had Saul merely desired to know the name of David's father, there would have been no need for any lengthy conversation. One word would have answered the question.

(ii) David is three times offered Saul's daughter in marriage 18:17–19; 18:22–29a; and 18:21b). But a careful reading of these passages removes the supposed difficulty here. In answer to his promise 17–25) Saul offers his elder daughter Merab. It was a crafty offer 18:17), and in true humility, without suspecting Saul's craftiness, David declares that he could not make pretension of becoming son-in-law to the king. Saul, however, did not keep his promise (verse 19). Then upon discovering that Michal loved David, Saul offered her to him. To this David, having discovered Saul's unreliability, did not reply. Saul therefore employed his messengers to approach David (verse 22). (In the LXX verse 21b is omitted.)

(iii) David is said to have escaped twice from Saul's court never to return (19:12; 20:42b), and although Saul is aware of David's first flight (19:17) he expresses wonder that David is not later present at dinner (20:25-29). Again the objection must be met by a careful reading of the relevant passages. In 19:12 Michal enables David to escape the messengers of Saul (the text does not say or imply that he escaped *never to return*), and in 19:17 Saul reproaches Michal for having deceived him. The Scripture then relates David's flight, first to Samuel at Ramah (19:18), then to Naioth in Ramah (19:18). David then left Naioth whither Saul had come and had been impelled to prophesy, and came to Jonathan (20:1). David then suggested that at the table Saul might miss him (20:6), and this is precisely what happens (20:25-29). Now, the reason for this is that when Saul at the table enquires for David, he is in a rational frame of mind. When he had pursued David previously, he had been in a fit of insanity (*cf.* 19:9, 'and an evil spirit from the Lord came upon Saul'). This condition was abnormal. It did not represent Saul's feelings toward David when he was rational. Hence, in his normal state of mind and unaware of the tragic things which had occurred when the evil spirit was upon him, Saul at the table could wonder at David's absence. Jonathan's conversation at the table with Saul enrages Saul, who now, in a state of sanity, realizes that in David he has a rival. Jonathan then carries out the pre-arranged plan of shooting the arrow, and David, now realizing that Saul is indeed determined to destroy him, flees.

(iv) Another evidence of composite authorship is supposedly found in an alleged duplicate account of David's sparing Saul's life (24:3-7 and 26:5-12). But these are not duplicate accounts at all. In 24:3-7, Saul hides in a cave (*me 'arah*) by the sheepcote (*gideroth hatsts'on*), for the purpose of covering his feet. David and his men were already in the cave, David cut off the skirt of Saul's robe in secret (*ballat*). Then David repented of his act and forbade his men to rise against Saul. In 26:5-12 on the other hand, David came to the place where Saul was (26:5). Saul lay in a trench (*ma'gal*, *i.e.*, a ditch, quite different from a cave), and about him the people were encamped. David then asks who will go down (*yeredh*) to Saul's camp. When they have descended, Abishai desires to smite Saul once, not twice. This David forbids, but they do take the spear and cruse of water. They are able to do this because a divinely imposed sleep was over the camp. The circumstances of the two events are quite different. But even so it is surely possible that David might spare an enemy twice. The genuineness of the accounts is shown in that David twice spares an enemy under *quite different* circumstances.

(v) David is said to have made a covenant with Jonathan *three* times (18:3; 20:16, 42; and 23:18). This objection disappears as soon as one reads carefully what the Scripture says. In 18:3 Jonathan and David made a covenant because Jonathan loved David as his own soul. In 20:12ff., when it has become apparent that Saul in his frenzy would destroy David, Jonathan renews the covenant with David by vowing that he will reveal Saul's intentions, whether good or bad, to David. He then (verses 14, 15) entreats David to show him everlasting kindness (*hesedh yehowah*) and to his house, implying therein that the house of David would surely prevail. In thus speaking, Jonathan emphasizes or renews the covenant already made, and in this covenant includes David's posterity. Lastly, in 23:18, when David was a fugitive, Jonathan went to David and strengthened his hand in God. Thus, they renewed the covenant already made. To insist that three distinct covenants were made is to force upon the text a meaning which it was never intended to bear.

(vi) David is said to have taken refuge with Achish twice (21:10–15 and 27:1–4). This is true. David did seek to take refuge with Achish twice, and the Scripture makes it clear why he did so. When David first fled to Achish, the remembrance of Goliath's death was evidently still vivid in the mind of the Philistines (21:11). This caused David to fear Achish and he feigned madness so that he could depart. During the time between 21:10 and 27:1, however, Achish could learn that David had been pursued by Saul, and would perhaps think that if a new war were to break out between Israel and the Philistines, David might fight for the Philistines. When David came to Achish, Saul refrained from further pursuit. Hence, we see that the narratives cannot in any sense be regarded as mere duplicate accounts of the same event.

(vii) The accounts of the slaying of Goliath are said to be confused. In chapter 17 (*cf.* also 19:5; 21:9; 22:10, 13) David is declared to have slain Goliath. In 2 Samuel 21:19, however, Elhanan is said to have slain Goliath. Furthermore, in 1 Chronicles 20:5, it is stated that Elhanan slew Lahmi, the brother of Goliath. What is the answer to these apparent discrepancies?

In the first place it should be noted that if the final 'redactors' of Samuel left such a glaring error, they must be regarded as incompetent.

But was there such a glaring error in the original? Careful examination will make it clear that 2 Samuel 21:19 and 1 Chronicles 20:5 are closely related. In the course of transmission some copyist's errors have evidently crept in, particularly into 2 Samuel 21:19. In the first place, we should remove the word *'oregim*, which appears as part of the proper name, and which is evidently a copyist's mistake, for the word appears again at the end of the verse (*-beam*). Secondly, the particle *'eth* (which introduces the direct object and is not to be translated) should, after Chronicles, be emended to read *'ahi* (the brother of). Thirdly, the name of Elhanan's father should be read Jairi (*y'r*).

Two alternatives now face us. We may read (both in Samuel and Chronicles), 'And Elhanan the son of Jairi smote Lahmi the brother of Goliath'; that is, we presuppose the text to read *wayyak 'eth lahmi' ah golyath*. If this is adopted, we must further emend the words for Bethlehemite (*beth hallahmi*) to Lama (*'eth lahmi*). Or, we may read, 'And Elhanan the son of Jairi the Bethlehemite slew the brother of Goliath.' If this is adopted, we must emend the Lahmi (*'eth lahmi*) of 1 Chronicles to agree with the word Bethlehemite (*beth hallahmi*) of 2 Samuel. Either of these alternatives is possible. The fact of the matter then is that David slew Goliath and that Elhanan slew the brother of Goliath.

A concluding word is in order. Some of the rough places in this section may be due to the condition of the text. It is the work of sober textual criticism to solve these difficulties. The Hebrew text has not been transmitted in as good condition as is the case with most of the other Old Testament books, and the LXX is often of tremendous help. But these minor textual difficulties are *not evidences* of composite authorship. Such evidences, we believe, are entirely lacking in the books of Samuel.

c. 2 Samuel 1:1–25:25. The reign of David
    1. 1:1–27. David's lament over Saul and Jonathan.
    2. 2:1–5:25. David established as king.
    3. 6:1–7:29. The announcement of the eternity of David's kingdom.
    4. 8:1–10:19. David's victory over Israel's enemies.
    5. 11:1–12:31. David's sin with Bathsheba.
    6. 13:1–19:43. Absalom's rebellion.
    7. 20:1–24:25. Sheba's rebellion; David's thanksgiving; his sin in numbering the people.

The essential unity of this section (*i.e.*, 2 Samuel) is generally admitted. These chapters are specimens of noble Hebrew prose, and from the literary standpoint alone may be regarded as incomparable master pieces. According to Bentzen, 2 Samuel exhibits a complex of tradition which parallel the *Landnahmetraditionen* (*i.e.*, the accounts of the conquest of the land) in Joshua. This is 'theological' literature, and a separation into documents is said to be 'problematic'.

The trustworthiness and historical character of the books of Samuel is seen from the fact that they are alluded to in other portions of the sacred Scripture. References to events in Samuel are found in 1 Kings (*e.g.*, 1 Ki. 2:27), 1 Chronicles, Jeremiah, Psalm 17; Christ referred to David's eating the shewbread (Mt. 12:3ff.; Mk. 2:25ff.; Lk. 6:3ff. – reference to 1 Sa. 21:6); and Paul gave a resumé of the contents of Samuel in Acts 3:20–22.

SPECIAL LITERATURE ON THE BOOKS OF SAMUEL

O. T. Allis, 'The Punishment of the Men of Bethshemesh',* in *EQ*, 15, 1943, pp. 298–307; William R. Arnold, *Ephod and Ark* (Harvard, 1917); Georg Beer, *Saul, David, Salomo* (Tübingen, 1906); James Oscar Boyd, 'Monarchy in Israel: The Ideal and the Actual',* *PTR*, 26, 1928, pp. 41–64; 'The Davidic Dynasty',*; 'The Davidic Covenant: The Oracle'*; 'Echoes of the Covenant with David',* in *PTR*, 25, 1927, pp. 215–239, 417–443, 587–609, respectively; S. R. Driver, *Notes on the Hebrew Text and the Topography of the Books of Samuel*[2] (Oxford, 1913); O. Eissfeldt, *Die Komposition der Samuelisbücher* (Leipzig, 1931); I. Hylander, *Der literarische Samuel-Saul-Komplex (I Sam. 1:15) traditionsgeschichtlich untersucht* (Uppsala, 1932); Richard Press, 'Der Prophet Samuel', in *ZAW*, 15, 1938, pp. 117–225; Martin Rehm, *Text-Kritische Untersuchungen zu den Parallelstellen der Samuel-Königsbücher und der Chronik* (Aschendorff, 1937); A. Fernandez Truyols, *I Sam. 1–15 Critica Textual* (Rome, 1917).

CHAPTER THIRTEEN

THE BOOKS OF KINGS

NAME

LIKE the books of Samuel, the books of Kings were originally one
In the LXX they are called the Third and Fourth Book of Kingdom
(*basileon trite kai tetarte*), and in the Vulgate, *Liber Regum tertius et quartus*.

AUTHOR

In *Baba Bathra* 15a we read, 'Jeremiah wrote his [own] book, the Book o
Kings, and Lamentations.' This ancient Jewish theory of authorship
very attractive, for there is much in Kings which seems to bear re
semblances to Jeremiah, and 2 Kings 24:18–25:30 is identical wit
Jeremiah. In recent times the Jeremianic theory has been held b
Steinmueller. The principal objection to this view is that the account o
the deportation and imprisonment of Jehoiachin was evidently writte
in Babylon, whereas Jeremiah was carried to Egypt (Je. 43:1–8
Jeremiah 52 and 2 Kings 24–25 seem to be abstracts (they contain min
verbal differences from each other) from a larger source of whic
Jeremiah was not the author. In all probability the author was
contemporary of Jeremiah, one who was a prophet and deeply concerne
because his people did not obey the voice of Jehovah.

This unknown author, since he was writing concerning events whic
had occurred long before his birth, made use of written records, and the
he mentions by name. In 1 Kings 11:41, after completing the descriptio
of Solomon's reign, the author mentions the Book of the Words o
Solomon (*divere shelomo*). The information for the accounts concernir
the kings of Judah was obtained from the Book of the Chronicles (*dive
hayyamim*) of the Kings of Judah (*e.g.*, 1 Ki. 14:29; 15:7, 23; *etc.*). Mentic
is also made of the Book of the Chronicles of the Kings of Israel (*e.g.*,
Ki. 14:19; 15:31; *etc.*).

Evidently these works were public annals of the kingdom which ha
probably been written down by the prophets. As an example, appe
may be made to the history of Uzziah's reign which Isaiah made (2 C

26:22). These sources, therefore, may be regarded as part of a prophetic history issued in the form of annals. Under divine inspiration the author of Kings made his choice from these written documents.

Advocates of the school of negative criticism believe that the book went through different redactions. This view has been well expressed in recent times by Pfeiffer. The first edition of Kings, according to this theory, was made about 600 BC, whereas the second appeared about fifty years later. The first edition is said to know nothing of the destruction of Jerusalem (586 BC) or of the exile. It also is supposed to recognize as legitimate the worship on the high places outside Jerusalem before the erection of the Temple. On the other hand, the second edition knows of the exile and is said to condemn Solomon for having sacrificed at Gibeon.

In accordance with this view Kings is regarded as a history which exhibits the philosophy and religion of Deuteronomy. This philosophy involved the doctrine of centralization of worship and of just retribution for human conduct on this earth. Hence, each king is said to be judged in accordance with his obedience to the law which centralized worship at Jerusalem and which ordered destruction of the high places (supposedly taught in Deuteronomy 12). Further, in order to explain the doctrine of earthly reward or retribution, the author found himself struggling with the facts and was willing to sacrifice the facts to his theory. The book of Kings then, on this view, is a theological history.[1]

One important modification of the above position should be noted. Eissfeldt and others hold to the existence of a pre-Deuteronomic book of Kings, which was made up of L, J, and E, or simply of J and E. The Deuteronomists, on this view, did not as it were create a new book but worked over the continuation of the narratives of the 'Octateuch'.

PURPOSE

The book of Kings aims to carry on the history of the theocracy until its end in the Babylonian exile. The kings of Judah are judged in accordance with the promise given to David in 2 Samuel 7:12–16, whereas those of the northern kingdom, all of whom are condemned, are condemned because they have continued in the sin of Jeroboam the son of Nebat who made Israel to sin.

[1] See Lindsay B. Longacre, *The Old Testament: Its Form and Purpose* (1945), pp. 36–57, and for a review of this work by the present writer, *WThJ*, VIII, pp. 246–250; *cf.* also *OT*, pp. 377–412.

Much stress is placed upon the prophetic ministry of Elijah and Elisha, who served as the link between the earlier period and prophetism. With respect to the southern kingdom the writer lays particular emphasis upon those kings who were true to the Davidic standard. Yet he condemns where condemnation is necessary, and he makes it clear that the exile is a divine chastisement.

ANALYSIS

a. 1 Kings 1:1–11:1–43. The reign of Solomon
1. 1:1–2:11. The last days of David; Adonijah usurps the throne; Solomon is anointed king; Adonijah flees, and then, upon condition of peaceable behaviour, obtains Solomon's forgiveness; David dies.

The introductory 'now' (Wᴱ) connects the narrative with the preceding history. 2:2–4 is ascribed by critics of the negative school to the Deuteronomic compiler. It need not be denied that these verses contain a Deuteronomic emphasis: that is to be expected in one who loved the law of the Lord; there is absolutely no warrant for denying these words to David.

2. 2:12–46. Introduction to the history of Solomon's reign. Some of the Fathers and one or two codices begin 1 Kings with 2:12.

3. 3:1–28. Solomon's marriage; his prayer at Gibeon; and his wise decision. Verses 2, 3 are considered to be an addition, conflicting with verse 4 in its teaching as to where one may sacrifice. But the three verses are from one author and do not exhibit different viewpoints. A redactor who would place verses contradictory to one another thus closely together, must have been careless indeed. His work would be detected in no time. Apparently, however, it was not detected until the advent of modern negative criticism. Verses 2, 3 present a general statement of the state of religion at the beginning of Solomon's reign. Since the Temple had not yet been built, people worshipped the Lord on the high places. Solomon (verse 4), who loved the Lord, also sacrificed on a high place even Gibeon. It is not just to say that verses 2, 3 disapprove of such worship, whereas verse 4 does not. Cornill thinks that chapter 3 has been subjected to drastic revision, and Driver would attribute verses 4:13, 15 16–28 to a 'pre-Deuteronomic' prophetical narrative. It may be that the final author has incorporated earlier material into his narrative, but the chapter does not present conflicting viewpoints, and it is utterly unwarrantable, with Gressmann, Pfeiffer, and others to look upon verses 16–28 as originally an oriental folk-tale which had nothing to do with Solomon.

4. 4:1–34. The administration of Solomon's kingdom. The list of officers belongs not to the beginning but to a later period of Solomon's reign and mentions the most distinguished officers during the entire reign. It serves to give an idea of the grandeur of the kingdom at this time and may have been taken from the annals of Solomon (11:41).

Cornill thinks that verse 20 is probably a legendary embellishment, and Driver regards verses 20–26 as a later insertion. Pfeiffer thinks that verses 1–19 and 27ff. are valuable sources, but that verses 22ff. and 26 are misplaced notices in a Deuteronomistic section, 4:20–26. But there is no reason why 4:20–26 should not be regarded as parts of the original narrative.

5. 5:1–7:51. The building of the Temple. Hiram of Tyre provides timber for the Temple, and the building commences. With the erection of the House of God, the people obtain a central place of worship, and Israel's early stage of dwelling in the promised land has come to an end. The promise made to David in 2 Samuel 7:10 has now been fulfilled. The event is solemnized by identifying it not only with the year of Solomon's reign but also by stating how many years had elapsed since the exodus from Egypt (6:1).

6. 8:1–66. The dedication of the Temple. (i) Verses 1–21. The removal of the furniture of the old Tabernacle into the new Temple. (ii) Verses 22–61. Solomon's prayer. In verses 23–53 Solomon prays, and in verses 54–61 he offers a blessing. This noble prayer is based upon Moses' words in Leviticus 26 and Deuteronomy 28. In fact, Haevernick is correct when he says that the language is 'only to be read and explained by the constant aid of the Pentateuch'. (iii) Verses 62–66. The offering of sacrifice.

There is no reason for denying this beautiful prayer to Solomon. It reveals a profound theology, based upon a reverent and intimate knowledge of the written Law. That such profound theology is too advanced for Solomon's day is a view which can appeal only to those who believe in a theory of the development of Israel's religion along lines of naturalistic evolution, a position for which there is no supporting evidence.

Verses 44–52 are said by some to contain a specific reference to the exile, and so cannot be from Solomon. However, there is no such specific reference, but rather a discussion of general principles. Even if Israel is far from Jerusalem and prays, then Solomon beseeches the Lord to hearken unto her.

7. 9:1–28. God makes a covenant with Solomon. Further remarks about Solomon's buildings and reign.

8. 10:1–29. The visit of the Queen of Sheba.

9. 11:1–43. The end of Solomon's reign; his sins and punishmen
Solomon's death.

The nature of the theocracy was peace, and the visible manifestatic
of the theocracy was the Temple. It was entirely fitting therefore that t**
Temple should have been constructed by Solomon (*Shelomo*), who:
name indicates the peace of his reign. The picture of Solomon which
given in Kings is straightforward and accurate, and the fact of t**
magnificence of his kingdom is being corroborated more and mo:
through archaeological discoveries.

Pfeiffer maintains that the Deuteronomic author admired Solomon**
building of the Temple but resented his violations of the Deuteronom**
law. He therefore rearranged the narratives of Solomon's wisdom ar.
magnificence so as to bring out the central importance of the Temp**
and then gave the account of the king's idolatry to point out his mor**
that punishment follows sin. He thus is said to give the reader t**
erroneous impression that Solomon first served the Lord in prosperit**
but later forsook God and suffered reverses (p. 389).

This theory, however, is based upon a certain preconceived vie**
namely, that the alleged Deuteronomist author has written a colour**
history. For this there is no real evidence. Rather, the picture of Solom**
is psychologically accurate. It is easily understandable that one who w**
thus entrusted with great wealth should take to himself many wives a**
turn his heart from Jehovah.

In the Hebrew text there are some secondary corruptions, whi**
appear particularly in the copying of numbers, but these do not affe**
the total picture of Solomon's reign which is given.[2]

b. 1 Kings 12:1–2 Kings 17:41. The divided monarchy
It is very difficult to determine the exact chronology of this period. T**
year in which each king began to reign is stated in relation to t**
reigning king in the opposite kingdom (*e.g.*, 15:1; 15:9; *etc.*), and wh**
the full numbers are compared, they do not always synchronize. T**
difficulty is one that we are not able completely to resolve.

It may be noted that with the aid of Assyrio-Babylonian literature
reliable chronology for many of the biblical events can be obtained. **
know, too, that in the Scriptures an uncompleted year was count**
either as the first year or as the last year of one king and the first ye**
of his successor (*i.e.*, twice). Furthermore, unless there is clear eviden**
of error in textual transmission, the numbers of the Scriptures are

[2] For the archaeological background of this period see Albright, *APB*, pp. 45–**
Jack Finegan, *LAP*, pp. 150–153; Nelson Glueck, *OSJ*.

be accepted as authentic. The difficulties are comparatively minor.

The dates of the kings as given below should be regarded as approximate, although they are fairly widely accepted at present.[3]

1. 12:1–16:28. The period of hostility between the two kingdoms.

(i) 12:1–14:20 (*cf.* 2 Ch. 10:1–11:4). The revolt of the ten tribes. Rehoboam forsakes the counsel of the old advisers, and answers the northern tribes harshly. As a result, Israel under Jeroboam rebels, verses 1–20; Shemaiah commands Rehoboam not to fight Israel, verses 21–24; the kingdom of Israel is founded; a man of God prophesies against the calf-worship introduced by Jeroboam, 13:1–34; Ahijah predicts the destruction of Jeroboam's family, 14:1–20.

According to Cornill, 12:1–20 draws a false picture of Rehoboam, and it also shows literary dependence upon 2 Samuel 20 (*e.g.*, *cf.* 1 Ki. 12:16 with 2 Sa. 20:1). He concludes, therefore, that it is of Ephraimitic origin. Chapter 13, he thinks, is a late production, bearing the same style as the miraculous stories in Chronicles and Daniel. This type of argument, however, is based upon groundless conjecture. There is no reason for doubting the correctness of the representation made of Rehoboam. As a punishment for Solomon's idolatry, God had determined to separate the ten tribes from the sovereignty of David's house. But this does not preclude the fact that Rehoboam's conduct was imprudent or that the ten tribes sinned in acting as they did. Jeroboam is known as the man who made Israel to sin (1 Ki. 14:16). Again, the fact that 2 Kings 12:1–20 may exhibit literary affinities with 2 Samuel 20 proves nothing as to authorship. Why may not the Israelites in their rebellion have employed words similar to those which were used by the Benjamite Sheba in his proclamation of rebellion (2 Sa. 20:1)? Does not the use of these words show that the real cause of the rebellion was not so much the supposed oppression of Solomon as it was the ancient and deep-seated aversion to and jealousy of Judah, which sprang from the basically untheocratic attitude of the northern tribes? Lastly, Cornill's attitude towards chapter 13 will not appeal to those who have not ruled out the supernatural from the pages of Scripture.

Driver thinks he finds an anachronism in 14:9 in the words 'all that were before thee'. But these words do not imply the existence of previous Israelitish kings. It is simply a general phrase to stress the wickedness of Jeroboam. Those who preceded him were probably elders and judges.

In discussing the divided monarchy the author combines the accounts

---

[3] For a thorough discussion of the Hebrew chronology and a solution which covers most of the difficulties, see Edwin R. Thiele, *The Mysterious Numbers of the Hebrew Kings* (1951).

of the two kingdoms, reverting from one to the other. The reigns are introduced and concluded with certain formulae. Thus:

Judah	Israel

1. The year of accession is synchronized with the reign of the king in the other kingdom, *e.g.*, 1 Kings 15:1 (for Judah); 1 Kings 15:25 (for Israel). In the case of Nadab (1 Ki. 15:28) and Elah (1 Ki. 16:10), the synchronized date of death is also given.

INTRODUCTION

Judah	Israel
2. The age of the king at his accession is next given, *e.g.*, 2 Kings 18:2. This is omitted in the case of Abijam and Asa.	2. The length of the reign is stated. The royal residence is also given, except for Jeroboam I and Nadab. This was Tirza, until Omri founded Samaria.
3. The length of the reign is stated, *e.g.*, 1 Kings 15:2.	3. Each king (except Shallum) is formally condemned, and reference is made to Shallum's conspiracy. Hence, he also is to be regarded as an evil king.
4. The name of the king's mother is given, *e.g.*, 1 Kings 15:2b. This is omitted in the case of Jehoram (2 Ki. 8:17) and Ahaz (2 Ki. 16:2).	4. The king's father is mentioned, *e.g.*, 1 Kings 15:25. This is omitted in the case of Zimri and Omri.
5. Judgment is passed upon the king's reign, *e.g.*, 2 Kings 18:3ff.	5. No stereotyped introduction is used for Jehu.

CONCLUSION

Judah	Israel
1. A concluding statement, *e.g.*, 'Now the rest of the acts of Rehoboam, and all that he did, are they not written in the book of the chronicles of the kings of Judah?' (1 Ki. 14:29).	1. A concluding statement, *e.g.*, 'And the rest of the acts of Jeroboam, how he warred, and how he reigned, behold, they are written in the book of the chronicles of the kings of Israel' (1 Ki. 14:19).

THE BOOKS OF KINGS

2. Generally there appears a statement of the king's death, 'And Rehoboam slept with his fathers, and was buried with his fathers in the city of David' (1 Ki. 14:31a). The words 'and he slept', are omitted, however, if the king died a violent death, e.g., Joash (2 Ki. 12:21). Also, in the case of Hezekiah, Josiah, and Jehoiachin, mention of the place of burial is omitted.

2. Generally a statement of the king's death, 'And he slept with his fathers.'

3. Then follows the statement, 'And his son reigned in his stead.'

3. Unless the king was followed by a usurper, it is stated that his son reigned in his stead.

Regarding Joash, two conclusions are given: 2 Kings 13:12, 13 and 2 Kings 14:15, 16. Regarding Ahaziah, Jehoahaz, Jehoiachin, Zedekiah, the conclusions are omitted entirely.

(ii) 14:21–31. Rehoboam's reign (cf. 2 Ch. 11:5–12:16). In the fifth year of Rehoboam's reign, Shishak (Sheshonk I, founder of the 22nd Dynasty) plundered Jerusalem and took the treasures of the Temple.

(iii) 15:1–24. Abijam and Asa of Judah.

(iv) 15:25–32. Nadab of Israel.

(v) 15:33–16:7. Baasha of Israel.

(vi) 16:8–14. Elah of Israel.

(vii) 16:15–22. Zimri of Israel.

(viii) 16:23–28. Omri of Israel. Omri established the capital of Israel at Samaria, and politically became one of the greatest of Israel's kings. Religiously, however, he continued the apostasy.

2. 1 Kings 16:29 – 2 Kings 10:36. A period of peace between the two kingdoms. This period extends from the reign of Ahab to the deaths of Joram of Israel and Ahaziah of Judah. During this period the kingdom of Judah recedes into the background, and the Scripture places its stress upon the kingdom of Israel. The reason for this is clear. Jehoshaphat's son had married Ahab's daughter, and Judah had taken Israel's part in struggles against Syria. But, above all, Jezebel had introduced the Tyrian Baal-worship into the land, and there ensued a life-and-death struggle between this heathenish idolatry and the pure worship of

Jehovah. Hence, at this time, God raised up the prophets Elijah and Elisha. This is the second great period of miracles in biblical history. The prophets, performing miracles in the name of Jehovah, were by God's grace enabled to prevent the Baal-worship from becoming the dominant state religion in Israel.

(i) 16:29–22:40. The reign of Ahab. The reign introduces a turning-point in Israel's history, for, not only did Ahab continue in the sin of Jeroboam, but he also raised the Tyrian Baal-worship to supremacy in Israel, and built in Samaria a temple and altar to Baal. Furthermore, he wished to persecute those who would not give up Jehovah for Baal. The apostasy from Jehovah became formal and official. The Lord, therefore, must intervene, and Elijah, His messenger, appears upon the scene. Elijah may be regarded as a second Moses, one in whom the prophetic power culminated. He is zealous for the law and the honour of God, and, like Moses, performs miracles. But he also serves as a model of that great Prophet whom Moses had predicted (Dt. 18:15), the One in whom both the Law and the Prophets would be fulfilled. 'His non-Israelitish ex-traction, his sojourn at Zarephath, bringing a blessing to the pious heathen woman, and several other things, point to the time when the Lord also will cause the heathen to partake in the blessings of the King-dom of God; and the raising of the dead child of the widow performed by him, as well as his ascent into heaven, are types of the raising of the dead and the ascension into heaven of Christ, before whose coming the spirit of Elijah was revived in John the Baptist' (Keil).

(ii) 22:41–51. Jehoshaphat of Judah (cf. 2 Ch. 17:1–21:3). He made peace with Ahab, gave his son Joram to Ahab's daughter Athaliah in marriage, and joined Ahab in war against Syria.

(iii) 22:52 – 2 Kings 2:25. Ahaziah of Israel. His reign resembled that of his father Ahab. Elijah (2 Ki. 2) is taken to heaven.

(iv) 2 Kings 3:1–8:15. Jehoram of Israel. Jehoram removed the pillar of Baal from Samaria. With Jehoshaphat he undertook an expedition against the rebellious Moabites. At this time occurs the ministry of Elisha. Elijah's influence is to be seen in the fact that Jehoram caused the Tyrian Baal-worship to cease as a state religion. It is also to be seen in the schools of the prophets (bene hannevi'im), which he founded for the purpose of religious and intellectual training to call the nation back to the Lord.

The miracles of Elisha, included in this section, are evidently arranged according to their nature rather than in a strictly chronological order. On the whole, the miracles performed for individuals and the schools of the prophets are related first and those for the king and nation last. The wondrous healing of Naaman, a foreigner, intervenes as a connecting link between the two.

Critics of the negative school are not at one in evaluating the relationship between Elijah and Elisha. They object to the supernatural element in the narratives and they seem agreed in maintaining that the Elisha narratives present not so much a history of Elisha as a number of anecdotes. In reply we would urge that this is indeed the case. The author selects incidents from the ministry of Elisha to show how through him God was at work in such crucial times.

(v) 8:16–24 (*cf.* 2 Ch. 21:2–20). Jehoram of Judah. He introduced the idolatries of Ahab into Judah. During his reign Edom and Libnah. (Jos. 15:42) revolted.

(vi) 8:25–29. Ahaziah of Judah.

(vii) 9:1–10:36. Jehu of Israel. This man utterly exterminates the Baal-worship of Ahab and Jezebel. Hosea (1:4, 5) condemns the bloodthirsty manner of Jehu, and this is in harmony with the present representation in Kings. The author relates vividly Jehu's bloodthirsty deeds. He is commended in so far as he obeyed the Lord (10:30), but he is condemned because his obedience was not complete (10:29, 31). Jehu was the type of man who would obey God in the manner most pleasing to himself.

3. 11:1–17:41. Renewed hostilities between the two kingdoms. The ministries of Elijah and Elisha were successful in bringing about the removal of the foreign idolatries. Israel, however, then sank back to where she had been before. Through Ahaz of Judah, the Syrian idolatry was brought even into Jerusalem. When Israel and Syria opposed Ahaz, he sought the help of Assyria. Thus, this great nation came into contact with Palestine, and in 722 BC Israel fell before her.

(i) 11:1–21. Athalia usurps the throne of Judah.

(ii) 12:1–21. Joash of Judah repairs the Temple.

(iii) 13:1–9. Jehoahaz of Israel. For a time Israel was captured by Syria.

(iv) 13:10–25. Jehoash of Israel recovered from Syria some of the cities which had been taken from his father.

(v) 14:1–22. Amaziah of Judah.

(vi) 14:23–29. Jeroboam II of Israel. During this reign Israel reached great material power and prosperity.

(vii) 15:1–7. Uzziah of Judah. Judah also at this time was outwardly prosperous.

(viii) 15:8–12. Zechariah of Israel.

(ix) 15:13–16. Shallum of Israel.

(x) 15:17–22. Menahem of Israel pays tribute to Tiglath-Pileser III (745–727 BC).

(xi) 15:23–26. Pekahiah of Israel.

(xii) 15:27–31. Pekah of Israel becomes an ally of Syria against Judah. Tiglath-Pileser invades northern Palestine and takes Naphtali captive.

(xiii) 15:32–38. Jotham of Judah.

(xiv) 16:1–20. Ahaz of Judah seeks the aid of Tiglath-Pileser III against Israel and Syria.

(xv) 17:1–41. Hoshea, the last king of Israel. The Assyrians besiege Samaria and take Israel captive.

c. 2 Kings 18:1–25:30. The kingdom of Judah to the captivity

1. 18:1–20:21. Hezekiah of Judah. Summary of Hezekiah's reign; its beginning, duration and general character, 18:1–8; the destruction of Israel by Shalmanezer, 18:9–12; from 18:13 to 19:37 the narrative of Sennacherib's invasion of Judah. This account is repeated almost verbatim in Isaiah 36 and 37 and is summarized, with some additional material, in 2 Chronicles 32. The original is the account in Isaiah, and upon this the accounts both in Kings and in Chronicles are based.[4] The historicity of the scriptural account is confirmed by the discovery of Sennacherib's own narrative of his conquest in Palestine. He relates that he conquered forty-six fenced cities of Judah, and carried away 200,150 inhabitants. As to Hezekiah, he says, 'Himself, like a caged bird [*kima issur ku-up-pi*] in the midst of Jerusalem his capital [*al sharru-ti-shu*] I shut up.'[5]

Hezekiah's sickness and recovery are related in 20:1–11; the arrival of the embassy from Merodach-Baladan in 20:12–19. These two events are also related in Isaiah 38 and 39. In Isaiah 38, however, the account of Hezekiah's sickness is followed by his song of praise upon his recovery (Is. 28:9–22). The account of Hezekiah's death follows in 2 Kings 20:20, 21.

2. 21:1–18. Manasseh. At this time those who were antitheocratic in principle gained power, with the result that pagan idolatry now flourished as never before.

3. 21:19–26. Amon. This king continued the idolatry of Manasseh, and was murdered during the second year of his reign.

---

[4] For the view that the account in Kings is original, see *LOT*[8], pp. 226–227.

[5] For literature on Sennacherib's invasion, see Daniel David Luckenbill, *The Annals of Sennacherib* (1924). This work contains the text and translation, and will serve as an introduction to the subject as well as to the royal Assyrian inscriptions generally.

TABULAR VIEW OF THE MONARCHY

e undivided monarchy (*approximate dates*): Saul 1050–1013; David 1013–973; Solomón 973–933

THE DIVIDED MONARCHY

JUDAH	ISRAEL	CHAPTER IN KINGS	PROPHETS	EGYPT (E) and BABYLONIA (B)	ASSYRIA
ehoboam 933–917	Jeroboam 933–912	12–15	Ahijah-Shemaiah	Sheshonk I c. 924 (E)	Adad-Nirari II 911–890
Abijam 916–914	Nadab 912–911	15			
Asa 913–873	Baasha 911–888	15	Jehu		Tukulti-Ninib II 889–884
	Elah 888–887	16			
	Zimri 887				
	Tibni *887–883				Assurnasirabal II 883–860
	Omri 887 (883) 877				
oshaphat 873–849	Ahab 876–854	16–22	Micaiah-Elijah		Shalmanezer III 859–824
	Ahaziah 854–853	2 Ki. 1	Elisha		(Battle of Karkar 854)
ehoram 849–842	Jehoram 853–842	3			
Ahaziah 842	Jehu 842–815	8			Shamshi-Adad V 823–811
Athaliah 842–836		9–12			
ehoash 836–797	Jehoahaz 814–798	13	Joel (?)		Adad-Nirari III 810–782
Amaziah 797–779	Jehoash 798–783	14			
	Jeroboam II 783–743				Shalmanezer IV 781–772
			Amos		Assurdan III 771–754
			Amos		Assur-Nirari II 753–746
Uzziah 779–740	Zechariah 743	15	Amos-Isaiah-Hosea		
	Shallum 743	15	Amos-Isaiah-Hosea		
otham 740–736	Menahem 743–737 (paid tribute to Assyria 738)	15	Isaiah-Micah-Hosea		Tiglath-Pileser III 745–727
			Jonah		
Ahaz 736–728	Pekahiah 737–736	16	Isaiah-Micah-Hosea-Jonah		
	Pekah 736–730	16	Isaiah-Micah-Hosea		
ezekiah 727–699	Hoshea 730–722	17–20	Isaiah-Micah-Hosea		Shalmanezer V 726–722
	(Fall of Israel 722)	20			
nacherib invaded alestine 701)					Sargon II 721–705
					Sennacherib 704–681
Manasseh 698–643		21	Obadiah (?)		Essarhadon 680–669
Amon 643–641		21	Nahum (?)		Assurbanipal 668–626
osiah 640–609		22–23	Jeremiah	Nabopolassar 625–605 (B)	Assuritililani 625–620
Jehoahaz 609		23	Jeremiah-Zephaniah		Sinshariskun 619–612 (Fall of Nineveh 612)
			Habakkuk (?)		Assur-Uballit II 611–609
eholakim 609–598		23–24	Jeremiah-Daniel	Pharaoh-Necho 609–594 (E)	
				Nebuchadnezzar 605–562 (B)	
Jehoiachin 598		24	Jeremiah-Daniel		
Zedekiah 598–587		24–25	Jeremiah-Daniel-Ezekiel		
l of Jerusalem 586)					
Gedaliah 587		25	Jeremiah-Daniel-Ezekiel		
		25	.	Evil-Merodach 561–560 (B)	

THE EXILE

cording to I Kings 16:21, 22, the people were divided between Tibni and Omri. In the 31st year of Asa, Omri prevailed, 'So Tibni died, and Omri gned.'

4. 22:1–23:30. Josiah. Characterization of the reign, 22:1, 2; the discovery of the Book of the Law during the eighteenth year of Josiah's reign, 22:3–20. This Book of the Law was the entire Pentateuch and not merely Deuteronomy. This would be an official copy of the Law, namely, that which belonged to the Temple itself and had been deposited beside the Ark in the Holy of Holies. The newly-found Law is read in the Temple, and the covenant is renewed, 23:1–3; the destruction of idolatry and celebration of the Passover, 23:4–24; the close of Josiah's reign, 23:25–30.

Some scholars think that in this section the Deuteronomic editors have naturally shown particular interest. But the account of Josiah is compact and straightforward, and there is every reason to believe that it is true to fact. If this section were a free creation, intended to exalt the 'Deuteronomic code', it is passing strange that sections such as 23:26, 27 should have been allowed to remain. These verses are clearly evidences of genuineness.

5. 23:31–35. Jehoahaz. This man reigned for three months, and then was taken to Egypt. (Cf. Je. 22:10–12, where we learn that Jehoahaz was also called Shallum.)

6. 23:36–24:7. Jehoiakim, or Eliakim. During this time (605 BC) Nebuchadnezzar first attacked Jerusalem, and Daniel was carried captive.[6]

7. 24:8–17. Jehoiachin, or Jechoniah, or Coniah. He reigned three months, and then was deposed to Babylon.

8. 24:18–25:26. Zedekiah and Gedaliah. This section is paralleled almost verbatim in Jeremiah 52, except that in Jeremiah the account of the murder of Gedaliah and the flight of the people to Egypt is omitted, but a statement of those whom Nebuchadnezzar carried into Babylon is inserted. Both the passage in Jeremiah and its parallel in Kings are best regarded as abstracts made from an original larger source (see discussion under Jeremiah).

9. 25:27–30. The last days of Jehoiachin. In the first year of his reign Evil-Merodach released Jehoiachin from prison. Thus was accomplished the divine purpose that David's royal line, although at times cast low, should never be utterly rejected (2 Sa. 7:14, 15 and also Gn. 49:10).

SPECIAL LITERATURE ON KINGS

Joachim Begrich, *Die Chronologie der Könige von Israel und Juda* (Tübingen, 1929); Immanuel Benzinger, *Jahvist und Elohist in den Königsbüchern* (Stuttgart, 1921); C. F. Burney, *Notes on the Hebrew Text of the Book of Kings* (Oxford, 1903); Johannes de Groot,

[6] For a discussion of the chronology of these events, see my *CD* (1949), pp. 295–297.

Die Altäre des salomonischen Tempelhofes (Stuttgart, 1924); Leo L. Honor, *Sennacherib's Invasion of Palestine* (New York, 1926); Ehrhard Junge, *Der Wiederaufbau des Heerwesens des Reiches Juda unter Josia* (Stuttgart, 1937); Erich Klamroth, *Lade und Tempel* (Guetersloh, 1932); Julius Lewy, *Die Chronologie der Könige von Israel und Juda* (Giessen, 1927); W. Milligan, *Elijah: His Life and Times** (New York, n.d.); Ernst Modersohn, *De Profeet Elisa** (Kampen, n.d.); Kurt Moehlenbrink, *Der Tempel Salomos* (Stuttgart, 1932); Sigmund Mowinckel, *Die Chronologie des israelitischen und jüdischen Könige* (Leiden, 1932); Otto Procksch, *König und Prophet in Israel* (Greifswald, 1924); D. W. B. Robinson, *Josiah's Reform and the Book of the Law* (London, 1951); Martin Thilo, *In welchem Jahre geschah die sog. syrisch-efraimitische Invasion und wann bestieg Hiskia den Thron?* (Barmen, 1918).

CHAPTER FOURTEEN

ISAIAH

NAME

THE book is named after the prophet himself. In the title the name appears as *yesha'yah* (also in *Baba Bathra* 14b). In the text of the prophecy, however, and elsewhere in the Old Testament, it occurs in a longer form, *yesha'yahu*, although the shorter form does occur (*cf.* 1 Ch. 3:21; Ezr. 8:7, 19; Ne. 11:7). This name may be a compound of *yesha'* (salvation), and *yahu* (Jehovah). Hence, it probably means, 'The Lord is salvation'. In the LXX the name is Hesaias, and the Latin has Esaias or Isaias.

AUTHOR

The question of the authorship of the prophecy of Isaiah is one that is widely discussed by modern scholarship. The position adopted in this book is that Isaiah himself wrote the entire prophecy, and the reasons for this position will shortly be given. In order to appreciate the nature and importance of the problem, it will be necessary briefly to survey the history of the literary criticism of the book.

1. The Talmud. *Baba Bathra* 15a states, 'Hezekiah and his company wrote Isaiah, Proverbs, the Song of Songs and Ecclesiastes.' What is the explanation of this statement? The context makes it clear that the verb 'wrote' (*ktb*) has a wide meaning, and evidently is employed in the sense of 'edited' or 'published'. Also, the phrase 'Hezekiah and his company' is evidently to be taken as referring to contemporaries of Hezekiah who outlived him, hence, equivalent to the expression 'men of Hezekiah' in Proverbs 25:1. According to the Talmud, therefore, the Isaianic authorship of the prophecy is not denied at all; only the collection of the prophecies is attributed to the company of Hezekiah.

Nor does the arrangement of the prophecies in *Baba Bathra* 14b in any sense deny Isaianic authorship. For we have already noted[1] the theological reason for this classification. Furthermore, the intention was

---

[1] See above, pp. 158f.

evidently to connect Jeremiah and Ezekiel as contemporaries on the one hand, and Isaiah and the Twelve as contemporaries (at least some of the Twelve) on the other. For the actual language of the passage is, 'Jeremiah and Ezekiel; Isaiah and the Twelve'.

2. Moses ben Samuel Ibn-Gekatilla (c. AD 110). This scholar is known from references to his commentaries in the works of Ibn Ezra. Apparently he regarded the prophecies in the first part of Isaiah as belonging to the time of Hezekiah. Those in the second part he assigned to the period of the second Temple. Ibn Ezra himself[2] wrote a brilliant commentary on Isaiah in which he denied the Isaianic authorship of chapters 40–66.

3. The period of modern destructive criticism. This period begins in 1780, twenty-seven years after the appearance of Astruc's book. About that year J. B. Koppe, in the German edition of Lowth's commentary, suggested in a note that chapter 50 might have been the work of Ezekiel or of someone else who lived at the time of the exile. In 1789 appeared the commentary of Doederlein, in which the Isaianic authorship of 40–66 was denied. Eichhorn made the same denial. Rosenmueller pointed out that if Isaiah was not the author of 40–66 he also could not have written the prophecies which deal with Babylon in the first part of the book.

For a time it was held that 40–66 were the work of many authors. There were also those who asserted the unity of these chapters, but denied their authorship to Isaiah. Such was Wilhelm Gesenius, who produced a strong defence of the unity of these chapters. He maintained[3] that the chapters were the product of an unnamed prophet who lived near the close of the exile.

During the nineteenth century, scholarship was basically divided into two groups. On the one hand, there were those who denied that Isaiah was the author of the entire prophecy. Chapters 40–66, at least, were attributed to the time of the exile, and were generally regarded as the work of a great unknown, the so-called 'Second Isaiah', hailed by some as the first proclaimer of true monotheism. The negative view was popularized in 1889 by George Adam Smith, whose lectures on Isaiah have passed through many editions and have exerted a tremendous influence throughout the English-speaking world. On the other hand, there were those who maintained the Isaianic authorship of the entire prophecy. Such were Moritz Drechsler, Carl Paul Caspari, H. A. Hahn,

---

[2] See p. 114.
[3] *Commentar*, II (1819).

Rudolph Stier, Franz Delitzsch (who later modified somewhat his opinion) and Joseph Addison Alexander. In the hands of these men the exegesis of Isaiah reached its greatest heights.

4. The school of Bernhard Duhm. In 1892 Duhm, Professor of theology at Basel, issued a commentary which proved to have a revolutionary influence in the study of Isaiah. Duhm maintained that there were three important steps in the compilation of Isaiah: the collection of 1–12 and 13–23, the uniting of the groups 1–12, 13–23, 24–35, and their completion through the addition of 36–39, and finally, the addition of 40–66. Each of these steps in the compilation is not necessarily to be regarded as the work of one man. Rather, each step may in itself have had a long history, and the final redactor probably lived about the first century BC. This late date is disproved by the discovery (1947) of the Qumran Scroll of Isaiah, which may possibly antedate the first century BC.

Of particular importance is the fact that Duhm restricted the compass of Second Isaiah to 40–55, and these chapters, with the exception of the famous 'Servant' passages, were thought by him to have been written by one who lived about 540 BC, not in Babylonia, but probably in the Lebanon or in northern Phoenicia. As for 55–66 Duhm declared that they were composed by someone who probably lived in Jerusalem just before the time of Nehemiah's activity. This unknown author Duhm would designate as 'Trito-Isaiah'. Basically, therefore, we have an Isaiah, a Second Isaiah and a Third Isaiah. This threefold division came to underly much subsequent study of the prophecy and, for the most part, the noble work of Isaiah was regarded as 'a little library of prophetical literature' (Marti).

5. The 'History of Tradition' school. Basic to this position is the assumption that the literature of the Hebrews fell into types and that each of these is clearly distinguished by certain characteristics. Each type exhibited certain introductory and concluding formulae, characteristic thoughts, and also some function in the life of the people. The original form of the prophetic utterance was the spoken word.[4] The influence of the study of comparative religion has often led the adherents of form-criticism to exhibit a correct exegetical insight that was lacking in some who wrote from the standpoint of the older liberalism.

6. Torrey's 'Second Isaiah'. In 1928 there was published a work by Charles Cutler Torrey of Yale, entitled *The Second Isaiah*. Torrey maintains that chapters 34–66 (with the exception of 36–39) were all the

---

[4] See p. 158.

work of one author who lived in Palestine. Torrey regards the two occurrences of the word 'Cyrus' and the words 'Babylon' and 'Chaldea' as interpolations which should be removed from the text. In Torrey's work we have a strong argument for the unity of 40–66 and also for Palestine as the place of its composition.

7. The work of Karl Elliger. Karl Elliger has written three important books on Isaiah. He has sought to defend the position that chapters 56–66 are from the hand of one author who lived towards the close of the sixth century BC, an author about whom we may learn something, and one who also composed the famous passage 52:13–53:12 and whose hand is found not only in the other 'Servant' passages but also elsewhere in 40–55.

The above sketch of the course of literary criticism has been based upon three articles in the author's *Studies in Isaiah* (1954). In this work an attempt has been made to trace in detail the course of literary criticism with respect to Isaiah from the time of Joseph Addison Alexander until the present. This work is intended to serve as an introduction to the study of the prophecy.

In the light of the long course of literary criticism, the present writer finds himself unable to accept the positions of the modern school. The viewpoint adopted in this book is that Isaiah the son of Amoz is the author of the entire prophecy. The reasons for accepting this position are the following:

1. In the New Testament Isaiah is quoted more than all the other prophets together, and this is done in such a way as to leave no room for doubt that, in the eyes of the New Testament, Isaiah was the author of the entire prophecy. In John 12:38 it is stated that despite the miracles which Jesus had performed, the people did not believe in Him, in order that 'the word of Isaiah the prophet' might be fulfilled. Then follows a quotation from Isaiah 53:1. This is followed by an explanation (verse 39) why the people did not believe, and this explanation is a quotation of Isaiah 6:9 ('Isaiah said again'). Then follows the remarkable statement. 'These things [*i.e.*, the quotations from both "second" and "first" Isaiah] said Isaiah, when he saw his glory and spoke concerning him' (verse 41). Thus in John 12:38–41 quotations are made from both parts of Isaiah and are attributed to the *man* Isaiah as author.

In Romans 9:27–33 Paul makes abundant use of Isaiah's prophecy. In verse 27 he says, 'Isaiah cries concerning Israel'. It is, according to Paul, *the prophet himself* who proclaimed this message, and his proclamation is described as crying. Next follows a quotation from Isaiah 10. A quotation from Isaiah 1:9 is then introduced with the words, 'And just as Isaiah had said before'. In verse 32 Paul uses the language of Isaiah 8:14 (in part) and in verse 33 he quotes Isaiah 28:16.

In Romans 10:16–21 Paul introduces the section with the words 'As it is written' (verse 15a), and this is followed by a quotation of Isaiah 52:7a. In verse 16 occur the words 'Isaiah says', and this is followed by a quotation of Isaiah 53:1. Then comes the statement 'Isaiah becomes bold and says', and a quotation from Isaiah 65:1. A quotation from Isaiah 65:2 is then introduced by the words 'he says'. This passage in Romans is instructive to show how Paul regarded the connection between Isaiah 52 and 53. At this point the New Testament refutes the idea that Isaiah 53 has no connection with what precedes it.

SUMMARY OF THE NEW TESTAMENT EVIDENCE
(Quotations from Isaiah by name)

NEW TESTAMENT PASSAGE	MANNER OF INTRODUCING QUOTATION	PASSAGE QUOTED	SOURCE OF QUOTATION
Mt. 3: 3	the prophet Isaiah	40: 3	II
Mt. 8:17	Isaiah the prophet	53: 4	II (III)
Mt. 12:17	Isaiah the prophet	42: 1	II
Mt. 13:14	the prophecy of Isaiah	6: 9, 10	I
Mt. 15: 7	Isaiah prophesied	29:13	I
Mk. 1: 2	in Isaiah the prophet	40: 3	II
Mk. 7: 6	Isaiah prophesied	29:13	I
Lk. 3: 4	in the book of the words of Isaiah the prophet	40: 3–5	II
Lk. 4:17	the book of the prophet Isaiah	61: 1, 2	III
Jn. 1:23	the prophet Isaiah	40: 3	II
Jn. 12:38	Isaiah the prophet	53: 1	II (III)
Jn. 12:39	Isaiah said again	6: 9, 10	I
Jn. 12:41	Isaiah – said – saw – spake	53: 1; 6:9, 10	I, II
Acts 8:28	reading Isaiah the prophet	53: 7–8	II (III)
Acts 8:30	reading the prophet Isaiah	53: 7–8	II (III)
Acts 8:32[6]	the passage of the scripture	53: 7–8	II (III)
Acts 28:25	Well spake the Holy Ghost through Isaiah the prophet[7]	6: 9, 10	I
Rom. 9:27	Isaiah cries	10:22, 23	I
Rom. 9:29[8]	As Isaiah said before	1: 9	I
Rom. 10:16	Isaiah says	53: 1	II (III)
Rom. 10:20	Isaiah becomes bold and says	65: 1	III

[5] *I.e.* whether in the alleged First, Second, or Third Isaiah, denoted by I, II, and III respectively.

[6] Note that the background of this incident illustrates and fulfils Is. 56:3–7, III.

[7] What a matchless statement of the biblical doctrine of verbal inspiration!

[8] Rom. 9 and 10 contain many allusions to, and echoes of, the language of Isaiah.

The nature of these quotations and the manner in which Isaianic language appears in the New Testament make it clear that the entire book was before the inspired writers of the New Testament and that they regarded it as the word of the prophet Isaiah. To every Christian believer this testimony of the New Testament should be decisive.

2. The tradition of Isaianic authorship appears as early as Ecclesiasticus. In 49:17–25 we read, 'He [*i.e.*, Isaiah] comforted them that mourned in Zion. He shewed the things that should be to the end of the time, and the hidden things or ever they came.' In speaking of Isaiah's comforting those that mourned in Zion (not, incidentally, in Babylon), the translation of Ben Sira employs the same Greek word for comfort (*parakalein*) that is used in the LXX of Isaiah 40:1 and 61:1, 2. So also does the Hebrew original employ the same word (*wayyinnahem*) as does Isaiah. It should be noted that this is the first appearance of any tradition concerning the authorship of Isaiah, and this first appearance of such tradition ascribes the work to Isaiah. Not a word is said of any 'prophet of the exile'. Thus, the so-called 'greatest' of Israel's prophets, the alleged 'Second Isaiah', is unknown to Ecclesiasticus. And if anyone was interested in the great prophets, it was Ben Sira. On the other hand, he does speak of 'Isaiah the prophet', 'who was great and faithful in his vision', 'who saw by the spirit of might'. Such language, based upon Isaiah 11:2, indicates the highest of praise. This also raises a problem.

If 'Second Isaiah' was so great, the greatest of the prophets according to some, a man who supposedly presented the most exalted doctrine of God which the world had ever witnessed, why had he dwindled so rapidly in stature that by the time of Ecclesiasticus his stature had disappeared entirely? On the other hand, why did the stature of the eighth-century Isaiah who, according to criticism, was by no means the greatest of the prophets, grow so tremendously that Ecclesiasticus would give to him such high praise? This is a phenomenon without parallel in the history of literature, and those who deny the Isaianic authorship must provide an explanation.

3. The heading of the prophecy (1:1) is intended to stand for the entire book. This heading describes the book as a vision (*hazon*) of Isaiah the son of Amoz, having to do with Judah and specially Jerusalem, and having been seen at a specific time. This title was probably added by Isaiah himself. If it was the work of later editors, then the question arises, What led them to be so definite in attributing the book to Isaiah the son of Amoz?

(i) In his *Geschichte der althebräischen Literatur* (1906, pp. 156–159), Karl Budde maintained that originally Isaiah's writings (1–39) and those of the 'great Unknown' had no relationship with one another. At this time books were divided into the categories of large, medium, and small. (This assumption of Budde's, by the way, is purely gratuitous. There is not one whit of evidence to support it.) The two *large* books, Jeremiah and Ezekiel, were each written on a single roll. The twelve *small* prophecies were also written on one roll. There were two *medium-sized* books, one by Isaiah, and one anonymous (*i.e.*, Isaiah 40–66). These two were written on one roll, with the following order as the result: Jeremiah, Ezekiel, Isaiah, the Twelve. Budde appeals to *Baba Bathra* 14b for evidence. But the theory is utterly without objective support, and it raises several questions. Why was the second *medium* book anonymous? When editors, according to criticism, were placing headings upon every other prophetical book, even one as short as Obadiah, why did they not give a heading to this greatest of all prophecies? And why did editors give to Isaiah 13 the heading, 'The burden of Babylon, which Isaiah the son of Amoz did see'?

(ii) It is often assumed that disciples writing in the spirit of Isaiah would include their own oracles in the collection of his prophecies. Thus, Second Isaiah is said to have been influenced by First, and Third Isaiah to have been influenced by Second. About each there grew up a body of disciples. Later editors incorporated all these utterances under the name Isaiah. This theory, with more or less modification, is probably most widely held today. In answer we would say that it is based upon guess-work and speculation. Furthermore, if the editors collected so many utterances which really were spoken by various persons, and issued them under the name of Isaiah, they did a very dishonest thing. For the heading (1:1) which these editors prefixed to the book is, as we have seen, very specific, and gives the impression that the entire book is the vision which Isaiah the son of Amoz saw concerning specific subjects and at a specific time.

(iii) According to E. J. Kissane, there was, apparently in Babylon, a prophet who had collected all of Isaiah's prophecies now found in 1–34. To these he appended chapters 36–39, and, for the benefit of the exiles, set forth the ideas of Isaiah in his own language. After the course of two centuries some of Isaiah's ideas had lost their appeal, especially his warnings of destruction. Hence, this unknown prophet stressed the prophecies of the return.

But Isaiah 40–66 is far more than a repetition of the earlier teachings of Isaiah. It is rather an expansion and development of some of these teachings. Furthermore, themes are introduced upon which Isaiah 1–39 is silent. In fact, the new ideas stand out so clearly that one would expect the name of the exilic author, rather than that of Isaiah, to adhere to the book. Again, the latter chapters contain denunciation as well as hope. Also, it must be noted that anonymity is contrary to the nature of prophecy. The identity of the prophet had to be known, in order that he be received as an accredited spokesman for the Lord. It was sufficient, in the case of the unnamed prophet who appeared to Eli, that Eli knew his name. But when the prophet *wrote* for the benefit of those with whom he might not have personal contact, it was essential that his identity as a prophet be known in order that his message might be received as the authoritative declaration of an accredited spokesman of the Lord. It is contrary to the whole genius of the biblical teaching to postulate the existence of anonymous writing prophets. The existence of the 'Former Prophets' does not modify the force of this statement.

By way of conclusion, if chapters 40–66 are not by Isaiah, how are we to account for their anonymity and for the fact that the heading attributes them to Isaiah? Negative criticism does not seem to have an appreciation of the tremendous problems which are involved at this point.

4. The author of Isaiah 40–66 was a Palestinian. The author does not show a familiarity with the land or the religion of Babylon such as we might expect from one who dwelt among the captives. But he does speak of Jerusalem and the mountains of Palestine, and he mentions some of the trees that are native to Palestine, *e.g.*, the cedar, cypress, oak (44:14; 41:19). In 43:14 the Lord speaks of sending *to* Babylon, a passage which is clearly addressed to those who are not in Babylon. In 41:9 the prophet addresses Israel as the seed of Abraham which the Lord has taken from the ends of the earth. Such a phrase as 'ends of the earth' could only have been employed by one who was writing in the promised land. The same may be said of 45:22. In 46:11 such phrases as 'from the east' and 'from a far country' are more understandable when spoken from a Palestinian viewpoint than from a Babylonian one. But 52:11 is conclusive. The phrase 'from thence' clearly shows that this passage was not uttered in Babylon.

5. There are passages in chapters 40–66 which do not fit the time of the exile. One or two may be mentioned now; others will be discussed under the subheading Analysis. In 62:6 the walls of Jerusalem are standing. In 40:9 the cities of Judah, as well as Zion, are yet in existence. How could such a passage as this have been penned during the exile? (*Cf.* also 43:6; 48:1–5; *etc.*)

6. If one begins to separate or divide Isaiah, it is impossible to rest with two or even three large divisions. One is compelled to continue analysing and dividing until only a conglomeration of fragments

remains. The history of the literary criticism of Isaiah had shown tha
the end of such divisive processes is really scepticism.

7. The arguments which are generally adduced for refusing to
attribute chapters 40–66 to Isaiah are the following: The name of Isaiah
is not mentioned in these chapters, they do not suit the time of Isaiah
and they are written in a style of Hebrew different from the genuine
prophecies of Isaiah. It is true that Isaiah's name is not mentioned in
40–66, but when one considers the aim of these chapters (see below under
Purpose) it is easily understandable why the name does not appear. With
respect to the claim that 40–66 does not suit the time of Isaiah, it may be
said that the theory which is most free from difficulty is that the aged
Isaiah, under the inspiration of the Holy Spirit, looked forward to the
time when his people should be in bondage and would be freed by a
mighty deliverance (see under Purpose). In other words, when the
purpose of these chapters is taken into consideration, this objection i
seen to be irrelevant. Lastly, the linguistic and stylistic differences are
not as great as is sometimes assumed. The reason for these differences i
to be found in the subject-matter, the prophetic and eschatological
character of the section.

8. There is a unity in the prophecy which is too often overlooked. Ther
are words and expressions common to both parts. Thus, the phrase 'Holy
One of Israel' as a designation of God reflects the great impression made
upon the prophet by the majestic vision seen in the Temple. So indelibl
is this impression that in 1–39 Isaiah uses the phrase twelve times and in
40–66 he employs it fourteen times. Elsewhere in the Old Testament i
occurs only five times. Other words also characterize both portions of the
prophecy, *e.g.*, 'thornbush', 'delusions', 'dross', 'saith the Lord' (*yo'mar*)
(*cf.* also 40:5 with 1:20; 43:13 with 14:27; 65:25 with 11:9; *etc.*). Further
similarities will be pointed out under Analysis. The importance of 36–3
should also not be overlooked. These chapters form a connecting bridg
or link between the earlier Assyrian period and the later Babylonian
They serve as a beautiful introduction to the last great section of the
book.

9. There are passages in Zephaniah, Nahum, Jeremiah, and
Zechariah which seem to reflect upon parts of 40–66 and hence indicat
that the latter portion of Isaiah was in existence when these prophet
wrote. Those who deny the Isaianic authorship of these chapters, how
ever, generally argue, in so far as they notice the point at all, that 40–6
made use of the other prophets. These passages will be discussed unde
Analysis (see also *SI*).

Our purpose in the above sketch has been to set forth in brief compa some of the principal reasons why we believe that Isaiah was the author of the entire book which bears his name (for the entire book, as it now stands, does bear his name). We are impressed with the fact that negative criticism, having denied to Isaiah the authorship of the entire book, has been unable to come to agreement as to who the author was. Of course, what settles the question is the unequivocal testimony of the New Testament. But we believe also that when the purpose of the entire book is taken into consideration, it will be seen that the theory which is most free from difficulty is that which posits Isaiah as the author of 40–66. We plan to set forth the purpose of the book merely in a few words since it is by an analysis that the deep underlying unity and harmony of the great prophecy can best be seen.

PURPOSE

The purpose of this noble prophecy is to teach the truth that salvation is by grace, that is, it is of God and not of man. This is embodied in the very name of the prophet, but it is clearly taught in his utterances. In the first chapter occur the words, 'Zion shall be redeemed with judgment and her converts with righteousness' (verse 27). This verse introduces the theme upon which the prophet continually expands. Indeed, chapters 40–66 may be regarded as a general exposition of this thought.

Isaiah's ministry occurred at a critical time in Judah's history. The Assyrian power was rising, and in the light of this fact two groups appeared within the nation. One sought alliance with Egypt and the other with Assyria. Isaiah, however, forbade human alliances and urged the nation to trust in God. As a sign of deliverance he proclaimed the birth of the Messiah and prophesied concerning the nature of His kingdom. In the latter portion of his prophecy (40–66) he set forth the spiritual walk and destiny of the people of God.

ANALYSIS

a. 1:1–12:6. Prophecies concerning Judah and Jerusalem
1. 1:1–31. The great arraignment (Ewald). Verse 1 is a general title, designed to serve as an introduction to the entire book and setting forth the character, author, subject, and date. The chapter serves the purpose of showing the relationship between the sins of the people and their sufferings, and the need of further punishments for purification. In verses 2–9 the corruption of the nation is shown to be the result of separation from God and the cause of the calamities that are coming

upon the people. In verses 10–20 the relationship of this corruption with religious practice is set forth to show that these rites, performed with a heart far from the Lord, are in themselves of no value. Verses 21–31 contrast the present moral corruption with the former glory of the city and also with the future in which the wicked rulers will be destroyed.

The first and second parts of the chapter are connected by the double reference to Sodom and Gomorrah (verses 9, 10). The third part (verse 21) is introduced by a cry which requires the preceding description for its proper understanding. This chapter, truly a continuous coherent composition, is best applied not to any one particular crisis, but serves as a general introduction, setting forth a sequence of events which God's people will have to experience in more than one crisis. Possibly Isaiah wrote it during Sennacherib's invasion of Judah.

As evidences of the unity of the book the reader should compare 1:11, 13 with 61:8; 1:14 with 43:24; 1:14–19 with 43:26; 1:15 with 59:3; 1:20 with 40:5 and 58:14; 1:29 with 65:3 and 66:17.

2. 2:1–4:6. Messiah's reign and judgments upon the people. 2:1 constitutes an introductory title for the present prophecy; verses 2–4, the exaltation of God's people as the source of instruction in the true religion; verses 5–4:1, the condition of the people in Isaiah's own time. Foreign alliances have brought about three great evils, and hence punishment will come. 2:9–11 refers to a humbling of the people; verses 12–17 introduce the day of the Lord in which God will be exalted, and that in which man trusts will be brought low; verses 18–21 state that the idols will be destroyed. The leading men of Judah are about to be taken away, 3:17; and this is because of the sin of the rulers, 8:15; and the women of Judah are shown to delight in pride and luxury, 3:16–4:1. In 4:2–6 Isaiah closes this section by returning to the Messianic theme showing the internal condition of the Church when Messiah reigns.

The following should be compared: 2:3 with 51:4; 2:2 with 56:7; 3:17 with 20:4 and 47:3. Chapter 2:2–4 is found, with some variation, in Micah 4:1–3. It is difficult to tell the precise relation of the two passages. Probably Isaiah based his utterance upon that of Micah, although in so doing he made minor variations. The similarity of the language with that of Joel 4:9–11 should also be noted. It is quite possible that there was current a prophecy from which Joel, Micah, and Isaiah drew. The point to be remembered is that in his choice of language each prophet was guided by divine inspiration. Each prophecy, therefore, is to be regarded as inspired and authentic.

3. 5:1–30. The prevalent iniquities of Judah. Verses 1–7 contain parable designed to set forth the highly favoured position of the natio

and her failure; verses 8–30 explain the parable. The sins of the people and the woe that will befall them are set forth, and this is followed by the announcement of the Lord's punishment.

According to Eissfeldt, 5:25–30 and 9:8–21 belong together, as do also 5:8–24 and 10:1–4a. This is because of the phrase 'for all this his anger is not turned away', *etc.* (5:25; 9:12, 17, 21), and the introductory woe (5:8, 11, 18, 20, 21, 22 and 10:1). But this idea (apparently first set forth by Ewald) is without merit. Why cannot an author use the same form of expression upon more than one occasion? Eissfeldt's dictum simply destroys the unity and purpose of chapter 5.

4. 6:1–13. Isaiah's vision of the Lord. The chapter is divided into two parts: the vision, verses 1–8, and the message, verses 9–13. The precise relation between these two parts is difficult to determine.

The following should be compared: 6:9 with 42:18–20 and 43:8; 6:9–12 with 53:1; 6:10 with 63:17. The phrase 'Holy One of Israel', so common to the entire book, is based upon this majestic vision. Eissfeldt maintains that this chapter originally stood at the beginning of the book, after the heading in 1:1 or 2:1. For this supposition there is not one particle of objective evidence. It is not necessary to assume that this chapter presents the account of Isaiah's prophetic call. It may do that, but it may also be a call to a special mission. There is, certainly, no reason for assuming that the chapter is not in its proper place.

5. 7:1–12:6. Prophecies uttered during Ahaz' reign. The passage 7:1–16 sets forth a promise of deliverance from Syria and Israel which is also set forth in symbolical form by the announcement of the miraculous conception and nativity of the Messiah; 7:17–25, the threat of the evils which will arise as a result of the alliance with Assyria sought by the unbelieving Ahaz; 8:1–4, a renewal of the prediction of the overthrow of Syria and Israel in the form of a symbolical name, to be applied to Isaiah's own son whose infant life is made the measure of the event. In 8:5–8 it is stated that Judah also shall be punished, because of her trust in man. In 8:9–22 the Messiah Himself speaks, urging the people to reverence the Lord and to consult His Word. 9:1–7 states that although darkness has come upon the land, it shall not be such as at the first vexation. A great light has shone, and there is universal peace and rejoicing brought about through the birth of the divine Messiah. In 9:8–12 the prophet reverts to his own time and again predicts the defeat of Israel; nevertheless (9:13–17), the people did not repent, hence (9:18–21), even though there were repeated strokes of God's displeasure, the nation was as it were devouring itself. Manasseh devoured Ephraim, and Ephraim Manasseh, and together they turned upon Judah. 10:1–4

continues the description of the nation's sinful state; 10:5–15 introduces the Assyrian, who is the rod which will be employed to execute God's wrath. The Assyrian does not realize this, but boasts as though he should conquer all in his own strength. 10:16–19 describes the doom of the enemy under the figure of a forest that is burned and almost entirely consumed; 10:20–23 shows that only a righteous remnant will escape God's judgments, and (10:24–34) to this remnant Isaiah utters encouragement. 11:1–4 says that a shoot will spring up, upon whom the Spirit of the Lord will come, and (11:5–9) the righteous reign of the Messiah will result in a complete peace. 10:10–13 sees the dispersed ones regathered, and 10:14–16 the ancient enemies of God's people spiritually conquered by the spread of God's kingdom. In 12:1–3, the first strophe of a psalm, the people praise God for His salvation, and in 12:5–6, the second strophe, they exhort each other to make known what God has done for them.

The following should be compared: 8:17 with 45:15 and 57:17; 9:2 with 42:7; 9:20 with 49:26; 11:1 with 60:21; 11:1, 10 with 53:2; 11:2 with 42:1 and 61:1; 11:4 with 49:2; 11:6 with 65:25; 11:9 with 65:25; 11:12 with 56:8 and 62:10. For Duhm's analysis of chapters 1–12 see *SI*, pp. 47–61. Eissfeldt rejects the following as non-Isaianic: 2:2–4; 9:1–6 (questionable, but probably Isaianic); 11:1–9 (questionable); 11:10–16; 12:1–6. The grounds for question or rejection are found in the ideas of the passages, rather than in objective evidence. There is no reason why Isaiah under divine inspiration might not have uttered all of chapters 1–12.

b. 13:1–23:8. Oracles of judgment upon the nations

1. 13:1–14:32. The fall of Babylon announced. The Lord commands His ministers to summon the invaders, the Medes, to come, 13:1–9; a fearful punishment is visited upon the Babylonians, expressed by the figure of the heavenly bodies ceasing to give their light, 13:10–18. Babylon is utterly destroyed and made desolate, 13:19–22. In chapter 14 the destruction of Babylon is again related and more definitely connected with Israel's release from bondage. The chapter begins with a song of triumph over the fallen enemy, 14:1–8; the startled unseen world sees the fallen tyrant in deep degradation, 14:9–20; Babylon is completely destroyed, 14:21–23; the preceding prophecy is concluded, 14:24–27; a warning is given to the Philistines who also had suffered from Babylon not to boast or rejoice prematurely, 14:28–32.

Compare 14:8 with 55:12, and 14:27 with 43:13. It is obvious that the school of negative criticism, if it is to be consistent with its principles must deny the Isaianic authorship of chapters 13, 14. Thus, *e.g.*, Pfeiffer attributes only 14:28–32 to Isaiah and regards the rest as having been written long after Isaiah's time. The denial of these chapters to Isaiah in spite of the clear testimony of the heading seems to be an evidence of disbelief in predictive prophecy. These two chapters introduce a series of discourses directed against the enemy nations of Israel. All objective evidence supports the view that they are the work of Isaiah under divine inspiration.

2. 15:1–16:14. The burden of Moab. Chapter 15 is a vivid description of Moab's destruction. The towns and cities of Moab – Ar-Moab, Kir-Moab, Heshbon – are represented as laid waste and as bemoaning their fate. In chapter 16 an exhortation is made to the Moabites to seek again allegiance with the house of David for deliverance, verses 1–6; then follows a description of Moab's desolation, verses 7–12; and finally the announcement that within three years the glory of Moab shall be destroyed, verses 13, 14.

Pfeiffer regards these chapters as the verbatim quotation, with some omissions, of an earlier non-Israelitic poem and, with the exception of the Maobite stone, 'the only remnant of Moabitic literature now extant', dating probably from 540–440 BC. This elegy, thinks Pfeiffer, was changed into a prediction by the Jewish author of the oracle, and finally a later editor added 16:13, 14. But the prophecy is best regarded as a generic prediction of the destruction of Moab, uttered by Isaiah himself without specific reference to any of the events by which it was brought about. Hence, it seems to me practically impossible to date the prophecy precisely.

3. 17:1–14. The burden of Damascus. A prophetic picture of the doom which lies in wait for the enemies of Israel. Syria and Ephraim shall both fall, verses 1–3, the destruction of Ephraim is described, verses 4–6; the nation, as a result of the judgment, returns to the Lord, verses 7, 8; the prophet describes further the judgment and sets forth the reason for it, verses 9–11; enemies of God's people shall gather together, but God shall disperse them, 12–14.

4. 18:1–7. The woe upon Ethiopia. The nation and all the world is informed of the impending catastrophe, verses 1–3; the catastrophe itself is then described under the figure of a vine, ripe with fruit, and suddenly destroyed, verses 4–7. Apparently this oracle is a divine announcement to the Ethiopians of the fact that the army of Sennacherib will be cut off by God's interposition.

5. 19:1–25. The burden of Egypt. The Egyptians are threatened with confusion, verses 1–4, and with physical calamities, verses 5–10, and a

perverse spirit has entered the land, verses 11–17; as a result of their sufferings they acknowledge the true God, verses 18–22, and future blessing is predicted, verses 23–25.

Pfeiffer would date 19:1–15 between 600–300 BC, and 19:16–25 even later, regarding the oracle in verses 16–22 as having reference to the third-century Jewish colony in Alexandria. But verses 1–17 are best taken as a metaphorical description by Isaiah of Egypt's downfall, and the second part (verses 18–25) describes under various figures the growth of the true religion. (*Cf.* the language of 19:25 with 45:11 and 60:21; and 19:23 with 11:16.)

6. 20:1–6. The approach of the Assyrian. Here is given a symbolical sign (the prophet walks naked and barefoot three years) of the defeat of Egypt and Ethiopia, the enemies of Assyria. (*Cf.* 20:4 with 47:3.)

7. 21:1–17. Three further burdens. The conquest of Babylon, verses 1–10; the burden of Dumah, *i.e.*, Edom or Arabia, verses 11, 12; the burden of Arabia, verses 13–17. It is best to regard the last two prophecies as generic visions seen and declared by the prophet. The first is a clear prediction of the downfall of Babylon by the Medes and Persians.

8. 22:1–25. The burden of the Valley of Vision. Verses 1–14 describe Jerusalem during a siege. It is difficult to say what siege is intended. Possibly it applies to the capture of Jerusalem by the Assyrians during the days of Manasseh, or, more likely, it is a generic description, the details of which have been drawn from various sieges which the people had to endure. Verses 15–25 predict the removal of Shebna from his position as treasurer of the royal household. The relationship between these verses and the preceding is that Shebna is to be regarded as a leader of the people, and the prophecy, while directed against the nation generally, concentrates on Shebna the leader specifically.

Compare 22:13 with 56:12. Driver suggests that Shebna may have been a friend of Egypt. This may have been the case; at any rate, this is the only prophecy of Isaiah specifically directed against an individual.

9. 23:1–18. The burden of Tyre. By means of addresses the destruction of Tyre is announced, verses 1–7; it is the Lord of hosts that has purposed this destruction, but the Chaldeans will be His instrument in carrying it out, verses 8–14; for seventy years Tyre will be forgotten, verse 15; then will she sing and be restored and her service devoted to the Lord, verses 16–18.

c. 24:1–27:13. The Lord's great judgments
These chapters form a continuous section, and the interpretations are almost legion. We may sum up the contents briefly, and then discuss the

nature of the section. We first note a description of the nation in distress as a result of the Lord's 'making the earth empty', 24:1–12; yet a few, 'as the shaking of an olive tree', shall glorify the Lord in a far land, 24:13–15; then follows a further description of judgment and of the exaltation of the Lord reigning in Zion, 25:16–23. A prayer of praise to God for His past judgments appears in 25:1–5; and this is followed by the announcement that the Lord will make a feast of fat things, removing the covering (*i.e.*, of spiritual blindness) cast over the people, will swallow up death in victory and will wipe away tears from all faces, 25:6–9; Moab, the enemy of Israel, will be cast down, 25:10–12. Then follows a song of praise to God, exalting His ways, 26:1–19, but apparently the victory has not yet come; there is to be a 'little moment', until the indignation be overpast. The destruction of the Lord's enemies is next set forth under the figure of the destruction of the sea-serpent, leviathan, 27:1–5; Israel shall flourish, for her sufferings were not as great as those of her enemies, 27:6, 7; Israel's punishment is in measure, for a time, 27:8, 9; the enemies, however, will receive no mercy, 27:10, 11; God's people will be regathered, 27:12, 13.

To apply these chapters to a specific period in Isaiah's ministry is very difficult. In fact, they do not have reference to specific events. Rather, the prophet here sets forth his philosophy of God's judgments. His purpose is to exalt God as sovereign Ruler over all. Hence, he seeks to show that God can and will visit the earth in judgment. In this visitation God's own people will suffer that they may ultimately be glorified, but the enemies of God will utterly perish. The future blessing is set forth in beautiful language as a blessing that is spiritual and evangelical. It may be that Isaiah never uttered these prophecies but merely wrote them down, as he may have done with chapters 40–66. They are a generic prophecy, a picture of judgment and salvation in its true nature, and there is no sufficient reason for denying their authorship to Isaiah.

Compare 26:1 with 60:18; 26:20 with 54:7, 8; 27:1 with 51:9 and 56:16. This section is denied to Isaiah by critics of the negative school. Pfeiffer, *e.g.*, regards it as even later than the fourth century BC; Driver refers it to the early post-exilic period; Kuenen to the fourth century; Duhm and Marti to the time of John Hyrcanus (134–104 BC). The basic reason for denying the section to Isaiah seems to be the presence of ideas which are thought to spring from a different (and later) vein of thought than Isaiah's (Driver). In reply we would point out that this apparent divergence of thought is based upon the nature of this section as a generic prophecy, which sets forth God's judgment and salvation in universal terms. It thus stands as a stepping-stone towards, or a preparation for,

Isaiah's great message in chapters 40–66. Why cannot these ideas have been revealed to Isaiah in the eighth century BC?

d. 28:1–35:10. Prophetic warnings

1. 28:1–33:24. Discourses dealing principally with the relation between Judah and Assyria. An announcement is made of the fall of Samaria, 28:1–6; Jerusalem is then addressed, and the folly of trusting in Egypt is pointed out, 28:7–22; God's purposes will surely come to pass, 28:23–29. Zion also will be attacked, 29:1–4; the enemy, however, will be defeated in its purpose, 29:5–8; the causes of judgment are given, 29:9–16; the final restoration is described, 29:17–24. The folly as well as the sin of relying upon Egypt is next set forth, 30:1–7; the relation between the people's lack of trust and their character and spiritual condition is depicted, 30:8–26; and, finally, the Assyrian will be halted by God Himself, so that reliance upon human aid is shown to be unnecessary 30:27–33. Reliance upon Egypt is foolish, for the Egyptians are mere men, 31:1–3; the Lord will certainly save His own, 31:4–5; hence, the people should turn to Him, 31:6–9. In the Lord are gracious blessings for the King will reign in righteousness, 32:1–8; the women are addressed for they had been indifferent; the desolation will continue until the Spirit be poured from on high, 32:9–20. The end of the invading Assyrian is announced, and the desolation will be followed by restoration, 33:1–24.

Compare 28:5 with 62:3; 29:15 and 30:1 with 47:10; 29:16 with 45:9 and 64:9; 29:23 with 60:21; 32:15 with 55:12.

2. 34:1–35:10. The contrasted future of Edom and Israel. The two chapters constitute one prophecy. Chapter 34 consists of a threat of God first against the nations generally, then particularly against Edom Edom is singled out, it would seem, as the representative of Israel' enemies, and the chapter is perhaps best regarded as a general threat against the spiritual Israel, the Church of God. In chapter 35 a picture of the glorious Messianic future is presented.

Torrey ascribes chapters 34, 35 to the author of chapters 40–66. Eiss feldt attributes them to the close of the sixth century BC, and thinks that their author modelled them after 40–66. Pfeiffer thinks that they may belong to the fourth century and in any case no earlier than the fifth Driver also denies the prophecy to Isaiah and apparently would assign it to the closing years of the exile. Compare 34:8 with 51:11; 35:1, 2 with 14:8, 32:15 and 55:12; 35:2 with 60:13; 35:6, 7 with 41:17, 18 and 43:19; 35:8–10 with 40:3, 4 and 49:11; 35:10 with 51:11 and 65:19.

e. 36:1–39:8. Historical appendix

Sennacherib invades Judah (chapter 36); Hezekiah the king sends for
Isaiah (37:1–5) who utters a message of comfort (37:6–35), and the
Assyrian army is destroyed by the Angel of the Lord (37:36–38);
Hezekiah is sick unto death, but his life is lengthened by the Lord
(38:1–8), and the thanksgiving of Hezekiah follows (38:9–22). From
Babylon come envoys who see the treasures of the Temple (39:1, 2), and
Isaiah announces the Babylonian captivity (39:3–8).

The reader should note that this section serves not only as a historical
appendix to chapters 1–35, but also as a bridge to connect these earlier
chapters with the latter half of the book. In the first portion of the prophecy the background has been the Assyrian period; in the latter half it
is the time of the Babylonian exile. These chapters serve as a remarkable
connecting link between the two. The Assyrian period closes, as it were,
with the account of Sennacherib's invasion. Then we are told of the
Babylonian envoys, and of Isaiah's prophecy of the captivity (39:3–8).
Thus we are prepared for the atmosphere which we find when we begin
to read chapter 40.

For this transition between the Assyrian and Babylonian periods, a
further preparation has also been made. As Delitzsch has pointed out,
the entire first half of the prophecy is like a staircase which leads up to the
latter half, bearing the same relation to it as the Assyrian background in
14:24–27 sustains to the burden of Babylon in chapters 13 and 14. This
Assyrian background is present throughout, but there are prophecies
which extend far beyond that time. Thus chapters 13–23 should be
compared with chapters 24–27, and chapters 28–33 with chapters 34–35.
In the series of prophecies concerning foreign nations (chapters 13–23),
those which relate to Babylon form the beginning, middle, and end
(chapters 13–14; 21:1–10 and 23). Thus the prophet, while living and
working in the days of Jotham, Ahaz, and Hezekiah, nevertheless was
given to see those things which would occur in the future, and thus, by
gradual glimpses into that future, the reader is prepared for the gracious
heights of chapters 40–66.

Chapters 36–39, with the exception of Hezekiah's psalm of thanksgiving, are repeated with minor variations in 2 Kings 18:13–20:19.
According to Driver, the original was the passage in Kings, and this was
used with slight variations by the compiler of the book of Isaiah. But
there are good reasons for believing that the original was that found in
Isaiah or at least that Isaiah was the author of both. From 2 Kings 16:5
it becomes clear that the author of Kings had Isaiah before him (*cf.* Is.
7:1). Again 2 Chronicles 32:32 shows that the events of the life of

Hezekiah were written in the book of Isaiah as well as in the book of Kings, which seems to show that the excerpt had been made from Isaiah ('*in* the vision of Isaiah, *upon* the book of the Kings'). The implication is that the original is to be found in the *hazon* of Isaiah. Lastly, the position of these chapters in the prophecy points to Isaiah as their author. It should be noted that the mention of the death of Sennacherib in 37:37, 38 does not militate against Isaianic authorship, since Isaiah probably outlived Hezekiah. According to tradition, Isaiah suffered martyrdom under the reign of Manasseh, who ascended the throne in 698 BC, and Sennacherib was murdered in 681 BC.

f. 40:1–66:24. The being and destiny of the Church of God

The last twenty-seven chapters of Isaiah's prophecy (and no other name than Isaiah has ever been connected with these chapters, not even by mistake or accident) are to be regarded as a unified whole. They were probably composed by Isaiah during his later life, and were written, not merely for the prophet's contemporaries, but also for the future Church of God. Whether Isaiah ever uttered any of these prophecies orally before committing them to writing is an open question.

According to many the theme of this section is the return from the Babylonian exile. But this is by no means the principal theme, for references to Babylon and the exile are far less frequent than is often supposed. For that matter, the prophet mentions Egypt more than he does Babylon. The theme of these chapters, rather, is the Church of God in its relations with God and man, and in its purpose, progress, design and vicissitudes. It is true that there are references to events in the life of the historical Israel, such as the calling of Abraham, the exodus from Egypt and the deliverance from exile. But the prophecy far transcends the limits of past historical events; it embraces also the advent of the Messiah and the fortunes of the spiritual Israel.

Hence, although the prophecy is a unit, it is very difficult to analyse. For there is an alternation between encouragement and threatening and a twofold sense in the use of the name Israel. Indeed, the section is desultory. This fact, however, in no sense militates against the position that the whole is the work of one man. Nor does this desultoriness in any sense indicate a haphazard or careless arrangement of the material, for there is an underlying unity of outlook and structure which preclude that.

J. A. Alexander has found five great subjects which he believes are treated in this section. They are: a description of the sinful nation, Israel; the spiritual Israel, weak in faith, but the object of Jehovah's favour; the deliverance from exile in Babylon, which serves as an example of God's future dealings with His people; the advent of the Messiah; the character of the new dispensation.

In the following we shall simply set forth the contents of each chapter.[9] The commonly accepted threefold analysis, 40–48, 49–57, 58–66, based upon the appearance of the phrase 'there is no peace, saith the Lord, unto the wicked', is too mechanical. In *SI* (pp. 47–61), I have sought to point out why there should be no separation after chapter 55. The principles of the history of tradition school[10] are based upon inadmissible presuppositions.

1. Chapter 40. Here is given a general promise of blessing and consolation. The people are commanded to prepare for a new and glorious appearance of the Lord, verses 1–8; who will come with a strong hand, yet as a tender Shepherd to His people, verses 9–11. That these promises are trustworthy is demonstrated by an appeal to God's wisdom and power and His absolute exaltation above, and independence of, man, verses 12–17. Furthermore, He is far above the idols of men, verses 18–25. His absolute power is present for the help of His people, verses 26–31.

2. Chapter 41. Although there are nations hostile to Israel, yet they shall perish before the chosen people, verses 1–16; Israel is weak but the Lord will protect and deliver, verses 17–29.

The reference to idols in these chapters is no indication of the place of composition, for what the prophet attacks is idolatry in general (*cf.* 41:7 with Je. 10:1–16). It may be that the fuller description in Jeremiah is indicative of the priority of Isaiah, but this is questionable. As for the relationship between Isaiah 40–66 and Jeremiah, the reader should compare the passages set out in the two columns below:

ISAIAH	JEREMIAH
44:12–15	10:1–16
46:7	10:1–16
48:6	33:3
53	11:19
56:11	6:15
56:9–57:11a	Jeremiah's reproaches
65:17	3:16
66:15	4:13

[9] The analysis of J. A. Alexander has been closely followed.
[10] See p. 204.

Too much cannot be made of this argument in defence of the priority of the Isaianic passages. It does appear, however, that in certain places, notably Jeremiah 50, 51, there is, as Delitzsch expressed it, a mosaic of Isaianic prophecies. On the whole, as far as this comparison in itself proves anything, it points to the priority of the Isaianic passages. (*Cf.* also Is. 47:8–10 with Zp. 2:15 and Is. 17:1, 7; 66:20 with Zp. 3:10.)

3. Chapter 42. The Servant of the Lord appears as the Saviour of mankind. His peaceful and quiet manner of working is described, verses 1–5, and the spiritual effects of that work are set forth, verses 6–9. This is really the work of God and for it He should be praised, verses 10–17. The nation, however, has been unfaithful and hence in trouble, a people robbed and spoiled, upon whom the fury of God's wrath has been poured, verses 18–25.

The figure of the 'Servant' in this chapter is probably the nation and its head, the Messiah. In verses 1–9 the head, the Messiah, is in the fore, but from verse 18 on the nation itself in its sinful condition appears. This idea of a group and its head in one is also found in the conception of the prophet, Deuteronomy 18:15. Within the compass of Isaiah 40–55 there are four passages which deal with the mysterious figure, the Servant of the Lord. These are 42:1–9; 49:1–6; 50:4–9; 52:13–53:12. According to Duhm and many others these passages have no immediate relation or connection with their present context. However, this position is untenable, as a serious exegesis of the passage will show.

Far more interest has attached to the problem of the identity of the Servant, and the interpretations broadly fall into two general groups, the collectivistic and individualistic. According to the first group, the Servant is the nation Israel or at least some portion or aspect of the nation. According to the second group of interpretations the Servant is an individual, either historical or ideal, past, contemporary, or one yet to come. The present writer is constrained to reject the collectivistic interpretation, except in a certain sense in 42:1–9 and 49:1–6. For one thing, in 50:4–9 and 52:13–53:12 the description of the Servant is such that it cannot be a personification and, furthermore, if the figure were intended as the personification of a group, that group could not possibly be the nation Israel. On the other hand, the descriptions do not apply to any individual except Jesus Christ.[11]

4. Chapter 43. Israel is the Lord's own people with whom He will be present in affliction, verses 1–4; the Lord will gather Israel to Himself, and the nations will be witness of His gracious dealings, verses 5–9; Israel

11 See Special Literature on Isaiah, pp. 226, 227 for an introduction to the literature upon the subject.

must know that there is no God like the Lord, who will for her sake destroy Babylon, verses 10–15, as He had once delivered her from Egypt, verses 16, 17; but His former deliverances are as nothing in comparison with what He will do for His people, and this He will do of His own good pleasure, and not because of any merit in the people, verses 18–28.

5. Chapter 44. Israel is God's servant, whom He will abundantly bless, verses 1–5; in support of this promise God appeals to His omniscience in contrast with the vanity of idols, verses 6–9; the idols are fashioned by men and hence of no value or profit, verses 10–20; but God has blotted out Israel's transgressions and redeemed her, and will send Cyrus as a deliverer, verses 21–28.

The structure of verses 24–28 clearly shows that Cyrus is regarded as one who is to come in the far future. For an analysis of the strophic structure of this prophecy and its relation to the important question of Isaianic authorship, consult Oswald T. Allis: 'The Transcendence of Jehovah God of Israel: Isaiah XLIV:24–28'*.[12] Concerning this passage Allis remarks, 'Thus we conclude that the most striking and significant features of the poem favour the view that while this utterance was significant in and of itself, it was chiefly significant in view of the exceptional circumstance under which it was spoken, *i.e.*, in view of its *early date*. The chronological arrangement of the poem assigns the restoration and Cyrus to the future. The perspective of the poem, together with the abrupt change of person in the second strophe, argues that this future is a *remote* future. And finally the carefully constructed double climax attaches a significance to the definiteness of the utterance which is most easily accounted for if this future was so remote that a definite disclosure concerning it would be of extraordinary importance' (p. 628).

6. Chapter 45. Cyrus will be victorious, being used of God for Israel's sake, verses 1–13; the Lord is then set forth as the only Saviour to whom Israel and all nations must look for deliverance, verses 14–25.

7. Chapter 46. As a specific illustration of the truths set forth in chapter 45 (namely, the absolute sovereignty of the Lord), this chapter relates the downfall of the Babylonian idols, verses 1–2; the Lord, however, cares for Israel throughout its entire existence, verses 3–4; the idols are indeed vanity, but the Lord is omniscient and He declares the future and raises up Cyrus, verses 5–11; hence, those that are far from righteousness should prepare for God's salvation, verses 12, 13.

8. Chapter 47. The judgments of God will fall upon Babylon, which is personified as a virgin, verses 1–3; Babylon is to fall because of her

[12] *BTS*, pp. 579–634.

oppression of Israel and her pride, her trust in wickedness, her wisdom and knowledge. These things cannot prevent her downfall, verses 4–15.

9. Chapter 48. Israel calls upon God the Lord but not in truth, verses 1, 2; hence, because of this obstinacy, former predictions were made; new things also are shown which Israel did not know, verses 3–8; in mercy God will spare His people from being cut off, verses 9–11; God is the Eternal One who has created the earth and who will accomplish His pleasure on Babylon, verses 12–16; Israel's sufferings have come because of her own sin, but she is to come forth from exile with rejoicing, verses 17–22.

It should be noted that the great basic theme of chapters 40–48 is the relationship which Israel sustains to God. Throughout the following chapters this doctrine is assumed as the basis for what is taught concerning Israel's relation to the world and her own calling.

10. Chapter 49. The Servant (here also the nation and its head, the Messiah) is set forth as the one who is to restore those who are in bondage, verses 1–6; the Lord has prepared the Servant that He may bless the earth, verses 7–12; the grace of the Lord has been manifested and God's enemies shall be destroyed, verses 13–26.

11. Chapter 50. The iniquities of the people have brought upon them their distress, verses 1–3; the Servant of the Lord is then introduced as meditating upon His sufferings, but the reason for these sufferings is not yet stated, verses 4–9; those that fear the Lord should trust in Him; thus the way of deliverance is set forth, and the doom of those that trust in themselves, verses 10, 11. In chapter 50 the Servant is best regarded, not as a corporate person, but as the Messiah alone.

12. Chapter 51. The righteous are exhorted to follow in the steps of Abraham, verses 1–3; the certainty of the Lord's salvation is assured, and the enemies of the righteous will perish, verses 4–8; the Lord brought the people through the Red Sea, therefore they may with confidence trust in His salvation, verses 9–16; weak Zion is commanded to awake and to trust in the Lord, verses 17–23.

13. Chapter 52. Here is set forth the future glory of God's people in comparison with their past state, a captivity, from which they are commanded to flee. God will deliver, and His people shall know Him, verses 1–6; the messenger of the gospel is already present, and there is to be a mighty exodus, verses 7–12; the Servant is the leader, and will be greatly exalted, an exaltation which is in proportion to the humiliation that He had to undergo, verses 13–15.

14. Chapter 53. Although Messiah had been proclaimed, few have believed concerning Him, verse 1; His appearance is lowly, verse 2; and

He is the object of contempt, verse 3; although He is One characterized by suffering, nevertheless this suffering is vicarious; He bears it because of the sins of others, verses 4–6; although innocent, the Servant is patient, even in unjust judgment, verses 7, 8; although innocent, His death is with the rich and wicked, verse 9; therefore, God will gloriously magnify Him, and He, as a substitute, the one Righteous in the stead of the many unrighteous, will justify them; and will continually make intercession for them, verses 10–12. In this chapter, the Servant is the Messiah.

15. Chapter 54. The future glory of God's people, verses 1–10, and the inviolability of the people of the Lord, verses 11–17, is set forth.

16. Chapter 55. The restrictions of the old dispensation are gone, and the Church stands open to the entire world, verses 1–5; the nations are then exhorted to seek the Lord, and are encouraged to do so by reference to God's mercy and to the infinite distance between God and man, verses 6–13.

17. Chapter 56. The righteousness of God will be fully revealed without the restrictions and distinctions of the old dispensation, verses 1–8; the sinful nation, however, is an unworthy one, verses 9–12.

18. Chapter 57. The righteous who have died are delivered from evil to come, verses 1, 2; the wicked are then addressed, and their idolatry condemned, verses 3–9; they will be destroyed because they continue in sin, verses 10–13; there will be deliverance for all who repent, verses 14–21. Verse 21 serves to show that even in Israel there will be no blessing for the unrepentant. The promises are only for true believers, the spiritual Israel, not for the unrepentant in the nation.

19. Chapter 58. Israel is a sinful nation, which exhibits hypocrisy rather than love to the needy, verses 1–7; had Israel been obedient, God's favour would have continued. She is invited to do well, keep the Sabbath, and delight in the Lord, verses 8–14.

20. Chapter 59. Israel's iniquities have separated her from God, verses 1, 2; these sins and their effects are set forth, verses 3–15; the Lord will intervene to save the true Israel by a Redeemer, verses 16–21.

21. Chapter 60. The change which awaits the spiritual Israel is a new and blessed light upon Zion, verse 1; from the entire world those that dwell in darkness shall come to Zion, verses 2–14; Zion is to be greatly glorified for ever, verses 15–22. The chapter presents a contrast between the new and the old dispensation.

22. Chapter 61. The Servant (here the Messiah) who is to bring about the great change is introduced as describing the object of His mission, verses 1–3; the blessings which flow as the result of His work are given, verses 4–11.

H

23. Chapter 62. The Servant will continue until righteousness and salvation shine forth, verse 1; God's people shall be recognized by the nations, and all the world will seek Zion, and she shall be called, 'Sought out; a city not forsaken', verses 2–12.

24. Chapter 63. The destruction of the enemies of the wicked is the work of the Messiah, verses 1–6; God has, however, been faithful to His people despite their unfaithfulness, verses 7–14; there follows a plea for God to show favour for the sake of His people, verses 15–19.

25. Chapter 64. Confidence is expressed in the mighty power of God, verses 1–3; God has done a blessed thing for His own, verse 4; Israel is unworthy, Zion is a wilderness, but because external prerogatives are lost, God will not cast off His own, verses 5–12.

26. Chapter 65. The Gentiles are called, verse 1; the Jews, because of their sins, are rejected, verses 2–7; there is, however, a chosen remnant, verses 8–10; the unbelieving Israel will be ashamed, but the true servants of God will sing for joy of heart, verses 11–16; the blessings of the new heaven and earth are cited, verses 17–25.

27. Chapter 66. The change between the old and new dispensations is described. The Lord dwells in the humble heart, not in an earthly temple, verses 1, 2; Zion will be blessed, verses 3–14; the old Israel will be destroyed but a remnant will go forth, verses 15–24.

SPECIAL LITERATURE ON ISAIAH

F. M. Th. Boehl, *De 'Knecht des Heeren' in Jesaja 53* (Haarlem, 1923); Charles Boutflower, *The Book of Isaiah (Chapters I–XXXIX) in the Light of the Assyrian Monuments** (London, 1930); Karl Budde, *Die sogenannten Ebed-Jahwe-Lieder und die Bedeutung des Knechtes Jahwes in Jes. 40–45*; *Ein Minoritätsvotum* (Giessen, 1900); Otto Eissfeldt, *Der Gottesknecht bei Deuterojesaja (Jes. 40–45) im Lichte der Israelitischen Anschauung von Gemeinschaft und Individuum* (Halle (Salle), 1933); Karl Elliger, *Die Einheit des Tritojesaia (56–66)* (Stuttgart, 1928); 'Der Prophet Tritojesaia', in *ZAW*, 59, 1931, pp. 112–141; *Deuterojesaja in seinem Verhältnis zu Tritojesaja* (Stuttgart, 1933); Franz Feldmann, *Der Knecht Gottes in Isaias Kap. 40–55* (Freiburg im Breisgau, 1907); Johann Fischer, *Isaias 40–55, und die Perikopen vom Gottesknecht* (Münster i. W., 1916); *Wer ist der Ebed?* (Münster i. W., 1922); Kemper Fullerton, 'Viewpoints in the Discussion of Isaiah's Hopes for the Future', *JBL*, XLI, 1922, pp. 1–101; Gerhard Fuellkrug, *Der Gottesknecht des Deuterojesaja* (Göttingen, 1899); Hermann Gunkel, *Ein Vorläufer Jesu* (Zürich, 1921); E. W. Hengstenberg, *Christology of the Old Testament and a Commentary on the Messianic Predictions**, II (Edinburgh, 1856), pp. 1–354; J. Meinhold, *Die Jesaja-erzählungen Jesaja 36–39. Eine historischkritische Untersuchung* (Göttingen, 1898); Sigmund Mowinckel, 'Die Komposition des deuterojesajanischen Buches', in *ZAW*, 49, 1931, pp. 87–112, 242–260; Ad. Neubauer, S. R. Driver, E. B. Pusey, *The Fifty-Third Chapter of Isaiah According to the Jewish Interpreters* (Oxford, 1877); C. R. North, *The Suffering Servant in Deutero-Isaiah* (Oxford, 1956); J. Schelhaas, *De Lijdende Knecht des Heeren** (Groningen, 1933); Ernst

Sellin, 'Die Lösing des deuterojesajanischen Gottesknechtsrätsels', in *ZAW*, 1937, pp. 177–217; Sidney Smith, *Isaiah Chapters XL–LV: Literary Criticism and History* (London, 1944); J. Steinmann, *La Prophète Isaie* (1950); Charles Cutler Torrey, *The Second Isaiah: A New Interpretation* (Edinburgh, 1928); J. S. van der Ploeg, *Les Chants du Serviteur de Jahve dans la Seconde Partie du Livre d'Isaie* (Chaps. 40–55) (Paris, 1936); Edward J. Young, *Studies in Isaiah* (Grand Rapids, 1945) and *The Prophecy of Isaiah**, I (Grand Rapids, 1964).

CHAPTER FIFTEEN

JEREMIAH

THE prophecy is named after the prophet himself, *yirmeyahu* or *yirmeyah*. In the LXX the name appears as Hieremias, and in the Latin Jeremias.

a. Authorship of the book

There is no satisfactory reason for doubting that Jeremiah himself was the author of the entire book. In chapter 36:1–2 we learn that in the fourth year of Jehoiakim the Lord commanded the prophet to take a book-roll and to write therein all the prophecies which had been revealed to him from the days of Josiah up to the present. In response to this command Jeremiah summoned his scribe, Baruch, who wrote all the prophecies down at dictation (*mippi yirmeyahu*) (verse 4). Baruch then went to the Temple and read there all that had been dictated to him (verse 8). A year later (*i.e.*, the fifth year of Jehoiakim) in the ninth month a fast was proclaimed and Baruch again read the prophecies publicly. This act was reported to the princes, who summoned Baruch to bring the roll before them. The princes then permitted Baruch and Jeremiah to escape but brought the roll to Jehoiakim who, upon hearing it read, cut it to pieces with a penknife and cast it into the fire (verses 9–23).

The Lord then commanded Jeremiah to take another roll and to write in it all that had been found in the previous book. Jeremiah dictated to Baruch all the contents of the former roll 'and there were added besides unto them many like words' (verse 32). Thus there came into existence the first written record of Jeremiah's prophecies from Josiah to Jehoiakim. It is obvious, however, that this dictated roll does not coincide with our present book of Jeremiah, since our present book contains many prophecies uttered at a time subsequent to the fifth year of Jehoiakim. It is quite possible that at later times Jeremiah dictated further to Baruch. Like Jeremiah, Baruch was taken into Egypt (43:6) and it is likely that in Egypt Baruch gathered and edited all of Jeremiah's prophecies. Even the arrangement of the prophecies may be due to the suggestion of Jeremiah, although actually carried out by Baruch. Hence, the inclusion of chapter 52 at the close, although not an original work of the prophet's, may nevertheless have been carried out at his suggestion. As to Baruch, all the evidence indicates that he was simply a scribe or an amanuensis, and whatever he did in the way of editing was doubtless at Jeremiah's direction.

The more important alternate views of authorship are those of Pfeiffer, and Oesterley and Robinson. According to Pfeiffer we have three groups of writings, the words which the prophet himself dictated or wrote, a biography of Jeremiah which was probably written by Baruch, and various additions by later authors and editors. Even Jeremiah's own work and, to a lesser extent, Baruch's biography are said to be subjected to editorial revision.

After the death of Jeremiah, or at least without Jeremiah's knowledge, Baruch is said to have prepared an edition in which he combined Jeremiah's book with his own, working over many of the prophet's speeches in his own 'Deuteronomic style'. Even this book of Baruch's was subject to later revision. Long prose interpolations were made and many poetic additions.

In answer to this position two observations may be made: All the evidence shows that Baruch was too pious and serious a man to have tampered with Jeremiah's speeches in the manner suggested above; and there is no evidence whatever to support the view that later additions and interpolations were made to the book. The idea that the biblical books are simply clusters of fragments originating from various sources is without foundation in fact.

According to the view of Oesterley and Robinson the compiler of the book (probably the fourth century BC) had before him material of three types: little collections of oracular material in poetry; descriptive material from the hand of Jeremiah's biographer; and oracular material worked over into rhetorical prose form in the first person. He would take each group of oracular utterances and prefix to it a suitable selection from one of the two prose sections. He preferred passages of the third type (*i.e.*, autobiographical prose) and did not use any of the second type (*i.e.*, biographical prose) until chapter 19, when he had nearly exhausted the other. According to *OR* it is possible to distinguish no less than fourteen of the collections of oracular poetry. The so-called Deuteronomic style of some of these passages is simply the form of Hebrew rhetorical prose in the latter seventh and early sixth centuries.

In characterizing the pieces of oracular poetry, *OR* call attention to the brevity of most of the independent pieces in the midst of poetical collections, and the number of these fragments which appear in other books of the Bible. As far as the date of the oracular poetical material is concerned, we are told that whereas some of it is of Jeremianic origin, some is much later and comes from the late fifth or early fourth centuries BC.

The biographical material comes for the most part from a contemporary and may be the work of Baruch. The autobiographical prose passages contain several which are the work of Jeremiah himself, although there are several, such as 3:14–17, which are not earlier than the close of the exile. Possibly these passages were found in the roll which Jeremiah dictated to Baruch in 605 BC.

From the above two theories of the composition of the book it is apparent that some scholars do not attribute all of the prophecies of the book to Jeremiah. Nevertheless there is for the most part considerable difference of opinion as to what is his and what is not. Duhm, for example, whose commentary is one of the most radical, thinks that about two-thirds of the entire book is the work of later supplementers whose labours continue even down to the first century BC.

Chapters 10:1–16 and 17:19–27 are generally denied to Jeremiah. Cornill, for example, thinks that 9:26 is continued in 10:17 and the intervening verses are out of place. Furthermore, he believes that they show dependence upon passages in the latter part of Isaiah, and so would regard them as an interpolation. But the theory of interpolations is very difficult to apply in connection with a book whose contents are arranged in the manner of Jeremiah. For our part, we cannot see that there is any real evidence of interpolation, and the dependence of these verses on Isaiah is significant for the early authorship of the latter.

Cornill further questions chapters 30 and 31 and denies 33 to Jeremiah. Also he finds that the oracles against the heathen nations have been worked over. Chapters 50 and 51 are denied to Jeremiah by practically all except conservatives.

b. Life of the author

More is known of the life of Jeremiah than of any other of the Old Testament prophets. Jeremiah was the son of Hilkiah, of the priests in Anathoth (the modern Anata, about an hour and a half's walk north-east from Jerusalem). While still a youth, about twenty years of age, he was called to be a prophet (1:6). This call came in the thirteenth year of Josiah (1:2; 25:3) *i.e.*, 627 BC. Jeremiah's ministry continued until after the final destruction of Jerusalem by Nebuchadnezzar, 586 BC, and altogether lasted for about fifty years.

In his call to the prophetic office Jeremiah learned that the destruction of Jerusalem was certain and that it would be accomplished through an enemy from the north (1:11–16). Five years after his call, in the eighteenth year of Josiah, the Book of the Law was discovered in the Temple (2 Ki. 22 and 23), and as a result Josiah instituted a religious reform designed to stamp out idolatry. Whether Jeremiah makes specific reference or allusion to this newly discovered Book of the Law is not certain, but it may be that he does so (11:1–8).

At first Jeremiah probably lived in Anathoth and only occasionally put in appearance at Jerusalem. At any rate, through his preaching he became the object of much hostility both in Anathoth and Jerusalem. At first this animosity broke out in his native town (11:18–23), and the prophet removed to Jerusalem. Apparently, even Jeremiah's family had dealt treacherously with him (12:6). Nevertheless, this period of Jeremiah's ministry was probably the happiest, and when Josiah died Jeremiah lamented for him (2 Ch. 35:25a).

Josiah was followed by Jehoahaz (also called Shallum), who reigned for three months. Against him Jeremiah prophesied in no uncertain terms, clearly announcing his doom (22:11–17).

After Jehoahaz the throne was occupied by Jehoiakim. During the fourth year of his reign (the third according to Dn. 1:1, which employs a different mode of reckoning) the famous battle of Carchemish was fought in which Nebuchadnezzar came forth victorious and then besieged Jerusalem, taking away both captives (among whom was Daniel) and vessels of the Temple. During this very year that the Chaldeans besieged Jerusalem, Jeremiah announced their coming and the seventy years of exile (25:1–14).

During the reign of Jehoiakim the prophet delivered his great address at the Temple (chapters 7–9). The priests now determined to have Jeremiah put to death (chapter 26). However, intervention was made for him. The Lord commanded him to gather his prophecies in a book-roll (36:1). These were dictated to Baruch, who read them before the people. Jehoiakim became so angry with the prophet that he cut the book into pieces with his penknife and burned it and commanded that Jeremiah and Baruch be seized, but the Lord hid them (36:26). Jeremiah then dictated to Baruch a second time, adding further prophecies.

Jehoiachin (also called Coniah, 22:24ff.) reigned for only three months and then was taken into captivity to Babylon, as Jeremiah had predicted (22:24–30). He was followed upon the throne by the third son of Josiah, Zedekiah, who had been appointed by the Babylonians (597–586 BC). After a time Zedekiah refused to pay further tribute to Babylon and sought alliance with Egypt (Ezk. 17:13; 2 Ch. 36:13), but Jeremiah urged him to continue to be faithful to Babylon (27:12–22). This would be the lesser of two evils, and would mean that the nation would not be destroyed. 'Bring your necks under the yoke of the king of Babylon, and serve him and his people, and live' (27:12b). Finally Nebuchadnezzar came, and after a long siege, took the city. This was a time of great suffering for Jeremiah. He was arrested as he sought to leave for Benjaminite territory and charged with deserting. As a result of this arrest he was placed in a dungeon where he remained for many days, but Zedekiah sent for him and asked, 'Is there any word from the Lord?' In response Jeremiah plainly announced that Zedekiah would be delivered into Nebuchadnezzar's hand, and he protested against his imprisonment, whereupon the king put him in the court of the prison. Jeremiah could now preach more freely, but his words aroused enmity, and he was placed in a slimy cistern from which he was rescued by an Ethiopian, Ebed-melech by name (38:7–13).

When finally Jerusalem fell Zedekiah was blinded and together with his people was taken into captivity. Nebuzaradan, the Babylonian general, set Jeremiah free and permitted him to remain in his own land (39:11–14). He went to the governor Gedaliah, but after a short time the governor was murdered by ruthless opponents, headed by a certain Ishmael (41:1, 2). The Jews now feared vengeance on the part of the Babylonians and sought to go to Egypt for safety (41:17, 18). Against this policy, however, Jeremiah protested most vigorously (42:9–22). His words proved to be of no avail and he was compelled to accompany the Jews to Egypt (43:1–7). At Tahpanhes, the place in Egypt where the Jews settled, the prophet continued his ministry, 43:8–13 and 44 being messages which were delivered there.

PURPOSE

The nature of Jeremiah's ministry is expressed in the words which the Lord uttered to him at the time of his call to the prophetic office. The great theme that runs through Jeremiah's messages is that of judgment against Judah. This judgment is to come in the form of a chastisement from the army from the north (the Babylonians). Furthermore, this punishment will come in the near future. It will come because the people are deserving of punishment. They have given themselves over to idolatry, to forsaking the Lord. Interspersed with these warnings against the chosen people of God are messages directed to the enemies of the theocracy.

Against this dark background of threat and punishment, however, there appear some of the most glorious Messianic prophecies of the entire Old Testament. Like Isaiah of the previous century, Jeremiah also was permitted to see Christ's day. These promises are not divorced from the background of warning. They rather are the outcome of a pleading with the nation to repent. For example, after a gracious reasoning with the rebellious people, the Lord through the mouth of His prophet says, 'Turn, O backsliding children, saith the Lord' (3:14). Then follows the promise, 'And it shall come to pass, when ye be multiplied and increased in the land, in those days, saith the Lord, they shall say no more, The ark of the covenant of the Lord; neither shall it come to mind; neither shall they remember it; neither shall they visit it; neither shall that be done any more. At that time they shall call Jerusalem the throne of the Lord: and all the nations shall be gathered into it, to the name of the Lord, to Jerusalem: neither shall they walk any more after the imagination of their evil heart' (3:16–17).

In chapter 23 we have the promise of the righteous Branch, and again in chapters 31 and 33. The climax of these Messianic promises in Jeremiah is perhaps the following, 'In those days shall Judah be saved, and Jerusalem shall dwell safely: and this is the name wherewith she shall be called, The Lord our righteousness' (33:16). This prophecy is God's great word of warning to the theocracy which had by its sinfulness so debased itself that its outward form must be broken up. The earthly city is to be destroyed, but one day she shall dwell safely – the Lord our righteousness.

ANALYSIS

a. *Logical arrangement*

It must be obvious even from a cursory examination that the contents of the prophecy are not arranged in what, to the western mind, would be called a logical order. It is true that there is a certain underlying plan to the book. Thus, chapters 1–25 form a unit in themselves, containing as they do prophecies, both of woe and weal, against Judah. But the order and arrangement are not strictly chronological. Again chapters 26–45, which deal with the personal life of the prophet, form a unit. Many critics refuse to attribute these to the prophet, but there is no sufficient reason for denying them to him. Chapters 46–51 also form a unit, being prophecies against the foreign nations. Incidentally, chapter 25, which closes the first unit, by its content prepares for the section of prophecies that deal with the foreign nations. Lastly, we have in chapter 52 a historical appendix. Thus, there is an underlying unity to the book.

Nevertheless, it is often difficult to see why certain passages occur at precisely the point where they do occur. Why were the prophecies arranged in the order in which they appear? In answer to this question it should be remembered that not only the personal, but also the national and racial characteristics of the writers of the Bible were preserved and employed by God in the composition of the biblical books. Now these writers were Orientals, and oriental writings do not always display the passion for logical and categorical arrangement which seems to characterize occidental. The Koran is a notable example. Jeremiah's prophecies may seem to be somewhat scattered, but their arrangement enables the prophet to emphasize *repetition*. The themes of Jeremiah are *recurring* ones – the sinfulness of the nation and the approaching doom. Into his book he weaves these thoughts, and as we read on we meet them over and over again until the impression which they have made upon us is truly powerful and tremendous.

These remarks on the arrangement of the prophecies are necessary in view of the fact that the LXX presents marked differences from the Hebrew text. In the first place, the order of the prophecies against foreign nations differs in the LXX from the Hebrew. In the LXX they occur as Elam, Egypt, Babylon, Philistia – Phoenicia, Edom, Ammon, Kedar – Hazor, Damascus, and Moab. Furthermore, they occur in a different place, namely, after chapter 25:13. It is not easy to tell why this classification was adopted. Possibly Elam (thought by the translators to represent Persia?) was placed first since at that time Persia was the dominant world power. Also, it may be that Babylon was placed after Egypt since Egypt and Babylon appear elsewhere as the combination of powers hostile to God's people. In the second place, the LXX is considerably shorter than the Hebrew. In fact, it is shorter by about one-eighth (about 2700 words, or six or seven chapters).

How are these divergences to be explained? It has been held that the LXX represents the original text (Workman) and therefore is superior to the Hebrew. On the whole, however, the Hebrew text is superior. It may be that in certain cases preference should be given to the LXX, but certainly not very often. The LXX translators, being Alexandrian Jews, were doubtless influenced by Greek philosophy. Hence, it may be that they deliberately sought to introduce what seemed to them a more logical arrangement of the prophecies. Evidently they were, to an extent at least, moved by such considerations. For example, in the phrase 'the

Lord of hosts', the words 'of hosts' are generally omitted by the LXX. Also, in the phrase 'Jeremiah the prophet' we find the words 'the prophet' often omitted. It is not accurate therefore to speak of two recensions of the text, nor is the LXX to be preferred over the Massoretic text.

b. Chronological arrangement

As they appear, Jeremiah's prophecies are not arranged in chronological order, and such a classification is difficult to make. However, the following will give a general idea of the order in which the prophecies were delivered.

1. Under Josiah. Only 1:1 and 3:6–6:30 are actually dated in the reign of Josiah. Nevertheless, they form an integral part of the section to which they belong. Hence, we may assign the following passages to Josiah's reign:

(i) 1:1–19. The time is the thirteenth year of Josiah, and Jeremiah receives his call to the prophetic office.

(ii) 2:1–3:5. The passage contains the prophet's first message to the sinful nation. The introductory phrase 'and the word of the Lord came unto me' (2:1) serves well to introduce the first prophecy after the general introduction, chapter 1. Hence, there is no reason for denying this introductory message to the time of Josiah.

(iii) 3:6–6:30. This is the prophet's second discourse, in which he announces the punishment of Judah by the coming of a nation from the north. This nation was long thought to be the Scythians, but more likely the reference is to the Babylonians.

(iv) 7:1–10:25. This message was delivered in the gate of the Lord's house. It is intended to arouse those who place a false trust in the Temple, and it condemns the people because of their idolatry, and threatens exile. It is difficult to date this prophecy. Some would place it under the reign of Jehoiakim. However, it may very well have been addressed to those who made an outward show of adopting Josiah's religious reform. Hence, it may have been uttered in support of the true nature of that reform. It is somewhat general in character, and seems not to reveal the Babylonian shadow ready to darken Judah. Hence, I am inclined to regard it as uttered during Josiah's days.

(v) 11:1–13:27. This section comprises a message in itself. Its stress upon violation of the covenant may be a clue as to its date. On the other hand, the terrible picture of Judah's moral condition herein painted may point to a time subsequent to Josiah.

(vi) 14:1–15:21. Here is given a representation of drought and dearth.

(vii) 16:1–17:27. This section belongs with the previous one. Both present pictures of Judah's desolation. These are general in character. Hence, it is difficult to tell whether they belong to the time of Josiah or Jehoiakim.

(viii) 18:1–20:18. The coming exile is symbolically represented. 19:14–20:3 gives an account of the prophet's arrest under Pashur. This incident, however, does not really enable us to date the passage. It is true that in 21:1 Zedekiah sends a certain Pashur to Jeremiah. However, this is evidently a different man (son of Melchiah) from the Pashur mentioned in 20:1–3 (the son of Immer).

2. Under Jehoahaz. No prophecies are dated under this reign, and the message concerning Jehoahaz, 22:11–12, was uttered while Zedekiah was king.

3. Under Jehoiakim. As already suggested, some of the prophecies which I have assigned to the time of Josiah may more properly belong to the reign of Jehoiakim. The following are dated as belonging to this time.

(i) 26. Jehoiakim's reign begins. Like chapters 7–10 this message was delivered in the court of the Lord's house. At this time Urijah, who prophesied in accordance with Jeremiah, was put to death (26:20–24).

(ii) 27. Verse 1 dates this chapter also at the beginning of Jehoiakim's reign, but as the content shows, it belongs to Zedekiah's reign. Evidently the word 'Jehoiakim' in verse 1 is a scribal error for 'Zedekiah'.

(iii) 25. This prophecy is dated in the fourth year of Jehoiakim, *i.e.*, the year in which Nebuchadnezzar later came to Jerusalem and besieged it (Dn. 1:1).

(iv) 35. This prophecy concerns the Rechabites and was delivered in the days of Jehoiakim.

(v) 36. This chapter belongs to the fourth year of Jehoiakim and relates the writing down of the prophecies, their destruction by Jehoiakim, and their re-writing.

(vi) 45. Jeremiah utters this brief message to Baruch in the fourth year of Jehoiakim.

(vii) 46–49 are difficult to date. That they were uttered after the defeat of the Egyptians at Carchemish is clear from 46:2. Driver suggests that (with the exception of 49) they may belong to the fourth year of Jehoiakim and may reflect the profound impression which Nebuchadnezzar's victory had made upon Jeremiah. This is quite possible, but it may also be that some of these prophecies were uttered later, when Jehoiakim had rebelled against the Babylonians and marauding bands

were sent against him. On the other hand, the prophecies may belong to
a later reign.

4. Under Jehoiachin. There are no prophecies expressly attributed to
this period. Jehoiachin is mentioned, however, in 22:24–30, a prophecy
uttered during the reign of Zedekiah.

5. Under Zedekiah.

(i) 21:1–22:30. These prophecies were uttered when Pashur and
Zephaniah were sent to Jeremiah by the king to enquire as to the outcome of the Babylonian siege. With verse 11 the prophet begins to set
before Zedekiah the need for justice. In chapter 22 he proceeds to
evaluate the three preceding kings: Jehoahaz, verses 11, 12; Jehoiakim,
verses 18–23; Jehoiachin, verses 24–30.

(ii) 23 continues the prophecy of 21 and 22. It consists for the most
part of denunciations against the false prophets, both those in Jerusalem
and those who had gone into exile, who had held out false promises of
peace and safety.

(iii) 24 is a symbolical message revealed to the prophet after the
captivity of Jehoiachin.

(iv) 27, although dated (verse 1) in the beginning of the reign of
Jehoiakim, belongs, as its context shows, to the reign of Zedekiah. The
chapter shows how the prophet thwarted the designs of five neighbouring
peoples, Edom, Moab, Ammon, Tyre, Zidon (verse 2), to induce the
Judaean king to unite with them in rebellion against Babylon. Jeremiah
further spoke to Zedekiah about the folly of such an action (verses
12–22).

(v) 28 also belongs to the beginning of Zedekiah's reign, the fourth
year and fifth month. It recounts Jeremiah's opposition to the false
prophet Hananiah.

(vi) 29 contains the letter which Jeremiah sent to the exiles in
Babylon after the captivity of Jehoiachin. It therefore belongs to the
reign of Zedekiah. Jeremiah informs the exiles that they should establish
houses in Babylon, for the exile will not be of short duration but will last
for seventy years.

(vii) 30 and 31 are not dated, but their content shows that the
deportation had already occurred, hence they probably belong with the
messages uttered during Zedekiah's reign. The chapters serve to teach
the nation that although her present suffering is grievous there will yet be
a glorious future. The Lord will make a new covenant in which there
will be a spiritual salvation (31:31ff.).

(viii) 32 belongs to the tenth year of Zedekiah. The prophet buys
the field in Anathoth of his cousin Hanameel and gave the evidence of

purchase to Baruch. This symbolical action was to show that the land would again be inhabited and cultivated.

(ix) 33 belongs, like 32, to the period of Jeremiah's imprisonment under Zedekiah. It contains a Messianic prophecy (also found with slight variations in 23:5ff.) and a promise of the perpetuity of David's throne.

(x) 34 was uttered during Nebuchadnezzar's siege. It relates the announcement to Zedekiah of his own captivity and the destruction of the city (verses 1–7). Zedekiah decrees that the people should free their Hebrew slaves. The people agree, but then go back on their word, hence the prophet severely denounces them.

(xi) 37 is historical, relating the accession of Zedekiah. Jeremiah announces that the Egyptians would not help the king but the Chaldeans would burn the city with fire. Jeremiah is imprisoned but later remanded to the court of the prison.

(xii) 38 continues the account of the prophet's imprisonment under Zedekiah.

(xiii) 39 is historical, relating the captivity of the king and the destruction of Jerusalem. It is dated in the ninth year of Zedekiah, the tenth month.

6. Under Gedaliah. Although no prophecies are expressly dated in the reign of Gedaliah, yet to this period must be assigned the following:

(i) 40 is a prophecy revealed to Jeremiah after the captivity (verse 1). Nebuzaradan releases Jeremiah, offering him the choice of going to Babylon or of staying in the land (verses 2–4). Jeremiah goes to Gedaliah and dwells with him (verses 6, 7). Gedaliah is warned that Ishmael seeks to slay him, but he does not believe the report.

(ii) 41 also belongs to this period. It is historical, relating how Ishmael slew Gedaliah, and how the people now feared the Chaldeans.

(iii) 42 continues the narrative, and contains the message of Jeremiah warning the remnant of Judah not to go down into Egypt.

Chapters 43:1–44:30 are largely historical, relating how the people refused to hearken to Jeremiah but set out for Egypt taking him with them. In Tahpanhes Jeremiah performs a symbolical act with stones to show that Nebuchadnezzar will yet smite Egypt. In chapter 44 Jeremiah explains the reason for the destruction of Jerusalem and the exile and also announces punishment to those that dwell in Egypt, except the remnant that will be saved.

Chapters 50–52 require special comment. 50 and 51 are said to be (51:59–64) the word which Jeremiah sent to Babylon with Seraiah when he went there with Zedekiah during the fourth year of the latter's reign.

Seraiah, upon arriving in Babylon, was to read this message, and then bind a stone to it and cast it into the Euphrates, thus symbolizing the downfall of Babylon, the great enemy of God's people.

A difficulty arises, however, in that, as it now stands the prophecy seems to imply that the Temple has already been destroyed (*e.g.*, 50:28; 51:11, 51), an event which had not occurred in the fourth year of Zedekiah. Either, then, Jeremiah is simply placing himself in the future and portraying the Temple as destroyed, or else we may assume that these two chapters present an expanded form of the prophet's message against Babylon, one that he himself had prepared in Egypt under divine inspiration after the sanctuary at Jerusalem had actually been destroyed.

There are other considerations which seem to support this last-mentioned view. For one thing, the exile seems to have taken place already, *cf.* 50:4 (note the force of the verb *yavo'u*, *i.e.*, they will come, from the bondage in which they now are), 7, 17, 33; 51:34ff. At any rate, there is no sufficient reason for denying the Jeremianic authorship of these chapters.

Chapter 52 is historical, being practically the same as 2 Kings 24–25. I do not believe that Jeremiah was the original author of the passage, but that he took it from the same source from which the passage in 2 Kings was taken.

SPECIAL LITERATURE ON JEREMIAH

Oswald T. Allis, 'A Modernistic View of Jeremiah',* in *PTR*, 23, 1925, pp. 82–132 (a review of G. A. Smith's Baird lecture, see below); Aage Bentzen, *Die Josianische Reform und ihre Voraussetzungen* (Kopenhagen, 1926); T. Crouther Gordon, *The Rebel Prophet. Studies in the Personality of Jeremiah* (London, 1931); H. L. Ellison in *Evangelical Quarterly** (London), XXXI, 1959 onwards; Friedrich Horst, *Die Anfänge des Propheten Jeremia* (Giessen, 1923); W. F. Lofthouse, *Jeremiah and the New Covenant* (London, 1925); John Skinner, *Prophecy and Religion: Studies in the Life of Jeremiah* (Cambridge, 1936); Sir George Adam Smith, *Jeremiah: Being the Baird Lecture for 1922* (New York, 1924); Alexander Stewart, 'Jeremiah – the Man and His Message',* in *PTR*, 26, 1928, pp. 1–40; J. G. S. S. Thomson, *The Word of the Lord in Jeremiah** (London, 1959); Geerhardus Vos, 'Jeremiah's Plaint and Its Answer',* in *PTR*, 26, 1928, pp. 481–495; Adam C. Welch, *Jeremiah: His Time and His Work* (Oxford, 1928).

CHAPTER SIXTEEN

EZEKIEL

NAME

IN Hebrew the prophet's name is *yehezqe'l*, which probably means 'God strengthens'. In the LXX it appears as Iezekiel, and in the Vulgate Ezechiel, from which the English is derived. No mention is made of the prophet in the Scriptures outside of his own book.

AUTHOR

In *Baba Bathra* 15a we read, 'The men of the Great Synagogue wrote Ezekiel and the Twelve.' Another ancient statement concerning the authorship of the book is found in Josephus.[1] 'But not only did he [*i.e.*, Jeremiah] predict to the people [the destruction of Jerusalem and the exile], but also the prophet Ezekiel who first wrote two books about these things and left them [for posterity]' (*duo biblia grapsas katelipen*). This passage is somewhat obscure and has occasioned discussion. Probably what Josephus had in mind by 'two books' was Ezekiel 1–32 and Ezekiel 33–48. Jerome also expressed doubts as to the homogeneity and genuineness of the prophecy.

Until recent years there was very little serious doubt that Ezekiel himself was the author of the book and was also responsible for the arrangement of the prophecies. Thus even Cornill could write, 'All these considerations compel the opinion that Ezekiel wrote down and elaborated his book as a whole in the twenty-fifth year, but for this purpose availed himself of earlier – and in some cases of much earlier – memoranda, which he has left essentially unaltered.'[2] And Driver wrote, 'No critical question arises in connection with the authorship of the book, the whole from beginning to end bearing unmistakably the stamp of a single mind.'[3]

Indeed, the reasons for holding to the authorship of the entire book by Ezekiel are rather strong. The book is autobiographical – the first person

[1] *Antiquities* x.5.1.
[2] *Intro.*, ET (1907), p. 318.
[3] *LOT*,[8] p. 279.

singular is employed throughout. The book does make the strong impression that it is the work of a single personality. Further, many of the prophecies are dated and localized. The similarity of thought and arrangement throughout make it clear that the entire book is the work of one mind. Hence, we may with confidence hold to the view that Ezekiel was the author. And it is quite interesting to note that one of the latest scholarly commentaries, that of Cooke, holds that Ezekiel is the basic author of the book.

HISTORY OF THE LITERARY CRITICISM OF EZEKIEL

The passage quoted above from *Baba Bathra* does not really deny the Ezekielian authorship of the book. It may mean to teach nothing more than that the men of the Great Synagogue edited and copied out the book. The school of Shammai thought that the teaching of the book was not in harmony with the Mosaic law and that the first ten chapters exhibited a tendency towards Gnosticism. Hence, they regarded it as apocryphal. Rabbi Hananyah ben Hezekiah, however, defended the book, and so it was retained as canonical.[4]

The first serious attack upon the unity and integrity of the book was made in 1756 by G. L. Oeder, in a work which appeared posthumously in 1771. Oeder thought that the real book of Ezekiel ended with chapter 39 and that chapters 40–48 were a later addition. His work fits in well with the spirit of doubt that prevailed in his day. And there had been preparation for the criticism of Ezekiel. Almost a hundred years earlier, Spinoza had denied the authorship of the book to Ezekiel.[5]

Oeder's work[6] introduced a thesis which from time to time has made its appearance. In 1798 (for this information I am indebted to Pfeiffer) an anonymous writer in the *Monthly Magazine and British Register* refused to attribute chapters 1–24 to the author of chapters 25–32, which author he thought was Daniel.

During the nineteenth century attack was made upon the authenticity but not upon the unity of the book. In his *Die gottesdienstliche Vortäge der Juden* (1832), Leopold Zunz sought to show that Ezekiel was a product of the early Persian period. Later, however,[7] he assigned it to a time

---

[4] The manner in which Hananiah restored the book is quite interesting. 'What did he do? They brought him three hundred jars of oil and he explained it.' See *Shabbath* 4b, *Hagiga* 13a, *Menahoth* 45a.

[5] *TTP*, p. 207.

[6] *Freie Untersuchung über einige Bücher des Alten Testaments* (1771).

[7] 1873 in *ZDMG*, XXVII, pp. 676–681.

between 440 and 400 BC. In 1857 Abraham Geiger[8] followed Zunz. Finally L. Seinecke attributed the book to the Maccabean age.[9]

R. Kraetzschmar (1900), influenced by the Talmudic tradition that Ezekiel was placed between Jeremiah and Isaiah and written by the men of the Great Synagogue, maintained that the book had been put together by a redactor from two recensions of the text.

Jahn (1905) opposed Kraetzschmar's hypothesis, and tried to reconstruct the text from the LXX. He thought that scribes had inserted notes in the margin which later came to be incorporated in the text. Jahn shows too much preference for the LXX.

J. Herrmann (1908, 1924) regarded the book as a collection of small prophecies which were largely edited and redacted by Ezekiel himself.

Gustav Hoelscher (1942) came out with the complaint that Ezekiel had too long escaped the knife of criticism ('*Fast an allen prophetischen Bücher des Kanons hatte man längst das Messer der Kritik gelegt, nur Hesekiel blieb unberührt.*'[10] He thought that Herrmann had presented the first methodical analysis of the book, but objected that Herrmann attributed so much to Ezekiel himself. Hoelscher thought that within the book there were two different worlds, that of Ezekiel and that of later editors. Ezekiel was the author only of certain parts; the rest, particularly where there is a literary relation with Leviticus and Jeremiah, is due to a later editor who lived about the time of Nehemiah. This later editor worked over the material of the original Ezekiel and thus intruded into the book his own attitude. The first editing of the book was between 500 and 450 BC. All told, of the 1273 verses of the book Hoelscher leaves to Ezekiel only about 143.

C. C. Torrey (1930) regarded the original prophecy as having been written in Jerusalem about 230 BC and as directed against the idolatries permitted under the reign of Manasseh. Thus it was a pseudepigraph, actually composed many centuries later. At a later time, not many years after the appearance of the original prophecy, an editor gave to the work the clothing of 'a prophecy of the "Babylonian Golah".' This editor may be regarded as a representative of a literary movement which had as its purpose the 'vindication of the religious tradition of Jerusalem'.[11]

James Smith (1931) also asserted that the prophecies appear to belong to Manasseh's age, being addressed to Palestinians. Furthermore, they

---

[8] *Urschrift und Uebersetzungen der Bibel*, p. 23.
[9] *Geschichte des Volkes Israel* (1884).
[10] *Hesekiel*, p. 1.
[11] *Pseudo-Ezekiel*, p. 102.

were uttered not in Babylon, but in Palestine by a true prophet, a
northern Israelite of the days of Manasseh.

Volkmar Herntrich (1932) thinks that the speeches of the book were
delivered to the inhabitants of Palestine. The Babylonian framework is
simply the work of some editor from the exilic period. Throughout the
book signs of the editor's work are to be seen. Thus the present form of the
book arose in Babylonia, where the editor sought to prove the unity and
superiority of the Lord to the Babylonian pantheon. Oesterley and
Robinson seem favourably inclined towards this view of Herntrich, and
so, for the most part, does J. Battersby Harford (1935), and also Alfred
Bertholet in his commentary (1936).

William A. Irwin (1943) seeks by a process of dissection to discover the
original oracles of the book. He begins with a study of chapter 15 and
leaves very little to Ezekiel. Chapters 40–48 are rejected, and of the rest,
about 251 verses, in whole or in part, are accepted as genuine. Ezekiel, it
is claimed, went to Babylon in the second deportation, and most of the
oracles were composed in Jerusalem.

Nils Messel (1945) put his finger on the weak spot in Herntrich's thesis
when he suggested that the exiles would have known the actual course of
Ezekiel's life and would have seen through the situation, had it been what
Herntrich proposed. According to Messel the Golah is not the exiles in
Babylon but those who have already returned to Palestine. Ezekiel,
therefore, belongs to Palestine, to a time after Nehemiah, probably about
400 BC, and the redactors of the book should be dated about 350 BC. In
a sense Ezekiel carried on the work of Nehemiah, his enemies having
come from the same Jewish circles as did those of Nehemiah. The
redactor sought to continue Ezekiel's battle against idolatry and used his
writings for this purpose, amplifying and correcting them.

The above survey will show how varied are the views of recent
negative criticism with respect to the book of Ezekiel. But the so-called
problems of the book are best solved upon the basis of the traditional
view, namely, that Ezekiel himself composed the entire book.

In 1953 H. H. Rowley[12] defended the essential unity of the book, and
pointed out in a most convincing manner that the 'theories that transfer
either the prophet himself or his literary creator to a post-exilic age are
unconvincing' (p. 182). This work of Rowley's is an excellent introduction to the study of modern criticism of Ezekiel.

---

[12] *The Book of Ezekiel in Modern Study.*

Ezekiel was a priest of Jerusalem, the son of Buzi, a man of whom little
more is known. With the deportation of Jehoiachin he also was taken into
exile to Babylon (1:1), where he resided at Tel Abib (3:15), on the river
Chebar (1:3; 3:16ff.). Ezekiel was married and had his own home
(24:16–18). His call to the prophetic office came in the fourth month of
the fifth year of the captivity (1:1–2), and the latest date given is the first
month of the twenty-seventh year (29:17), hence his ministry lasted at
least twenty-two years. On the day that the siege of Jerusalem began his
wife died (24:1, 15–18), and it is not known whether he himself lived to
see the release of Jehoiachin under Evil-Merodach. That he knew Daniel,
his contemporary in Babylon, is evident from 14:14, 20 and 28:3.

It was Ezekiel's task to impress upon the exiles the fact that calamity
had come because of their own sinfulness. 'The soul that sinneth, it shall
die.' Thus, the prophecy inculcates the great doctrine of personal
responsibility. Even the theocracy in its outward form must come to an
end, if the chosen nation persists in sin. God, however, does not delight in
the death of the wicked. He freely and sincerely offers deliverance to all.
'Turn ye, turn ye, for why will ye die?' One day Israel will be regathered
into her own land, and will have one king. There will be true worship of
the Lord, and then the city will be called *Jehovah shammah* (the Lord is
there). Thus, the book reveals the faithfulness of God to His eternal
purposes. The sinful nation must be destroyed, but yet God will not
forsake His own.

a. 1:1–24:27. Prophecies uttered before the overthrow of Jerusalem
1. 1:1–3:21. Introduction. The prophet relates how, in the fifth year of
Jehoiachin's captivity (*i.e.*, *c.* 592 BC) he received a vision and beheld the
majesty of the Lord.

In 1:1 he mentions the thirtieth year. It has been suggested that this is
the thirtieth year after Josiah's reformation. Others have said that it is
the thirtieth year after the father of Nebuchadnezzar, Nabopolassar
ascended the throne. However, these opinions appear to be refuted by
1:2, which speaks of the fifth year of Jehoiachin's captivity. In all
probability, therefore, the phrase 'the thirtieth year' has reference to the
thirtieth year of the prophet's life. If this is correct Ezekiel was probably
born just after the accession of Nabopolassar to the throne. Quite
probably, also, he was about five years older than Daniel.

The whirlwind approaches from the north, thus signifying that it is from the north that judgment will come upon the nation. After the manifestation of God there follows the divine call, and Ezekiel (3:14, 15) goes to Tel Abib, where he waits for seven days. Then comes the call to begin his ministry, and the character of his position is set before him. He is a 'watchman unto the house of Israel'.

2. 3:22–27. A second vision of the glory of the Lord.

3. 4:1–7:27. By means of symbolical actions the destruction of Jerusalem is set forth. Ezekiel is symbolically to represent the siege of Jerusalem (4:1–3); by lying on his side, he is to announce the punishment of the nation's sins (4:4–8); by the kind of food he eats, he is to set forth the consequences of the siege. In 5:1–4 he shows symbolically what will become of the inhabitants of the city, and in 5:5–17 the prophet clearly explains the guilt of the people. Chapters 6 and 7 are two additional oracles, treating of judgment upon the idolatrous land and, finally, upon the entire kingdom.

4. 8:1–8. In the sixth year, sixth month, fifth day (c. August/ September 591 BC) the prophet is transported in the spirit to Jerusalem and beholds a vision of its destruction.

5. 9:1–11:25. The punishment of Jerusalem. The Lord's ministers pass through the city to destroy all who remain. He prepares to take His final departure from the sanctuary. The ungodly rulers of the nation will be destroyed.

6. 12:1–14:23. The Lord forsakes the city because of its unbelief and its following after false prophets.

7. 15:1–17:24. The certainty and necessity of the punishment.

8. 18:1–32. The love of God towards sinners.

9. 19:1–14. A lamentation over the princes of Israel.

10. 20:1–24:27. The last utterances of warning before the downfall of the city.

5. *25:1–32:32. Prophecies of judgment which are uttered against foreign nations* Ammon, 25:1–7; Moab, 25:8–11; Edom, 25:12–14; Philistia, 25:15–17; Tyre, 26:1–28:19; Sidon, 28:20–26; Egypt, 29:1–32:32.

7. *33:1–48:35. Prophecies concerning the restoration which were uttered after Nebuchadnezzar had taken Jerusalem*

1. 33:1–22. The new covenant and the love of God for the sinner. Formal instruction for the prophetic mission.

2. 34:1–31. The time will come when the people will recognize the Lord and there will be among them a true prophet.

3. 35:1–15. The devastation of Edom.

4. 36:1–38. The restoration of the people of Israel.

5. 37:1–28. The vision of the dry bones, symbol of the resurrection of Israel.

6. 38:1–39:29. The prophecy of Gog and Magog.

The chapters containing this prophecy follow immediately Ezekiel's vision of the dry bones and the glorious statement that the children of Israel shall be returned to their land where David will be their king, and they shall truly be the Lord's people, and He will be their God (chapter 37). This state of things is to endure for ever.

In our opinion, these three chapters (37, 38 and 39) form a unit. Thus, the reading of chapter 37 raises in our minds certain questions: Will there be no enemies who will seek to overthrow and destroy God's people, and so to sever them from their God? It is to chapters 38 and 39 that we must turn to discover the answer. There it is made plain that such enemies will exist and that they will be mighty and powerful, but the Lord knows His own. With them He has made an everlasting covenant that cannot be broken, and as for their enemies, He Himself will destroy them utterly. The prophecy is, therefore, above all a message of comfort to God's people.

Ezekiel tells us when the enemy will appear. It is to be 'after many days' (38:8), 'in the latter years' (38:8), and 'in the latter days' (38:16). The primary reference of these phrases is to this present New Testament age, which was ushered in by the appearance of our Lord upon earth (Read carefully, in this connection, the following New Testament passages, and note the use which they make of such phrases as 'in the end of these days', 'in the last days', and so forth: Acts 2:17; Heb. 1:1–2; 1 Pet. 1:20; 1 Jn. 2:18; Jude 18.)

When, therefore, these latter days have come and Israel is again established in her land (38:8), when, to use other words, the promised Messiah has appeared and the Tabernacle of God is among men (cf 48:35) and the incarnate Son of God has wrought our peace upon the cross, then ferocious enemies will appear who will attempt to destroy those for whom He died. Yes, even the very gates of hell will seek to prevail against His Church. But God is God and He will destroy the enemies of His people. Through Him, and through Him alone, the redeemed shall prevail.

But how is Ezekiel to present these truths? Surely not through the medium of New Testament language, for he was an Old Testament prophet. He spoke, therefore, as an Old Testament prophet, and used the thought-forms of his day as vehicles for his truths. Characteristically he employed imagery for this purpose. How better could he convey the truth that enemies would attack God's people, even after the promised redemption had come, than by employing the names of contemporary nations which were known to him, as symbols to represent a great alliance of the hosts of evil? It is precisely this, so it seems to us, that he does. He uses the figure of a great confederacy of nations of his day which seeks to destroy God's people 'upon the mountains of Israel'. This confederacy, headed by Gog, represents the allied forces of those who would oppose the Lord and His redeemed. In their enterprise, however, these enemies are ingloriously defeated. Indeed, so inglorious and complete is their defeat, that Ezekiel symbolically represents the fact by saying that Israel shall be seven years in burning their weapons and seven months in burying their dead. Thus, God's people may truly be convinced that God can defend them from all ill.

Which, however, are the nations that Ezekiel names as taking part in the confederacy against Israel? The answer to this question is difficult. Not all of these nations can be identified with certainty, and there is serious disagreement among devout students of the Bible as to the proper identification. Ezekiel seems to place at the head of the conspiracy Gagaia, by which he may have had in mind Carchemish. From the name of this land, Gagaia, he seems to build the names Gog and Magog. He next chooses nations which were near to Gagaia, namely, the Moschi and Tibareni (Meshech and Tubal). Then, from the world as it was known to his hearers, he mentions nations which were both near and remote, Persia, Ethiopia, Phut (possibly the East Africans), Gomer (perhaps the Cimmerians) and Togarmah (probably the ancient district corresponding to Armenia). These nations serve merely as the symbols by which Ezekiel seeks to portray the power and might of the enemies of God's redeemed people.

The prophecy, therefore, does not refer primarily to any one particular historical event, nor was it intended to do so. Hence, to seek to find its fulfilment in events taking place in the world today is to miss the point entirely. To treat it as though it were merely history written in advance is to betray an ignorance of its true nature. On the other hand, how rich and comforting is this prophecy when properly understood. It reveals clearly to us Christians how strong are the principalities and powers that would overthrow us. Yet this fact should not cause us discouragement, since the greatness of our foes only serves to reveal to us again how much greater our God is. 'Their rock is not as our Rock.'[13]

---

[13] The foregoing explanation of chapters 38:1–39:29 has been taken from an article by the author, 'Gog and Magog: Does the Bible Predict the Russo-German Alliance?', which appeared in *The Presbyterian Guardian*, Feb. 25, 1940.

This comforting prophecy of God and Magog prepares the way for the glorious vision which is revealed in the last nine chapters of the prophecy

7. 40:1–48:35. The vision of the Church of God upon earth symbolized by the description of the Temple.

With respect to the interpretation of these chapters it may be said tha part of the ministry of the prophet was to comfort the exiles and to remind them of the coming salvation. The exile was truly a punishment for their sins, but the exile would have an end. God had not forgotten His promises. There would come a day when Israel would return to her land and would worship the Lord in spirit and truth. How was Ezekiel to present these truths to the people? He, both a priest and a prophet would present these truths by the employment of symbols chosen from the priestly service. Hence, he sets forth in elaborate detail the description of the Temple and its worship.

It is obvious that the prophet never intended these descriptions to be taken literally. It is clear that he is using figurative or symbolical language. Every attempt to follow out his directions literally leads to difficulty. A literal construction of chapter 48, for example, would result in placing the Temple outside the city of Jerusalem. The whole description (chapters 40–48) comes to a striking climax in the very last words of the prophecy. 'The Lord is there', and this is the heart of the entire description. The prophet is depicting a time when there will be true worship of the Lord. In an earthly temple? No, for the prophet does not even mention an earthly high priest. But in spirit and in truth. In other words, this elaborate representation is a picture of the Messianic age. The Lord dwells in the midst of His people. Such is the chief characteristic of this picture.

To us this may seem a strange way of setting forth the truth. We should probably be inclined to employ straightforward, narrative prose. But we must never forget that the prophets of the Old Testament often employed dark speeches and figurative language. They spoke in th shadowy forms of the old covenant. But they spoke of Christ, and Ezekiel also, under this strange symbolism, was speaking of Christ. Hence, he was not in conflict with the Pentateuch, nor was he describing a literal temple, to exist during the millennium. He was, in a manner peculiar to himself, preaching Jesus Christ.

SPECIAL LITERATURE ON EZEKIEL

James Oscar Boyd, 'Ezekiel and the Modern Dating of the Pentateuch',* in PTR, 6 1908, pp. 29–51; Millar Burrows, The Literary Relations of Ezekiel (Philadelphia, 1925) C. H. Cornill, Der Prophet Ezechiel (Heidelberg, 1882); Lorenz Duerr, Die Stellung de

Propheten Ezechiel in der israelitisch-jüdischen Apokalyptik (Münster, 1923); John Battersby Hartford, *Studies in the Book of Ezekiel* (Cambridge, 1935); Volkmar Herntrich, *Ezekiel-probleme* (1932); J. Hermann, *Ezechiel Studien* (1908); Gustav Hoelscher, *Hesekiel: der Dichter und das Buch; eine Literarkritische Untersuchung* (Giessen, 1921); G. Jahn, *Das Buch Ezechiel auf Grund der Septuaginta hergestellt* (Leipzig, 1905); R. Kraetzschmar, *Das Buch Ezechiel* (1900); C. M. Mackay, 'The City and the Sanctuary',* 'Ezekiel's Sanctuary and Wellhausen's Theory',* in *PTR*, 20, 1922, pp. 399–417 and 661–665 respectively; 'The City of Ezekiel's Oblation',* *PTR*, 21, 1923, pp. 372–388; 'Ezekiel's Division of Palestine Among the Tribes',* *PTR*, 22, 1924, pp. 27–45; Nils Messel, *Ezechielfragen* (Oslo, 1945); James Smith, *The Book of the Prophet Ezekiel: A New Interpretation* (London, 1931); Charles Cutler Torrey, *Pseudo-Ezekiel and the Original Prophecy* (New Haven, 1930).

CHAPTER SEVENTEEN

THE TWELVE

AS early as Ecclesiasticus, the twelve Minor Prophets were grouped together (49:12). They were evidently thus regarded also by Josephus (*Contra Apionem* i. 8.3). *Baba Bathra* 15a states that the men of the Great Synagogue wrote the Twelve, and the early Church Fathers spoke of them as 'The Twelve' or 'The Book of the Twelve Prophets'.

In the manuscripts of the LXX a different order of books is followed, at least as far as the first six are concerned, namely: Hosea, Amos, Micah, Joel, Obadiah, and Jonah. Probably because it was the longest, Hosea was placed first, but it is difficult to account for the arrangement of the other books. Further, in some manuscripts (A and B) the Twelve are placed before the Major Prophets.

Probably chronological considerations governed to an extent the arrangement of the Twelve in the Hebrew Canon. Thus, we read: 'But indeed! Hosea was the first, because it is written, The beginning of the word of the Lord of Hosea. Now, did he first speak with Hosea? Were there not many prophets from Moses to Hosea? Rabbi Johanan says that he was the first of the three prophets that prophesied at the period, namely, Hosea, Amos and Micah, and would not Hosea be placed at the head? [Answer]: His prophecies were placed by the side of Haggai, Zechariah, and Malachi; and Haggai, Zechariah, and Malachi were the end of the prophets; it is reckoned with them. It should be written in part and [placed] at the head. Since it is short, it might have become lost.'¹ Hence, in the Twelve, according to the Talmud, there are the three oldest prophecies, more or less contemporary with Isaiah, those which closed the collection being later. Evidently the others were regarded as having prophesied before the destruction of the Temple and so were placed in the middle of the collection. But too much weight should not be given to this Talmudic tradition. We do not really know why this arrangement of the Twelve was adopted.

---

1 *Baba Bathra*, 14b.

HOSEA

NAME

The book is named after the prophet *hoshe'a*. In the Greek and in the Latin this appears as *Osee*.

AUTHOR

Hosea was the son of Beeri and prophesied in the kingdom of the ten tribes. His work falls within the lifetime of Isaiah. He is author of the entire book bearing his name.

Some scholars have denied to Hosea various parts of the book. Volz and Marti, for example, do not attribute to him the prophecies of blessing or salvation, such as 11:8–11 or 14:2–9. A second type of passage which has often been denied to Hosea is that which contains some mention of the southern kingdom. Marti, Nowack, and others thus considered such passages (with some exceptions) to be secondary interpolations. These older views are clearly set forth in Harper's Commentary.

At present, however, there seems to be a modification of this tendency. Thus Eissfeldt points out that even in the certainly genuine portions of the book (chapters 1–3) there is mention of salvation after punishment, and he appeals to 5:8–6:6 to show that not every mention of Judah must be denied to Hosea. Eissfeldt regards the following as the principal glosses: 4:3, 9; 7:10; 14:10; and parts of chapter 12. Bentzen here adopts essentially the same position as Eissfeldt.

But there is no sufficient reason for denying to Hosea any of the prophecy. We may expect him to mention Judah since (8:4) he clearly regards the northern kingdom as a usurpation. In the light of this viewpoint (*cf.* also 3:5) we may understand why he dates his prophecy according to the southern rulers.

PURPOSE

In the ministry of Hosea to the ten apostate northern tribes there is manifest the grace of God. It is to these tribes, ripe for destruction, that the prophet is sent. His great purpose is to reveal the love of God for a sinful and rebellious nation. He pictures that nation, under the symbolism of a faithless wife, as a nation that has committed spiritual adultery, and he pleads with the people to repent and to turn from their ungodly ways. There must come a time of refining, when Israel shall dwell for many days in an unusual condition. Then, after the exile, mercy will again be shown.

Hosea's call probably occurred towards the close of the reign of Jeroboam II. He evidently witnessed the last days of this monarch's reign, the declining days and the destruction of Israel, and her departure into exile.

ANALYSIS

a. Hosea 1:1–3:5. God's relations with His people

In studying the prophecy of Hosea the reader is almost immediately confronted with a problem of exceeding difficulty. The prophet begins his message by the announcement that the Lord has commanded him: 'Go, take unto thee a wife of whoredom and children of whoredom: for the land hath committed great whoredom, departing from the Lord.' At first sight it appears that Hosea is being commanded to do something that is wrong. In answer to the Lord's command, Hosea relates that he married Gomer and that she bore him several children. Each of these children bore a symbolical name and was made the object of instruction. For example, one of the children was called Lo-Ammi (*i.e.*, not my people), and this name stood as a symbol for the message of the Lord: 'Ye are not my people.'

Throughout these first three chapters of the prophecy there runs a tender strain of sadness. Christian commentators, therefore, have paused to reflect upon the precise meaning of the prophecy. According to some devout students of the Scriptures, we are to understand these things as actually having taken place. Hosea did, therefore, according to this interpretation, actually marry a woman who was an adulteress, and she bore him children which might bear the terrible name, children of whoredom. As each child was born, Hosea took the occasion to proclaim to the people the message which God had given him. For example, when Hosea's little daughter was born, he called her name Lo-ruhammah (*i.e.*, not has mercy been shown), and he took the occasion of her birth to announce to Israel: 'I will no more have mercy upon the house of Israel; but I will utterly take them away' (1:6).

There is much to be said in defence of this literal interpretation. For one thing, the prophecy reads as straightforward narrative. At first sight, we receive the impression that these things are to be understood as actually having taken place. It is perfectly understandable, then, that many Christian expositors would regard the literal interpretation at this point correct.

As one reflects further upon the passage, however, questions begin to rise in his mind, and the questions are of so arresting and compelling a nature that they cannot lightly be brushed aside. For one thing, if Hosea had actually married an adulterous woman, would he not by that act have destroyed the effectiveness of his ministry? To make the matter plainer: When a present-day minister of the Gospel becomes entangled with a woman of loose character, do not people look askance at him? Do they not question the sincerity of his profession? So with Hosea. If he had actually married such a woman, would not people have refused to listen to him? This consideration is weighty, and it cannot lightly be brushed aside. Again, would not the time element have destroyed the effectiveness of the prophet's message? A number of months would have elapsed before the birth of the first child. At the birth of this child the prophet would have spoken his message. Would not its continuity with the message which was uttered at the time of the prophet's marriage have been destroyed? So much time would have elapsed that people would have forgotten what Hosea had proclaimed to them at the time of his marriage. Then, months must again elapse before the birth of the next child, and so on. These are only two of the compelling considerations which have caused many devout students of the Bible to ask whether, as a matter of actual fact, we are to regard this account as literal.

Consequently, in company with many biblical students, the present writer has become more and more convinced that the whole episode has a symbolical significance. The entire message was revealed to the prophet, and the prophet related this revelation to the people. If this is the case, then we can immediately perceive the forcefulness and the effectiveness of the message. It is forceful and direct. It portrays the love of God for the sinful and adulterous nation and reaches its climax in the announcement that the children of Israel shall be as the sand of the sea.

This symbolical interpretation, of course, is not without difficulty, but seems to be correct. In this connection we may note that again in chapter 3 Hosea is commanded to marry, and it is not clear whether this woman is Gomer or not. There are good reasons for believing that this woman is Gomer. At any rate, the episode serves to reveal the tender love of Jehovah for His erring people.

Wellhausen embraced what might be called a semi-literal interpretation. On this view Hosea did not realize the true nature of his wife until the birth of the children. Modifications of this position have been advanced. This interpretation, however, cannot be carried through consistently. It could not well apply to chapter 3.

b. Hosea 4:1–14:10. Various discourses of the prophet
As Driver has stated, in this section particularly Hosea reveals himself
as the prophet of 'the decline and fall of the Northern Kingdom'.
Chapters 4–8 lay special stress upon the guilt of the sinful kingdom;
9–11:11 emphasize the punishment that is to come to Israel, and 11:12–
14:10, while also continuing these thoughts, point to the future blessing
that awaits a repentant nation. The background of these prophecies is
the threat of the Assyrian Empire. Hosea shows himself to be a man of
deep feeling, and at times his anger against sin manifests itself in language
that is harsh and somewhat vehement. On the other hand, when the
prophet sets before the nation the sublime love of the Lord the language
of the book is filled with beautiful imagery.

JOEL

NAME

The book is named from its author, *yo'el*, who is said to be the son of
Pethuel, and this is all that the book states concerning him.

ANALYSIS

It is best first to consider the contents of the book in order better to
understand the questions of authorship and composition.

a. Joel 1:1–2:27. The plague of locusts
1. 1:1. Superscription. Although the superscription does not state the
fact, there is more or less general agreement that Joel exercised his
ministry in Judah.
   2. 1:2–20. The book opens with the description of a devastating plague
of locusts (verses 2–4); this is followed by a command to repentance. The
priests are bid to proclaim a fast and solemn assembly at the house of the
Lord (verses 5–14); with the words 'Alas for the day!' the prophet
announces the coming of the day of the Lord, a day of trouble and
visitation.
   3. 2:1–17. The prophet commands that a trumpet be blown since the
day of the Lord is coming. It is a day of darkness in which the enemy will
enter the city. In verses 3–10 Joel gives a description of this invading
army, and announces that the Lord with His army will meet the invader
(verse 11); therefore, the people should repent and fast and turn to the

Lord (verses 12–17); the Lord will respond to this repentance by a mighty deliverance.

b. Joel 2:28–3:21. The blessing and judgment of the Lord

In the Hebrew, chapter 2 ends with verse 27. Verses 28–32 are regarded as chapter 3, and chapter 3 in the English is chapter 4 in the Hebrew. Thus, English 2:28–32 is Hebrew 3:1–5; English 3:1–21 is Hebrew 4:1–21.

1. 2:28–32. A prophecy of the Messianic age, when the Spirit of God is poured out upon all flesh, and the gospel will be offered to all. 'Whosoever shall call on the name of the Lord shall be delivered.' The fulfilment of this prophecy of grace occurred when the Holy Spirit was poured out at Pentecost (Acts 2:17).

2. 3:1–21. The prophet now proceeds further to characterize the time of His people's blessing by the use of metaphorical language. The captivity of Judah and Jerusalem will be brought again, but for the nations there will be judgment in the valley of Jehoshaphat (verses 1–8); it is to be announced to these nations that it will be a time of war and judgment (verses 9–16); for God's people, however, there will be everlasting blessing, 'Judah shall dwell for ever, and Jerusalem from generation to generation' (verses 17–21).

AUTHOR

The basic problem to be considered is whether chapters 1 and 2 are to be considered as a prophecy or as a description of events which have already taken place. In modern times Merx[2] and Eissfeldt have shown clearly that these chapters contain prophetic material pointing to the future. However, it is best to regard the two chapters as *complete* prophecies. Thus, they fit in well with the latter half of the book. The author of the entire book was Joel himself, and his ministry is best placed in the pre-exilic period, possibly during the reign of Joash. In favour of this view it may be noted that the enemies of Judah which are mentioned are not those of the exilic period, such as the Syrians, Assyrians and Babylonians, but rather the Philistines, Phoenicians (3:4), Egypt, and Edom (3:19). At the time of Joash, Syria and Assyria had not begun to attack Judah, but Egypt was evidently still an enemy, having invaded Judah during the days of Rehoboam. And during the reign of Jehoram, shortly before, Edom and Philistia had been at war with Judah (*cf.* 2 Ki. 8:20–22; 2 Ch. 21:16–17).

[2] *Die Prophetie des Joel und ihre Ausleger* (1879).

Again, the position of the book between Hosea and Amos seems to show that Jewish tradition considered it to be ancient. Furthermore, the literary style is quite different from such post-exilic prophecies as Haggai, Zechariah, and Malachi. It should also be noted that the king is no mentioned, but rather the elders and priests. Such practice would be quite understandable in Joash's days, since upon ascending the throne he was but seven years of age (2 Ki. 11:21). The prophet Amos was apparently acquainted with Joel's prophecies (cf. 3:16 with Am. 1:2, and 3:18 with Am. 9:13).

Oesterley and Robinson believe that the narrative portions must be post-exilic, chiefly because there is no reference to the northern kingdom, Jerusalem is the only sanctuary, there is no mention of the high places, or of a king, and there is the threefold reference to the meal offering and drink offering (1:9, 13; 2:14) – which is said to be conclusive, since it i the Tamid or 'continual' offering, supposed to be a sign of post-exilic times – and, lastly, the style itself. All of this, together with some arguments of lesser importance, convince these writers that the narrative portions are post-exilic.

Some of these arguments have already been considered. In addition, however, to what has already been indicated, it may be noted that there was in the prophecy no particular occasion for using the name of the northern kingdom, and the name of Israel belonged to the southern as well as the northern kingdom. The absence of mention of the *bamoth*, or high places, proves nothing as to date, since there seems to be no particular reason why they should have been mentioned. And even Oesterley and Robinson do admit that such absence might apply to a time considerably before Amos. Hence, nothing can really be made of the lack of such mention. Again the reference to meat and drink offering cannot be used as an indication of date, unless one also accepts the dating which negative criticism applies to Exodus and Numbers, which introduce the drink offering (cf. Ex. 29:38–42; Nu. 28:3–8).

As to the apocalyptic portions, Oesterley and Robinson believe that they belong to about 200 BC. Hence, these authors (as also did Duhm) hold to a dual authorship of the prophecy. The apocalyptical context i said to be similar to that of the apocalypse of the two centuries before Christ, and the mention of 'the sons of the Grecians' (3:4) is supposed to refer to the Seleucid line. But that this phrase has any reference to th Seleucid line is mere assumption. It is perfectly possible that, even a early as the days of Joash, Jewish captives were sold to the Greeks. Also the apocalyptic sections of Joel have some similarities with those o Isaiah. Apocalyptic literature is not necessarily an indication of late date

Pfeiffer regards the book as a unit, the product of one author, and would place it about 350 BC. All in all, however, the pre-exilic date has most in its favour.

PURPOSE

Joel's purpose is to warn the nation of the need for humility and repentance and the certainty of coming judgment. At the same time, he seeks to keep the heart of the people faithful to the promises of God by reminding them of the coming salvation and of the destruction of their and God's enemies.

AMOS

NAME

The prophet's name was *'Amos*, not to be confused with the name of Isaiah's father, *'Amoz*.

AUTHOR

The author of the entire prophecy was Amos himself. The prophet was from Tekoa, a town about five miles south-east of Bethlehem, where he was a herdsman (*nogedim*, sheep-raiser, see 1:1) and also a dresser of sycamore trees (7:14). While he was in the course of his ordinary occupation the Lord called him to be a prophet (7:14–15). He himself describes this call in the words, 'And the Lord took me from [following] after the flock, and the Lord said unto me, Go! Prophesy unto my people Israel.' From the book itself we learn the type of people to whom Amos preached. They were a rich people, self-confident and sure that no evil would befall them. The rich oppressed the poor, and justice was sadly lacking in the courts. With true courage Amos rebuked these evils and pleaded with the nation to turn to the Lord.

It is generally held that Amos was the author of the book. A number of critics maintain, however, that there are annotations and additions made by later editors or writers. An attempt to identify these was made in 1935 by R. E. Wolfe. Pfeiffer thinks that the glossators were Jews from Jerusalem who were active between 500 and 200 BC. He believes that there are numerous glosses, the most important of which are the doxologies and the Messianic promise of 9:9–15.

I

Eissfeldt also believes that there are numerous additions, and, apart from individual verses and phrases, regards 1:9 ,10; 1:11, 12; 2:4, 5 (insertions in Amos' denunciation of the nations), 4:13; 5:8, 9; 9:5, 6 (doxologies) and 9:11–15 (the Messianic promise) as three important types of addition.

However, these additions are generally regarded as having been made for theological reasons, and the assumptions upon which they are regarded as additions are based upon a particular theory of the religious development of Israel. There are no objective grounds for denying to Amos any portion of the book which bears his name.

PURPOSE

The prophecy of Amos is an example of the goodness of God to an unworthy nation. The Israelites of the north had rejected the Davidic covenant and hence any claim to the promises of Jehovah. At the same time, they were smug and confident in the belief that, since they were the chosen people, no calamity could come upon them. They worshipped the Lord with their lips, but their hearts were far from Him. Their lives were characterized by selfishness, greed, immorality, oppression of the poor. There was no justice in the land. To such a people came Amos, in order that he might warn them of the impending doom. He does not mention the Assyrian by name, but clearly predicts the exile. His purpose is to warn, but also to promise deliverance through Christ.

It has sometimes been held that Amos' message was one of woe alone and, hence, the blessing predicted in chapter 9 could not have been his. But this is to misunderstand the prophet. In proclaiming blessing, he is showing the faithfulness of God to His covenant, a faithfulness which will be realized when God brings again the captivity of His people (9:14).

ANALYSIS

a. *Amos 1 : 1–2 : 16. The announcement against the nations*
1. Superscription. Possibly Uzziah is mentioned first in order to show that Amos regarded only the Davidic line as legitimate (*cf.* Ho. 1:1). The earthquake occurred two years after Amos had prophesied (*cf.* Zc. 14:5) but before he committed his messages to writing.
2. 1:2. Theme of the section. Note that the Lord speaks from Jerusalem, for Zion was the legitimate sanctuary.
3. 1:3–3:3. Prophecies against the nations: Damascus (1:3–5),

Philistia (1:6–8), Phoenicia (Tyre) (1:9, 10), Edom (1:11, 12), Ammon
(1:13–15), Moab (2:1–3).

Note that the first three nations were not blood-relatives of Israel,
whereas the last three were. Step by step Amos approaches nearer to
Israel.

4. 2:4–16. Prophecies against the chosen people: Judah (2:4, 5),
Israel (2:6–16).

In these prophecies Amos employs a certain framework to give
strength to his message. First the statement 'For three transgressions, yea,
for four, I will not turn away.' Then follows mention of a characteristic
sin, then the announcement of judgment. This scheme holds the
attention of the reader, until, having finally come to Israel, the prophet
breaks forth in all his vehemence to proclaim the coming of exile.

b. Amos 3:1–6:14. The judgment against Israel

1. 3:1–15. God's quarrel with His people.

2. 4:1–13. Despite past punishments Israel has not returned to the
Lord.

3. 5:1–27. The Lord laments over Israel as over a virgin that is fallen.

Each of the above three addresses is introduced with the phrase 'hear
ye this word'. In 5:18 a woe is introduced which prepares for the
continuation of the third address, found in 6:1–14.

4. 6:1–14, continuation of the third address, introduced by a cry of
woe.

c. Amos 7:1–9:15. Five visions of the coming judgment

1. 7:1–3. The first vision, the plague of locusts.

2. 7:4–6. The second vision, fire devours the great deep.

3. 7:7–17. The third vision, the plumbline. To this vision there is
added in verses 11–17 the historical account of the command of Amaziah
to Amos to leave the land.

4. 8:1–14. The fourth vision, the basket of summer fruit.

5. 9:1–10. The fifth vision, the destruction of the sanctuary.

The first four visions are introduced by the words, 'thus hath the Lord
shewed me', the fifth by 'I saw'.

6. 9:11–15. The promise of Messianic blessing.

Verses 11, 12 form the basis of a quotation by James in Acts 15:16–18.
In this quotation James, under the inspiration of the Holy Spirit, makes
this passage, in the LXX version, the basis of his summing-up of Old
Testament prophecy regarding the Messianic age. He definitely applies
these words to the purpose of God in calling out the Gentiles.

OBADIAH

NAME

This little prophecy is named from its author '*Obhadhyah*, which appears in the LXX as *Obdiou*, and in the Vulgate as *Abdias*.

AUTHOR

Various views have been held concerning the authorship of Obadiah. According to Oesterley and Robinson, the book is a collection of oracles directed against Edom, the age and author of which are unknown. Pfeiffer holds that the original oracle against Edom has come down in two recensions (Ob. 1–9 and Je. 49:7–22). Apparently verses 10–14 and 15b never existed apart from verses 1–9, and all these verses (*i.e.*, 1–14, 15b) Pfeiffer would date about 460 BC. The second part he would place even later. Rudolph divides the prophecy into two oracles, verses 1:14, 15b, and verses 16–18, both of which he attributes to Obadiah. As to the concluding verses, he admits that they may be derived from Obadiah.

Eissfeldt has insisted that verses 2–9 present an actual threat, not a mere description, and that 11–14, 15b belong with verses 1–10 as an actual unity, since verses 11–14, 15b contain the basis or reason for the threat of the earlier verses. This part he would date after 587 (the destruction of Jerusalem). Verses 15a plus 16–18 do not belong with the preceding and are divided into two sections, verses 15a plus 16–18 and verses 19–21. Possibly these two utterances come from Obadiah but more likely they are from later hands.

But in opposition to the above views we would assert that it is best to regard the entire prophecy as having been written by Obadiah and that he lived before Jeremiah. It is not necessary to interpret verses 11–14 as does Eissfeldt, namely as referring to the end of Jerusalem. They may also refer, as Raven and others have suggested, to the events which occurred during the reign of Jehoram when Philistines and Arabians invaded Judah (2 Ch. 21:16–17, *cf.* also Am. 1:6). How long after this Obadiah prophesied, we cannot tell. It has been suggested (Davis, Raven) that his ministry is to be placed in the reign of Ahaz when Edom was particularly hostile to Judah. This may be; it seems best to maintain that he prophesied in Judah sometime before the ministry of Jeremiah (Je. 49:7–22 is similar to Obadiah, and probably dependent upon it).

PURPOSE

The prophet's purpose is to show that Edom's actions towards Judah will be punished, but Judah herself will be glorified. 1–14 contain the heading (verse 1), and the general threat against Edom. Edom trusted in her pride, but God will bring her low, confounding her mighty men. Edom's conduct was unbrotherly (verse 12) and the Lord points out to her what she should not have done. 15–21 announce the coming of the day of the Lord when Edom, like other nations, will be visited for her sin. Nevertheless, there will be deliverance in Zion and the kingdom will belong to the Lord.

JONAH

NAME

The book takes its name from the author, *yonah* (a dove). In the LXX the word has the form *Ionas*, and in the Vulgate *Jonas*.

AUTHOR

Jonah was an Israelite, the son of Amittai, from Gath-hepher in Galilee. The only mention of him outside the prophecy is in 2 Kings 14:25, which states that Jeroboam II restored the coast of Israel from the entering of Hamath unto the sea of the plain as God had spoken by Jonah. We are not told at what precise time Jeroboam thus followed out the words of Johan, but we do at least learn the time of Jonah's ministry, since Jeroboam, under whom he exercised that ministry, reigned from 783–743 BC. While the prophecy itself is not dated, it is quite probable that Jonah wrote shortly after his return from Nineveh. It is also quite possible that the prophet's visit to Nineveh occurred shortly before the reign of Tiglath-Pileser.

According to Eissfeldt it is questionable whether the Jonah of the prophecy and the Jonah of 2 Kings are to be identified. The present book, he thinks, contains two legends, one of which (chapters 1–3) deals with Jonah's conflict with the divine command, and the other (chapter 4) shows how Jonah's dissatisfaction with God's grace is reduced to absurdity. Included in the first legend is a mythological, fairy-tale (*märchenhaftes*) motif, found throughout the whole world, which deals with a fish swallowing a man and spewing him out again.

An unknown composer has taken this material and formed it into our present book, although it is difficult, thinks Eissfeldt, to tell how much is his own. One thing appears clear, namely, that the universalistic ideas in the book are those of the composer, and this fact enables us to determine the age in which he lived. This was the post-exilic age (possibly the time of Ezra-Nehemiah, since the book might have been a protest against their measures) as is also thought to be shown by the fact that the Assyrian kingdom and its capital are regarded as long since passed away (*dahin*), and the Aramaisms (*e.g.*, 1:7, *beshellemi*, through whom? and 3:2, *qeri'ah*, preaching). We do not, however, possess the book as it left the hand of the composer. In the course of time it received certain changes, the most notable of which was the inclusion of the 'thanksgiving song' (2:3–10) and verse 2 as an introduction to the song. Otherwise the book is a unit, and the attempts at source analysis, such as those of Hans Schmidt, must be regarded as unsatisfactory.

Eissfeldt presents a position which in its essentials is widely held. Oesterley and Robinson appeal more in detail to the presence of Aramaisms and to the style of the language as evidences for a post-exilic date. Pfeiffer thinks that he finds historical inaccuracies in the designation 'king of Nineveh' (3:6), and the description of Nineveh as 'an exceeding great city of three days journey' (3:3), and he states that it is 'physiologically improbable' for a man to survive three days in the belly of a fish.

In answer it should be noted that Christ believed in the historicity of the miracles recorded in Jonah (*cf.* Mt. 12:39–40; Lk. 11:29–30) and the historicity of the prophet's mission to the Ninevites. Hence, we cannot regard the book as legendary and unhistorical in character. With those who disbelieve in miracles or in the deity of Jesus Christ there is no common meeting-ground. For the believer in Jesus, it is sufficient that in God's miraculous power the prophet was kept alive in the belly of the fish for three days.

The presence of Aramaisms in the book cannot be made a criterion for determining the date, since Aramaisms occur in Old Testament books from both early and late periods. Furthermore, the recently discovered texts from Ras Shamra contain Aramaic elements (*c.* 1400–1500 BC).

Nor can the phrase 'journey of three days' (3:3, 4) be evidenced as an inaccuracy. The phrase may be intended as a designation of the city's diameter, but possibly it is nothing more than a rough expression to indicate that the city was a large one. Verse 4 states that Jonah 'began to enter into the city (*ba'ir*) a journey of one day'. This does not mean that he walked as far as it is possible to walk in one day. It merely means that he entered the city and went about, doubtless here and there, preaching his message. It is furthermore possible that this designation of the city as a 'journey of three days' had reference, not to the diameter of the city proper but to the complex of villages which clustered about Nineveh. If so, there can be no objection to this description.

Nor can exception be justly taken to the designation 'king of Nineveh'. The writer merely intends to refer to the ruler as such, as, *e.g.*, the king of Damascus (2 Ch. 24:23) or the king of Edom (2 Ki. 3:9, 12). Ordinarily the Israelites spoke of the ruler as king of Assyria. The usage here is similar to the designation of Ahab as king of Samaria (1 Ki. 21:1, *cf.* with 20:43) and Benhadad as king of Damascus (2 Ch. 24:23), whereas he is generally called king of Syria.

Furthermore, 3:3 does not describe Nineveh as a city that had existed long ago in the past but simply indicates the condition or size as Jonah found it. Moeller appeals to Luke 24:13 as a parallel. Certainly the words 'which was from Jerusalem about threescore furlongs' simply describe the location and do not imply that Emmaus was a city which had existed in the distant past but was no longer in existence.

As to the universalistic ideas of the book, they are in perfect keeping with the universalistic emphasis which appears throughout the Old Testament. This emphasis appeared early (*e.g.*, Gn. 9:27). There is no objective warrant for regarding such teaching as characteristic of post-exilic times alone.

PURPOSE

The fundamental purpose of the book of Jonah is not found in its missionary or universalistic teaching. It is rather to show that Jonah being cast into the depths of Sheol and yet brought up alive is an illustration of the death of the Messiah for sins not His own and of the Messiah's resurrection. Jonah was an Israelite and servant of the Lord, and his experience was brought about because of the sins of the nations (Nineveh). The Messiah was *the* Israelite and true Servant of the Lord whose death was brought about by the sins of the world.

'For as Jonas was three days and three nights in the whale's belly; so shall the Son of man be three days and three nights in the heart of the earth. The men of Nineveh shall rise in judgment with this generation and shall condemn it: because they repented at the preaching of Jonas; and, behold, a greater than Jonas is here' (Mt. 12:40, 41). Thus the experience of Jonah has as its basic purpose to point forward to the experience of that One who is 'greater than Jonas'.

Furthermore, this experience of Jonah's had great didactic value for the Israelites of his day. Jonah, an Israelite, was cast into the sea and delivered in order that he might fulfil his mission. So the nation, because of its disobedience, would have to pass through the waters of affliction, that a remnant might return to accomplish Israel's mission in the world.

The ministry of Jonah also serves to point out the stubborn and rebellious character of the Israelites. Many prophets had arisen, and the nation had not repented, but when Nineveh heard the words of one prophet, it repented in sackcloth and ashes.

Lastly, the mission of Jonah served to impress upon the Israelites the fact that the Lord's salvation was not to be confined to one nation. Israel was the servant to bring the knowledge of the Lord to the world.

THE UNITY OF THE BOOK

As will be seen from the sketch of Eissfeldt's view given above, the psalm in chapter 2 is attributed to a different original source from the remainder of the book. The basic question, therefore, as far as the unity of the book is concerned is that of the relation of this psalm to the three other chapters.

Those who believe that the psalm is from a different source from the other chapters advance the following arguments. In 2:1 it is said that Jonah prayed, but what follows is not a prayer but a psalm of thanksgiving for deliverance. Furthermore, it is maintained, this psalm of thanksgiving for deliverance occurs *before* the deliverance has taken place, for only in verse 10 are we told that the fish 'vomited out Jonah upon the dry land'. Nor is there anything in this psalm, it is argued, which suggests its connection with Jonah's experiences. Wellhausen even thought that verse 5 with its mention of weeds, excluded the idea that Jonah was in the fish's belly, for he remarked that 'weeds do not grow in a whale's belly'.[3] Lastly, it has been maintained that the text reads smoothly without this psalm, if 2:10 be placed immediately after 2:1.

In the first place it may be remarked, however, that if 2:2–9 be removed, the symmetry of the book is destroyed. The book obviously falls into two halves, chapters 1 and 2, and chapters 3 and 4. It should be noted that 3:1–3a and 1:1–3a correspond to one another with only minor verbal differences. Furthermore, 4:2 and 2:2 correspond in that both mention Jonah's praying (*wayyithpallel*). In one case there is a psalm of thanksgiving, in the other a complaint. The removal of 2:2–9, therefore, simply destroys the symmetry of the book. Furthermore, there is no

[3] *Die Kleinen Propheten* (1898), p. 221.

conflict between the statement that Jonah prayed, and a psalm of thanksgiving. For is not thanksgiving of the very essence of prayer? (*Cf.*, *e.g.*, Psalm 86, a prayer, *tephillah*, which contains elements of thanksgiving.)

But Wellhausen and other objectors to the genuineness of 2:2–9 do not understand the meaning of the psalm at all. Of course weeds do not grow in whales' bellies. But this is *not* a psalm of thanksgiving for deliverance from a whale's belly. It is rather a psalm of thanksgiving for deliverance from drowning; the figures of speech employed in this psalm have reference to drowning, not to a whale's belly. Furthermore, there is not one scintilla of evidence which makes this psalm purport to have reference to deliverance from the belly of the fish. The school of negative criticism has unjustly imputed to this psalm a meaning which it never was intended to bear.

The psalm, therefore, is to be regarded as in its proper place. Jonah had been cast into the sea, into the belly of Sheol – the depth, the heart of the seas, the flood, the waves and billows, the waters, the deep, the weeds, the bottoms of the mountains, the bars of the earth, the pit. (To what else could such phrases refer but to the sea?) From this terrifying experience, however, Jonah had been rescued by the great fish which the Lord had prepared (*wayeman* – this act of the Lord's should be taken into account before one proceeds to deny the possibility of the miracle). While in the belly of the fish, Jonah uttered his thanksgiving. Then, at the proper time, the fish spewed him out.

The psalm contains reminiscences of many psalms which by their titles are attributed to David and of others which are from his time. Moeller offers the following table for comparison:

JONAH	PSALMS
2:3b	18:7; 120:1
2:4b	18:6; 30:4
2:5	42:8
2:6	31:23; 5:8
2:7	18:8; 69:2f.
2:8	18:17; 30:4; 103:4
2:9	142:4; 143:4; 18:7; 5:8
2:10	88:3
	31:7
	26:7; 50:14, 23; 42:5; 116:17

MICAH

NAME

The book is named after the prophet Micah, whose name appears in a longer form in Judges 17:1, 4, *Michayahu*. In the LXX it appears as *Michaias* and in the Vulgate as *Michaeas*.

AUTHOR

The entire prophecy is the work of the prophet himself. He was from Moresheth, which is probably to be identified with the Moresheth-Gath of 1:14. His ministry took place in the days of Jotham, Ahaz, and Hezekiah. In the light of Jeremiah 26:18, which asserts that Micah uttered the words of 3:12 during the reign of Hezekiah, it may be inferred that Micah was a younger contemporary of Isaiah. The background of the book is the same as that found in the earlier portions of Isaiah, although Micah does not exhibit the same knowledge of the capital's political life as Isaiah. This may be due to the fact that Micah was from the country (Moresheth is generally equated with Beth Jibrim).

That Micah himself is the author of the entire prophecy is not accepted by the school of modern negative criticism. Eissfeldt, for example, regards the authorship of the book as follows. Chapters 1 to 3 are genuine, the work of Micah, with the exception of 2:12, 13. The heading (1:1) is secondary, but 1:2–8 were uttered before the destruction of the northern kingdom. 1:9–16 come from the situation either of 701 or 711. The remainder of this section contains no allusion to any specific situation.

It is very difficult, thinks Eissfeldt, to decide about the genuineness of 4:1–5:8 and 2:12, 13. The arguments adduced for their genuineness are worthy of notice, but Eissfeldt believes it best to pronounce against their genuineness. For one thing, threats such as 3:12 are weakened by the addition of secondary promises. 4:1–5 also appears in Isaiah, and most likely this was originally an anonymous prophecy which was attributed in one book to Isaiah and here to Micah. Furthermore, according to Jeremiah 26:18, Micah proclaimed only threat, not promise of restoration.

As to the remaining parts of this section, they contain thoughts which elsewhere occur only in passages from a later time, thus 4:6, 7 and 5:6, 8,

the gathering together of God's dispersed people; 4:8–14, the eschatological expectation of the destruction of Jerusalem's foes.

The passage 5:9–14 reminds us of Isaiah 2:6–8 and has probably been
changed from an original threat against the nation to a threat against the
foreign peoples; 6:1–8 also is probably from Micah, as well as 6:9–16 and
7:16. On the other hand, 7:7–20 belongs to a later time, probably in the
second half of the sixth century BC when the poems of Isaiah 56–66 arose.
In fact, there are similarities between the two. Furthermore, just as
4:1–5:8 plus 2:12–13 (promise) was related to 1–3 (threat), so also
7:7–20 (promise) stands in relation to 5:9–7:6 (threat). This double
series of threat and promise may be explained on the one hand by the
assumption that there were at first two collections of Micah's prophecies
of woe. Each of these was then later supplemented with a conclusion of
promise. Or, it is possible that there was one collection of genuine
material which was enlarged not only with a conclusion of deliverance
(*Heilsweissagung*), but enlarged also in the middle, since 3:12 seemed also
to require such a conclusion. At first 4:1–5 was inserted, and then other
similar prophecies of salvation.

In reply to this position of Eissfeldt's the following considerations may
be adduced.

The character of the book is somewhat desultory. Micah does not
present one long, sustained argument, but like Isaiah (in the latter
portion of his book) passes from one subject to another. It is this fact
which seems to support (although in reality it does not) a plural authorship of the prophecy.

We cannot grant the validity of any position which, for theological
reasons, would deny to the period of Micah the ideas of salvation which
are found in the book. There is no objective evidence to show that such
ideas were not present in Micah's day. Indeed, there are passages in
Micah very similar in character to those in the writings of his contemporaries. To insist, in the interests of a certain naturalistic theory of the
development of Israel's religious views, that these latter passages must
also be ascribed to a later time is an utterly unwarranted procedure.

Lastly, appeal to Jeremiah 26:18 cannot legitimately be made to show
that Micah's messages consisted only of threats. Jeremiah, be it remembered, had been judged worthy of death because he had proclaimed
the coming destruction. Some of the princes, however, said in effect that
since Jeremiah had spoken in the name of the Lord, he was not worthy of
death. And certain of the elders declared that in the days of Hezekiah
Micah had spoken in similar vein. The reference to Micah, therefore,
was only to institute a comparison between Micah's action at a certain

time and the present situation with Jeremiah. It in no sense can be regarded as a characterization of all Micah's prophecies, and to appeal to this passage in order to demonstrate that Micah spoke only threat is certainly unwarranted.

ANALYSIS

a. Micah 1:1–2:13. Threats against Israel and Judah

1. 1:1. The superscription. This superscription may be regarded as the work of Micah himself. At least there is no sufficient reason for denying it to him. If Micah did not write it, we may regard it as the work of a scribe who inserted it under divine inspiration.

2. 1:2–16. God's anger against Samaria and Judah. Both Samaria and Judah are evil and the Lord will punish them.

The introductory 'hear' of 1:2 appears also in 3:1 and 6:1. There is not sufficient reason for denying 1:5b, 6, 8, 9 to Micah. The figurative language of this description is not to be pressed so as to bring it out of harmony with the historical facts of 722 BC. The forceful picture of the destruction of Samaria which Micah paints is to be applied to the fate of the nation itself, not to be regarded as a minute description of what will happen to the physical city.

3. 2:1–13. The reasons for the divine displeasure. 2:1–11 contains a description of the sinful practices of the people and a statement of the Lord's purpose to bring punishment. In verses 12, 13 there is an announcement of future deliverance.

There is no sufficient reason for denying to Micah the promise of 2:12, 13. These verses form a climax to the first section of the book. The change of subject may be explained from the fragmentary character of the book.

b. Micah 3:1–5:15. Judgment followed by restoration

1. 3:1–12. A second denunciation in which the prophet further describes the people's sinfulness, culminating in the announcement of Jerusalem's destruction (verse 12). (Note the similarity of phraseology, 'mountain of the house', between the passage which is acknowledged to be genuine and the disputed passage 4:1.)

2. 4:1–5:1. The establishment of God's glorious kingdom. 4:1–3 occurs, with slight variations, in Isaiah 2:2–4. It is possible that Micah has the original, but it may also be that both prophets drew from an earlier prophecy. At any rate, the prophecy in Micah has a closer connection with the verses which follow than is the case in Isaiah. With-

out doubt such glorious promises of the future salvation were current in the eighth century BC. If these remarkable promises be denied to the prophets of the eighth century, then those prophets remain little more than fault-finders, men who condemn sin and demand repentance but who have no hope to hold out to the nation. (Compare also 4:3 with Joel 3:10; 4:7 with Is. 24:24; 4:9 with Is. 13:8 and 21:3; 4:13a with Is. 41:15, 16; 4:13b with Is. 23:18.)

3. 5:2–15. The birth of the new King and His kingdom. In verse 2 the future birth of the Messianic King is declared. His humanity is set forth in that He is to come forth out of Bethlehem, and His true deity, in that the places of His going forth (*motsa'othau*) are from of yore (*miqqedem*), from days of eternity (*mime 'olam*). (Compare 5:5 with Is. 9:6; 5:13 with Is. 2:8.)

c. Micah 6:1–7:20. Punishment of the people and God's final mercy
1. 6:1–16. God's complaint about His people. The Lord's controversy consists in the fact that He has done much for the people, but they are rebellious. The people, evidently personified or represented by an unknown speaker, asks how it may approach the Lord. The answer is then given that humble obedience to His will is what is required.

Compare 6:2 with Hosea 4:1 and 12:2; 6:4 with Amos 2:10; 6:7 with Isaiah 1:11; 6:8 with Isaiah 1:17 and Hosea 6:6; 6:11 with Hosea 12:7; 6:14 with Hosea 4:10. These comparisons, suggested by Raven, clearly show the relationship of the chapter to contemporary prophecy.

2. 7:1–20. Reproof and promise. (Compare 7:1 with Is. 24:13 and Ho. 9:10; 7:2 with Is. 57:1; 7:3 with Is. 1:23 and Ho. 4:18; 7:10 with Joel 2:17; 7:11 with Am. 9:11.) It should be noted that there is a similarity between 7:7–20 and Isaiah 40–66. This does not mean that either is post-exilic. I confess that I can find no legitimate reason for denying these verses to Micah. Wellhausen seeks to find a great gulf between verses 1–6 and verses 7–20. But it is unwarrantable to maintain that the consolation of the people is unthought of in verses 1–6. The real explanation is that here, as elsewhere, there is an interchange between denunciation and blessing. Why could not one individual have employed such a method?

PURPOSE

The purpose of this short book which apparently, because of its fragmentary or desultory character, presents a summary of Micah's ministry, is to set forth the nature of God's complaint against His people, to announce the certain punishment of sin and the sure salvation to come, which salvation will centre about the appearance of the divine Messiah.

NAHUM

NAME

The book is named from its author Nahum. In the LXX this appears as *Naoum*, and in Vulgate *Nahum*.

AUTHOR

Nahum is said to be an Elkoshite. The exact location of Elkosh is unknown but Jerome identified it with a certain Elkesi in northern Galilee. Some have sought to identify it with Alkush, a few miles north of Mosul, but this is extremely questionable. According to Pseudo-Epiphanius[4] it was in Judah near Eleutheropolis. This may be correct, as 1:15 with its reference to Judah may imply that the prophet was from Judah.

Nahum seems to have exercised his ministry between the time of Assyria's capture of Thebes (No-ammon, 3:8 – the event is regarded as having already occurred), 664–663 BC under Assurbanipal, and the destruction of Nineveh itself in 612 BC. More precisely than this the date cannot be fixed.

Nahum's subject is the downfall of Nineveh. He begins in chapter 1 with an introductory psalm, in which he praises the majesty of God and announces the punishment of the Lord's enemies, and His goodness to those who trust in Him. In vivid language he then proceeds in chapter 2 to describe the siege of Nineveh and her destruction, and in chapter 3 sets forth reasons for the city's downfall. The book, therefore, is a complete unit, and may be regarded in its entirety as the work of the prophet himself.

Pfeiffer, however, would limit the actual material of Nahum to a triumphal ode (2:3–3:19). To this ode a redactor of about 300 BC prefaced an alphabetic psalm which he wrote down from a somewhat faulty memory. This psalm (1:2–10) had nothing to do with the fall of Nineveh, but was inserted because it seemed appropriate to the context. The intervening material (1:11–2:2) is thought to be partially redactional, and partly an original section of Nahum's ode.

In answer it must be said that Pfeiffer's theory is subjective, and without evidence. Why may not the prophet himself have prefixed chapter 1

---

[4] *De vitis prophetarum* xvii.

with its magnificent description of the glory and power of God as a fitting prelude or prefix to his message?

HABAKKUK

NAME

The book takes its name from the prophet Habakkuk. In the LXX the name appears as *Ambakouk*, and in the Vulgate *Habacuc*.

AUTHOR

Little is known of the life of the prophet, except what may be inferred from the book itself. Nor can the date of the prophecy be determined precisely. However, 1:5, 6 seems to refer to a time just before the Chaldeans came to power. The Chaldeans were in power from 625 to 539-538, hence Habakkuk's ministry might have taken place under Manasseh. It may be, however, that 1:6 has reference to the Chaldeans as a threat to Judah, and since a threat seemed first to materialize at the battle of Carchemish (605), it has been thought by many that Habakkuk prophesied during the reign of Jehoiakim.

In recent times Duhm, Torrey, and others have emended the word Kasdim (Chaldeans) of 1:6 into Kittim (Cypriotes) and maintained that the prophecy was directed against Alexander the Great and the Macedonians. This procedure is subjective and without textual support.

Bruno Balscheit maintains the novel view that the word Chaldean (in 1:6) is used in a metaphorical sense, as today in Europe many people are called Huns. The book, therefore, would fit very well in the time of Alexander. But this interesting suggestion is also without objective support. Micah and Isaiah had already predicted the downfall of Judah at the hand of the Chaldeans. Hence, the people would be known to the Jews. It may be, therefore, that the prophet began to preach when first the Chaldean power appeared upon the horizon.

According to the school of negative criticism the book is of composite authorship. In the first place the psalm (chapter 3) is separated from the first two chapters. According to Pfeiffer the author of this poem lived in the fourth or third century and deliberately wrote in an archaic style imitating Deuteronomy 33 and Judges 5. One of the first to insist upon a post-exilic date for this chapter was Bernhard Stade (1884), and in this he has been followed by many.

As to chapters 1 and 2 there is considerable difference of opinion. Giesebrecht insisted that 1:5–11 was out of place and that 1:12 should follow immediately after 1:4. Karl Budde agrees with this and would place 1:5–11 after 2:4. It is this passage (1:5–11, with its mention of the Chaldeans) which has been the *crux interpretum* in discussing the book. For our part, we regard this passage as referring to an actual historical event (there is no reason for not doing so) and hence as in its right place.

Lastly, there are no sufficient reasons for divorcing chapter 3 from chapters 1 and 2. For one thing, the theme in both sections is the same. Also, there are important similarities in language. Both in 1:4, 13 and 3:13 the enemy is designated as wicked (*rasha'*). 3:2 seems to have reference to the vision of 2:3–5. Furthermore, chapter 3 is said to be a prayer of Habakkuk (verse 1). The fact that it is introduced and concluded with technical musical terms is no reason for denying it to Habakkuk, since such terms were evidently used in pre-exilic times in connection with the Psalter. In an important study of Habakkuk's psalm, W. F. Albright maintains that the book is a substantial unit to be dated between 605 and 589 BC.[5]

The three short chapters of this little prophecy contain a message of supreme beauty. The prophet begins with a complaint. He has cried out against wickedness and violence, but his cry appears to go unheeded (1:24). In reply to this complaint the Lord speaks. The Lord will not allow the people to go unpunished. He is taking action. He is raising up a people – a bitter and hasty nation – which will punish the people. This nation, the characteristics of which are described in forceful fashion, will serve as God's instrument in the punishment of His people. However, this nation itself will become presumptuous and will be punished (1:5–11).

The prophet then acknowledges the righteousness of the Lord and His purity. However, there yet remains a problem the answer to which he does not see. This enemy nation will indeed punish the people, but it will be punishing those that are more righteous than itself. 'Thou art of purer eyes than to behold evil, and canst not look on iniquity: wherefore lookest thou upon them that deal treacherously and holdest thy tongue when the wicked devour the man that is more righteous than he?' (1:13). Why, asks the prophet, does the Lord, since He is pure, permit this to go on?

The answer is forthcoming. It is found in the matchless passage: 'Behold, his soul which is lifted up is not upright in him: but the just shall live by his faith' (2:4). The thought is that those who are proud, namely,

[5] See 'The Psalm of Habakkuk' in *Studies in Old Testament Prophecy* (1950), pp. 1–18.

the Chaldeans, have no faith, and therefore are condemned.   ιe only one that will live is the one who has faith. There is thus presented a contrast; it is the contrast between those who have faith (the just) and those who are puffed up with pride. It is the contrast which separates not only the Chaldeans and the elect of Israel, but all mankind, into two classes. The fact that a man is filled with pride is in itself an evidence of his doom. So it was with the Chaldeans; these people were being used of God but they were proud of their accomplishments; they would not, therefore, live. This verse, then, has a primary reference to the situation immediately at hand but it is also very correctly used by the apostle Paul to express the truth that 'the just shall live by faith'. Essentially, the situation is one and the same, for the life of which Habakkuk speaks is not mere earthly life, but life in the deepest sense, life with God. Many modern critics have missed the deep meaning of the prophet at this point.

In the light of this profound statement of the prophet we may understand the series of five woes which are pronounced against the enemy nation and also the song of praise (chapter 3).

ZEPHANIAH

NAME

The book is named after its author, *Tsephan-yah*, a name which is borne by three other individuals in the Old Testament (see 1 Ch. 6:36–38; Je. 21:1; Zc. 6:10). In the LXX the name appears as *Sophonias*, and likewise in the Vulgate.

AUTHOR

According to 1:1 the prophecy was received by Zephaniah during the days of Josiah. While it cannot definitely be determined, nevertheless it is probable that Zephaniah uttered his message at some time before Josiah's reformation had occurred. From passages such as 1:4–6, 8–9, 12 and 3:1–3 and 7 we learn that the religious and moral condition of the people was very low.

The ancestry of the prophet is traced back four generations to Hizkiah. Since Zephaniah is the only prophet who traces his ancestry back through so many generations, there must be some particular reason, and it may be that this reason is to be found in the thought that Hizkiah and King Hezekiah were one and the same. If this were the case, then

Zephaniah is seen to have been of royal ancestry. Zephaniah, therefore, probably had easy access to the royal court to gain a hearing for his message.

Some modern scholars believe that the book has been revised by editors, but there is not too much agreement among them as to details. Eissfeldt may be regarded as representative. He suggests that apart from the possibility of minor glosses and reworkings (*Uebermalungen*) there can be no doubt about the genuineness of 1:2–2:3. On the other hand, the genuineness of 2:4–15 is thought to be not so sure, and at least it must be acknowledged that exilic and post-exilic additions have been made, notably the beginning and end of verse 7. In 3:1–13, however, thinks Eissfeldt, we do have a genuine poem, and only in verses 8–10 does there appear a reworking of the material. Verses 14–17 may have come from Zephaniah, but since it was customary to make such eschatological additions, it is also probably to be regarded as such. Likewise verses 18–20 should be denied to Zephaniah and assigned to either the period of the exile or later.

In answer to all this we would simply remark that it is largely subjective. There is no sufficient reason for denying to Zephaniah any portion of his prophecy.

PURPOSE AND ANALYSIS

Zephaniah's purpose is to warn the nation of approaching doom. He depicts the day of wrath but also points forward to the coming deliverance. The book falls into three main divisions:

1. The day of the Lord, 1:1–2:3. The general theme is set forth in 1:2, namely, that God will consume all things from off the land. The prophet then shows the specific application of this theme, referring it to Judah and to Jerusalem and to all that is found there, man and beast, the whole system of idolatry, the royal seed; it will be an utter destruction, 1:3–13. After this vivid description of the coming punishment Zephaniah announces that the day of the Lord is near. This terrible day he describes in agonizing terms of great force, a description which has furnished the basis for the medieval hymn '*Dies Irae*', 1:14–18. In 2:1–3 the Lord's mercy is set forth in the appeal to repent and seek the Lord with which the prophet closes this section.

2. Prophecies against the heathen nations, 2:4–15. Like many other prophets Zephaniah also turns his attention to the heathen or pagan nations in order both to reprove them for their sins and thus to leave them without plea when wrath comes and also to reveal to them the fact

that the sovereign disposition of the destinies of nations lies in the hands of the Lord and that He will surely punish those who have ill-treated His chosen people. Hence these prophecies against the nations are an integral portion of the prophetical message, and it is only a lack of understanding of their true nature and function that would attribute them to later redactors.

Zephaniah speaks first of Gaza and the Philistine plain, verses 4–7, and then condemns Moab and Ammon because of their hostility to Israel, verses 8–11; Ethiopia and Assyria, particularly Nineveh, shall also come to an end, verses 12–15.

3. The sin of Jerusalem and the future salvation, 3:1–20. In the first seven verses the prophet announces a woe (*hoi*) upon Jerusalem and characterizes her sin. He then proceeds (verses 8–20) to announce the coming deliverance. There will be a remnant of Israel, a pure remnant, and the daughter of Zion will sing, for the mighty Lord is in the midst and He will save.

HAGGAI

NAME

The book is named from its author, Haggai, which name appears in the LXX as *Aggaios* and in the Vulgate as *Aggaeus*.

AUTHOR

There are not sufficient reasons for denying the authorship of the entire prophecy to Haggai. Rothstein has suggested that 2:15–19 should follow 1:15a, and then be dated on the twenty-fourth day, sixth month; 2:10–14, however, would belong to the twenty-fourth day, ninth month. This rearrangement would relieve what some scholars think is a confusing or mixing of the subject in 2:10–19. Some scholars have also thought that the text has been enlarged or altered in 1:1–11. Eissfeldt suggests that possibly parts from two small collections have been added.

These suggestions are not necessary, however, since the prophecy as it stands presents a unified message. When the exiles returned to Palestine from Babylon, they came with high hopes. Cyrus the Great had issued an edict in which he granted full permission to the Jews to rebuild the Temple in Jerusalem. Under his protection and permission, therefore, they came back to the land of promise. But difficulties were in store. Adversaries appeared upon the scene, who did much to discourage the work. For about fifteen years work on the Temple ceased, and affairs generally were in a discouraging condition.

It was duing the second year of the reign of the Persian king, Darius (*i.e.*, 520 BC) that two great prophets appeared. These were Haggai and Zechariah. According to the book of Ezra (5:1 and 6:14) the Jews built and prospered through the prophesying of these two men. Of the man Haggai, however, practically nothing is known. In all probability he was born in Babylonia during the exile, and returned to Palestine with the first exiles. If this is the case, then it is quite possible that he had known Daniel in Babylon.

ANALYSIS

The brief prophecy which Haggai has left falls into four divisions.

1. 1:1–15. This section was uttered on the first day of the sixth month of the second year of Darius (about August-September). Haggai addressed his message to the leaders, Zerubbabel the governor and Joshua the high priest. He begins with a statement of the attitude of the people. The people had been saying that the time was not yet ripe for the rebuilding of the Lord's house. This attitude is rebuked. The people dwelt in ceiled houses, whereas the Temple of the Lord lay waste. The people saw to it that their own houses were well covered and protected, in fact, sumptuously built, but they exhibited little real concern for the house of God. Therefore the time had come to consider their ways.

The blessing of the Lord had been withheld from the people because of their neglect. 'Ye have sown much, but bring in little; ye eat, but ye have not enough; ye drink, but ye are not filled with drink; ye clothe you, but there is none warm; and he that earneth wages earneth wages to put it into a bag with holes' (1:6). Haggai urges the people to resume their work upon the Temple, and the Lord will take pleasure in it and be glorified. As a result of this earnest message the leaders of the people and the people themselves feared the Lord and on the twenty-fourth day of the sixth month (*i.e.*, just twenty-three days after Haggai delivered his message), they began again the work on the neglected Temple.

2. 2:1–9. The second message was received by Haggai from the Lord on the twenty-first day of the seventh month. It is essentially a message of comfort and of hope. Apparently there were some who remembered the glory of the first Temple, *i.e.*, the Temple which Solomon had built and which Nebuchadnezzar in 587 had destroyed. This present Temple is as

nothing when compared to that magnificent structure. Yet in this fact there should be no cause for discouragement. The Lord is still with His people, even as He had covenanted with them when He brought them out of the land of Egypt. There is to come a glory even greater than that of the first Temple. The Lord will send the 'desire of the nations' and 'I will fill this house with glory, saith the Lord of hosts.' The result will be that 'the glory of this latter house shall be greater than of the former, saith the Lord of hosts: and in this place will I give peace, saith the Lord of hosts' (2:9). This promise is Messianic. The 'desire of the nations' is none other than the Messiah Himself. It must be obvious to a careful reader of this promise that the blessings which the Lord is here promising are spiritual in nature. It may be that this second Temple could never equal the first in material splendour and glory, but there was to come a glory far greater than that of the first, even a glory which would be brought about following a shaking of the heavens, the earth and the sea, and the dry land (*cf.* Heb. 12:26–28).

3. 2:10–19. The third revelation came to Haggai on the twenty-fourth day of the ninth month (*i.e.*, two months after the previous revelation). In this section the prophet endeavours to explain to the nation that just as a clean thing would become polluted by touching the unclean, so the former attitude of the people towards the Lord and His house polluted their own labour and as a result the blessing of the Lord was withheld. However, from this time forth, the Lord will indeed bless. 'Is the seed yet in the barn? yea, as yet the vine, and the fig tree, and the pomegranate, and the olive tree, hath not brought forth: from this day will I bless you' (2:19).

4. 2:20–23. This last revelation, a message of comfort, was received on the same day as the preceding. The Lord will establish Zerubbabel. This means that the Lord has set His affection upon the chosen line, and He will surely fulfil His promises of blessing to that line. The strength of the kingdoms of the heathen will be broken by the Lord and He will truly show His mercy to His people.

ZECHARIAH

NAME

The name of the book is derived from the prophet himself, *Zekar-yah*. It appears in the LXX as *Zacharias* and thus also in the Vulgate.

AUTHOR

Zechariah is said to be the son of Berechiah, the son of Iddo (1:1). Probably this Iddo is to be identified with the levitical Iddo who returned to Palestine (Ne. 12:1, 4, 16). If so, it would follow that Zechariah was a priest and to be identified with the Zechariah of Nehemiah 12:16. It was doubtless as a young man that the prophet began his ministry, and his early contemporary was Haggai. Zechariah's ministry began two months after that of Haggai.

The position adopted in this book is that Zechariah was the author of the entire prophecy. However, as this opinion is widely controverted, it will be necessary to give some attention to the subject of the authorship of the prophecy.

One of the first to question the genuineness of the entire prophecy was Joseph Mede (1653), a scholar of Cambridge. Mede was troubled by the quotation of Zechariah 11:12, 13 in Matthew 27:9, 10, where the prophecy is attributed to Jeremiah. His solution of the difficulty was to maintain that chapters 9–11 were not the work of Zechariah, but were from the time before the exile and were written by Jeremiah. This directed attention to the question, and scholars began to consider it as they had not done before. In 1700 Richard Kidder came out in defence of Mede's view and asserted that chapters 12–14 were also the work of Jeremiah.

In 1785 William Newcome declared that chapters 9–11 were written before the downfall of Samaria, probably about the time of Hosea, but that chapters 12–14 were later, having been composed sometime between the death of Josiah and the destruction of Jerusalem. Thus, Newcome thought that he had found within the compass of chapters 9–14 two pre-exilic fragments.

H. Corrodi (1792), on the other hand, writing in opposition to the pre-exilic hypothesis, suggested (as Grotius earlier had done, 1644) that chapters 9–14 were written long after the time of Zechariah. Between the pre-exilic and post-Zecharian date scholarship was divided, and some stoutly maintained the unity and genuineness of the entire prophecy. In 1824 Eichhorn, in the fourth edition of his *Introduction*, attributed chapters 9–14 to a very late date. He thought that in 9:1–10:12 he found a description of the invasion of Alexander the Great (322 BC), and in 13:7–14:21 a song of comfort over the death of Judas Maccabaeus (161 BC). 11:1–13:6 he attributed to the intervening period. Others followed Eichhorn in maintaining the origin of these chapters in the late Grecian period, while still others, such as Rosenmueller and Hitzig, argued for their pre-exilic origin. Indeed, defenders of the pre-exilic view become more and more numerous, and, from 1840 on, criticism was more or less divided between those who argued for the unity of the entire prophecy and those who urged a pre-exilic date for chapters 9–14.

Stade, however (1881–2), gave a new turn to the course of criticism by declaring that chapters 9–14 were written during the period of the Diadochi (306–278 BC), and thus the post-Zecharian hypothesis was revived. At the present time scholarship is divided between those who hold to the unity of the entire book (Robinson, Davis, Moeller) and those who would place chapters 9–14 in the Grecian period, for the most part in the third centry BC. The pre-exilic hypothesis, once triumphantly proclaimed as one of the 'surest results of modern criticism' (Diestel, in 1875), has, as far as the present writer knows, no defenders in the present day.

In considering the argument for the post-Zecharian authorship of chapters 9–14 it will be well if we examine this view as it has recently been set forth by one of its most able and learned defenders, Otto Eissfeldt.

The passage 9:1–17 and probably 10:1–2, we are told, contain certain archaisms, such as the references to the king in Gaza (verse 5), but they also have certain evidences of a very late time, such as the mention of Greece (*yawan*) in verse 13. The passage is regarded by Eissfeldt as a threat against the power of the Seleucids in Zion and a promise of the Messianic kingdom for Zion. However, one cannot decide definitely whether it has reference to the beginnings of the Seleucid power (*c.* 300 BC) or to the Maccabean period.

The passage 10:3–11:3 contains even clearer marks of a later period, although even here there are archaisms to be found. Particularly in verses 6–10 do we find the exile and a great diaspora presupposed. The passage is to be regarded as a threat against the Diadochi, both the Seleucids and the Ptolemaic line. Since this passage recognizes the same contemporary situation as 9:1–10:2, it may be from the same author as that section.

The passages 11:4–17 and 13:7–9 contain no archaisms, and are clearly from the Grecian period. More than that, from two decades just before the Maccabean uprising and from the Maccabean period itself are events which would suit this passage. Two possible interpretations, each of which has its difficulties, commend themselves. One is that of Marti, who identifies the good shepherd of chapter 11 as Onias IV, the evil shepherd as Alcimus, and the three shepherds of verse 8 as Lysimachus, Jason, and Menelaus. The other view is that of Sellin, who refers the good shepherd to Onias III, the evil shepherd to Menelaus, and the rejection of the three to the driving out by Onias III of Simon,

Menelaus, and Lysimachus.[6] The first of these views would place the passage about 160, the other about 150–140 BC.

The passage 12:1–13:6 contains, according to Eissfeldt, a particularly rich number of indications of a very late period of composition, particularly the eschatological outlook. The one that is pierced (12:10–12) evidently has reference to a concrete event, but it is difficult to tell what the event is.

Chapter 14 also is late, and may be the work of several hands, since it presents somewhat conflicting views of the day of the Lord. The period of its origin is difficult to determine.

In answer to the above exposition of the post-Zecharian view and to this view generally we would adduce the following considerations.

1. The principal and strongest argument adduced in favour of the post-Zecharian hypothesis is the mention of the sons of Greece in 9:13. Thus, Greece (*i.e.*, the Seleucids) is thought to be a threat against Zion and is regarded as the dominant world power of the day. But there are serious objections to this interpretation. The prophecy is one of a defeat, not a victory, for Javan. In this connection the prophet has just appealed to the exiles to return to the stronghold (verse 12). Thus, the situation wells fits the time of Zechariah, but not a later time. What we have is not the description of an actual battle, but an apocalyptic vision of a future victory. There is no question but that in Zechariah's day Greece was a nation of considerable importance.

2. In both portions of the book there is no reference to an actual king in Israel. It is true that in 12:7–13:1 mention is made of the 'house of David', but a careful exposition of this passage will show that it is not a reference to an actual ruler. The one king that is recognized in both parts of Zechariah is the Messiah (*cf.* 6:12, 13 and 9:9). Furthermore, in the picture of the Messiah which each part gives, there are no essential differences. Rather, all that is said could easily be the work of one mind.

3. It is also important to note that in both portions of the book the houses of Israel and Judah are regarded as one, a fact which well accords with Zechariah's time. (*Cf., e.g.,* 1:19; 8:13 and 9:9, 10, 13; 10:3, 6, 7.)

4. Certain peculiar expressions occur in both portions of the book. Thus 'from passing through and from returning' (*me'over umishshav*) occurs in 7–14 and 9:8. 'Saith the Lord' (*ne'um yehowah*) appears in 10:12; 12:1, 4; 13:2, 7, 8; and some fourteen times in the first part of the book. The providence of God is designated 'the eyes of the Lord' in 3:9; 4:10 and also in 9:1. The phrase 'Lord of hosts' occurs in 1:6, 12; 2:9 and

[6] For the historical references to these events, see 1 Macc. 7:5–25; 9:54–57; 2 Macc. 4–5; 13:1–8.

also in 9:15; 10:3; 12:5, *etc*. Further, *kal of yashav* (to dwell) is used in a passive sense in 2:8; 7:7 and 12:6; 14:10; and only rarely outside of this prophecy. There are also similarities of expression (*cf*. 2:10 with 9:9). While these phenomena do not prove the literary unity of the prophecy, they do at least go a long way towards establishing such unity.

5. Zechariah, like Isaiah before him, is an evangelical prophet, and this evangelical emphasis appears in both portions of the book.

6. The purity of the language in both parts should be stressed. The language is remarkably free from Aramaisms. Pusey remarks, 'In both [parts] there is a certain fullness of language, produced by dwelling on the same thought or word: in both, the whole and its parts are, for emphasis, mentioned together. In both parts, as a consequence of this fullness, there occurs the division of the verse into five sections, contrary to the usual rule of Hebrew parallelism.' As illustrations of this principle, Pusey adduces 6:13; 9:5; 9:7; 12:4. The principle becomes clear when we examine one passage:

> Ashkelon shall see, and shall fear;
> Gaza, and shall tremble exceedingly;
> And Ekron, and ashamed is her expectation;
> And perished hath a king from Gaza,
> And Ashkelon shall not be inhabited (9:5).

Thus from the above considerations, it becomes clear that in the book of Zechariah there is a deeper, underlying unity than is at first sight apparent.

7. Lastly, it should be noted that those who reject the Zecharian authorship of chapters 9–14 have not been able to agree upon the alternate theory of composition. On the one hand we have been told that chapters 9–14 are a unit, either pre- or post-exilic, but not from Zechariah. On the other, chapters 9–11 have been said to come from the eighth century, and chapters 12–14 from about the beginning of the sixth century, or else from the period of the Diadochi or even the Maccabees. Others have placed all of chapters 9–14 in the third and second centuries and have regarded them as the work of an apocalyptic author who wrote in the vein of a pre-exilic prophet. Still others have divided the entire prophecy into four parts. This lack of agreement as to just what these disputed chapters are is of force in showing that a satisfactory alternative to Zecharian authorship has not been discovered.

ANALYSIS

a. Zechariah 1:1–6. Introduction

In the eighth month of the second year of Darius the word of the Lord
was made known to Zechariah, who begins his message with a command
to repent and not to act as the sinful ancestors of the nation had done.
The principal theme of the book, therefore, appears in the words,
'Return unto me and I will return unto you.'

b. Zechariah 1:7–6:15. The visions of the night

1. 1:7–17. The introductory vision. Through His messengers God
observes the events on earth. The man upon the red horse (verse 8) is the
Angel of the Lord, and the riders are the Lord's servants who have ridden
through the earth to do His bidding. The earth is found to be quiet and
at peace, but Jerusalem and Judah still suffer the effects of God's
indignation. To the question as to how long this state of things would
continue, the Lord answers through the interpreter (verse 13, 'the angel
that talked with me', to be distinguished from the Angel of the Lord),
that in due time the Lord's wrath will be poured out upon the nations,
and Jerusalem and the Temple will be rebuilt.

2. 1:18–21. The first vision. The four horns represent the enemies of
the kingdom of God, and the four smiths are to break these in pieces.
These four horns represent the four empires of Daniel's visions, Babylon,
Medo-Persia, Greece, Rome. The picturing of these nations as horns
evidently goes back to Daniel 7:7, 8.

3. 2:1–13. The second vision. The prophet sees a man engaged in
measuring the future dimensions of Jerusalem, since its present size is not
large enough for the enlargement which God's salvation will bring
about.

4. 3:1–10. The third vision. The prophet beholds the high priest in the
Temple, clothed in filthy garments (symbolical of sin), and praying for
the mercy of the Angel of the Lord. Satan beholds the scene with jealous
eyes.

5. 4:1–14. The fourth vision. The prophet sees a golden candlestick
(the people of God) and by it two olive-trees (the Spirit). Whatever
mountain of obstacles there will be to the erection of God's kingdom will
be removed only by the Spirit of God, through grace.

6. 5:1–4. The fifth vision. The flying roll is a symbol of divine judgments.

7. 5:5–11. The sixth vision. Israel will fill up the measure (*ephah*) of its

iniquity, and the Lord will restrain (the weight of lead) the course of sin in the nation.

8. 6:1–8. The seventh vision. The winds of heaven serve as divine judgments.

9. 6:9–15. The eighth vision. A general prophecy of restoration under the Messiah.

c. Zechariah 7:1–8:23. The question of fasting

This section, revealed to Zechariah in the fourth year of Darius, ninth month, fourth day, serves to answer the question of the men of Bethel whether the day of the destruction of Jerusalem and the Temple should still be kept as a day of fasting. The answer is that the Lord delights in obedience rather than in fasting. God will now turn again towards His people with abundance of blessings if they will but walk in His ways.

d. Zechariah 9:1–14:21. The future of the world powers and of God's kingdom

1. 9:1–10:12. Zion shall be delivered, and will triumph over the heathen world. This shall be accomplished through her King, the Messiah.

2. 11:1–17. The good and foolish shepherd.

3. 12:1–13:6. A further picture of Israel's future turning unto the Lord.

4. 13:7–14:21. A judgment to purify Israel, and the future glory of Jerusalem.

PURPOSE

Zechariah serves to encourage the nation in its divinely appointed task. The indignation of the Lord has come, he teaches, because of the people's sin. If then the nation will humble itself before God, it will have a glorious future. The heathen nations will one day be cast down, and Jerusalem will prosper. This future spiritual blessing will be brought about through the Messiah.

MALACHI

NAME

The book is named from its author, *Mal'achi*. In the Targum of Jonathan ben-Uzziel there are added the words 'whose name is called Ezra the scribe'. The LXX regards the word, however, as a common noun, not a proper name, and translates, 'The burden of the word of the Lord to Israel by the hand of his messenger [*aggelou autou*]', although it does have the title *Malachias*. It is better, however, to regard the word as a proper name, for the prophetical books are not anonymous, and it would be strange to find this book an exception. At any rate, even if Malachi be a proper name, there does seem to be a connection between it and the 'my messenger' of 3:1.

AUTHOR

The entire book is a unit, the work of one author. Of the life of Malachi, however, nothing is known, although there are certain indications in the book itself which enable one to determine the approximate date of the prophecy. Thus, the Temple had evidently been completed and sacrifices were offered, 1:7–10; 3:8. A governor (*pehah*), *i.e.*, a Persian governor, was ruling in Jerusalem (1:8). These considerations show that the prophecy is subsequent to Haggai and Zechariah.

The early zeal connected with the building of the Temple seems now to have died out, and the religious laxities and abuses which Malachi condemns are the same as those present under Ezra and Nehemiah. Thus, as 2:10–12 shows, mixed marriages were present, the payment of tithes had been neglected (3:8–10) and blemished sacrifices had been offered (1:6ff.). But the 'governor' mentioned in 1:8 was probably not Nehemiah, hence it is quite possible that the book was written during Nehemiah's visit to Susa. At any rate, it dates from about this time.

The genuineness of the prophecy is not doubted by modern negative criticism, with the exception of the title, 1:1. Cornill, however, follows Marti in regarding 2:11, 12 as an interpolation, since elsewhere in the book different thoughts respecting the heathen are expressed. But these verses simply reflect the conditions then existent and the people's sinfulness. Cornill's argument is not convincing. He also discusses at some length the title. He points to the similarities (the oracle [*massa'*] of the word of the Lord) which occur also in Zechariah 9:1 and 12:1. He assumes that the original is Zechariah 9:1 and that the other passages are imitations, the superscription in each case being secondary in character, having arisen in Malachi 1:1 through a misunderstanding of Malachi 3:1.

Both Zechariah 9–14 and Malachi, thinks Cornill, were originally anonymous prophecies which were appended at the close of the collection of minor prophecies. Thus Zechariah 9–14, being the longer, was added first, and 'Malachi', the shorter, followed. This latter appendix (*i.e.*

'Malachi') could now be provided with a superscription, and this had the added advantage of securing the significant and favoured number twelve.

Next, according to Cornill, it was perceived that Zechariah 12–14 differed somewhat from Zechariah 9–11, and so was provided with a specially framed superscription. (Strange, is it not, that this anonymous minor prophecy should have gone about as a unit, and the difference between its first and second part only noticed after it had been appended to Zechariah? Why, if this difference between chapters 9–11 and 12–14 is so great, was not 12–14 regarded as a separate book just as the other anonymous prophecy, 'Malachi', was so regarded? Or why were not all three added as one grand appendix to Zechariah? Was it the desire to secure the number twelve that led these so-called editors thus to act?)

But all of this is mere fancy and without any objective evidence to support it. We are not at all compelled to assume that 1:1 is based upon 3:1. Why may not the reverse be the case? And why may not Malachi have himself formed his title in conscious imitation of Zechariah 9:1 and 12:1?

PURPOSE AND ANALYSIS

The purpose of the book is best made clear through a study of its contents. It falls into two principal parts: chapters 1 and 2 describe the sin and apostasy of Israel, and chapters 3 and 4 point to the judgment that will come upon the sinner and the blessing reserved for those who repent. After the superscription, the prophet plunges into the heart of his message by showing that in the election of Israel God's love was manifested (1:2–5). But Israel has not manifested the honour to God which is His due. The priests have shown themselves lax and neglectful in their liturgical duties (1:6–2:4). Furthermore, the priests have given faulty instruction in the law, and have caused many to stumble (2:5–9). The people also were like the priests, and exhibited their faithlessness in the mixed marriages ('hath married the daughter of a strange god') and divorces (2:10–17).

The Lord, however, will send His messenger to prepare the way before Him, and the Messiah will come. But who may abide the day of His coming, for His coming will purge the nation (3:1–6)? If the people wish to delight in the blessing of the Lord, they must be obedient to the laws which He has revealed (3:7–12). However, when the day of the Lord comes, there will be a distinction between the righteous and the wicked (3:13–4:3). The conclusion, therefore, is that the nation should be obedient to the law of Moses, and that Elijah will come before the appearance of the great and terrible day of the Lord (4:4–6).

SPECIAL LITERATURE ON HOSEA

Joh. Lindblom, *Hosea: Literarisch untersucht* (Abo, 1927); H. S. Nyberg, *Studien zum Hoseabuche* (Uppsala, 1935); Felix E. Peiser, *Hosea* (Leipzig, 1914); Norbert Peters, *Osee und die Geschichte* (Paderborn, 1924); Franz Praetorius, *Bemerkungen zum Buche Hosea* (Berlin, 1918); *Die Gedichte des Hosea* (Halle, 1926).

SPECIAL LITERATURE ON JOEL

H. Holzinger, 'Sprachgebrauch und Abfassungszeit des Buches Joel', in *ZAW*, 1889, pp. 88–131.

SPECIAL LITERATURE ON AMOS

Karl Cramer, *Versuch einer theologischen Interpretation* (Stuttgart, 1930); Ludwig Koehler, *Amos der älteste Schriftprophet* (Zurich, 1920); 'Amos-Forschungen von 1917 bis 1932', in *ThR*, 4, 1932, pp. 195–213 (this survey article, for those who can read German, will serve as an excellent introduction to the study of recent trends in the investigation of the prophecy of Amos); Julian Morgenstern, 'Amos Studies', in *HUCA*, Cincinnati, 1936–1940; Franz Praetorius, *Textkritische Bemerkungen zum Buche Amos* (Berlin, 1918); Hans Schmidt, *Der Prophet Amos* (Tübingen, 1917); A. S. Kapelrud, *Central Ideas in Amos* (1956); J. W. Watts, *Vision and Prophecy in Amos* (1958).

SPECIAL LITERATURE ON OBADIAH

George A. Peckham, *An Introduction to the Study of Obadiah* (Chicago, 1910).

SPECIAL LITERATURE ON JONAH

R. D. Wilson, 'The Authenticity of Jonah',* in *PTR*, 16, pp. 280–298, 430–456; G. Ch. Aalders, *The Problem of the Book of Jonah** (1948).

SPECIAL LITERATURE ON MICAH

A. Bruno, *Micha und der Herrscher aus der Vorzeit* (Leipzig, 1923); Joh. Lindblom, *Micha literarisch untersucht* (Helsingfors, 1929); Copass and Carlson, *A Study of the Prophet Micah** (1950).

SPECIAL LITERATURE ON NAHUM

W. R. Arnold, 'The Composition of Nahum 1:2–2:3', in *ZAW*, 21, pp. 225–265; Walter A. Maier, *The Book of Nahum** (1959).

SPECIAL LITERATURE ON HABAKKUK

Karl Budde, 'Habakkuk', in *ZDMG*, 84, pp. 139–147; Giesebrecht, *Beiträge zur Jesajakritik* (1890), pp. 196–198; Bernhard Stade, 'Habakkuk', in *ZAW*, 4, pp. 154–159; C. C. Torrey, 'The Prophecy of Habakkuk', in *Jewish Studies in Memory of George A. Kohut* (New York, 1935), pp. 565–582; H. H. Walker and N. W. Lund, 'The Literary Scripture of the Book of Habakkuk', in *JBL*, 53, pp. 355–370.

SPECIAL LITERATURE ON ZEPHANIAH

C. V. Pilcher, *Three Hebrew Prophets and the Passing of Empires* (London, 1931); F. Schwally, 'Das Buch Sephanja', in *ZAW*, 1890, pp. 165–240; H. Weiss, *Zephanja Kap. 1 und seine Bedeutung als religionsgeschichtliche Quelle* (Koenigsberg, 1922).

SPECIAL LITERATURE ON HAGGAI

Karl Budde, 'Zum Text der drei letzten kleinen Propheten', *ZAW*, 1906, pp. 1–28; article, 'Haggai',* in *ISBE*.

SPECIAL LITERATURE ON ZECHARIAH

John D. Davis, 'The Reclothing and Coronation of Joshua',* *PTR*, 18, pp. 256–268; B. Heller, 'Die letzten Kapital des Buches Sacharja im Lichte des späteren Judentums', *ZAW*, 1927, pp. 151–155; W. D. Munro, 'Why Dissect Zechariah?'* in *EQ*, X, 1938, pp. 45–55; George L. Robinson, *The Prophecies of Zechariah** (Chicago, 1896 – this work is by far the best introduction to the study of Zechariah); J. W. Rothstein, *Die Nachtgesichte des Sacharja* (Stuttgart, 1910); M. F. Unger, *Zechariah** (Grand Rapids, 1963).

SPECIAL LITERATURE ON MALACHI

A. von Bulmerincq, *Der Prophet Maleachi*, I, *Einleitung* (Dorpat, 1926); II, *Komment a* (Dorpat, 1932); C. C. Torrey, 'The Prophecy of Malachi', *JBL*, 1898, pp. 1–15.

PART THREE

The Hagiographa

CHAPTER EIGHTEEN

THE POETICAL BOOKS

IN the third division of the Old Testament Canon there are three books which were regarded by the Jews as poetical: Psalms, Proverbs, and Job. They were designated by a mnemonic word, 'Books of *'Emeth* [truth]', the word *'emeth* being composed of the first letter of the names of each of the poetical books, thus: *'iov, meshallim, tehillim* (Job, Proverbs, Psalms). These three books were provided by the Jews with a special system of accents.

It must not be thought that the poetry of the Bible is confined to the three major poetical books. Indeed, throughout the Bible there are bits of poetry. To mention but a few, we may refer to Genesis 4:23–24; 49:1–27; Exodus 15:1–18; Judges 5; 2 Samuel 1:17–27.

The poetry of the three great poetical books is for the most part didactic and lyrical, although there are traces of epic and dramatic poetry also. But since these books are the Word of God, they are intended primarily to *teach* sinful men. For this reason they are preponderantly didactic, although, as in the Psalms, this didactic element is set forth in beautiful, lyrical form.

THE CHARACTERISTICS OF HEBREW POETRY

1. *Parallelism.* Hebrew poetry is distinguished by certain peculiarities and characteristics of its own. Its principal feature is not rhyme, but parallelism (*parallelismus membrorum*). This phenomenon had long been noticed but it was first subjected to a careful scrutiny and investigation by Bishop Robert Lowth in 1753.[1] According to Lowth the 'verses' of poetry consisted of two or more members, the thought of which exhibited a 'parallel' relationship to one another. The unit of poetry is the line, and two such lines usually constitute a verse (distich), although there are tristichs (3 lines), tetrastichs (4 lines) and even pentastichs (5 lines). An example of parallelism may be seen in Psalm 83:1.

> Keep not thou silence, O God:
> Hold not thy peace, and be not still, O God.

[1] *De sacra poesi Hebraeorum.*

Here it will be seen that the second expresses a thought that is parallel in meaning to the first line.

Lowth identified three basic forms of parallelism, and even today these three are recognized as standard, although other types also have been recognized. These types are:

(i) Synonymous, in which the same thought is repeated in almost the same words, *e.g.*, Psalm 49:1:

> Hear this, all ye people,
> give ear, all ye inhabitants of the world.

(ii) Antithetical, in which a thought is expressed by means of contrast with its opposite (this form is particularly frequent in Proverbs), *e.g.*, Proverbs 15:1:

> A soft answer turneth away wrath:
> but grievous words stir up anger.

(iii) Synthetic, in which the second member completes or fills out the thought of the first, *e.g.*, Proverbs 4:23:

> Keep thy heart with all diligence;
> for out of it are the issues of life.

Other forms of parallelism also have been noted, most of which are essentially variations of the three basic types. Attention, however, should be called to Chiastic parallelism, in which the arrangement ab, ba occurs, *e.g.*, Psalm 51:1:

> a. Have mercy upon me, O God,
> b. According to thy lovingkindness:
> b. According unto the multitude of thy tender mercies
> a. Blot out my transgression.

The first and fourth members correspond, and likewise the second and third. Thus the passage is given a peculiar forcefulness of expression. The parallelism found in Psalm 29:1, *e.g.*, may be called climactic, in that it proceeds, step by step, to a climax. In reality, however, this is but a form of synthetic parallelism.

In 1915 George Buchanan Gray[2] pointed out that in some instances, *e.g.*, Isaiah 3:1, the two stichoi of the line were in exact parallelism,

[2] *Forms of Hebrew Poetry.*

whereas in others, *e.g.*, Deuteronomy 32:2, this was not the case, but an additional term had been inserted in the second member or stichos.

Oesterley and Robinson, who in their *Introduction*, pp. 139–142, have written a very helpful discussion of parallelism, point out that there are also instances in which only a portion of the first stichos is repeated in the second.

2. *Acrosticism, assonance, alliteration.* There are certain minor characteristics which are sometimes exhibited by Hebrew poetry. One of these is the acrosticism, the most notable example of which is Psalm 119. In this Psalm, verses 1–8 begin each with an *'aleph*, verses 9–16 each with a *beth*, and so on throughout the entire twenty-two letters of the alphabet. Other examples may be found in Psalms 9, 34, 37; Proverbs 31:10ff. and Lamentations 1–4. Poetry also at times exhibits a certain amount of assonance (words which sound alike) as in Genesis 49:17; Exodus 14:14; Deuteronomy 3:2; and of alliteration, such as in Psalm 6:8; 27:7.

3. *Metre.* From what has been written above concerning parallelism it will be seen that the balance in thought is all-important. Indeed, every other peculiarity or characteristic of Hebrew poetry must be regarded as secondary to this parallel expression of thought. This phenomenon lends a peculiar intensity of force and beauty to the poetry of the Old Testament and admirably serves as a vehicle for the communication of truth. In other words, it is a true handmaid of didactic poetry, for it serves to impress upon the mind the *content* of the poetry. While parallelism appears also in other languages – Egyptian, Accadian, Ras Shamra, Syriac – nowhere does its peculiar grace and strength appear so clearly as when it serves to express the divinely inspired words of the Old Testament.

When, therefore, we come to consider the question whether there is metre in the Old Testament, we must ever keep in mind the basic parallel structure of the poetry. Josephus in his *Antiquities* ii. 16.4, remarked that Moses had composed the song of triumph (Ex. 15:1–18) in hexameters and in the same work (iv. 8.44) he speaks of the song in Deuteronomy 32:1–43 as poetry written in hexameters. Josephus' purpose was to cause his non-Semitic readers to understand the nature of Hebrew poetry and so he applies to this poetry a non-oriental concept, namely, that of the classical metre.

Such testimony as this of Josephus, however, does not in reality decide the question. To answer the question whether there is metre in Hebrew poetry, we must ourselves examine that poetry. There is no tradition about Hebrew metre; the Talmud is silent on the subject. And there appears to be no evidence of the presence of regular metre in the recently discovered texts from Ras Shamra. Upon the basis of a recent examination of the Ras Shamra texts, G. Douglas Young writes, 'That regular metre can be found in such poetry is an illusion'.[3] On the other hand, those who argue in favour of the presence of metre point to the fact that some of the Psalms were apparently sung to the accompaniment of musical instruments, and to the presence of metre in Accadian and Egyptian (in which language even the pronunciation of the vowels is not fully known).

Gustav Bickell (1882), a profound student of the Syriac language, recognized that classical concepts of poetry should not be applied to an oriental language.[4] He appealed to the Syriac, therefore, in which language the verses consisted of feet of two syllables, one long and one short, following each other in alternation. In classical terminology these would be called trochees or iambs. Bickell sought to apply this principle to Hebrew, but the attempt was not successful. Gustav Hoelscher adopted this system but insisted that the ultima should everywhere be accented (iambic). This resulted in the frequent appearance of the following scheme: x — x — | x — x — (i.e., the acatalectic dimeter). A pair of these dimeters is regarded by Hoelscher as the characteristic form of the Hebrew poetry. Hoelscher called attention further to the combination of an acatalectic dimeter with a brachucatalectic dimeter (i.e., a dimeter in which the second member was incomplete), which resulted in the scheme

$$x — x — \;|\; x —x —$$
$$x —x — \;|\; x —$$

In addition to the 'Syriac' system of Bickell, there is another, which has much more to commend it. According to Julius Ley (1875), the character of the verse is to be determined through the number of accented (tone) syllables, it being unimportant how many unaccented syllables there are. The foot is therefore the smallest metrical unity, which usually exhibits a climactic (anapaest) rhythm ∪ ∪ —, although at the end of the verse there is often an extra short syllable. Ley called attention to the frequent presence of an 'elegiac pentameter', in which the caesura appears after the third accent, thus:

$$xx — \;|\; xx — \;|\; xx — \;\|\; xx — \;|\; xx — \quad i.e., 3 + 2.$$

Karl Budde studied this structure exhaustively, and it came to be

---

[3] 'Ugaritic Prosody' in *Journal of Near Eastern Studies*, IX, 1950, pp. 124–133.
[4] In writing this section I have been guided to a great extent by Eissfeldt's excellent discussion (*Einleitung*, pp. 65–69).

known as the Qinah (lamentation) measure, although it is found in other types of poetry as well.

A further exploration of the results of Ley's work was undertaken by Edward Sievers in his famous *Metrical Studies* (1901). Sievers, by this thorough investigation, seemed to establish the results of Ley as sure. But he also went further. Ley had felt that the number of unaccented syllables was unimportant. Sievers believed that every foot or measure must always consist of four beats. Thus, the measure xx — is really the equivalent of xx xx, *i.e.*, one accented is the equal of two unaccented beats. If, however, between two accented beats there were no unaccented, or only one, Sievers thought that the requisite number of missing unaccented beats should be counted in with the accented, so that each measure would always consist of four beats. However, this simply does not work out in practice.

Sievers maintained that there were rows of 2, 3, and 4 feet, and that the lines might consist of 2+2; 3+3; 4+4; 4+3 or 3+4; 3+2 or 2+3; and 2+2+2.

The question now arises, do these metres actually appear in the poetry of the Old Testament? In answer we would say that it does not seem possible to discover any consistent metrical system. It is true that certain forms appear, notably the 3+2, but the appearance is, as it were, accidental. The poet seems to slip into such a measure and then to abandon it. And the designation Qinah is not entirely accurate. Various types appear, and this fact should serve as a caution. The Hebrew text *must never be emended*, merely in order to fit it into a certain metrical scheme. In other words, *metrical considerations are not sufficient to serve as criteria for textual criticism*. This fact cannot be sufficiently stressed. The commentaries of Bernhard Duhm and others are vitiated by a failure to observe this principle. In conclusion, therefore, it may be said that we do not know enough about Hebrew poetry to discover in it definite metrical systems, that if metre does appear here and there, such appearance is somewhat accidental or secondary, and in no case can metrical considerations justify us in emending the text. The real state of the matter is that the poetical writers of the Old Testament under the stress of strong emotion expressed themselves rhythmically, and thus at times produced those phenomena which later could be classified as forms of metre.

4. *Strophic structure.* In recent times there has been much discussion of the question whether there are stanzas or strophes in Hebrew poetry. In the strict sense of the word a strophe must contain the same number and kind of two or more verses which occur two or more times. Such metrically constructed stanzas are very rare, if indeed they really appear

at all. On the other hand, if a strophe be regarded merely as an arrangement of lines, characterized by external marks, then doubtless strophes are to be found. For example, a frequently recurring refrain is regarded as indicating the close of a stanza. So also is the word Selah, *e.g.*, in Psalm 87. Lastly, the acrostic has been thought to indicate strophic structure, as in Psalm 119. There does indeed seem to be strophic structure in Hebrew poetry, but the principles upon which such structure is built do not appear to be uniform.

SPECIAL LITERATURE ON METRE

W. F. Albright in H. H. Rowley (ed.), *Studies in Old Testament Prophecy* (Edinburgh, 1957), pp. 1–18; O. T. Allis, 'The Transcendence of Jehovah God of Israel',* in *BTS*; J. Begrich, 'Zur hebräischen Metrik', in *ThR*, 1932, pp. 67–89; Gustav Bickell, *Carmina VT metrice*, 1892; *Dichtungen der Hebräer zum ersten Male nach den Versmassen des Urtextes übersetzt*, 1882–83; William Henry Cobb, *A Criticism of Systems of Hebrew Metre* (Oxford, 1905); Gustav Hoelscher, 'Elemente arabischer, syrischer und hebräischer Metrik', *BZAW*, 1920, pp. 93–101; Julius Ley, *Grundzüge des Rhythmus, des Vers und Strophenbaus in der habräischen Poesie* (1875); *Leitfaden der Metrik der hebräischen Poesie* (Halle, 1887).

SPECIAL LITERATURE ON THE STROPHE

Francis Brown, 'The Measurements of Hebrew Poetry as an Aid to Literary Analysis', *JBL*, 1890, pp. 71–106; Albert Condamin, *Poèmes de la Bible avec une introduction sur la strophique hébraïque* (Paris, 1833); L. Desnoyers, *Les Psaumes* (Paris, 1935); Kemper Fullerton, 'The Strophe in Hebrew Poetry and Psalm 29', *JBL*, 1929, pp. 274–290; Fred. T. Kelly,' The Strophic Structure of Habakkuk', in *AJSL*, 1902, pp. 94–119; Charles Franklin Kraft, *The Strophic Structure of Hebrew Poetry* (Chicago, 1938 – this book will serve as an excellent introduction to the subject); Hans Moeller, *Strophenbau der Psalmen* (Zella-Mehlis-Thuer., 1931); 'Strophenbau der Psalmen', in *ZAW*, 1932, pp. 240–256; *cf.* also Moeller's remarks in his father's *Einleitung*, pp. 175–176; Felix Perles, *Zur althebräischen Strophik* (Vienna, 1898).

CHAPTER NINETEEN

THE PSALMS

NAME

THE Hebrew name of the entire collection of Psalms was 'the book of praises' (*sefer tehillim*), or simply 'praises' (*tehillim*). This corresponds with the designation in the New Testament as 'book of Psalms' (*biblos psalmon*, Lk. 20:42; Acts 1:20). In the Greek manuscripts the book is known as *Psalmoi*, although in some it appears as *Psalterion* (a collection of songs). The Vulgate follows the LXX, *Liber Psalmorum*, and from this the English term is derived.

AUTHOR

The statement of the Beraitha (*Baba Bathra* 14b) is as follows: 'David wrote the book of Psalms [*sefer tehillim*] with the help of ten elders; with the help of Adam, the first, and Melchizedek, and Abraham, and Moses, and Heman and Jeduthun, and Asaph, and the three sons of Korah.' We must first seek to interpret this passage and then discuss its value. Evidently this statement must be understood not in the sense that David composed the Psalms with the assistance of (although the phrase '*al yedhe* means 'upon the hands of') the elders, but rather that David collected the Psalms which had already been composed by the elders. According to this view, therefore, there were no Psalms composed after the time of David. All of the Psalms were written either by the ten elders, or by David himself.

When we examine the list of ten elders, we note that while seven of them are mentioned in the titles of the Psalms, three of them, Adam, Melchizedek, and Abraham, are not, and two others, Ethan the Ezrahite (Ps. 89) and Solomon (Ps. 72), who are mentioned in the titles do not appear in the Talmudic list at all. Evidently Ethan was regarded as Abraham, and the Solomonic Psalms as composed *for* Solomon and not *by* him. In *Sanhedrin* 38b, Adam is called the author of Psalm 139, and possibly Melchizedek the author of Psalm 110.

This view, however, must be rejected as not having historical foundation. It is correct in the prominence which it gives to David, but apart from that it must be regarded as confused.

There can be no doubt that some Psalms were composed after the time of David, and some Psalms as late as the exile. Furthermore, the title and content of Psalm 139 shows that it could not have been the work of the first man. In the New Testament certain Psalms are clearly ascribed to David as the author. Thus Acts 4:25 ascribes Psalm 2 to David; Acts 2:25–28 and 13:36 ascribe Psalm 16 to him; Romans 4:6–8, Psalm 32; Acts 1:16–20a and Romans 11:9ff., Psalm 69; Acts 1:20b, Psalm 109; Matthew 22:42ff., Mark 12:36ff., Luke 20:42-44, and Acts 2:34, Psalm 110; Hebrews 4:7, Psalm 95. This witness of the New Testament ascribes the authorship of some Psalms to David. David did, therefore, compose some of the Psalms. Of that fact there can be no doubt.

The tradition of Davidic authorship, to which infallible expression is given in the New Testament, appears also in Ecclesiasticus 47:8, 'In every work of his, he gave thanks to the Holy One Most High with words of glory; with his whole heart he sang praise, and loved him that made him.' In certain passages of the Old Testament (1 Ch. 6:31; 16:7; 25:1; Ezr. 3:10; Ne. 12:24, 36, 45, 46; Am. 6:5) David is represented as arranging the liturgical song of the sanctuary.

Furthermore, many of the Psalms are attributed to David by their titles. In the Hebrew titles some seventy-three Psalms are ascribed to David, in the LXX eighty-four, and in the Vulgate eighty-five. In the Hebrew titles the phrase *ledhavidh* occurs, and this phrase, while it need not necessarily refer to authorship, is generally regarded as so referring.[1] The contents of some of the titles, *e.g.*, 3, 7, 18, 30, 34, 51, 52, 54, 56, 57, 59, 60, 63, 142, refer to some event in David's life, and here the phrase *ledhavidh* is clearly intended to indicate authorship by David. If that is the case here, it would seem also to be the case with the other occurrences of the phrase. The titles, therefore, do ascribe the authorship of many Psalms to David. The value of this witness will be discussed later.

There are certain other considerations which should be taken into account when one seeks to evaluate the tradition that David composed many of the Psalms.

1. David himself was a skilful musician. This is seen by the fact that he was able to play well before Saul. Furthermore, the prophet Amos makes reference to this ability of David's (Am. 6:5). In ancient Israel, David did have the reputation of playing well. Evidently David possessed

---

[1] It is possible that in some cases the title may mean merely 'belonging to David' and thus indicate that the Psalm in question is Davidic in character, or is like David's Psalm. I fail to see any evidence for the view that the word David in such a connection could be used to indicate a collection of Psalms.

the requisite musical knowledge for the composition of the Psalms.

2. David was also a true poet. There is extant one of his poems, the genuineness of which is admitted by many who do not acknowledge the Davidic authorship of some of the Psalms. This is the lament over Saul and Jonathan (2 Sa. 1:19–27). These words were uttered after word had been received concerning the death of David's former enemy. It will be well to remember the situation. During his lifetime Saul had, in a most unfair and jealous manner, sought the life of David. Now that Saul is dead, David has the opportunity to utter his thoughts with complete freedom. We find that David here exhibits the greatness of his heart. There is not one word of criticism of Saul. David says nothing about those unfortunate traits in Saul's character which might very well have called forth vengeful remarks on the part of a person of lesser stature. If we ask why there is no mention of religion in this poem, the answer is probably to be found in the fact that to mention religion would have been to call attention to Saul's defection. It is better to let this go unmentioned. David says what he truthfully can say, just that and no more. One cannot read these words without admiration for the magnanimous character and great heart of David. No mere crude warrior-chieftain would have spoken this way. No *little* soul composed this lament. Rather, we are here face to face with one who is truly great in spirit. If David was able to compose this remarkable poem – and it is indeed remarkable – why may he not also have composed some of the Psalms? Surely he shows himself capable.

3. David was a man of deep feeling and of rich imagination. The lament over Saul and Jonathan, to which we have just made reference, shows that he was a true poet. His imagination here expresses itself in figures that are rich indeed. David at one time sinned deeply, but he did not sin with impunity. He grieved over the sin which he had committed. His intense love for his children also shows his greatness. Hence, we must reject the idea that he was a man of a mere primitive nature.

4. David was a true worshipper of the Lord and a man of genuine religious feeling. The Psalms could not have been written by one who did not love the Lord. Throughout his life, despite the reality of his sinfulness, David never lost faith in the Lord God.

5. David was a man of rich and varied experience. The author of the Psalms must have been such an one. As we read over David's life, we may think of him as shepherd boy, warrior, leader of men, king, administrator, musician, writer, poet, religious man, parent, sinner. Only a person with such background would have had the experience requisite for composing some of the Psalms.

6. It should be noted also that the Bible represents David as endued with the Spirit of God (1 Sa. 16:13).

This tradition of Davidic authorship we may conclude, is founded upon fact. The witness of the New Testament abundantly establishes that point. This does not mean that David composed every Psalm in the Psalter. The Psalter itself does not make such a claim. It does mean, however, that the book of Psalms is basically Davidic, and that there is no sufficient ground for denying that those Psalms which are said to come from David are, as a matter of fact, his compositions.

The witness of the titles

According to the titles which stand before the Psalms in the Hebrew Bible, seventy-three Psalms are ascribed to David. Twelve (*i.e.*, 50, 73–83) are given to Asaph (*cf.* 1 Ch. 15:17; 16:5). The sons of Korah (*i.e.*, descendants) (Nu. 16; 26:11; 1 Ch. 9:19) are mentioned as the authors of ten Psalms (42, 44–49, 84, 87, 88). Two Psalms are ascribed to Solomon (72, 127). One Psalm is attributed to Heman the Ezrahite (88), Ethan the Ezrahite (89), and Moses (90).

For the most part, the titles are rejected by modern criticism as being of practically no value. It is rather generally held that the titles were added at a much later time, and that the titles which refer to an event in David's life were simply taken from the books of Samuel. Further, the basic philosophy of the development of Israel's religion which underlies so much of the modern treatment of the Psalter necessarily precludes attributing much value to the witness of the titles. Thus, Pfeiffer thinks that 'the real question with regard to the Psalter is not whether it contains Maccabean psalms of the second century, but rather whether any psalms are pre-exilic psalms'.[2] The Psalter, he thinks, represents on the whole the religious situation of post-exilic Judaism. Hence, as far as the titles are concerned, the names mentioned in them, with the exception of Heman and Ethan, are irrelevant.

With this denial of value to the witness of the titles the present writer cannot agree. For example, it is certainly not permissible to derive the Abimelech of Psalms 34:1 from the Achish of 1 Samuel 21:11ff. Also, as Moeller has pointed out, Psalm 60:1 contains details which are not found in Samuel, and it is difficult to determine what is the historic reference of Psalm 7:1. It is true that in the remaining eleven titles, there is similarity between the title and the account in Samuel. The titles aid in the understanding of the Psalm, and there is no objective reason for denying their value as a witness. If the Psalms had been composed at a much later date,

2 *IOT*, p. 629.

it is difficult to see why such titles would have been added. This is especially so because often in the Psalm itself there is little that would lead one to think of the situation expressed in the title. Why, for example, would one, judging from the contents alone, ever think that David sang Psalm 7 concerning the words of Cush the Benjamite? Why would one be justified in regarding Psalm 18 as sung when David was delivered from Saul, or Psalm 30 as sung at the dedication of David's house? Do not these considerations point to the fact that the titles were early added by those who knew the actual circumstances in which the Psalm arose? If the titles were merely made up of whole cloth by 'pious' and 'devout' editors of a post-exilic age, why did not these editors compose titles for all the Psalms? The fact that there are orphan Psalms (*i.e.*, without titles) is in itself an evidence of the value and antiquity of the titles. Further, when we consider the manner in which Psalm 18 is reproduced in 2 Samuel 22, it is quite possible that the books of Samuel are dependent upon the Psalms and their titles. Hence, unless the testimony of the title is actually contrary to the contents of the Psalm the title may be regarded as trustworthy.

The denial of Davidic authorship
If the Davidic authorship of the Psalms be denied, what alternative theories are offered? These alternative theories have this in common, that they regard the Psalter as growing out of the needs of the Hebrew religious community. According to Eissfeldt the Israelites took over their cult songs from the Canaanites, who in turn were dependent on Egypt, Babylon, and Asia Minor. Thus the beginnings of Israel's cult-poetry go back to the beginning of Israel's settlement in Canaan. This does not mean, however, thinks Eissfeldt, that the individual examples are so old. Some Psalms are certainly pre-exilic and some, notably the royal psalms, are early pre-exilic, but most of them are of post-exilic origin. David was regarded by the post-exilic nation as the founder of the cultic arrangements and the composer of the songs of the Temple, and for this reason the titles, which are suspicious and have no claim to credibility, were attributed to him. Eissfeldt will admit that at the most one or two Psalms may have come from David, but this is not to be determined from the titles, and a closer examination shows that the Psalms presuppose a much more developed religious and ethical situation than can be admitted for David and his time.

Bernhard Duhm placed most of the Psalms in the post-exilic age and even in Maccabean times. The view that there are Maccabean Psalms is an old one. Theodore of Mopsuestia considered seventeen Psalms to be

Maccabean, and Calvin admits that some are from this age. Cornill asserts that the title of Psalm 30 must be later than 165 BC since he thinks that it refers to the festival of Hanuchah. But even if the title were later, it does not follow that the Psalm itself is Maccabean. Two possibilities suggest themselves. Either this Psalm was sung at the festival of Hanuchah, as *Sopherim* 18:2 says was the case, and because of this the words 'song of the dedication of the house' were added to the title of this Davidic Psalm,[3] or else the Psalm was composed by David for the dedication of his own house, and because of this the phraseology of the title was also used at the rededication of the Temple by Judas Maccabaeus.

Cornhill also appeals to Psalms 44, 74, 79 and 83 as Maccabean, for he thinks the sufferings which they mention have the character of a religious persecution brought upon innocent sufferers. There are other passages also, thinks Cornill, which might be regarded as Maccabean, but these four are certain. Cornill thinks that to regard even the majority of the Psalms as Maccabean is 'grossly extravagant'.

Fortunately, the view that many Psalms are Maccabean is being more and more rejected. This was an extravagant theory which, along with many other extravagant theories, gained its prominence in connection with the liberal view of the Old Testament. For one thing 1 Maccabees 7:17, in citing Psalm 79 as Scripture, clearly shows that the Psalter was already in existence. Furthermore, the internal evidence to which appeal is made for the Maccabean date is irrelevant.

The view of Eissfeldt, presented above, may be regarded as a fair representative of those views which deny much credibility to the titles. In denying the Davidic authorship of the Psalter the following arguments are principally used (based upon Sellin):

1. Psalms which address the king directly or speak of him in the third person cannot be by David, *e.g.*, 20, 21, 61, 63, 72, 110.

2. Some Psalms imply that the Temple is already in existence, *e.g.*, 5, 27, 28, 63, 68, 69, 101, 138.

3. Some Psalms, such as 139, exhibit Aramaisms.

4. David's religious opposition was combined with private or political

---

[3] If this were the case, the original title would be 'A Psalm of David'. In defending the essential trustworthiness of the titles, I do not mean to suggest that as they stand they are above investigation or criticism. But a cautious and reverent criticism, it seems to me, will be unable to dismiss them in their entirety as valueless witnesses of authorship. In support of the opinion here expressed concerning the title of Psalm 30, there is nothing in the content of the Psalm that makes it more fitting for the festival of Hanuchah than for the dedication of David's house. Rather, the individual character of the Psalm makes it more appropriate for the latter occasion.

conflict. Hence, Psalms which imply a purely religious opposition to the godless who are in power cannot be by David, *e.g.*, 9, 12, 14, 27, 35, 38, 101, *etc.*

In answer to these objections, the following should be taken into consideration:

1. Of the Psalms listed in 1 above, Psalm 72 is ascribed to Solomon and therefore not relevant for the discussion. That David might speak of himself in the third person as king, however (*e.g.*, Ps. 21:7), by no means excludes Davidic authorship. When speaking of his official capacity, David uses the third person, a device which is far more effective and self-effacing than would be the first person pronoun. Nor does the use of the second person necessarily exclude Davidic authorship. Indeed, no objection was found to such self-address in ancient times, for Acts 2:34 clearly attributes Psalm 110 to David.

2. It is, of course, true that if a Psalm actually contained a reference to the Temple, it would be difficult to see how David could have written it, since the Temple was built after David's death. The question, therefore, is whether Psalms which are attributed by the titles to David actually contain references to the Temple. It should be noted that the Tabernacle is called the holy place (*qodhesh, e.g.*, Ex. 28:43; 29:30) and the house of the Lord (Jos. 6:24); and the Tabernacle at Shiloh is called the house of God (Jdg. 18:31), the house of the Lord (1 Sa. 1:7), and the temple (*hechal*, 'palace', 1 Sa. 1:9; 3:3). In employing these designations in the Psalms, therefore, David most likely was referring to the Tabernacle (*cf.* also 2 Sa. 12:20). In this connection we may note that the place of worship which in Psalm 27:4 is called 'the house of the Lord' (*beth yehowah*) and 'temple' (*hechal*) in verse 5 receives the designation 'booth' (*sukkah*) and 'tent', descriptions which were never applied to the Temple of Solomon.

3. The presence of Aramaisms in a composition is in itself no indication of date. David had conquered tribes which spoke Aramaic. The presence of an Aramaic element in the recently discovered texts of Ras Shamra may show that Aramaisms were evidence of early as well as of late date.

4. The suggestion that Psalms which imply a purely religious opposition to the party in power cannot have been written by David is based upon a misunderstanding of the situation itself. The question arises, Who are the enemies mentioned in the Psalms? In recent times Sigmund Mowinckel has declared that these enemies were magicians or workers of magic who had brought sickness and calamity to the nation. But the Psalms themselves attribute this calamity to the Lord or to the

sin of the individual himself. Basically, therefore, the enemies and the calamities are to be regarded as actual and real. That David had such real and actual enemies is clear from passages such as 1 Samuel 18:27 and 2 Samuel 15:18, 20, 22, and it is true that in this enmity political and private factors appeared. But this is true also of the enmity depicted in the Psalms. Hans Moeller points out how difficult it is to account for this enmity if David is not the author of these Psalms. First of all, the complaining 'I' (e.g., 'Hear, O Lord, when I cry with my voice'; Ps. 27:7a) was taken by scholars to refer to the congregation of the Maccabean age, because at this time the entire congregation was oppressed, and only at this time did there seem to be present political and religious Psalms. More and more, however, and, of course, rightly, the opposition of a nature sufficient to justify the complaints of the Maccabean background was given up, and the enemies and complaints of the Psalms were taken in a typical or symbolical manner. One of Mowinckel's contributions was the rejection of this position and the identification of the enemies as actual magic workers. But, as indicated above, this view also is attended with difficulties. When, on the other hand, the Davidic authorship is assumed, the Psalms in question yield good sense.

In the light of the above considerations, therefore, we are constrained to reject the position that the contents of the Psalms are often in conflict with the titles, and we believe that the titles are trustworthy indications of authorship.[4]

The authorship of non-Davidic Psalms

There is no valid reason for denying the credibility of the titles which indicate authors of Psalms other than David. What, however, may be said about the so-called 'orphan' Psalms which have no title? Mowinckel has designated Psalms 47 (ascribed to the sons of Korah) and 93–99 (all without a title except Psalm 98) as Psalms which were used in the cult at a supposed yearly festival of the ascension of the throne. But no such festival is mentioned in the Old Testament. Doubtless when the ark was first brought into the sanctuary Psalms were used. Such occasions would be David's introduction of the ark into the city (2 Sa. 6 and 1 Ch. 13:15ff.) or Solomon's dedication of the Temple (1 Ki. 8; 2 Ch. 5–7). From the book of Chronicles we learn what Psalms were sung on these occasions (see 1 Ch. 16:22–33 and 2 Ch. 6:41, 42), and it is interesting to note that among these is Psalm 96 and Psalm 132, the latter also regarded by

---

[4] It is by no means necessary to assume that verses 18, 19 were added to Psalm 51 by a post-exilic editor. Rather, these words should be taken in a figurative sense, namely, by doing good to Zion God will build the walls of Jerusalem.

Mowinckel as a cultic Psalm. It is quite likely, therefore, that Mowinckel has hit upon the purpose of these Psalms, and, if so, they are to be regarded as coming from the time of either David or Solomon.

With respect to the anonymous Psalms which appear in a Davidic cycle, such as 10, 33, 66, 67, 71, it is quite possible that they also are of Davidic authorship. Thus, from Acts 4:22ff. we learn that Psalm 2 is by David. From internal evidence we learn that Psalm 137 belongs to the time of the exile, and probably also Psalm 126. It is very difficult, if not impossible, however, to date a Psalm if it has no title, and there is no clear internal evidence such as that found in Psalm 137.

DIVISION AND NUMBER

In the Hebrew text as well as in the most ancient versions the Psalter is divided into five books, each of which terminates in a doxology, the last Psalm forming a fitting concluding doxology to the entire Psalter. Thus:

> I. Psalms 1–41
> II. Psalms 42–72
> III. Psalms 73–89
> IV. Psalms 90–106
> V. Psalms 107–150

In Book I the divine name Jahweh (the Lord) occurs 273 times, and Elohim (God) only 15 times. In Book II Elohim appears 164 times, and Jahweh only 30. In Book III Jahweh occurs 44 times and Elohim 43. In Book IV only Jahweh is used (103 times) and in Book V Jahweh is used 236 times and Elohim 7. Note that Psalm 53 is essentially a repetition of Psalm 14, but uses Elohim in place of Jahweh.

The division of the Psalter into 150 Psalms does not appear in the earliest Hebrew manuscripts, some of which count more, some less, than that number. According to *Berachoth* 9b, Psalms 1 and 2 were counted as one. And Jerusalem Talmud (*Shabbath* 16) speaks of the number as 147, corresponding to the years that Jacob lived.[5]

The LXX unites Psalms 9 and 10 and also 114 and 115 into one Psalm each, but on the other hand it divides Psalms 116 and 147 into two Psalms each. In addition it adds an extra Psalm which, according to its title, is said to be 'without the number' (*exothen tou arithmou*). Thus the LXX has 151 Psalms. This extra Psalm, however, is apocryphal.

---

[5] 'The 147 Psalms which are written in the Psalter [*tehillim*] correspond to the years of our father Jacob. Each of the praises which Israel addressed to the Lord corresponds to the years of Jacob.' *Cf.* also *Sopherim* 16:11, and elsewhere.

The Psalms are not arranged in chronological order, but related Psalms do occur together. Thus, 3–4, 9–10, and 42–43 are related; also larger groups such as 95–100 and 146–150 belong together, and so also, by reason of their alphabetic acrostic, do 111 and 112. Again, groups are sometimes arranged according to author, as 42, 44–49 (sons of Korah) and 73–83 (Asaph). Psalms which bear similar descriptive inscriptions are placed together, as 50–60 (Michtam) and 120–134 (Songs of Ascent).

At the close of Psalm 72 appears the statement, 'The prayers of David the son of Jesse are ended.' These words occur at the close of a Solomonic Psalm, and even beyond this point, we may note, there are Davidic Psalms. This statement evidently intends us to understand, not that there are no further Davidic Psalms in the Psalter, but that we have now reached the conclusion of a section which had been predominantly characterized by Davidic Psalms. Thus, it sets these works of David off from the Psalms of Asaph (73–83).

A similar statement appears also in Job 31:40, 'The words of Job are ended.' But words of Job do appear later. The statement indicates that a certain point in the book has been reached, and distinguishes what precedes (Job's discussions with his three friends) from what follows (the section in which Elihu appears).

THE COLLECTION OF THE PSALTER

It is difficult to determine how the present Psalter took its form, but there were earlier collections of Psalms. Furthermore, there seems to be little doubt that the present fivefold division is earlier than the time of the LXX.

It is probable that David himself began a formal collection and arrangment of the Psalms. David instituted the liturgical use of a few Psalms at least (e.g., 1 Ch. 16:4ff.) and he also instituted the service in song at the sanctuary (1 Ch. 6:31; cf. also 2 Ch. 7:6; 23:18; 29:30; Ezr. 3:10ff.; Ne. 12:24, 27ff.). But it is impossible to tell to how great an extent David collected and arranged his Psalms. There is no evidence that David had *all* his Psalms used at the sanctuary.

Hezekiah may have been responsible for arranging the first three books of the Psalter. At least in his time there were collections of David's and of Asaph's Psalms (2 Ch. 29:30). It is impossible to tell how or when Book IV was collected, but probably Ezra was the final editor of the entire collection.

THE TITLES OF THE PSALMS

There are thirty-four Psalms in the Hebrew text which do not have a title, but in the LXX only two lack titles (the word Alleluia being counted as a title). The Vulgate follows the LXX in this respect. It is also clear that the LXX translators did not always understand the language of the titles, a fact which argues for their great antiquity. The titles of the Hebrew text, when studied with the aid of a legitimate textual criticism,[6] are to be regarded as trustworthy and of great value in determining the Psalm in question. Many Christian scholars have regarded them as inspired, but whether they are inspired or not, they are an ancient, and a valuable source of information concerning the Psalter.

As the titles appear in the LXX they cannot be original. There are some manuscripts which do not contain them, and some titles (*e.g.*, those to 51, 52, 54, 57, 63, 142) are evidently in part of later origin. And in the various manuscripts of the LXX there is considerable divergence.

In the Syriac text there is a divergence from both the Hebrew and Greek, which expresses the view of the Psalms held by the Antioch school of exegesis. Evidently, therefore, the superscriptions were not regarded as inspired by those who produced the LXX and Syriac translations of the Psalter.

We have already considered the titles which indicate authorship. It should also be noted that the titles may indicate the following.

1. *Type or poetic characteristic.* Fifty-seven Psalms are designated as *mizmor*, which is the common title for individual Psalms. The root of the word means 'to pluck' and so refers to the plucking of the strings of a musical instrument. Quite likely, therefore, we are to understand by this designation a Psalm which was sung to the accompaniment of a stringed instrument.

Shir, a song, occurs thirty times, twelve of which are in connection with *mizmor*. Whereas *mizmor* may apply only to Psalms used in religious worship, *shir* is used of both sacred and secular songs.

Maschil occurs in the titles of thirteen Psalms. The word has several connotations; thus, a meditative Psalm, a didactic Psalm, a skilful Psalm.

Michtam occurs in six titles, but its meaning is by no means clear. Since *kethem* means gold, it has generally been assumed that *michtam* means a golden Psalm. Mowinckel appeals to the Assyrian *ka-ta-mu* ('to cover') and suggests that the *michtam* would be a song of covering, or atoning for sin.

Shiggayon occurs once, in Psalm 7, and its meaning is not clear.

Tephillah appears in five titles. The word means 'prayer'.

Tehillah ('praise') appears but once (Ps. 145) although the entire

---

[6] Thus, the two titles of Psalm 88 are obviously not original.

Psalter is called 'the Book of Praises' (*Tehillim*). The word itself is used in the body of several Psalms.

2. *Musical directions or setting.* The word *lamnatseach* appears in the titles of fifty-five Psalms, and also in Habakkuk 3:19. The Vulgate renders it *in finem*, but the AV translates it 'to the chief Musician'. The RV renders it 'for the chief musician'. In 1 Chronicles 15:21 the verbal form is used with respect to musical service in the sanctuary, and hence it is often supposed to have reference to a director or leader of the music. But the ancient translations did not thus understand it. Some would slightly emend the text so that it should be translated 'musical rendering', but there are difficulties also in this view. Mowinckel has suggested that the term indicates that the Psalm is to be used to propitiate God. The suggestion is interesting, but questionable. It seems best to admit that we do not know the meaning of the term.

Selah does not occur in the titles, but at the end of a section (*e.g.*, Ps. 46:7). It appears seventy-one times in thirty-nine different Psalms. The meaning is not known. Some take it to mean 'lifting up' of the voices; others that the music was to increase in volume. But if it is a musical term, why is it used in so few Psalms? The LXX renders it by *diapsalmon*, which shows that the translators did not understand its meaning.

Neginoth, in six titles, is always combined with *lamnatseach*. The terms means 'stringed instruments', and its infrequent use is surprising. Four of the titles in which it appears also have the term *mizmor*.

'*Al hashsheminith*, in Psalms 6 and 12, is generally taken to mean 'on the octave'. *FAP*, however, has shown rather convincingly that this is not the meaning. Its meaning is not known.

'*Al 'alamoth*, occurring in Psalm 46, possibly occurred also in the title of Psalm 49, but now appears as the last word of Psalm 48. In 1 Chronicles 15:20 it is used of stringed instruments, but its exact meaning is not known.

Gittith occurs in three titles. It may be connected with the word *gath* ('wine-press'). If so, it could be called a tune or melody of vintage. This is, however, questionable.

Nechiloth in Psalm 5 is rendered in the RV by 'with wind instruments'. *FAB* suggests that it may refer to a reed-pipe (1 Sa. 10:5; 1 Ki. 1:40; Is. 30:29). *Machalath*, 'sickness, grief', possibly indicates that the Psalm is to be sung to a mournful tune. In the title of Psalm 88 it appears as *machalath leannoth*.

3. *Melodies.* *Al-tashcheth* ('do not destroy') appears in four titles. *FAP* suggests that the reference is to the 'vintage-song' quoted in Isaiah 65:8 ('destroy not the cluster'), and that these Psalms were to be sung to the

tune of this song which was so well known that it could be identified
merely by its opening words. However, it is by no means clear that the
words in Isaiah 65:8 are those of a song. More likely they are not. We
must acknowledge that we do not understand the precise force of this
phrase.

Ayyeleth hashachar, in the title of Psalm 22, means 'the hind of the
morning'.

Shoshanim, in the titles of Psalms 45 and 69, means 'anemones'.

Shushan 'Eduth ('an anemone is [my] testimony'?) occurs in the titles
of Psalms 60 and 80. (*Cf.* also Ps. 45, 'a song of loves'.)

Jonath elem rechokim in Psalm 56 possibly means 'the dove of the
faraway terebinths' (*elyem*). Joachim Begrich emends this title so that it
reads 'after the mode of Greece [*javanith*] of the distant isles' and appeals
to Isaiah 56:19. But this is mere conjecture.

Al muth labben appears in the title of Psalm 9.

4. *Songs of Ascent (Ma'aloth)*. It has been suggested that these (Pss.
120–134) were sung as the pilgrims journeyed to Jerusalem to celebrate
the three annual feasts. This may have been the case (*cf.* Ps. 122:1–3),
but we cannot be certain.

PURPOSE

According to Cornill, the Psalter in its present form is 'the hymn-,
prayer-, and religious instruction book of the community of the Second
Temple'.[7] This view is based upon the assumption that the Psalter
represents the devout feeling of old Israel in protest to the rising Judaism
of Ezra and the Pharisees. But such an opinion is without foundation in
fact.

Moreover, we are mistaken when we regard the entire Psalter as
designed for the usage of the Temple. That some Psalms were so used
cannot be denied, but it is interesting to note that liturgical directions are
lacking for many of the Psalms. The Psalter, rather, is primarily a
manual and guide and model for the devotional needs of the individual
believer. It is a book of prayer and praise, to be meditated upon by the
believer, that he may thereby learn to praise God and pray to Him. As
Calvin has remarked, it is ' "An Anatomy of all the Parts of the Soul," for
there is no emotion [*affectum*] of which any one can be conscious
[*reperiet*] that is not here represented as in a mirror. Or rather, the Holy
Spirit has here drawn to the life [*repraesentavit*] all the griefs, sorrows, fears,
doubts, hopes, cares, perplexities, in short, all the distracting emotions

[7] *Intro.*, ET, p. 399.

[*turbulentos motus*] with which the minds of men are wont to be agitated. The Psalms in which the first person pronoun is employed are obviously designed to express primarily the experience of an individual. This fact is more and more being recognized (by, *e.g.*, Mowinckel, Balla and others). Of course, this does not preclude the usage of these Psalm in divine worship, but such usage is secondary. While today Christian should sing Psalms in the worship of the Church, they do great wrong to neglect the Psalter in individual devotions.

SPECIAL LITERATURE ON THE PSALMS

Oswald T. Allis, 'The Bearing of Archaeology upon the Higher Criticism of the Psalms', *PTR*, 15, 1917, pp. 277–324; Karl Budde, *Die Schönsten Psalmen* (Leipzig, 1915); H Gunkel und J. Begrich, *Einleitung in die Psalmen*, 2 vols (Göttingen, 1928 and 1933); H Gunkel, *Ausgewählte Psalmen* (Göttingen, 1917); Max Haller, 'Ein Jahrzehnt Psalmen forschung', *ThR*, 1929, pp. 377–402; Fleming James, *Thirty Psalmists* (New York, 1938) H. L. Jansen, *Die spätjüdische Psalmendichtung: ihr Entstehungskreis und ihr 'Sitz im Leben* (Olso, 1937); Robert De Laughe, *Le Psautier* (Louvain, 1962); M. Loehr, *Psalmen studien* (Stuttgart, 1922); Chambers Martin, 'The Inscriptions of the Psalms',* *PRR* XI, 1900, pp. 638–653; 'The Imprecations in the Psalms',* *PTR*, I, 1903, pp. 537–553 Sigmund Mowinckel, *Psalmenstudien: I. Awan und die individuellen Klagepsalmen* (Kristiana 1921); II. *Thronbesteigungsfest Jahves und der Ursprung der Eschatologie* (1922); III. *Kult prophetie und prophetische Pss.* (1923); IV. *Die technischen Termini in den Psalmenüberschrifte* (1923); V. *Segen und Fluch in Israels Kult und Psalmendichtung* (1924); VI. *Die Psalmen dichter* (1924); W. O. E. Oesterley, *A Fresh Approach to the Psalms* (New York, 1937); J. P Peters, *The Psalms As Liturgies* (New York, 1922); N. H. Ridderbos, *De 'werkers de ongerechtigheid' in de individuele Psalmen** (Kampen, 1939); O. C. Simpson, *The Psalmist* (Oxford, 1926); Johannes Vos, 'The Ethical Problem of the Imprecatory Psalms',* *WThJ*, IV, pp. 123–138; A. C. Welch, *The Psalter in Life, Worship and History* (London 1926); Robert Dick Wilson, 'The Headings of the Psalms',* *PTR*, 24, 1926, pp. 1–37 353–395; Elmer A. Leslie, *The Psalms* (1949).

CHAPTER TWENTY

PROVERBS

NAME

IN the Hebrew Bible the title is 'The proverbs [*mishele*] of Solomon, the son of David, king of Israel' (1:1). The word *mashal* indicates a brief, pithy saying which expresses wisdom. It is, strictly speaking, a representation or comparison. Raven well defines it as 'a sententious, synthetic or antithetic statement of a principal which covers many cases'[1] (*Introduction*, p. 267). The word has a wider force than the English 'proverb'. It is not to be restricted to a 'maxim' but is rather more closely akin to a saying. The LXX has the title *paroimiae Salomontos* ('proverbs' or 'parables' of Solomon), and the Vulgate, *Liber Proverbiorum* (the Book of Proverbs).

AUTHOR

The book of Proverbs itself is not without some indication of its authorship, since the authorship of at least six parts is mentioned. Apart from the general title in 1:1 we find: 'the proverbs of Solomon' (10:1), 'the words of the wise-men' (22:17), 'also these belong to the wise-men' (24:23), 'also these are the proverbs of Solomon which the men of Hezekiah, king of Judah, copied out' (*heʿ-ti-qu*) (25:1), 'the words of Agur, the son of Jakeh, the burden, saith the man to Ithiel, to Ithiel and Ukal' (30:1), 'the words of Lemuel the king, the burden which his mother taught him' (31:1).

From a survey of these indications it will be seen that the book does not claim in its entirety to be the work of Solomon. On the other hand, here is no reason for doubting the trustworthiness of these titles and not assuming that the bulk of the book is indeed from Solomon. According to Kings 4:32, 'he spake three thousand proverbs: and his songs were a thousand and five'. Evidently, then, Solomon spoke many more proverbs than those recorded in Scripture. But Solomon himself probably wrote down at least one section of the present book. In Proverbs 22:21, 22 there is a passage which seems to be of particular importance in this connection. In verse 20 the writer asks, 'Have I not written to thee excellent

[1] *Introduction*, p. 267.

things?' (*halo' chathavti lecha shalishim*). It is true that the exact meaning of *shalishim* is in doubt, but this does not affect the main point. Here, the writer, who has just quoted some sayings uttered by the wise men,[2] declares that he has written. The singular points to an individual who has written many things. Further, the one addressed by the writer is also an individual ('to thee'), and the singular here is in agreement with the 'my son' of the Solomonic portions. It is quite possible, then, that Solomon himself wrote out chapters 10–24.

During the reign of Hezekiah, his scribes edited this section and appended chapters 1–9, which were Solomonic. This activity of the men of Hezekiah made such an impression in Jewish tradition that we read in *Baba Bathra* 15a, 'Hezekiah and his company wrote the Proverbs.' However, they probably looked upon these men merely as editors who also added 25–29, and such a view is probably correct. The last two chapters were in all probability added later by the final editor of the book. Who the authors were, *i.e.*, Agur and Lemuel, we do not know.

Those sections of the book which are attributed to the wise men evidently represent inspired wisdom which had previously been uttered by devout men in Israel. As indicated above, these men were probably earlier than Solomon, and he himself may have written this section in its earlier form. On the other hand, it must be admitted that too much weight cannot be placed upon 22:20 and the person who speaks there may have been one of the wise himself. If so, then these sections, *i.e.*, 22:17–24:34, were inserted by the editors, and their date is unknown. At any rate, they must be regarded as inspired proverbs.

It should be noted that the view of the early Church Fathers, namely, that Solomon was the author of the entire book, is incorrect. This view was adopted because of the obscurity or absence of the titles of chapters 30 and 31 in the Greek and Latin manuscripts.

For the most part modern critics deny the Solomonic authorship of Proverbs. According to Eissfeldt the latest portion of the book is 1:1–9:18. This section contains long periods such as chapter 2, which is basically one sentence. In addition to this, the manner in which wisdom and folly are personified probably betrays Grecian influence. Probably *'etun* (7:16) is a Hebraized form of Greek *othone* ('tapestry'). Hence, this section cannot be earlier than the third or fourth century BC, and since

---

2 It may be that this reference to the wise men is not an indication of authorship but merely shows that the words which the writer utters are words which have been approved and followed by wise men or are in agreement with the utterances of wise men.

his is the most recent section, the book in its present form cannot have
risen before the fourth century BC.

A few remarks must be made concerning this position. The personi-
cation of wisdom and folly does not necessarily indicate Greek philo-
ophical influence. The Hebrews, too, had a philosophical sense,
lthough it was directed to the practical affairs of daily life. Possibly in
ıe book of Proverbs we do see a developing philosophy. But the form of
xpression is purely Semitic. Hence, the length of a passage, *e.g.*, chapter
, is not to be explained as due to Greek influence, but to the subject-
ıatter. As for the word *'etun*, its etymology is uncertain; it is interesting to
ote that Solomon speaks of an Egyptian *'etun*. The word may have been
ıe common property of several languages.

As for 10:1–22:16, Eissfeldt thinks that the presence of Aramaic words
.g., *hesedh*, 'reproach', 14:34; *nahath*, 'to go down', 17:10; *racac*, 'to
reak', 18:24; *gibbel*, 'to receive', 19:20) precludes a pre-exilic date for
ıe compilation of the section. Yet there may be in this section proverbs
hich themselves are very ancient. But it must ever be stressed that the
resence of Aramaisms in the Old Testament is no indication of the date
`the document in question. Thus, *nahath* appears on the text from Ras
hamra (Gordon [8:31, 'thy rod is falling']). *Racac* occurs in Isaiah 8:9
ıd Psalm 2:9 as well as Job 34:24, all of which are pre-exilic. *Qibbel*
ppears with a different force in Exodus 26:5 and 36:12, which is very
ose to its meaning in Accadian. This linguistic appeal, therefore, does
ıt really support Eissfeldt's contention.

The third collection (22:17–24:22) is thought, at least as far as 22:17–
3:12 is concerned, to have been based upon the Egyptian Wisdom of
menemope. Ten of the eleven proverbs of this section, thinks Eissfeldt,
'e taken in part literally from Amenomope. The Egyptian collection
thought to be a standard for the entire collection in that it has thirty
ıapters (houses), and Eissfeldt thinks that we are to understand 22:20 as
xpressing the writer's purpose of presenting thirty proverbs.[3] He
lmits that only about a third of the section corresponds to Amenemope,
ıd that the other two-thirds are either of Israelitish origin or else are
ırrowed from elsewhere (*e.g.*, 23:13, 14, from the teaching of Achikar).
nce the imitation of an Egyptian original is clear, we must assign this
ction to the pre-exilic age.

In reply to this position a few remarks must be made. That there is a
rmal relation between Proverbs 22:17–23:12 and the Wisdom of

---

[3] He would follow Erman and Gressmann in emending the present *shilshom* to
loshim ('thirty').

Amenemope seems clear, but that Proverbs is based upon this Egyptian source is by no means clear. For one thing, although these Egyptian proverbs themselves may go back to the beginning of the first millennium BC, the language in which they occur seems to show that they were written down somewhat later. If then Proverbs 1–24 was regarded as Solomonic at Hezekiah's time (and I think this conclusion may legitimately be drawn from 25:1, even if 25:1 be dated at a considerably later period, which seems to be unwarranted), it would certainly seem that Proverbs was earlier than Amenemope.

It must be noted that in Amenemope there is present a polytheism which would have been repulsive to the strict monotheism of Israel. How would the author of Proverbs, who must have been a man of high character, have been attracted to such a source? And further, we may note in passing, since the Wisdom of Amenemope is a document of advice to young men seeking civil service and is more or less connected in thought, why did the writer of Proverbs simply compose his proverbs in such an unsystematic manner? If he was so attracted to Amenemope in the first place as to use it, how do we explain such use? Again, it is surely difficult to believe the writer would have taken 22:17–23:12 from Amenemope and then 23:13, 14 from a Babylonian source, Achikar. Just what would have been the point of this?

Evidently, therefore, the borrowing, if there was any, was on the part of Amenemope. This is supported also by the fact that the contents of 22:17–23:12 contain direct relation to other parts of Proverbs. Compare 22:17, 'incline thine ear', with 5:1 and 7:1; 22:17, 'word of the wise', with 1:6 and 24:23; 22:17, 'apply thy heart', with 2:1ff.; 22:20, 'excellent things', with 8:6; 22:27, 'take away', with 20:16; 23:4, 'weary not thyself to be rich', with 15:27; 23:4, 'cease from thine own wisdom', with 3:5, 7 and 26:12; 23:5, 'riches pass away', with 27:24; 23:6, 'evil eye', with 28:22.

The phrase 'ancient landmark' (22:28; 23:10), which occurs nowhere else in Proverbs, is obviously derived from Deuteronomy 19:14 and 27:17, and Amenemope seems to have misunderstood it, apparently having read 'almana ('orphan') for 'olam.

It should further be remarked that Eissfeldt's interpretation of 22:20 is questionable. In the first place, it is by no means clear that there are thirty proverbs in 22:17–23:12. I am inclined to think that there are but twenty-seven. Amenemope apparently read the word shilshom ('adjutant'?) as sheloshim ('thirty'). The misunderstanding, therefore, was upon the part of the Egyptian. Since there were approximately thirty proverbs in this section, Amenemope composed his work in thirty parts.

It seems most in accord with the evidence to regard Amenemope as dependent upon Proverbs rather than the reverse.

Eissfeldt admits that the collection, 25–29, may be as old as the title indicates. Agur (30:1) is identified as a member of the Arabian tribe Massa (Gn. 25:14), to which Lemuel (31:1) also is said to belong. We cannot tell how old these two sections are.

The actual part which Solomon played in all this is said to be very small. The tradition of Solomonic authorship, it is maintained, is not a trustworthy guide, but is simply based upon the remark in 1 Kings 4:32. Eissfeldt's statement may be regarded as fairly representative of modern criticism. As we have tried to point out, we do not believe it to be a justifiable position.

POSITION IN THE CANON

According to a statement in the Talmud (*Shabbath* 30b) there was some question among the Rabbis as to the canonicity of Proverbs. The statement reads: 'And the book of Proverbs also they sought to hide [*lgnwz*], because its words contradicted one to another. And for what reason was it not hidden?' Then follows the statement that Ecclesiastes also was examined and found satisfactory. The supposed contradictions in Proverbs were the statements 'Do not answer a fool according to his folly' (26:4) and 'Answer a fool according to his folly' (26:5). Then the statement continues, 'There is no difficulty; one refers to the things of the Law and the other to secular affairs.' The rabbinical objection to which mention is made in this Talmudic passage is hardly worthy of serious note.

The New Testament evidently uses language from the book. (Compare Rom. 3:15 with Pr. 1:16; Heb. 12:5 with Pr. 3:11; Jas. 4:6 with Pr. 3:24; 1 Pet. 4:8 with Pr. 10:12; 1 Pet. 4:18 with Pr. 11:31; 1 Pet. 5:5 with Pr. 3:34; 2 Pet. 2:22 with Pr. 26:11.)

In the Hebrew Bible Proverbs stands between Psalms and Job, but in the LXX and Vulgate Psalms stands between Job and Proverbs.

ANALYSIS

1. 1:1–9:18. The praise of wisdom

The contents of this section are as follows: introduction to the section, pointing out its purpose, namely, to impart true, i.e., divine, wisdom and knowledge, verses 1–6; restatement of theme of the whole section (verse 7), indeed, of the entire book, and warnings against sins of violence,

1:7–19; wisdom personified: she cries aloud against her enemies, 1:20–33; inculcation of wisdom and understanding urged, 2:1–22; the blessings which true wisdom brings set forth, 3:1–20; promises of divine care for those who have true wisdom, 3:1–26; practical advice on man's relations with his neighbour, 3:27–35; practical admonitions of a father to his son, 4:1–5:6; admonition to faithfulness in marriage, 5:7–23; the folly of becoming another's surety pointed out, 6:1–5; the folly of the sluggard described 6:6–11; the evil nature of the troublemaker shown, 6:12–19; a general warning against adultery, 6:20–35; an illustration of the preceding warning, 7:1–27; wisdom again personified; she points out the blessings she brings to those who possess her, 8:1–36; wisdom and folly both personified and contrasted, 9:1–18.

This section bears the character of instruction delivered by a father to his son (*cf.* 'my son'). The thoughts are developed somewhat at length and presented from different points of view. Delitzsch has pointed out a similarity between this section and Deuteronomy: 'As Dt. would have the rising generation lay to heart the Mosaic *Torah*, so here the author would impress upon his hearers the *Torah* of wisdom.'

b. 10:1–22:16. Miscellaneous proverbs of Solomon

This section is characterized by the fact that each verse contains a complete proverb, consisting of two members, each member having (in Hebrew) only three or four words, *e.g.*, 10:1:

> A wise son maketh a glad father:
> But a foolish son is the heaviness of his mother.

There is one exception, 19:7, which contains three members. Perhaps this form (*i.e.*, the distich) is the characteristic Solomonic form for a proverb. As is seen from 10:1 the two members exhibit an antithetic parallelism, and this type of parallelism characterizes the entire section.

Driver points out that the second member states a reason (16:12, 26), or purpose (13:14, 15, 24), or completes the thought (12:9; 15:16, 17), or commences with 'how much more' (11:31). Driver also points out that in this section the happier aspects of life predominate; 'prosperity seems to prevail, and virtue is uniformly rewarded.' Many of the proverbs also warn against the wrong use of the tongue. In this life men are rewarded according to their actions.

c. 22:17–24:22. Sundry duties and rules

The admonitions herein are described as 'words of the wise'. In form, these proverbs are for the most part tetrastichs (four members) and ever longer. These proverbs also are addressed to 'my son', and exhibit a more or less consecutive argument, hortatory in its emphasis. The maxims herein contained deal with many subjects and are of a practical character.

d. 24:23–34. Further sayings of the wise
This section serves as an appendix to 22:17–24:22, and exhibits the same variety in form as that section.

e. 25:1–29:27. Miscellaneous sayings by Solomon
In reality this is an appendix to 10:1–22:16. As far as arrangement can be discerned, these proverbs seem to be grouped according to similarity of subject. Again, the antithetic parallelism is not predominant here, but comparison prevails, e.g., 26:8:

> As a bag of gems in a heap of stones,
> So is he that giveth honour to a fool.

Many of these proverbs are identical with those in 10:1–22:16.

It has been objected that the verb translated 'copied out' ('thq) in 25:1 never has this sense in the earlier language, where it always means 'to remove' (e.g., Gn. 12:8). Hence, it is sometimes concluded, the presence of this verb indicates a late date for the title. But this does not necessarily follow. In Ras Shamra 'thq has still a different sense, 'to pass' (of time). The verb, therefore, may have been used all along with various connotations. Its occurrences are not sufficiently frequent to enable one to speak with certainty.

f. 30:1–33. The words of Agur
Verses 1–4 are introduced as an oracle, and point out the conclusion of a sceptic as to the impossibility of knowing God. This is answered, verses 5–6, by an appeal to consider God's revelation, and a prayer, verses 7–9, that the supplicant be preserved. Verses 10–33 consist of nine groups, the so-called 'numerical' proverbs, in which the number four is conspicuous, e.g., 30:15b:

> There are three things that are never satisfied,
> Yea, four that say not, Enough.

g. 31:1–9. The words of Lemuel
These proverbs are addressed to the king by his mother, who urges upon him moderation, chastity, and uprightness.

h. 31:10–31. An acrostic in praise of the virtuous woman
The verses in this beautiful section are arranged in alphabetical order.

SPECIAL ,LITERATURE ON PROVERBS

W. Baumgartner, 'Die Israelitische Weisheitsliteratur,' in *ThR*, 1933, pp. 259–288 (contains a survey of recent study); G. Bostroem, *Proverbiastudien, Die Weisheit und das fremde Weib in Sprüche 1–9* (Lund, 1935); T. K. Cheyne, *Job and Solomon or the Wisdom of the Old Testament* (London, 1887); S. du Toit, *Bybelse en Babilonies-Assiriese Spreuke** (Johannesburg, 1942 – this work, written in Afrikaans, contains a thorough discussion of the relation between the biblical Proverbs and the proverbial literature of Babylon and Assyria. Those who do not read Afrikaans will find a brief summary of its contents in *The Calvin Forum*, IX, Oct. 1943, pp. 54, 55); O. Eissfeldt, *Der Maschal im Alten Testament* (Giessen, 1913); F. James, 'Some Aspects of the Religion of Proverbs', *JBL*, 1932, pp. 31–39; F. D. Kidner, *Proverbs** (*TC*, London, 1964); K. A. Kitchen in C. Henry (ed.), *The Bible Expositor** (Grand Rapids, 1960), II, pp. 71–73, and *Tyndale House Bulletin,** v–vi, 1960, pp. 4–6; D. B. Macdonald, *The Hebrew Philosophical Genius: A Vindication* (Princeton, 1936); O. S. Rankin, *Israel's Wisdom Literature: Its Bearing on Theology and the History of Religion* (London, 1936); H. Rannston, *The Old Testament Wisdom Books and Their Teaching* (London, 1930).

CHAPTER TWENTY-ONE

JOB

THE book receives its name from its principal character *'iyyov*, which appears in the LXX and in the Vulgate as *Iob*. It is from this latter source that the English name is derived.

AUTHORSHIP AND COMPOSITION

There are two problems which must be carefully distinguished in a study of the book of Job. In the first place, it is necessary to determine, in so far as this is possible, who wrote the book and when the author lived. Secondly, we must discover when Job himself lived and the events recorded in the book transpired. It is to the first question that we must address our attention in this section. The question of the authorship of the book, however, is a very complicated one, and there are many views advanced. For the sake of clarity, therefore, it will be best to state our own view of authorship and then the other views which have been held.

The view of the date and authorship of the book which seems to be most free from objection regards the book as composed at some time during the reign of Solomon. This is a view which has antiquity te commend it. It was held by some of the Jewish doctors, and also by Gregory Nazianzen (died *c*. AD 390). It was advanced again by Martin Luther, and during the nineteenth century was defended by Haevernick, Keil and Delitzsch.

The positive arguments in its favour are: (1) This was an age of leisure in which literary pursuits were practised. It was, therefore, a fitting time for the composition of such a book as Job. (2) The book of Job bears the character or stamp of Wisdom (*Chokma*) literature. As Delitzsch remarks, 'It bears throughout the stamp of that creative, beginning-period of the Chokma – of that Solomonic age of knowledge and art, of deeper thought respecting revealed religion, and of intelligent, progressive culture of the traditional forms of art – that unprecedented age, in which the literature corresponded to the summit of glorious magnificence to which the kingdom of the promise had then attained.' These are the two principal arguments for placing the time of composition during the age of Solomon. They are not, of course, conclusive, but they have their place.

According to one alternate view, expressed in *Baba Bathra* 14b, Moses was the author of Job. Those who have supported this view have been accustomed to point to the presence in Job of certain words which also occur in the Pentateuch, such as *'ulam, tnu'ah, netz, pelilim, qshitah, yeret*.

But in opposition to this is the consideration that part of Job is written in the style of Proverbs. Further, it is unlikely that a book of the reflective nature of Job would have been written before the giving of the Law and by one whose chief occupation was Law-giver. However, even among some of the Church Fathers this view was held.

Cornill maintains that in the light of Jeremiah 20:14–18, compared with Job 3, Job must be regarded as later. Further, Ezekiel 18 is thought to show that Job is later than Ezekiel, since, according to Cornill, this passage denies the existence of the problem with which Job strives. Job 42:17 exhibits a distinct reminiscence of Genesis 25:8 and 35:29. Lastly, Proverbs 1–9, the latest part of Proverbs, is presupposed in Job. (Thus, Job 15:7 is dependent on Proverbs 8:25). In addition, the presence of what he calls the 'Aramaeo-Arabic' linguistic character of the book leads Cornill to place the work in the latest period of Hebrew literature.

Like many others Cornill would separate the prologue and epilogue from the poetical section. He believes that the prose narrative was earlier than the poem. It had, he thinks, assumed so fixed a form in the tradition that the poet dared not modify anything in it.

Pfeiffer believes that the question whether the prologue and epilogue were written by the author of the book is academic. We have, he thinks, a folk-tale or legend which had an oral history before it was committed to writing. This tale was familiar in some form to Ezekiel (Ezk. 14:14, 20), although, as its background shows, the story originated among the Edomites. In its original form the tale probably lacked the Satan episodes (1:6–12; 2:1–7a), and the visit of the three friends (2:11–13; 42:7–10a) was probably introduced when the tale became a framework for the poem. As we have it, the folk-tale has been adapted by means of slight touches to the poem.

The tale is Israelitic according to Pfeiffer, for the mention of Jehovah in the mouth of the Edomite hero is inconsistent. This tale was probably added to the poem by a Jewish redactor, who reproduced the tale as he heard it from storytellers in Judaea. The folk-tale was a vehicle for the expression of a popular pessimistic philosophy, and the poet (an Edomite) merely used the tale as an illustration of his thought, although he investigated problems far beyond the scope of the story.

With respect to chapter 28, Pfeiffer believes that it was an independent composition of the author and not an integral part of the book. The speeches of Elihu (chapters 32–37) are a polemical interpolation designed to defend Jewish orthodoxy and to condemn much of the previous teaching of the poem.

The final editor of the book worked about 200 BC, and the prose prologue and epilogue were not earlier than the sixth century BC. As for the poet, we may place him sometime between 700 and 200 BC, probably at the time of Jeremiah (605–580 BC).

The views of individual critics vary greatly, and we perhaps best understand the attitude of recent criticism by a survey of the various positions which are expressed. The reader may find the different work surveyed in the commentaries, the works by Dhorme being particularly valuable.

1. The prologue is a redactional addition. Schultens in his learned commentary (1737) adopted this view. Koenig rejects the prologue.

2. The prologue and epilogue were originally a popular book, separate from the poem. Wellhausen, Budde, Cheyne, Bickell, Duhm, and Volz held that the poet himself used these narratives as a framework for his poem.

3. The Satan passages in the prologue may be the work of the poet. It is an open question to Koenig whether these passages are not interpolations on the part of the poet.

4. The original introduction to the book is chapters 29–31. This view was advanced by Studer in 1881.

5. The prologue is the work of the poet – Dhorme, O'Neill, Hoelscher, and, of course, conservative Protestant scholars such as Green.

6. The poem itself (chapters 3–31, omitting chapter 28) is the work of more than one man.

(i) Baumgaertel regards as original only 4:1–5:7, 27; 6:1–30; 8:1–11, 20–22; 9:1–3, 11–23; 32–35; 11:1–5, 10–20; 13:1–19 and 16:6, 9, 12–17, 18–21; 19:2–29; 23:2–7,10–17; 31:35, 37. This is one of the most drastic treatments of the poem. But there are others also (*e.g.*, Volz, Fullerton, Jastrow) who recognize secondary hands in this section. Complaints, as 3:3–12 and certain other passages which are regarded as unsuitable, are exscinded. This procedure, however, is subjective. It presumes to declare what the poem should have been and then sets to work with the paring knife.

L

(ii) Chapters 24–27 are accepted as genuine by Budde and, of course, by conservative Protestant scholars. On the other hand, some have tried to rearrange the text to produce what they believe to be a harmonious order. In his procedure Torczyner seems to me to be one of the most radical. Duhm has also made rearrangements and likewise Dhorme. Some have regarded the section as containing various interpolations, the principal one being chapter 28. It is thought to be unlikely that Job would have uttered the words of this chapter, since, if he had, there would be no need for the divine message which follows (chapters 38–41). Also, if Job rose to such sublime heights in this chapter, how explain his lapse into complaining (30:20–23)? Furthermore, how should we then explain the ironical tone of the divine speeches (38ff.)? We shall discuss these arguments under the heading Analysis.

7. The speeches of Elihu (chapters 32–37) are original and genuine. Budde, Rosenmueller, Thilo, Wildeboer, Cornill, O'Neill, and conservative scholars hold to this. Cornill even went so far as to consider this section the crown of the book and as presenting the only solution of the problem that could be given from the Old Testament standpoint.

8. The speeches of Elihu must be rejected. Driver, Pfeiffer, and many others thus argue. The reasons usually adduced for this are: (i) These speeches exhibit an independent character and disturb the connection between the earlier poem and the Lord's discourses. (ii) 38:1–2 and 40:6 presuppose that Job, not Elihu, has spoken. (iii) This section exhibits far more Aramaisms than the remainder of the book. (iv) The theoretical explanation of suffering presented in these speeches is said to be regarded as impossible by 38:1–42:6 and thus these speeches destroy the artistic structure of the book. These arguments will be discussed under Analysis.

9. The double speaking of the Lord and Job's abasing himself twice are genuine. Dillmann and conservative Protestant scholars so believe.

(i) 38:1–40:2 alone is regarded as genuine. Thus Siegfried.

(ii) The original form of the divine speeches is thought to be 38,39 plus 40:2,8–14 and 40:3–5 plus 42:2–5. So Bickell, Budde, Duhm. The reason for this is that these speeches are regarded as having been interpolated. Thus 39:13–18 is rejected by some, e.g., Duhm, Cheyne, Hoelscher. 40:15–24 (the section about the hippopotamus) is rejected, as is also 40:25–41:26 (the crocodile). It is contended that these two sections have an independent character and do not serve as illustrations of pride such as the context was discussing.

(iii) The speeches of the Lord are rejected in their entirety. Thus Cheyne, Volz, Hempel, Baumgaertel.

(iv) 40:1–4 is considered to be the conclusion of the book. So argues Hans Schmidt, while Fullerton maintains 40:3–5 is the conclusion.

10. The time of composition cannot be established with certainty.

(i) The age of Solomon – Keil, Delitzsch, Haevernick.

(ii) The eighth century (before Amos) – Hengstenberg.

(iii) The beginning of the seventh century – Ewald, Riehm.

(iv) The first half of the seventh century – Staehelin, Pfeiffer.

(v) The time of Jeremiah – Koenig, Gunkel, Pfeiffer.

(vi) The exile – Cheyne, Dillmann (1891).

(vii) The fifth century – Moore, Driver and Gray, Dhorme.

(viii) The fourth century – Eissfeldt, Volz.

(ix) The third century – Cornill (later held to a more indefinite date).

The brief survey of critical opinion on Job which has just been given will show the student how varied are the viewpoints held. We believe that any view which would destroy the unity of the book must be rejected. If the unity of the entire book be granted, then it would seem that the Solomonic age was as fitting a time for its composition as any. At the same time it must be admitted that, as we have it, certain portions, *e.g.*, the prologue, may exhibit a more recent linguistic revision. If so, this would account for some of the grammatical constructions of the chapter, which seem to be reflections of a later period. But this is difficult to determine.

There remains the further question as to the time when the action of the book took place. And in consideration of this problem we must note that Job was a historical personage, as is proven by Ezekiel 14:14 and James 5:11. There are certain indications in the narrative which seem to point to a time before the giving of the Sinaitic legislation. The patriarchal description in chapter 1 seems to support this, and also the absence of mention of any of the distinctively Israelitish institutions. It seems to me, therefore, that Job was probably a contemporary of the patriarchs, but of this we cannot be certain.

ANALYSIS

a. 1:1–2:13. The prologue

1. 1:1–5. In the midst of great prosperity Job is a truly pious man. This section gives the setting of the narrative, which takes place east of Palestine in the Arabian desert. This prologue is essential to the further understanding of the book. Job appears as the priest of the household, and offers an *'olah* (burnt offering), two factors which point to a pre-

Mosaic age. In these remarkably direct verses we are introduced to the chief character. The introductory words ('there was a man', '*ish hayah*) evidently show that this is not a narrative of a portion of the Israelitish history, but rather a beginning of an extra-Israelitish history.

2. 1:6–12. The Lord determines to try Job. The scene now transfers to heaven, and the truth is illustrated that whatsoever comes to pass upon earth has been decreed of God in heaven. The mention of Satan is thought by some to show that the book cannot be as early as Solomon's time, since the mention of Satan by name first appears in post-exilic writings (Zc. 3 and 1 Ch. 21:1). But this proves nothing. The adversary had already been present in Eden, and the knowledge of such a being was not derived from contact with eastern nations but was present also in Israel itself (*cf*. Ps. 109:6). If, then, the author of Job was acquainted with the narrative of Genesis, it is difficult to understand why he may not now have designated the wicked one as Satan. There is no point in mentioning Satan in the poem itself, since the earthly characters would have had no knowledge of the heavenly scene which had gone before. Note well that Satan is subject to the omnipotent God; he can go only so far as God permits.

3. 1:13–22. The four messengers. Like repeated strokes the four come to Job. In all this Job sins not. His true piety is thus manifested.

4. 2:1–10. Satan again turns his attention to Job and grievously afflicts him, probably with the disease of elephantiasis, a loathsome and dangerous form of leprosy. Yet Job refuses to curse God, as his wife had commanded, but rather exhibits a magnificent patience in the midst of his suffering.

5. 2:11–13. Job's three friends visit him to comfort and sympathize. They are affected by his grief and show respect for his suffering by a seven days' silence.

b. *3:1–26. Job's complaint*

The contrast between Job's grand patience in chapter 2 and his complaint in chapter 3 is not because the two chapters are from different authors. At first Job does not complain. But the visit of his friends and their long silence, coupled with the increasing severity of his pains, lead Job to break forth in heart-rending complaint. It may be, too, that Job had an idea what his friends would say, and so could restrain himself no longer. Job first complains (verses 3–5) against the day of his birth. Then he desires that that night (verses 6–9) be destroyed; he asks why he was born (verses 10–12), and wishes such had not been the case (verses 13–16), for in the grave there is rest (verses 17–19). Why should the suffering man live (verses 20–23) when life is unbearable (verses 24–26)?

c. 4:1–31:40. The discourses with the three friends
1. *4:1–14:22. The first cycle of discourses.* (i) 4:1–5:27. Eliphaz' first speech. Eliphaz begins with an apparent show of sympathy for Job. But he soon sets the keynote for the whole discussion by implying that Job's suffering is because of his guilt. 'Who, being innocent, has ever perished, or when have the upright ever perished?' (4:7b). Eliphaz assumes that material prosperity will follow those who are upright and adversity will come upon evildoers. This he apparently regards as an ultimate principle to which even God seems to be subject. On this ultimate principle Job is in perfect agreement. The debate seems to start out then upon the basis of an assumption that not God but a certain principle of ethics is ultimate. Eliphaz therefore hints that Job must have done some great sin to bring upon himself such suffering (verses 1–12). Eliphaz also is religious; he has had visions, which have told him that sinful man will perish (verses 13–21). It is only the foolish man, therefore – since one cannot change this principle – who resents God's dealings with him. Eliphaz suggests that it would be wise for Job to seek the Lord.

(ii) 6:1–7:21. Job's first reply. Job does not deny the principle which Eliphaz has suggested. In fact, he himself holds to that principle as of an ultimate nature. He now does not see that this element in his thinking is inconsistent with his *worship* of God as sovereign. He therefore complains that God has afflicted him and will not grant him death (6:1–13). He regards his friends as unfaithful, and begs them to consider whether iniquity is on his tongue. He expostulates upon the miseries of life (7:1–10), and bitterly commands God to let him alone! He is so inconsequential before God – why does God not pardon him, for he shall soon perish?

(iii) 8:1–22. Bildad's first speech. Bildad is more outspoken than Eliphaz, but his speech, beautiful as it is, is based upon the same low plane as that of his friend. Bildad thinks that the death of Job's children is a divine judgment (verse 4). He thus betrays his ignorance of the true state of affairs and also his adherence to the false principle that death or suffering must be in punishment for specific sin. God cannot do otherwise; apparently He is bound to this rule. Hence, Bildad urges Job to repentance and points out the pleasant consequences which would follow.

(iv) 9:1–10:22. Job's second reply. Job begins by admitting the truth of the principle underlying Bildad's words (verse 2), and then launches into a severe tirade against God, regarding Him as an irresponsible

Power. He seems to look upon God as a blind, irresistible Power, something like the Allah of the Moslems. Job is compelled to adopt this position – he is driven into it, in fact – by the rationalistic principle which he holds in common with his friends. In his heart he evidently has begun to doubt, or at least to question the validity of this principle: hence he attacks the justice of God. The situation is not just, he feels; there should be a *mochiah* ('arbiter', 'umpire') between them, so that God would be compelled to deal fairly with him. Job pleads with God and utters a cry of despondency. He even criticizes God for having brought him into existence.

(v) 11:1–20. Zophar's first speech. Zophar is more impetuous than the others, but like them argues upon the same low level. He condemns what he calls the 'multitude of words' (*cf.* Pr. 10:19 and Ec. 5:3) and thus reveals that he has not begun to understand the depth of conflict that has gone on in Job's mind. At the same time, part of his speech (verses 7–20) is of unsurpassed beauty. If his words are to be understood in accordance with the basic philosophy which has undergirded the discussion thus far, they are but empty sounds. If, however, Zophar is inconsistent with his underlying philosophy and is speaking as a true believer in God, we have in his expressions profound and beautiful teaching of God's incomprehensibility.

(vi) 12:1–14:22. Job's third reply. Job tells Zophar that his pretensions to superior wisdom are not impressive. They are making him, an innocent man, to be a laughing-stock. Yet Job still feels that God's rule is arbitrary, and not in accord with justice (12:7–25). Job regards his friends as ill-advised counsellors. He desires to speak with God, and to plead with Him. This seems to be the first real step in advance (13:3). Hitherto, Job has accepted the pagan philosophy of his friends, namely, that in this life the good are rewarded and the evil punished. His own terrible sufferings, however, have caused him to doubt the validity of the principle. He therefore turns on God in bitter complaint. Now, however, he wants to discuss the matter with God. This shows both that he begins to recognize in reality that God is greater than he and also that there is justice in God, for he expects God to listen to him. More and more he begins to realize that God is essentially just (13:10, 11). Job will prove his ways to God, even before His face. God will slay him, he fears, but he is prepared for that, he will await what God will do, and resigns himself to it, even though it be death.[1] A hypocrite would not thus wish to come

---

[1] 13:15 should best be translated, 'He will slay me: I wait for him.' Thus, I read *lo*, 'to him' and not *lo'*, 'not'. The AV rendering, 'Though he slay me, yet will I trust him', while not literally correct, nevertheless seems to reflect rather well the attitude of Job.

before God. Job then pleads with God and pours out (chapter 14) a lament over the weakness and frailty of man.

2. *15:1–21:34. The second cycle of discourses.* (i) 15:1–35. Eliphaz' second speech. Eliphaz repeats his platitudes, and regards Job's words as empty. He appeals to the wise and ancients as authorities.

(ii) 16:1–17:16. Job's fourth reply. Job realizes the vanity of the position adopted by his friends. Were he in their place, he also would be able to confuse with words. But what can Job do, for God has come upon him? He still wishes that there were one to judge between God and himself (16:21), and thus, for a time, overcome by the severity of his suffering, he sinks back into complaining hostility to God. In the midst of such laments, however, he confesses that the 'righteous shall hold on his way, and he that hath clean hands shall wax stronger and stronger' (17:9).

(iii) 18:1–21. Bildad's second speech. Bildad begins by reproaching Job and then graphically describes the terrors and ruin that await the wicked. He has not abandoned the basic pagan philosophy with which he began.

(iv) 19:1–29. Job's fifth reply. Job breaks out in a powerful complaint against his friends and charges them with slandering and persecuting him. Thus, emboldened, he protests his innocence, and expresses the clear-cut conviction that his Vindicator is living. Furthermore, this Redeemer (*go'el, i.e.*, one who will defend his good name) will stand upon the earth and have the last word, which word will be in defence of Job and in attestation of his innocency. After Job himself has died, he nevertheless in the flesh (*min* is best taken as indicating the standpoint or position *from* which one sees) will see God with his eyes. For this Job eagerly waits.

This magnificent statement of a bodily resurrection – for that is precisely what it is – raises a question. How did Job come to such a belief? Could he have attained it by mere reflection? I think not. It seems to me that God gave him a special revelation of consolation, a revelation also which showed him how false was the principle upon which he had begun to reason. In the light of this revelation Job now comes to clear reflection.

(v) 20:1–29. Zophar's second speech. In lines of awe-inspiring force, Zophar describes the fearful punishment of the wicked. He ignores Job's appeal to a final judgment, since he says the wicked have already been judged (verses 4, 5). It may be that Job's remarkable declaration seemed to Zophar and the others to be merely the ravings of a madman. At any rate, it is ignored, and the three continue on blindly, as before, not understanding the true nature of the case.

(vi) 21:1–34. Job's sixth reply. Job becomes more and more emboldened, and with confidence points out the fallacies in the position which he had held to at the first. The facts of life are against it, since wicked men do prosper in this life. The ways of God, thinks Job, are inscrutable, and the three friends are, as it were, speaking lightly and dogmatically of them.

3. *22:1–31:40. The third cycle of discourses.* (i) 22:1–30. Eliphaz' third speech. Eliphaz seems to reach the height of blasphemy in this discourse. God, he thinks, has no interest in or concern over human sufferings, except in so far as they vindicate His justice. Eliphaz then repeats Job's own words and urges him to repent.

(ii) 23:1–24:25. Job's seventh reply. Job is perplexed and saddened by his grievous sufferings, but the fierce note of complaining bitterness is absent. He knows that God is just and that He will render justice. Although Job himself is in the dark, he yet has confidence in God.

(iii) 25:1–6. Bildad's third speech. These words are difficult to understand. Bildad seems to have no argument, and his words therefore are best regarded as a mere protest against Job's statements hitherto.

The brevity of this speech has caused some to consider it as out of place. Some would assign 26:5–10 to Bildad, so that in its entirety Bildad's speech would consist of 25:1; 26:5–10; 25:2–6. Job's reply to Bildad is then said to consist of 26:1–4 and 27:2–6. Chapter 27:7–23 would then be regarded as the third speech of Zophar. But the absence of a third speech of Zophar is an evidence of genuineness. The extreme brevity of Bildad's last speech seems to show that the three friends had exhausted their argument. The principal reason for arranging the text seems to be that as it stands it contains statements that are out of place in the mouth of Job and seem more fitting in the mouth of his friends. But it must be remembered that Job has not yet completely thought through the implication of his position, and it is to be expected that in the agony of his suffering he might utter words which were inconsistent with his basic belief in the true sovereignty of God. For fuller discussions of the order of the text, consult the various recent commentaries.

(iv) 26:1–14. Job's eighth reply. Job regards Bildad's reply as useless and besides the point. Job, too, is conscious of God's greatness and majesty, and again describes God's power in the created world. Thus Job gives expression to what he now sees more clearly and firmly believes – the infinite distance between the Creator and His creation.

(v) 27:1–31:40. Job's final reply to his friends. Job now takes up his proverb (*mashal*), which here has the nature of a final setting forth of his position. He again insists that he is speaking the truth (27:1–6), and expresses his utter detestation of the wicked (27:7–23). Although some of these words are similar to those previously uttered by Zophar (20:29), yet, I think, Job places a different content in them. It is not merely that the wicked suffer in accordance with an inscrutable principle, but as enemies of God. He reveals a deeper understanding (*cf.* 27:14 with 21:8), for he seems now to have in mind the ultimate end of the wicked. Job then launches into a consideration of the problem how and where true wisdom is to be obtained (chapter 28). This wisdom is not so much in the realm of everyday life but rather in the knowledge of God's ways in control of His creation. While man can explore certain aspects of the physical universe (*e.g.*, 28:1–11, the depth of the mines), yet man is limited. Ultimate and absolute knowledge belong to God alone. Hence, for man, true knowledge consists in thinking God's revealed thoughts after Him, *i.e.*, 'The fear of the Lord, that is wisdom; and to depart from evil is understanding' (28:28). To sever this chapter from its context seems to me to betray a lack of true exegetical insight.

Job's argument appears now to be complete, and there is left to him only to sum up his life. This he does in chapter 29. He then contrasts his former happiness with a picture of the present contempt in which society holds him (chapter 30). Lastly, he utters a final protestation of innocence (chapter 31). He has kept himself from impurity (verses 1–4), has exhibited uprightness and honesty in his dealings (verses 5–8); he has been true to his wife (verses 9–12) and fair to those who worked for him (verses 13–15); he has steadfastly shown kindness and humaneness (verses 16–23) and has turned from greed (verses 24–28), exhibiting, rather, generosity to all (verses 29–34), and now he would commit his way to God (verses 35–40).

Some would place 31:35–37 after 31:38–40, since the latter seems to present a climax. It is possible that this transposition is correct, and that verses 35–37 do form the conclusion.

d. 32:1–37:24. *The speeches of Elihu*
The change in the book is indicated by a short introduction in prose (32:1–5, the poetical accents are here retained, however), in which it is stated that the three friends cease because they think Job is self-righteous. Elihu was angry with Job because he thought that Job justified himself at the expense of God, and he was angry with the three friends because, although they condemned Job, they had no answer to the problem.

The Aramaisms and other peculiarities of the language of this section are probably due to the individuality of the speaker. They do not indicate that this portion should be severed from the remainder of the book. Nor need we expect a reply to these speeches from Job. It is time that the Lord intervene in defence of His servant, and this He graciously does. The absence of a reply on Job's part to Elihu is but an evidence of genuineness and originality. Nor is there any particular reason why Elihu should be mentioned either in the prologue or epilogue. His speeches seem at points to show a misunderstanding, but the speeches of the three were based upon an ultimate wrong philosophy, and they were in need of forgiveness. Furthermore, the curt dismissal, as it were, of these speeches, seems to indicate that they were not as harmful or important as were those of the three. Finally, the fact that Elihu addresses Job by name and refers to the preceding discourses simply shows that he had been present. O'Neill suggests that he may have been a note-taker.

Elihu asserts that wisdom does not belong alone to the old. He is dissatisfied with the arguments of the three, and cannot keep silence. He refers to Job's innocence (33:6-9) and then seeks to point out that God speaks to man in various ways. There is a purpose in the discipline that has been inflicted upon Job. Hence, Elihu urges Job to listen and to consider that God does not act unfairly. Job has shown ignorance, then, in criticizing God, for God is righteous and has designed suffering for man's benefit; men should therefore revere Him.

There is a severity and harshness in Elihu's speeches which is even stronger than in those of the three friends. Elihu does not seem to share belief in the vicious principle upon the plane of which the debate began. He seems rather to believe in the true sovereignty of God, but his words are words of ignorance. What he says seems to be true enough in itself, but it is here beside the point.

e. 38:1–42:6. The Lord speaks

These wondrous words of the Lord constitute both the answer to Job's prayer and desire that he might confront God and also the true answer to the problem. By constant appeal to the creation and the incomprehensible nature of the created universe God brings to the fore the infinite, absolute distance between the Creator and the creature. Man, being a creature and hence finite, cannot comprehend the infinite wisdom of God or the mystery of His rule. By these words Job is more and more abased to the point where he sees that it is futile for man to think that he can penetrate the mysteries of God's providential dealings with His creatures. He has found peace – a God-given peace – even though all his questions have not been answered. He now knows that 'all things work together for good [even though he cannot understand how] to them that love God, to them that are called according to his purpose'. His pride has been abased and his spirit humbled, but by beholding God affirm his integrity, Job has by God's grace attained to a true victory and triumphant faith. Job breaks completely with the narrow theology which he had once held. He now sees that God is sovereign. Job and his sufferings have their place in God's all-wise, incomprehensible disposition of things. All is well. Why should Job seek to penetrate the mystery? God is upon the throne. That is enough. Job therefore abhors his words and repents.

God's grace is further manifested in that He commands the three to take sacrifices and to go to Job that Job may pray for them. Job's innocence is thus further attested. Indeed, one of the purposes of this remarkable book is to defend the integrity and innocency of Job. Finally, Job is richly blessed of God and dies 'being old and full of days'.

SPECIAL LITERATURE ON JOB

G. C. Bradley, *Lectures on the Book of Job* (Oxford, 1887); Karl Budde, *Beiträge zur Kritik des Buches Hiob* (1876); Foster, 'Is the Book of Job a Translation from an Arabic Original?', *AJSL*, 49, 1932–33, pp. 21–45; K. Fullerton, 'The Original Conclusion of Job', *ZAW*, 42, 1924, pp. 116–135; William Henry Green, *The Argument of the Book of Job Unfolded** (New York, 1881); M. Jastrow, *The Book of Job* (Philadelphia-London, 1920); O'Neill, *The World's Classic Job* (Milwaukee, 1938); E. Sellin, *Das Problem des Hiobbuches* (1919); W. B. Stevenson, *The Poem of Job* (London, 1947).

CHAPTER TWENTY-TWO

THE SONG OF SOLOMON

NAME

IN the Hebrew the book is named in accordance with its first verse, 'The Song of Songs' (*shir hashshirim*), *i.e.*, the best of songs. The LXX translates with *asma asmaton*, and the Vulgate, *Canticum Canticorum*. In the German Bible since the time of Luther the book has been called *Das Hohelied*.

AUTHOR

The book claims to be by Solomon, and this opinion is not contradicted by *Baba Bathra* 15a, which relates that 'Hezekiah and his company wrote . . . the Song of Songs'. There is no sufficient reason for denying such authorship, since the book does have some points of contact with other writings of Solomon. Furthermore, the work seems to reflect a time before the division of the kingdom, since the author speaks of various places throughout the country as though they all belonged to the same kingdom (*e.g.*, Jerusalem, Carmel, Sharon, Lebanon, Engedi, Hermon, Terzah, *etc.*). The author also shows a knowledge of animals and exotic plants. According to Steinmueller, he mentions fifteen species of animals and twenty-one varieties of plants. The comparison of the bridegroom with 'a company of horses in Pharaoh's chariots' (1:9) is interesting, since Solomon introduced horses from Egypt (1 Ki. 10:28).

The modern school denies the Solomonic authorship of the book. It believes rather that there are linguistic indications present which point very clearly to a later date as the time of composition. Thus, appeal is made to the use of the short relative particle *she* in connection with '*adh* in the sense of 'so that' (*e.g.*, 1:12; 2:7; *etc.*). In addition, the Persian word *pardes* ('paradise', 'orchard', AV) is thought to point to the Persian period, and '*appiryon* (3:9, 'bed', 'couch' – *phoreion*), a Greek loan word, is thought to point to a later time. Hence, it is argued, the book, at least as we have it, must come from the third century BC.

But it must be noted, as Eissfeldt so well points out, that this can refer only to the Song in the form in which it has come to us. It is quite possible that the book itself is the work of Solomon, and that the few linguistic phenomena which seem to point to a later date may have been mere editorial changes to make the book understandable to a later generation. At the same time, I do not think that the presence of a Greek and Persian word is in itself determinative of a later date. It must be remembered that Solomon's commerce and trade were very extensive, and foreign words might travel widely (*cf.*, *e.g.*, the widespread use of *chai* [tea] in the Near East today). The presence of Aramaic words is, of course, no indication of date.

INTERPRETATION OF THE BOOK

Students of the Song of Solomon have differed widely as to its form and its interpretation. It will be necessary, therefore, briefly to survey the various interpretations which have been advanced.

   1. Jewish allegory. In passages of the Mishnah, Talmud, and Targums an allegorical interpretation appears which expounds the Song in terms of Israel's history, as representing the love of God for, and His dealings with, His chosen nation. Thus 1:13 has been interpreted (*e.g.*, by Rashi) as a reference to the Shekinah between the cherubim.

   2. Christian allegory. The allegorical method was introduced into the Christian Church principally by Origen and Hippolytus. For the most part, however, Christian scholars who have used this method have seen the book not as the history of the people of Israel, but of Christ's dealings with His Church. This view has been very popular in Christendom; indeed, it might be called the dominant position. It is essentially this view which has been advocated by Hengstenberg and Keil, and it may be found in the chapter headings of the AV, thus: 1–3, The mutual love of Christ and his church; 4, The graces of the church; 5, Christ's love to it; 6–7, The church professeth her faith and desire; 8, The church's love to Christ.

Rowley gives some interesting examples of this type of exposition.[1] He points out how in the twelfth century this method became a favourite one to interpret certain phrases of the Virgin Mary. Certain other strange views which Rowley mentions as having been advanced are the following: (i) 1:5 means black with sin, but comely through conversion (Origen). (ii) 1:12, 'between my breasts', refers to the Scriptures of the Old and New Testaments, between which is Christ (Cyril of Alexandria).

---

[1] H. H. Rowley, 'The Interpretation of the Song of Songs', *JTS*, 38, 1937, 337–363. This article gives an excellent survey of the history of the interpretation of the Song of Solomon. In writing this section I have received much help from Rowley's article.

(iii) 2:12 refers to the preaching of the apostles (Pseudo-Cassiodorus). (iv) 5:1 refers to the Lord's supper (Cyril of Alexandria). (v) 6:8 has a reference to the eighty heresies (Epiphanius).[2]

In defence of the allegorical interpretation it has been argued that if the book does not have a religious meaning it would not have been accepted into the Canon. In reply we would say that this consideration in itself does not justify an allegorical interpretation. When we come to see what the true meaning of the book is, we shall readily enough understand why God has placed it in the Canon.

It is further argued that elsewhere in the Scriptures the figure of a marriage relationship between the Lord and His people is used. This is true enough, but elsewhere this figure is used as a symbol and is always made the basis of didactic explanation. That is not the case in the Song of Solomon. We must remark that there is a distinction between allegorical interpretation and the interpretation of allegory. There is no justification for allegorical interpretation unless there is first of all an allegory to be interpreted, and there is no evidence to show that the Song of Solomon is an allegory. In other words, the arguments generally used to support the allegorical interpretation are really irrelevant.

3. A drama. Franz Delitzsch advocated the view that the Song is a drama in which King Solomon falls in love with a Shulamite girl and takes her to his capital Jerusalem, his love being purified from sensual to pure love. Otto Zoeckler held essentially this same interpretation.

Others, notably Heinrich Ewald, and also Strack, Koenig, Driver, advocate what has been called the Shepherd hypothesis, namely, that the Shulamite girl remains faithful to her shepherd husband despite the temptations of Solomon.

But drama did not make its way to any extent among the Semitic peoples. Also, the Song does not purport to be a drama any more than it does an allegory. It is unlikely that the pious of the ages would have regarded the Song as a divinely inspired composition if it were merely a drama of such nature.

4. A collection of love songs. This view appears in different forms. Thus, Eissfeldt thinks that in the book we have a collection of independent songs. Eissfeldt appeals to J. G. Wetzstein, who for many years was consul at Damascus. Wetzstein says that on the day before her marriage the bride dances a sword dance in accompaniment to a song in which her beauty is described (*wasf*). For a week after the marriage the couple is celebrated as king and queen, and during this time many

---

[2] Rowley, *op. cit.*

songs are sung, among which is a *wasf* ('description') of the young couple.

Eissfeldt thinks that this same custom prevailed in Israel, and that 4:1–7, 5:10–16, and 7:1–6 correspond to the *wasf* described by Wetzstein. On this view, then, the book is a collection of love songs which may best be understood by a comparison with similar collections recently made by Dalman, Littmann, and others.[3] Pfeiffer, Lods, Reuss, Dussaud hold essentially this view, which was advocated by the German poets Herder and Goethe. But it is questionable whether the practice described by Wetzstein was also observed in Palestine.

5. A type. Honorious of Autun (twelfth century) and others have insisted upon a literal interpretation of the Song. In addition, however, they think that there is a typical meaning which indicates the love of Christ for His Church. This view has been held by some Catholic scholars, such as Peter Schegg and Vincent Zapletal. But since there is no warrant for finding this typical meaning, this view must be rejected.

6. An adaptation of a pagan liturgy. Theophile J. Meek thinks that the Song was originally a liturgy of the Tammuz-Adonis cultus. In this cult the god died and the goddess descended to the underworld in search of him, thus signifying the dying of nature. Upon their return their marriage was represented in this rite. As we have the Song, however, it has been revised and purified to bring it into the harmony with the religion of Israel.

But it is extremely unlikely that, had such been the origin of the Song, it would have been accepted into the Canon. While the Song may contain some allusions to this cult, which was found in Israel, it was never a mere cult song. This explanation is naturalistic.

7. A scene in a harem. According to Leroy Waterman the Song (1:2–8:4) presents a harem scene in the royal palace at Jerusalem. In this scene Solomon speaks to the girl from Shunem, whom Waterman identifies with the maiden who was brought from Shunem to act as David's nurse (1 Ki. 1:1–4). In the harem scene there is interchange of discourse among three parties: Solomon, the girl, and the harem. The passage is a village scene at Shunem. This interpretation is based upon a rearrangement of the text as follows: 1:1; 3:6–11; 4:1–6; 1:2ff. The passage 4:7ff. then comes after 3:5.

8. A parable. The Second Council of Constantinople (AD 533) con-

---

[3] Gustav Dalman, *Palästinischer Diwan* (Leipzig, 1901); Enno Littmann, *Neuarabische Volkspoesie* (1902); Alois Musil, *Arabia Petraea*, III (Vienna, 1908); and St. H. Stephan, 'Modern Palestinian Parallels to the Song of Songs', in *Journal of the Palestine Oriental Society*, 1922, pp. 199–278.

demned Theodore of Mopsuestia, not because he questioned the canonicity of the Song, but because he held to a literal interpretation. He regarded it as a mere song of human love, written by Solomon upon the occasion of his marriage to the daughter of Pharaoh.

There is certainly an important element of truth in this interpretation of Theodore's. The Song does celebrate the dignity and purity of human love. This is a fact which has not always been sufficiently stressed. The Song, therefore, is didactic and moral in its purpose. It comes to us in this world of sin, where lust and passion are on every hand, where fierce temptations assail us and try to turn us aside from the God-given standard of marriage. And it reminds us, in particularly beautiful fashion, how pure and noble true love is.

This, however, does not exhaust the purpose of the book. Not only does it speak of the purity of human love; but, by its very inclusion in the Canon, it reminds us of a love that is purer than our own. By its very presence in the Canon (for, in the last analysis, it is God who has put these books in the Canon, not man), it reminds us that God, who has placed love in the human heart, is Himself pure. In my opinion, we are not warranted in saying that the book is a type of Christ. That does not appear to be exegetically tenable. But the book does turn one's eyes to Christ. This is certainly shown by the history of interpretation in the Christian Church. The book may be regarded as a tacit parable. The eye of faith, as it beholds this picture of exalted human love, will be reminded of the one Love that is above all earthly and human affections – even the love of the Son of God for lost humanity.

THE CANONICITY OF THE SONG

Because of the nature of its contents some among the school of Shammai expressed doubts about the canonicity of the Song. But the view which was expressed by Rabbi Akiba prevailed: 'No man in Israel has ever contested that the Song of Solomon defiles the hands [*i.e.*, is not canonical]. For in the entire world there is nothing to equal the day on which the Song of Solomon was given to Israel. All the Writings [*i.e.*, the Hagiographa] are holy, but the Song of Songs is most holy, and if there has been dispute, it has only been about Ecclesiastes' (Mishnah, *Yadaim* 3:5). Nevertheless, as Rowley points out, the fact that such a statement as this of Rabbi Akiba should be preserved, implies that even in his day there was some question about the book.[4]

But if the Song is primarily a love song, and not an allegory, what

[4] *Op. cit.*, p. 337.

reason is there for its inclusion in the sacred Canon? In answer we would say that God has placed this Song in the Canon in order to teach us the purity and sanctity of that estate of marriage which He Himself has established. When we read the Song of Solomon, our hearts will be purer, and we shall realize all the more the heinousness of that temptation which would lead to unfaithfulness among those who are married. Since the purpose of the book is not mere entertainment, but is ethical and didactic, we may understand why God has given it to us. For even the faithful servant of the Lord is tempted to break the seventh commandment. In the polygamous ancient world and in the sophisticated modern world, unfaithfulness may easily be regarded as something light and trivial. But when we occidentals turn from the callous sinfulness of our daily world and carefully read the oriental imagery of this portion of Holy Scripture, we are blessed, and we are helped. So long as there is impurity in the world, we need, and need badly, the Song of Solomon.

ANALYSIS

It is very difficult to analyse the Song, but perhaps the following will serve to give an idea of its general structure.

1. 1:1–2:7. The bride longs for the bridegroom. They meet and praise one another. In 1:5,6 the bride describes herself 'black but comely'. From 1:8 on, the two sing one another's praises.

2. 2:8–3:5. Their love increases. The maiden, using beautifully expressive figures from nature, e.g., 2:11–13, sings the praises of her beloved.

3. 3:6–5:1. This passage contains the espousal, e.g., 4:8ff., and praise of the bride.

4. 5:2–6:9. The bride longs for her beloved and sings his praises while he is gone from her.

5. 6:10–8:4. The beauty of the bride is described.

6. 7:5–14. Here the beauty of love is shown.

SPECIAL LITERATURE ON THE SONG OF SOLOMON

K. Habersaat, 'Glossare und Paraphrasen zum Hohenlied', Biblica, XVII, 1936, pp. 348–358; K. Kuhl, 'Das Hohelied und seine Deutung', ThR, 9, 1937, pp. 137–167; W. Riedel, Die Auslegung des Hohenliedes in der jüdischen Gemeinde und der griechischen Kirche (1898); H. H. Rowley, 'The Meaning of the Shulamite', in AJSL, LVI, 1939, pp. 84–91; The Song of Songs. A Symposium (Philadelphia, 1924); A. Vaccari, 'Il Cantico dei Cantici nelle recenti publicazioni', Biblica, IX, 1928, pp. 443–457; P. Vulliaud, Le Cantique des Cantiques d'après la tradition juive (Paris, 1925); Leroy Waterman, The Song of Songs (Ann Arbor, 1948).

CHAPTER TWENTY-THREE

RUTH

NAME

THE book receives its name from its principal character. In the LXX the name appears as *Routh*.

DATE AND AUTHORSHIP

In recent times several critics, *e.g.*, Eissfeldt, Pfeiffer, Oesterley and Robinson have regarded the date of composition of Ruth as post-exilic. The author is said to have been familiar with the 'Deuteronomic' edition of Judges (supposed to be *c.* 550). This post-exilic date was also maintained by some of the older writers such as Kuenen and Wellhausen.

The arguments in support of a post-exilic date are extremely weak. To defend it, some have even sought to regard the book as a counterblast to the stern measures of Ezra and Nehemiah against mixed marriages. This, however, is rightly rejected by Pfeiffer and others. Again, appeal has been made to the linguistic data in support of a post-exilic date.

On the other hand, *Baba Bathra* 14b tells us that 'Samuel wrote his book and Judges and Ruth'. This view, however, while possible, is unlikely, since the genealogy in Ruth 4:22 seems to imply that David was a well-known person.

What then shall we say about the question of authorship? On the whole, the evidence seems to favour an early, pre-exilic date. The language and style are different from those of the post-exilic books. There are two words to which appeal may with justification be made as supporting a later date. These are *lahen* ('therefore') and *mara* ('bitter').

Lahen (1:13) is thought to be an Aramaic form. It is very questionable, however, whether this word with the meaning 'therefore' actually does occur in Aramaic. Also, it may be that in Ruth 1:13 the word should be emended to read *lahem* ('to them'), a reading which is favoured by the principal versions. Again it must be stressed that the presence of an Aramaic form is no indication of the date of the document in which it occurs. Lastly, it may be noted that the form *lahen* need not be translated 'therefore', but can be taken with the meaning 'for those [things]'. If so, the difficulty disappears. *Mara* (1:20) has also been appealed to as Aramaic. But these two words are not sufficient in themselves to prove a late date, for we must remember that from the beginning the Hebrew language contained Aramaisms, as does the Ugaritic.

Again, we may note that David is mentioned by name. This does not mean that the book was written long afterwards, when David's fame had become a legend, for then we should probably also find Solomon's name. Hence, the absence of Solomon's name seems to lend support to the view that the book was written sometime during the life of David the king. Furthermore, the straightforwardness of the narrative, given without any apology, as it were, shows that it was not a 'tendency' writing, but seems rather to point to the fact that it was pre-exilic in origin. In 4:7 mention is made of the custom of taking off a shoe to symbolize the renunciation of one's claims. 'Now this was the manner in former time in Israel concerning redeeming and concerning changing, for to confirm all things a man plucked off his shoe, and gave it to his neighbour; and this was a testimony in Israel.' Obviously, this custom no longer applied when the book was written. It did apply, however, in the period of the Judges, and in the earlier Mosaic period, though with a different connotation (*e.g.*. Dt. 25:9,10).

While, therefore, it is impossible to assign the composition of the book to a definite age, it seems likely that it was composed at some time during the reign of David.

THE HISTORICITY OF THE NARRATIVE

Pfeiffer[1] believes that the book is fiction, and points to the following arguments: (1) the significant names of some of the characters, *e.g.*, Mahlon ('sickness'), Chilion ('wasting'), Orpah ('stiff-necked'), Naomi ('my sweetness', 1:20); Ruth may mean 'companion'; (2) the noble character and conduct of Ruth, Naomi, Boaz; (3) the picturesque details of life with no unpleasantness; (4) the strong religious faith.

But it should be noted that the book purports to be history. We read the opening words, 'Now it came to pass in the days when the judges ruled, that there was a famine in the land' (1:1). This is the language of simple, historical narrative. It points to a certain time and to certain conditions in history. We are prepared by these words for the narration of a historical event. The narrative proceeds throughout with this same simplicity and straightforwardness. In other words, it purports to be the

[1] *IOT*, p. 718.

account of something that actually happened. Again, we may note that in so far as the book of Ruth speaks upon the customs of the time, it shows itself to be accurate and true to fact. During the early period there was friendly intercourse between Israel and Moab (*cf.* 1 Sa. 22:3, 4). At this time marriage with a Moabitess was not forbidden. From the book of Ruth we may see how it was that David at a later time sought asylum with the king of Moab. Again, it is hardly likely that a writer of fiction would seek to trace the origin of David's ancestry to a Moabitess. If this book is not historical, but merely the work of someone who sought to account for the origin of David's line, is it not more likely that such a writer would endeavour to discover the origin of that line in an Israelitess and not in a foreigner? The very fact that Ruth, the ancestress of David, was a Moabitess, is in itself an argument for the historicity of the book.

What is of decisive significance, however, is the fact that in the genealogy of David, given in Matthew (1:5), the name of Ruth is included. And the genealogy in Luke 3:32 agrees with that of Ruth. This is conclusive evidence. The New Testament, which is the infallible Word of God, speaks of Ruth as a historical person. This rules out any possibility that the book of Ruth is a mere romance and not true history.

PURPOSE

This little book endeavours to trace the ancestry of David to the Moabitess, Ruth. It thus has a historical aim. However, it also seeks to inculcate the lesson of filial piety and devotion. There is a wealth of such devotion and unselfishness in Ruth's words: 'Intreat me not to leave thee or to return from following after thee: for whither thou goest, I will go; and where thou lodgest, I will lodge: thy people shall be my people, and thy God my God: where thou diest, will I die, and there will I be buried: the Lord do so to me, and more also, if ought but death part me and thee' (1:16, 17). The book also serves to show that the true religion is supranational, and not confined to the bounds of any one people.

POSITION IN THE CANON

The early date for Ruth seems further to be supported by the fact that it was early placed after Judges, rather than in the Hagiographa. It appears thus in the LXX and Vulgate. Josephus also (*Contra Apionem* i.8) apparently counted Ruth with Judges and Lamentations with Jeremiah when he spoke of twenty-two books of Scripture. Jerome in his *Prologus Galeatus* seems also to imply that the Jews thus placed Ruth with Judges, but he also says that some place Ruth and Lamentations among the Hagiographa.

How Ruth came finally to be placed among the Hagiographa is not known. Possibly its usage in the synagogue may have put it there, but this is mere conjecture.

ANALYSIS

a. Chapter 1. Ruth comes to Bethlehem
1. 1:1–7. Introduction.
2. 1:8–18. Ruth's determination to remain with Naomi.
3. 1:19–22. The arrival in Bethlehem.

b. Chapter 2. Ruth meets Boaz
1. 2:1–7. Ruth gleans in the fields.
2. 2:8–16. The kindness of Boaz.
3. 2:17–23. Ruth returns to Naomi.

c. Chapter 3. Ruth's appeal to Boaz
1. 3:1–5. Naomi's advice.
2. 3:6–13. Ruth speaks to Boaz.
3. 3:14–18. Ruth returns to Naomi.

d. Chapter 4. The marriage of Ruth and Boaz
1. 4:1–8. The goel (kinsman).
2. 4:9–12. Boaz takes Ruth.
3. 4:13–17. Ruth bears a son.
4. 4:18–22. The ancestry of David.

Verses 18–22 are thought by some to be a later addition based upon 1 Chronicles 2:4–15 (Eissfeldt, Sellin). Eissfeldt goes farther and thinks that 4:14b, 'and they called his name Obed', is also secondary, and that originally some other name stood here. He also questions 17a, but without sufficient ground. Why must a genealogy be a later addition? Why may not the writer of Chronicles have employed this genealogy as well as *vice versa*?

SPECIAL LITERATURE ON RUTH

W. W. Canon, 'The Book of Ruth', in *Theology*, 16, 1928, pp. 310–319; H. Gunkel 'Ruth', in *Reden und Aufsätze* (1913), pp. 65–92.

CHAPTER TWENTY-FOUR

LAMENTATIONS

NAME

IN the Hebrew Bible the book is named after its first word *'echah* (how!). In the LXX, however, it is named after its content, The Tears of Jeremiah (*threnoi*), and so in the Vulgate *Threni* ('tears'), with the interpretation, The Lamentations of Jeremiah (*Threni, id est lamentationes Jeremiae prophetae*). Our English title is derived from the Latin.

AUTHOR

According to tradition, both Jewish and Christian, Jeremiah was the author of Lamentations. This tradition first appears in the title of the book in the LXX, which reads, 'And it came to pass after Israel had been taken away into captivity and Jerusalem had been laid waste that Jeremiah sat weeping and lamented this lamentation over Jerusalem and said'. The Vulgate repeats these words and adds 'with a bitter spirit sighing and wailing'.

Baba Bathra 15a presents the same tradition: 'Jeremiah wrote Lamentations' (the book is here called Lamentations, *Qinoth*). This tradition was very widespread in antiquity. However, the book itself does not claim to be the work of Jeremiah. In fact, no author is named. What then was the origin of this tradition? In all probability it arose from a misreading of 2 Chronicles 35:25. This latter passage states that Jeremiah composed lamentations over Josiah and that these are written in the Lamentations (*wehinnam kethuvim 'al-haqqinoth*). Now it is obvious that the lamentations of which Chronicles speaks are not our present book, for the reason that our present book does not contain any lamentations over Josiah, although Cornill thinks that Lamentations 4:20 ('the anointed of the Lord') may be a reference to Josiah. But this is most unlikely. Lamentations 4 is not a lament over the loss of a person, but an outpouring of grief over the tragic conditions of Zion itself. Hence, the passage in 2 Chronicles simply teaches us that upon one occasion Jeremiah did compose lamentations. From this, it seems to me, the tradition must have arisen that Jeremiah was also the author of the canonical book.

Too much weight, therefore, cannot be placed upon this tradition as a witness to authorship. In its earliest manifestation, this tradition is several hundred years later than the book itself. In seeking to answer the question of authorship, therefore, we must turn to other considerations.

The author of the book seems to have been an eyewitness of the destruction of the city (assuming that that is the cause for lamentation in, *e.g.*, 1:13–15; 2:6, 9ff.; 4:10). This seems to be borne out also by the general vividness of the description and by the fact that the poet seems to identify himself with the fortunes of the city.

Furthermore, there are striking similarities of style and phraseology between Lamentations and Jeremiah. The following are particularly interesting:

'The oppressed virgin daughter of Zion' (La. 1:15; Je. 7:21; *etc.*); 'the prophet's eyes flow down with tears' (La. 1:16a; 2:11; Je. 9:1, 18b; 3:17b; *etc.*); 'fears and terrors surround' (La. 2:22; Je. 6:25; 20:10); appeal to God for vengeance' (La. 3:64–66; Je. 11:20). Driver also suggests the following comparisons: Lamentations 1:2 with Jeremiah 30:14. Lamentations 1:8b–9 with Jeremiah 13:22b, 26. Lamentations 2:11; 3:48; 4:10 with Jeremiah 6:14; 8:11, 21. Lamentations 2:14; 4:13 with Jeremiah 2:8; 5:31. Lamentations 2:20; 4:10 (women eating their own children) with Jeremiah 19:9. Lamentations 3:14 with Jeremiah 20:7. Lamentations 3:15 (wormwood), 19 with Jeremiah 9:15; 23:15. Lamentations 3:47 with Jeremiah 48:43. Lamentations 3:52 with Jeremiah 16:16b. Lamentations 4:21b with Jeremiah 25:15; 49:12. Lamentations 5:16 with Jeremiah 13:18b.

In addition we may note that both expect a similar punishment to come upon those nations which rejoiced in the downfall of Jerusalem (*cf.* La. 4:21 with Je. 49:12). Driver also points out that in both books the national calamity is attributable to the same causes (*cf.* 1:5, 7, 14, 18; 3:42; 4:6, 22; 5:7, 16 with Je. 14:7; 16:10–12; 17:1–3; *etc.* [national sin]; *cf.* La. 2:14; 4:13–15 with Je. 2:7, 8; 5:31; 14:13; 23:11–40; *etc.* [guilt of prophets and priests]; *cf.* La. 1:2, 19; 4:17 with Je. 2:18, 36; 30:14; 37:5–10 [the nation's vain confidence in weak and treacherous allies]).

Driver further remarks, although he does not himself accept Jeremianic authorship: 'The same sensitive temper, profoundly sympathetic in national sorrow, and ready to pour forth its emotions unrestrainedly, manifests itself both in Lam. and in Jer. (*e.g.*, c. 14–15).'

I have thus constantly referred to Driver, since he has given such a complete survey of the arguments for Jeremianic authorship.[1]

---

[1] *Cf.* also Mas Loehr, 'Die Sprachgebrauch des Buches der Klagelieder' in *ZAW*, 1894, pp. 31–50, and particularly 1904, pp. 1–16.

In the light of these arguments it seems most likely that Jeremiah did compose Lamentations. Of this, however, we cannot be certain, and it seems best to admit that we do not really know who the author was.

The principal arguments urged against the Jeremianic authorship are the following:

1. Jeremiah looked upon the Babylonians as the instruments of God's punishment, whereas Lamentations 1:21 and 3:59–66 present different ideas. This objection betrays a profound lack of understanding of the true situation. The Chaldeans, in God's providence, were the instruments of God in punishing Judah. But God makes even the wrath of men to praise Him. And the thing that the Chaldeans did was an evil thing for which they should be punished. Why could not one man believe that the Chaldeans were God's instrument of punishment and at the same time desire that they, too, should be recompensed for what they had done?

2. Jeremiah would not have spoken of the cessation of the prophetic oracles, as in 2:9c. In answer, however, it may be said that this verse does not mean to assert that there is no more prophetic revelation. The writer has just said that there is no more law (*'en torah*), which is a strong expression to teach that since the city is destroyed (9a) there is no law to be obeyed, or rather, no-one to obey the law. Also, says the writer, the prophets of the city have found no revelation from the Lord. Is not this merely a forceful way of declaring that the old order is completely changed? If this clause be pressed to the limit, so should the preceding one. I can see no reason whatsoever why Jeremiah could not have written these poetical words.

3. Jeremiah would not have blamed the prophets generally for the calamity (2:14; 4:13). As a matter of fact, however, Jeremiah condemns the false prophets even more strongly than does Lamentations (*cf.* Je. 14:14; 23:16).

4. The acrostic arrangement is not to be expected from Jeremiah. But why not? Who is to say that a prophet may not employ different styles and forms of expression when he so desires?

5. Jeremiah did not expect help from Egypt (4:17). But 4:17 does not teach that the author himself had individually looked to Egypt for help. In using the 1st person plural, the author is simply speaking of the nation as such. He is not necessarily at this point stating his own political views.

6. Jeremiah did not look for safety under the shadow of Zedekiah (4:20). But it is quite possible that at first Jeremiah did place his confidence in Zedekiah, a confidence later to be disappointed. Although Zedekiah had been appointed by Nebuchadnezzar, he was nevertheless a descendant of Josiah and so a legitimate claimant of the throne, and the

phrase 'the anointed of the Lord' could perfectly well apply to him.

7. Most important is the argument that the phraseology of Lamentations differs from that of Jeremiah. Yet, in itself this cannot be conclusive. Arguments of this kind are generally precarious, and it must be remembered that because of the acrostic arrangement and peculiar subject-matter and also the poetical style, particular words may have been chosen which do not appear in Jeremiah.

In conclusion we would maintain that the arguments offered against Jeremianic authorship are not sufficiently cogent.

PURPOSE

The book of Lamentations represents the attitude of a devout believer in the theocracy towards the destruction of that theocracy. The nation has become so vile that the Lord has left His sanctuary, and evil forces have destroyed it. The poet laments deeply that the nation has become thus iniquitous, but he realizes that the Lord is righteous. He thus calls upon the people to repent. At the same time he sees how evil has been the action of those who have destroyed the holy city, and calls for their punishment.

This is one of the most tragic books in the Bible. The nation from whom salvation was to come has become so filthy that God would destroy her outward theocratic form. Against the background of this fact we may understand the cry, 'How doth the city sit solitary, that was full of people! how is she become as a widow! she that was great among the nations, and princess among the provinces, how is she become tributary!'

ANALYSIS

. Chapter 1. The desolate and forsaken Jerusalem. The poet pictures vividly the lamentable condition of the forsaken city. This description climaxes in verse 11b, where the city, personified, speaks: 'See, O Lord, and consider; for I am become vile.' In verse 18 the city again speaks, proclaiming the Lord's righteousness, her own desolation, and uttering a plea that her enemies be punished.

2. Chapter 2. The reasons for the Lord's anger with the city are now set forth. The poet urges the nation to seek the Lord, and it responds to this plea, verses 20-22.

3. Chapter 3. This chapter contains a remarkable acrostic. Each letter of the alphabet begins three verses. Thus, verses 1-3 begin with Aleph, verses 4-6 with Beth, etc. The nation is herein personified. In verses 1-20 it laments or bewails the tragic condition that has come upon

it. Then (verses 21–39) it recalls the Lord's mercies that it is not entirely consumed, and trusts in His goodness. In verses 40–54 the people of the nation are exhorted to search and try their ways and to turn again to the Lord, and finally (verses 55–66), after the acknowledgment that God has heard its cry, the nation calls to Him for vengeance upon its foes.

4. Chapter 4. This chapter exhibits a contrast between Zion's former splendour and her present condition.

5. Chapter 5. The nation appeals to the Lord to remember its affliction. This affliction is truly great, but the nation would trust in the eternal God (verse 19). This chapter is not written in the acrostic form.

Cornill remarks, 'The attempt to explain Lam. IV and V as Maccabean is a pure curiosity.' This statement should be taken to heart.

SPECIAL LITERATURE ON LAMENTATIONS

Of particular importance are the articles of the Catholic scholar H. Wiesmann, which have appeared in *Biblica*, 'Der planmässige Aufbau der Klagelieder des Jeremias', VII 1926, pp. 141–161; 'Der Zweck der Klagelieder des Jeremias', VII, 1926, pp. 412–428; 'Die Textgestalt des 5. Kapitels der Klagelieder', VIII, 1927, pp. 339–347; 'Der Verfasser der Klagelieder ein Augenzeuge?', XVII, 1936, pp. 71–84; and the following two which have appeared in *BZ*: 'Zu Klagelieder 3, 1a', XVIII, 1928, pp. 38ff.; 'Der geschichtliche Hintergrund des Büchleins der Klagelieder', XXIII, 1935, pp. 20-43.

CHAPTER TWENTY-FIVE

ECCLESIASTES

NAME

IN the Hebrew the book bears the title, 'The words of the preacher [*divere qoheleth*], the son of David, king in Jerusalem' (1:1). The word *oheleth* is a Qal active participle, feminine singular. The reason for the eminine is probably to be found in the fact that the word denotes an ·ffice. This seems to be substantiated by analogous forms such as *ofereth* (Ezr. 2:55, Ne. 7:57); *pochereth* (Ezr. 2:57). It is also possible that he feminine is to be explained in a neuter sense, with an intensive force. As applied to an individual, therefore, the word would denote one who ealized or fulfilled the idea completely.

Evidently the participle is derived from the root *qahal*, which else-vhere appears in the Hiph'il in the sense 'to assemble'. It probably ndicates one who holds or addresses an assembly. The LXX rendered it ·y *ekklesiastes*, from which the English title comes, and Jerome translated as *concionator* (*i.e.*, one who gathers an assembly). The word thus esignates the function of the leader who speaks in the assembly. Hence, he translation 'preacher' is approximately correct.

AUTHOR

The actual name of the author is not mentioned in the book. It has been ssumed, however, because of the words 'the son of David, king in erusalem' in 1:1, that Solomon was intended, and hence it has been held y some that Solomon was the actual author. This appears to be upported by the reference to great wisdom (1:16) and great works 2:4–11), allusions which seem to refer to Solomon. However, the olomonic authorship is not widely held, and is rejected by most rthodox Protestant scholars.

The reason for this widespread rejection of the Solomonic authorship to be found in the following considerations.

1. The name Solomon does not occur. The book does not make the xplicit claim that Solomon was its author. If it did, that fact in itself ould settle the question.

2. All the writings of Solomon bear his name in their titles. Here
however, the unusual designation, *qoheleth*, appears, and thus it would
seem to be evident (note the feminine construction in 7:27) that Solomon
is not intended to be regarded as the author.

3. At the same time, by the addition of the words 'the son of David
king in Jerusalem' there would seem to be a reference to Solomon. In
what sense, however, is this reference intended? In the light of the
preceding remarks (see under 1 and 2) and of the discussion to follow, it
is clear that the reference is not for the purpose of showing that Solomon
was the author of the book. Solomon, however, was known for his great
wisdom and so is here regarded 'as a representative . . . of that mind
which is alone capable of uttering such things as are of thorough and
lasting importance for the people of God' (Hengstenberg). Wisdom
therefore, is here presented as embodied in a person, and that person is
Solomon. Hence, it is in an ideal sense that Solomon is introduced, and so
the author is not guilty of a literary deception (*cf*. Lk. 11:49, 50 with Mt
23:24).

4. Again, in 1:16 the writer says that he had increased wisdom 'over
all who were before me over Jerusalem'. This seems to refer to former
kings, and if it does, it would not well apply to Solomon. It is true that
Hans Moeller[1] thinks the reference is only to the city-kingdom
Jerusalem, but to confine or restrict the reference in this manner is not
convincing. It is not likely that the author, were he Solomon, would thus
have compared himself with previous city rulers of the Jebusites, or that
he would have included his father David in such a line. Hence, 1:16
seems to imply that the writer lived at some time after Solomon.

5. In 1:12 the writer says, 'I *Qoheleth* was king in Jerusalem.' The past
tense seems to imply that the writer was no longer king. It is true that the
verb (*hayithi*) might be translated 'I was and still am', but that is very
unnatural. The clear implication is that the writer had been and no
longer is king. This, of course, would not apply to Solomon, who was king
to the end of his life.

6. The background of the book does not fit the age of Solomon. It was
a time of misery and vanity (1:2–11); the splendour of Solomon's age
was gone (1:12–2:26); a time of death had begun for Israel (3:1–15);
injustice and violence were present (4:1–3); there was heathen tyranny
(5:7, 9–19); death was preferred to life (7:1); 'one man ruled over other
men to their hurt' (8:9). The foregoing is based on Hengstenberg. See
also 4:13, 'Better is a poor and a wise child than an old and foolish king
who will no more be admonished', and 8:2; 9:14–16; 10:16, 17, 20.

---

[1] *Einleitung*, p. 216.

The language and diction of the book apparently point to a time later than that of Solomon. Some of the words seem to be Aramaic, which in itself would be no indication of date, but others seem to approach the region of the Mishnah. In all probability the book is to be dated about the time of Malachi. The political background is satisfactory, and this period would also satisfy the linguistic phenomena.

There is a statement in *Baba Bathra* 15a to the effect that Hezekiah and his company wrote Ecclesiastes. However, this is not to deny Solomonic authorship, for the meaning is probably that Hezekiah and his company merely edited the text.[2] Early Christian and Jewish tradition ascribed the book to Solomon, and Luther seems to have been the first to deny that Solomon wrote the book.

L. Wogue maintained that the original author was Solomon, but that at a later time, before the exile, the book was edited and enriched with additional expressions. In this editorial work one or more editors took part. Thus, the foundation or basis is Solomonic, but the developments and perhaps a large part of the redaction come from another age.

The Solomonic authorship is maintained today by Hans Moeller and by the Romanist scholars Gietmann and Schumacher. Those who believe that the author lived later than Solomon are agreed that this later writer lived in the post-exilic period. But when, precisely? Here opinions differ. Many would date the book about 200 BC, since they think that it shows unmistakable signs of Hellenistic influence. Others have wished to place it as late as 100 BC, and Graetz even went so far as to regard the book as belonging to the time of Herod the Great.

UNITY OF COMPOSITION

Among some of the Church Fathers, such as Gregory the Great, Gregory Thaumaturgus, Gregory of Nyssa, Jerome, as well as among some medieval writers, Bonaventura, Thomas Aquinas, Nicholas of Lyra, and some modern writers, the view is held that the book consists of a dialogue in which various problems are discussed. The unity of the book, however, is not denied by those who maintain this view.

Some have regarded 12:13-14 as an addition which was intended to obscure the true contents of the book and for the same reason 11:9b, 12:1a and 7 have been suspected. The reasons for regarding these verses as additions, however, are really based upon a misconception of the true teaching of the book.

[2] *Cf.* also *Megilla* 7a, *Shabbath* 30, where Solomon is expressly said to be the author.

Eissfeldt regards the following as later insertions: 2:26; 3:17; 7:26b; 8:5, 12b, 13a; 11:9b, 12:7b and 12:12–14.

PURPOSE

There are those who assert that the book contains the influences of Grecian philosophy, and parallels are supposed to have been found in Aristotle, Heraclitus, the Stoics, and the Epicureans. These supposed parallels, however, are not real. Nor do we find parallels in Egyptian literature, nor anywhere else in the ancient pagan world.

There are also those who assert that the teaching of Ecclesiastes is at variance with the teaching of the gospel. The book is said to present mere human reasoning; it is the best that man can do; it is legal, and apart from redemption man can do no better. The book, it is said, does not anticipate the gospel. Of course, we may ask, if this low view of Ecclesiastes is correct, why did the Lord God cause it to be placed in the Canon?

The key to the proper understanding of the book is to be found in the words of the conclusion: 'Fear God and keep his commandments, for this is the whole duty of man. For God shall bring every work into judgment, with every secret thing, whether it be good or whether it be evil' (12:13, 14). There can be no higher purpose in life than this. This is the same great goal that our Lord laid down in the Sermon on the Mount. It is the divine demand for absolute perfection, the goal for which God's people must ever strive.

Nevertheless, although the goal for which we should strive is clear, we fall far short of attainment. And the reason for this is stated in Ecclesiastes: 'Lo, this only have I found, that God hath made man upright; but they have sought out many inventions' (7:29). The word translated 'inventions' (*hishshevonoth*) means 'thoughts, reckonings, devices'. The idea is that God has made man perfect (*i.e.*, straight, right), but man has deviated from this condition in discovering for himself devices of his own that are contrary to his original condition. In other words, we learn here that man has fallen from the original state of uprightness in which the Lord God had created him. There is nothing similar to this in Grecian philosophy. It is the pure biblical teaching. It represents the reflection of one who had had rich and varied experience in the world, and who as a result of his experience was profoundly convinced of the fact that man now was not what he had been when God created him. No unaided human reason would ever come to such a conclusion, for unaided (*i.e.* unregenerate) human reason is filled with pride and looks upon man as the ultimate reference-point for the interpretation of life.

We are now ready to consider the import of the entire book. The writer relates his experiences of life. He has tried now this, now that, in an endeavour to arrive at the true interpretation of life. He finds, however, that all is vanity. Nevertheless, he does give good advice for the practical enjoyment of life. For example he says, 'There is nothing better for a man, than that he should eat and drink, and that he should make his soul enjoy good in his labour' (2:24). Such passages as this show clearly that the author is not a pessimist. But such passages do not teach that the enjoyment of the things of this life is an end in itself. They are but practical directions to the God-fearing soul for his guidance through life. Life, however, in all its many aspects is completely without meaning apart from God. That is the grand theme of the book. Life apart from God can have no meaning, for God alone can give life meaning. To state the matter in a slightly different way we may say: God is the ultimate standard and point of reference by which every aspect of life must be interpreted. If man or the world be regarded as the ultimate standard or point of reference, all is vanity. All then becomes without meaning, and can lead only to despair. The only possible interpretation of the world then is to regard it as the creation of God and to use and enjoy it for His glory.

ANALYSIS

a. *1:1–11. The prologue*
  1. 1:1. Heading.
  2. 1:2–11. Introduction to the entire book. The basic theme is introduced in verses 2, 3, namely, the vanity of all things. This is not to be construed in a materialistic sense as though life is in itself evil. The remainder of the book shows that, in themselves, apart from God and when not used for His glory, all things are vain. Even those things which are good and praiseworthy in themselves become without meaning, and vain when pursued for their own sakes, and not for God's sake. This basic theme is substantiated by an appeal, verses 4ff., to the changes which also appear upon earth and in human life.

b. *1:12–6:12. The vanity of all things*
  1. 1:12–18. To search after human wisdom is vain. The preacher here begins the 'I' sections, *i.e.*, he employs the first person singular pronoun. The preacher has undertaken an investigation, the result of which is stated.

2. 2:1–11. Pleasures also are vain. This appears to be the first point of the investigation. Pleasures, luxuries and great wealth also prove to be empty.

3. 2:12–23. Wisdom and riches are vain. The second point of the preacher's investigation.

4. 2:24–3:15. This seems to be the third point of the investigation. Even human efforts are in vain, and one cannot always enjoy the fruit of his labours.

5. 3:16–4:6. The fourth point is that wickedness and oppression are prevalent in the earth.

6. 4:7–12. The fifth point is that two can succeed in various endeavours better than one.

7. 4:13–16. The sixth point is that wisdom and poverty are better than folly and riches.

8. 5:1–7. The seventh point consists of general advice. Man must observe his responsibility and fear God.

9. 5:8–6:12. The purpose of this section is to exhibit the vanity of riches. It develops certain themes which had already been introduced in order to accomplish this end.

c. 7:1–12:7. The words of wisdom

1. 7:1–14. Practical advice for a well-ordered life.

2. 7:15–22. All men are sinners, but the strength of the wise lies in wisdom.

3. 7:23–29. The conclusion of the preacher's investigation. Mankind is sinful: 'One man among a thousand have I found, but a woman among all these have I not found.' God has made man upright, 'but they have sought out many inventions' (7:29).

4. 8:1–8. The king is to be respected.

5. 8:9–17. Although it seems as though the wicked may fare better than the righteous, yet the preacher knows that before God this is not so.

6. 9:1–10. Thoughts on the order and administration of the world.

7. 9:11–10:3. Observations on wisdom and folly.

8. 10:4–20. Comparison of the wise and foolish.

9. 11:1–12:7. Sundry practical observations.

d. 12:8–14. Epilogue
The conclusion. Man should fear God and keep His commandments.

SPECIAL LITERATURE ON ECCLESIASTES

G. Bickell, *Der Prediger über den Wert des Daseins* (Innsbruck, 1884); S. Euringer, *Der Masorahtext des Koheleth kritisch untersucht* (Leipzig, 1890); Robert Gordis, *The Wisdom of Ecclesiastes* (New York, 1945); Paul Humbert, *Recherches sur les sources Egyptiennes de la littérature sapientale d' Israel* (Neuchatel, 1929); Morris Jastrow Jr., *A Gentile Cynic, Being a Translation of the Book of Koheleth* (Philadelphia-London, 1919); Duncan B. Macdonald, *The Hebrew Philosophical Genius* (Princeton, 1936); A. H. McNeile, *An Introduction to Ecclesiastes with Notes and Appendices* (Cambridge, 1904); H. Ranston, *Ecclesiastes and the Early Greek Wisdom Literature* (London, 1925); J. Stafford Wright, 'The Interpretation of Ecclesiastes',* *EQ*, 1946, pp. 18–34.

CHAPTER TWENTY-SIX

ESTHER

THE book takes its name from its principal character *'ester*. This is a Persian word meaning 'star'. The Hebrew name of Esther was Hadhassah, meaning 'myrtle' (2:7).

AUTHOR

According to *Baba Bathra* 15a, 'the men of the Great Synagogue wrote ... the roll of Esther.' Josephus (*Antiquities* xi.6.1) considered Mordecai to be the author, and this opinion seems also to have been held in the synagogue. In favour of this there has sometimes been urged the fact that in the last two chapters of Esther mention is made of letters and writings of Mordecai. But there is no evidence that these letters or writings are the book of Esther or even a part thereof. Furthermore, in the light of 10:3 it seems rather clear that Mordecai was not the author of the book.

Ibn Ezra suggested that the original author was Mordecai. Mordecai, he thought, realized that the Persians would desire a copy of the book for their official archives, and would also substitute the name of their idols for the name of God. To prevent this from happening, Mordecai deliberately omitted the name of God altogether. This is ingenious, but certainly betrays a low view of the nature of Scripture.

The fact is that we do not know who the author was. It seems clear that he lived in Persia rather than in Palestine, since he exhibits such an intimate acquaintance with Persian life and customs. Doubtless, in composing Esther he made use of some of Mordecai's writings (9:20) and the books of the chronicles of the kings of Media and Persia (2:23; 19:2) and probably also of oral tradition. Such were evidently his historical sources.

It is difficult to tell precisely when this unknown author of Esther lived and worked. According to 10:2, the book was written after the death of Ahasuerus (Xerxes). In fact, when it was composed the official state history of Xerxes had been written. The date of Xerxes' assassination is commonly accepted as 465 BC.

1:1 seems to indicate that Xerxes would be well known to the readers. Further, the accurate knowledge of Persia seems to point to a time shortly after the death of Ahasuerus. Hence, it is best to regard the author as having lived sometime during the latter half of the fifth century BC. But of this we cannot be certain.

HISTORICITY OF THE BOOK

Among the Jews the book of Esther is naturally regarded with high favour. Indeed, in the Jerusalem Talmud (*Megilla*) it is said that whereas the Prophets and the Writings might come to naught (*yivtol*), the Pentateuch and Esther (and the *Halachot*?) would never perish. There are, however, some Talmudic statements to the effect that Esther does not defile the hands (*i.e.*, is not canonical).

By many modern scholars, the historicity of the book is completely denied, and it is regarded as nothing more than a historical romance. Thus Cornill remarks, 'The Christian expositor of the O.T. would prefer to pass over the Book of Esther altogether, and at any rate does not care to occupy himself with it more than is absolutely necessary; for, valuable as this book is to us as a document for the history of religion, in receiving it into the collection of the sacred writings the framers of the canon committed a serious blunder. All the worst and most unpleasing features of Judaism are here displayed without disguise; and only in Alexandria was it felt absolutely necessary to cover up the ugliest bare places with a couple of religious patches.'[1]

Not all writers are as strong in their condemnation of the book as is Cornill. Ewald has said that in passing from the other Old Testament books to Esther, we 'fall from heaven to earth'. Driver is far more cautious, and while he, too, regards the book as mainly a story, he does believe that 'the writer shows himself well informed on Persian manners and institutions; he does not commit anachronisms such as occur in Tobit or Judith; and the character of Xerxes, as drawn by him, is in agreement with history'.[2]

What then are the principal objections to the historicity of the book?

1. The author regarded Xerxes as following immediately after, or at least as one of the immediate successors of Nebuchadnezzar. This objection is based upon 2:5, 6, which is supposed to teach that Mordecai had been carried away from Jerusalem by Nebuchadnezzar in the deportation of Jehoiachin. Hence, at the time of Xerxes, Mordecai would be over a hundred years old. Now, continues the objection, since

[1] *Intro.*, p. 257.
[2] *IOT*, p. 453.

the author did not want to represent Mordecai as over a hundred years old, it is obvious that he did not know his history. He evidently thought that Xerxes reigned shortly after the time of Nebuchadnezzar. But this does not follow at all. If one will only read 2:5, 6 carefully he will see that the one who was carried away from Jerusalem was not Mordecai but Kish, Mordecai's great-grandfather. The relative pronoun 'who' of verse 6 refers not to Mordecai but to Kish. Hence, this supposed difficulty vanishes into thin air.

2. More important is the objection that, according to Herodotus iii.84, Xerxes could have only one wife, taken from the family of 'seven', hence the Jewish Esther could not be his queen. Technically, it may have been true that the king in his choice of a wife was limited to the seven noble families, but as a matter of fact the king did very much as he pleased (*cf.* Herodotus iii.31). Further, these regulations in Herodotus iii.84 seem to have reference only to the actual successor of Pseudo-Smerdis, namely, Darius, and he apparently had for wife not only a daughter from the 'seven' but also several others.

3. The wife of Xerxes is said to have been Amestris, not Esther. This woman was noted for her cruelty, and is not to be identified with Esther, although some critics seem to think that Esther was cruel enough. In Xerxes' second year he went against Egypt and subdued it. In the third year of his reign he called together an assembly to consider an expedition against Greece.[3] In 480 Xerxes made the expedition against Greece and returned defeated. According to Herodotus ix.108 he now paid attention to his harem. In the seventh year of the king, Esther was made queen (Esther 2:16ff.). Considering the position and character of Xerxes, we may well believe that he could have had more than one wife.

4. It is said to be unlikely that the king would send out decrees in many different languages, as stated in 1:22; 3:12; 8:9. But objections to this procedure are subjective. It is becoming evident that the Jews were widespread throughout Persia, and there seems to be no sufficient reason for denying the historicity of these statements.

5. It has been objected that it would have been incredible for 75,000 enemies of the Jews to have been slain (9:16 and also 9:6, 12, 15). The LXX gives the number as 15,000 and hence is preferred by many scholars. At the same time, a massacre or pogrom such as this is not a rarity in the Near East.

6. The origin of the feast of Purim, as set forth in Esther, is thought to

---

[3] Herodotus vii. 8; *cf.* Esther 1:3; this seems to be the assembly mentioned by Herodotus, the year being 483 BC.

be inaccurate, since the word *pur* is not used in this sense in Persian.[4] It may have been the custom at Persian feasts to give gifts. It may well have been that in their celebration, the Jews did follow some of the Persian customs. But apart from that there is no reason for denying the accuracy of 9:22.

P. Jensen and Zimmern have assumed that there is a mythological basis for the narrative. This had to do with the conquering of the Elamite deities by the gods of Babylon and also with Marduk's victory over the chaos. Thus, Haman corresponds to Human, Vashti to Mashti, Esther to Ishtar, Mordecai to Marduk. Haman also is supposed to stand for the deity of the chaos. Gunkel, however, has called this opinion into question. The name Esther probably comes from the Persian *stara* ('star'), and Mordecai is a fairly common personal name.

The mythological theory is not widely held today, but the view that Esther is a romance is widely held. Eissfeldt thinks that it is the same type of story as the narratives in Daniel 1–6. However, in the light of the remarkable historical and geographical accuracy of the book, and in view of the extremely weak character of the arguments adduced against that historicity, in view of the fact that the book purports to be straightforward history and is lacking in the fancy that characterizes mere romances, we believe that the only correct interpretation is to regard the work as strictly historical.

PURPOSE

It is perfectly true that the name of God is not mentioned in Esther. However, this is not sufficient reason for doubting its canonicity. It should also be noted that prayer is not mentioned, nor praise, nor is there any *direct* mention of the worship of God. On the other hand, the ordinance of fasting (5:16) must be regarded as at least having religious connotations, and in 9:31 'the matters of the fastings and their cry' is a phrase which also probably has religious connotations. Particularly do the words 'their cry' seem to imply a cry for help, presumably addressed to God. At any rate, 4:14 certainly seems to teach the doctrine of an overruling providence. In the light of these facts, it is not correct to say that the book of Esther is of a purely secular character.

But why is the name of God omitted? Why is there not more emphasis upon the service and worship of the Lord? The answer is not an easy

---

[4] Zimmern held that *pur* was related to the Babylonian word *puhru* ('assembly'). But Gunkel pointed out that the relationship could not be established. Probably *pur* is derived from the Assyrian *puru* ('lot').

one. The following line of thought may possibly suggest the correct answer.

When in 539 Cyrus conquered Babylon he found the Jews ready to return to Palestine. He also gave them permission to return and to rebuild their Temple in Jerusalem. Many of the Jews did return. But many did not. For long centuries after, even into the Christian era, Jews were found in the Mesopotamian valley. Among those Jews who remained, Daniel is probably to be reckoned.

In the eighth chapter of Daniel, the prophet in vision sees himself in Susa, the palace, which is in Persia. It may very well be that the Babylonian kings had sent Jews to Persia or even had permitted some of them to emigrate there. We read that when Israel was taken captive, the Assyrian king placed some of them in the city of the Medes (2 Ki. 17:6). Hence, there may have been a Jewish population in Persia even from the times of the first captivity.

These Jews in Persia apparently showed no desire to return to Palestine. They did not wish to leave Persia and set out again for the promised land. Their theocratic spirit, we may say, was weak. Yet they were still God's chosen people. It was not through them, however, that the promised salvation was to come to the world, but, despite that fact, God had not rejected them. He would still watch over them and protect them from their foes and from unjust oppression. And from them there would come the great feast of Purim. But, since these Jews were no longer in the theocratic line, so to speak, the *Name* of the covenant God is not associated with them. The book of Esther, then, serves the purpose of showing how divine providence overrules all things; even in a distant, far country, God's people are yet in His hands. But since they are in this distant, far country, and not in the land of promise, His name is not mentioned. By causing us to behold the workings of providence, the book does, after all, turn our eyes to God who determines the destinies of men and nations.

UNITY OF THE BOOK

Several scholars (*e.g.*, Eissfeldt, Steuernagel) regard 9:20–32 as a gloss. 9:19 is thought by them to form a suitable conclusion to the book. The Jews in the country celebrated the fourteenth and those in the city the fifteenth of Adar. But a difference is said to appear in 9:20–32. The language is thought to be more affected and clumsy (Eissfeldt) than in the preceding part of the book. Also, the distinction between country and city Jews is thought to be made no longer, but all are to celebrate on the fourteenth and fifteenth of Adar. The practice, we are told, had been changed, and 9:20–32 was added to justify this changed practice.

Chapter 10:1–3, too, must go, for its annalistic style does not fit well with the romance-narrative. The phrase 'book of the history of the kings of Media and Persia' is said to sound like the 'book of the history of the kings of Israel and Judah' in the book of Kings. Hence, some have denied the historicity of this reference.

In answer to these assertions we may remark that in so far as there is a change in style in 9:20–32, it is because of the summary character of the section. Nor can we detect any change in the prescriptions regarding the celebration of Purim. 9:21 simply sums up what had been said before. In 9:17–19 we have been told that the country Jews are to celebrate the fourteenth and the city Jews the fifteenth. Then 9:20–21 (*cf.* also verses 22, 27, 'these two days', 28, 31) relates that Mordecai sent letters to all the Jews – nigh and far – to keep these two days. I simply fail to see evidence for the supposed change in practice. If the supposed change is there, why did not the Jews, who for so long have been keeping this feast, note the discrepancy long ago? As to the annalistic character of chapter 10, its very presence shows that the book of Esther is not a mere story. If its presence is so incongruous with a 'romance', why would a redactor have placed it there? There seem to be no objective grounds for rejecting 9:20–32 or 10:1–3.

SPECIAL LITERATURE ON ESTHER

O. T. Allis, 'The Reward of the King's Favorite (Esther 6:8)',* in *PTR*, 21, 1923, pp. 621–632; J. Hoschander, *The Book of Esther in the Light of History* (Philadelphia, 1923); W. Scott Watson, 'The Authenticity and Genuineness of the Book of Esther',* *PTR*, 1, 1903, pp. 62–74.

CHAPTER TWENTY-SEVEN

DANIEL

NAME

THE book is named after its principal character *dani'el*. This name was also given to David's second son (1 Ch. 3:1; *cf.* also Ezr. 8:2 and Ne. 10:6).

AUTHOR

According to *Baba Bathra* 15a, 'the men of the Great Synagogue wrote . . . Daniel.' By this statement, however, the Jews did not mean to deny that Daniel himself was the author of his book. In fact, it is the testimony of both Jewish and Christian tradition that Daniel, living at the royal court in Babylon, composed his book during the sixth century BC. That this traditional thesis is correct may be seen from the following considerations.

1. Jesus Christ quoted from Daniel (*cf.* Mt. 24:15 with Dn. 9:27 and 12:11). Whether Christ's reference be to Daniel 9:27 or to 12:11, He says that the abomination of desolation was spoken of by Daniel the prophet. This is the more interesting since both 9:27 and 12:11 are thought by modern negative criticism to have come from the time of the Maccabees. Both these passages in Daniel must be taken in their contexts. Hence, it is evident that Christ regarded at least a portion of the book as having come from Daniel himself.

An attempt to resolve this difficulty has been made by Cartledge,[1] who says, 'Jesus may have known that the book was written by someone else and still have spoken of it in a popular way. Or the "emptying" of which Paul spoke may have kept the incarnate Jesus from having complete knowledge about certain non-essential things; He may simply have used the current tradition.' This language, however, is unguarded. It is true that in His human nature our Lord did not have knowledge of some things. Cartledge himself points out that Christ had said that He did not know the time of His own coming again. This is true, but we must note that Christ was perfectly silent upon these things of which He had no knowledge. He did not speak of the day and hour, except in a general way.

---

[1] *A Conservative Introduction to the Old Testament* (1943), p. 221.

Nor can it be said that He simply used the current tradition. For, this implies either that He was ignorant, or that He deceived. If, in His human nature, Jesus Christ had been ignorant of the identity of the author of Daniel, He would not have spoken upon the subject. And if, knowing that Daniel had not spoken of the abomination of desolation, He had lent His voice to the erroneous view that Daniel had spoken thereof, He was certainly guilty of deception. He ought to have corrected the erroneous view.

If He did not correct this erroneous view, it follows that He was not trustworthy. And if He is not trustworthy in a matter as important as this, how do we know that He is trustworthy when He sets Himself before us as our only hope for salvation?

Such a view of our Lord must be rejected. The question of the authorship of Daniel is important, for the book deals with the destinies of men. If Daniel wrote the book and spoke of coming events which would affect the well-being of mankind, as our Lord said, we should pay serious heed to what the book says. If, however, Daniel did not write the book, and our Lord was mistaken or deliberately allowed us to think that Daniel did write the book, then what warrant have we for believing that the contents of the book are true?

2. The witness of Jesus Christ is borne out by the claims of the book itself. Daniel speaks in the first person and claims to have been the recipient of the divine revelations (*cf.*, *e.g.*, 7:2, 4, 6ff., 28; 8:1ff., 15ff.; 9:2ff.; 10:2ff.; 12:5–8). In 12:4 he is commanded to preserve the book in which the words are found.

In this connection it may also be noted that the entire book is obviously the work of one writer, and if Daniel is named as the recipient of the revelations, it follows that he is the author of the entire book. The arguments for the unity of the book are as follows.

(i) The first part of the book prepares for the second, and the second looks back to the first. Thus, chapter 7 develops more fully what is introduced in chapter 2 as also does chapter 8, yet neither chapter 7 nor 8 is fully understandable without chapter 2. Chapter 2 also prepares the way for the revelations in chapters 9, 10, 11 and 12, and all of these chapters are based upon the earlier revelation in chapter 2 (*cf.* also 2:28 and 4:2, 7,10 with 7:1, 2, 15).

(ii) The several sections of the same part also stand in mutual relationship. The reader should compare 3:12 with 2:49; the carrying away of the sacred vessels (1:1, 2) prepares us for the understanding of Belshazzar's feast in chapter 5; 9:21 should be compared with 8:15ff.; 10:12 with 9:23; *etc.* If the reader will read the book carefully, he will be deeply impressed with the remarkable manner in which the various parts of the book interlock and depend upon one another.

(iii) The historical narratives uniformly have the purpose of revealing how the God of Israel is glorified over the heathen nations.

(iv) The character of Daniel is everywhere seen to be the same. It is one Daniel who appears throughout the entire book.

(v) The literary unity of the book has been widely acknowledged by scholars of all schools of thought. It is naturally maintained by conservative scholars, but in recent times the following also have regarded Daniel as a unit: Driver, Charles, Rowley, Pfeiffer.[2]

3. In the following passages of the New Testament, there is at least an indirect approval of the genuineness of the book of Daniel: Matthew 10:23; 16:27ff.; 19:28; 24:30; 25:31; 26:64.

4. The book reflects the background of the Babylonian and Persian empires. Historical objections have been raised against the book, but they do not seem to be valid.

One of the first critics to deny that Daniel wrote the book bearing his name was Porphyry, a neo-Platonic philosopher of the third century AD. On a visit to Sicily Porphyry, then about forty years of age, wrote a work in fifteen books entitled *Against the Christians*. This work is completely lost, but parts of the twelfth book in which Porphyry attacked Daniel have been preserved in Jerome's commentary on Daniel. Porphyry denied that Daniel in the sixth century BC was the author of his book, and asserted that it was written by someone who lived in Judaea during the times of Antiochus Epiphanes. The reason which led Porphyry to this conclusion was that the book of Daniel speaks so accurately about the times of Antiochus. Hence, it must be history, not prophecy, since, according to Porphyry, predictive prophecy is impossible (*si quid autem ultra opinatus sit, quia futura nescient, esse mentitum*). The author of Daniel lied (*mentitum*) for the sake of reviving the hope of the Jews of his time.

Porphyry's criticism of Daniel, therefore, was based upon his anti-theistic philosophical presuppositions. He thought that predictive prophecy was impossible, hence he denied that Daniel could have uttered such prophecy. But there is one thing that must be said to Porphyry's credit. He clearly recognized that if an unknown person wrote under the guise of Daniel's name, this unknown person was a deceiver. In fact, this is the principal objection to holding the view that some unknown Jew wrote the book of Daniel and simply used Daniel's name as a guise. This is deception, and there is no escaping the fact. As Pusey has well said,

---

[2] The foregoing arguments for the unity of the book are taken from my *Prophecy of Daniel* (Grand Rapids, 1949), pp. 19, 20.

'The book of Daniel is especially fitted to be a battle-ground between faith and unbelief. It admits of no halfway measures. It is either Divine or an imposture'.[3]

In this connection I would quote what I have written elsewhere: 'The book of Daniel purports to be serious history. It claims to be a revelation from the God of heaven which concerns the future welfare of men and nations. If this book were issued at the time of the Maccabees for the purpose of strengthening the faith of the people of *that* time, and the impression was thereby created that Daniel, a Jew of the sixth century were the author, then, whether we like it or no – the book is a fraud. There is no escaping this conclusion. It will not do to say that the Jews frequently engaged in such a practice. That does not lessen their guilt one whit. It is one thing to issue a harmless romance under a pseudonym; it is an entirely different thing to issue under a pseudonym a book claiming to be a revelation of God and having to do with the conduct of men and to regard such a book as canonical. The Jews of the inter-testamental period may have done the first; there is no evidence that they ever did the second.'[4]

Uriel Acosta (1590–1647), a Jewish rationalist, considered the book of Daniel to have been forged for the purpose of favouring the doctrine of the resurrection of the body. In 1727 the English deist, Anthony Collins, in an appendix to his work *Scheme of Literal Prophecy Considered*, attacked the integrity of the prophecy. But probably the earliest carefully wrought out attack on Daniel was made by Leonhard Bertholdt (1806–8). From that time on two viewpoints have been struggling to maintain the ascendancy. One of these – the position herein set forth – maintains that Daniel himself, under the inspiration of God, wrote his book in Babylon in the sixth century BC. The other position is that the book was written by an unknown Jew in Palestine at the time of the Maccabees in the second century BC.

In recent times this theory has received a slight modification at the hands of Gustav Hoelscher.[5] Hoelscher maintained that the actual composer of the book lived at the time of the Maccabees. He himself wrote Daniel 8–12. Before him was an old collection of five narratives (*i.e.*, Dn. 2–6) which, because of the background in them, are evidently earlier than the Maccabean age. The composer took these five narratives, provided them with an introduction (chapter 1), inserted chapter 7 as a

[3] *Daniel*, p. 75.
[4] *CD*, p. 25.
[5] 'Die Entstehung des Buches Daniel' in *Theologische Studien und Kritiken*, xcii, 1919, pp. 113–138.

connecting link, and thus produced the present book of Daniel. Others
have also adopted essentially this position.

Why is it, therefore, that scholars refuse to attribute the authorship of
the book to Daniel?

1. In the first place, the eleventh chapter of Daniel (apart from verses
36–45) exhibits such an accurate picture of the wars between Syria and
Egypt and of the times of Antiochus Epiphanes, that it without doubt
influences and has influenced many to consider the book the work of an
eyewitness of these events. Likewise, these times are so clearly portrayed
in chapter 8 that many feel it also must have been written after the events
had occurred. It would not be just to say that all who believe the book to
have been written after the occurrence of the events therein described,
follow Porphyry in disbelieving in predictive prophecy; but there are
many advocates of this view who have thus disbelieved. At any rate, the
character of these chapters has exerted a strong influence, I believe, in
moulding the views of some as to the date of authorship.

2. In the second place, many scholars do not believe Daniel wrote the
book because they think that there are historical inaccuracies or in-
consistencies which would not be found if the book really had been
written by Daniel. The following are cited.

(i) The remark in Daniel 1:1 with reference to the third year of
Jehoiakim is said to be an anachronism, since Jeremiah, in the fourth
year of Jehoiakim, speaks of the Chaldeans in a manner which shows that
they had not yet attacked Jerusalem (cf. Je. 25:1, 9; 46:2. Je. 25:1 shows
that the fourth year of Jehoiakim was the first year of Nebuchadnezzar).
Some think that the author of Daniel was confused and that he had in
mind the siege of Jerusalem in 597 BC when Jehoiakim was king. But was
the writer of Daniel confused? Several attempts have been made at
answering this supposed difficulty.

a. Aalders[6] suggests that since in the Hebrew manuscripts the
letters of the alphabet represented numerals a mistake was made by the
substitution of *gimel* ('three') for *waw* ('six'). Thus, he would hold that
the expedition took place in the sixth year of Jehoiakim. This is a possible
solution, but since all the versions support the present Hebrew text, the
error must have been very ancient.

b. Keil and others would translate the Hebrew word *ba* in
Daniel 1:1 as 'he set out'. Thus, the verse would state only that in the
third year of Jehoiakim Nebuchadnezzar set out for Jerusalem. If this
translation be correct it is not necessary to suppose that Nebuchadnezzar
actually arrived at Jerusalem and laid siege to it in Jehoiakim's third

[6] *EQ*, 2, No. 3.

year. This translation, despite the strictures of Driver and others, is perfectly possible (*cf.* Gn. 45:17; Ex. 6:11; 7:26; 9:1; 10:1; Nu. 32:6; 1 Sa. 20:19; 2 Ki. 5:5; Jon. 1:3). However, the occurrence of the statement 'and besieged it', in such close connection with the verb 'came', as well as the mention of the date, gives the impression that the siege also occurred in the third year.

c. The correct solution, it seems to me, is to be found in the fact that Daniel here reckons the years according to the Babylonian method and Jeremiah according to the Palestinian. The year in which the king ascended the throne was designated on the Babylonian system not the *first* year, but 'the year of the accession to the kingdom'. Hence, in mentioning the third year of Jehoiakim, Daniel has reference to the same year which Jeremiah calls the fourth. This point may be illustrated as follows:

Babylonian	*Palestinian*
Year of Accession	First Year
First Year	Second Year
Second Year	Third Year
Third Year	Fourth Year

This assumption entirely removes the difficulty which is supposed to be created by the mention of the third year. It may be noted in passing that this mention of the third year is really an evidence of genuineness. For the author of Daniel was familiar with the book of Jeremiah (*cf.* Dn. 9:2). Not only was he familiar with the book of Jeremiah, but he had also read the very chapter (25) which equated the fourth year of Jehoiakim with the first year of Nebuchadnezzar (*cf.* verse 11, which mentions the length of the exile as seventy years). Now, if the author of Daniel were an unknown Jew of the second century BC, why did he substitute 'third year' for Jeremiah's 'fourth year'? If he desired his book to appear authentic, here is one place at which he failed. Why did this unknown author make such a mistake?[7]

In this connection it may be pointed out that some critics assert that Jerusalem was not captured in 605 BC (the third year of Jehoiakim) but only in 597 BC. In reply to this we may say that Daniel does not state that Jerusalem was captured in the third year of Jehoiakim.

Again, it is said to be an error that Nebuchadnezzar *as king* took Jerusalem. But the word 'king' is used here proleptically, as we say, 'In the childhood of President Washington'.

(ii) In the book of Daniel the term 'Chaldean' is employed in an

[7] See Special Literature at the end of this chapter.

ethnic sense and also in a more restricted sense denoting a group of wise men. This twofold usage of the term does not appear elsewhere in the Old Testament, nor upon the inscriptions. The first extra-biblical occurrence of the restricted sense of the term is to be found in Herodotus (c. 440 BC). Hence, it is argued, the twofold usage is an inaccuracy and is indicative of a later date. But does this conclusion necessarily follow? It will be of value to consider the language of Herodotus. He remarks (i.181), 'as the Chaldeans, being priests of this god, say'. Again (i.183), 'In the greater altar the Chaldeans burn also 1000 talents of frankincense every year, when they celebrate the festival of this god.' This same chapter also contains the phrases, 'as the Chaldeans said', and 'I did not see it, but I say what is said by the Chaldeans'. Herodotus obviously regards these Chaldeans as priests. Furthermore, the festival which they celebrate is not an innovation, but a long-established practice. It would seem, in fact, that this practice had been in existence for a very long time. For, says Herodotus, the Chaldeans told him that *in the time of Cyrus* the temple had contained a huge golden statue of a man. Xerxes, the son of Darius (486–465 BC) had wanted this statue and had killed a priest who forbade him to remove it.

The natural impression which one receives from these words of Herodotus is that the order of things described had been in existence since the time of Cyrus. The sanctuary had been standing since that time, and it appears to be a justifiable inference that the sanctuary priests, the Chaldeans, had also been in existence since that time. It seems also to be a warrantable inference that the priest who had opposed Xerxes was of the same order as the priests whom Herodotus met, namely, a Chaldean.

Thus, a careful reading of Herodotus gives the impression that the Chaldeans had served as priests long before his time. The mere fact that to date no extra-biblical material of the sixth century BC has appeared which employs the term 'Chaldean' in the restricted sense, does not seem to be a sufficient warrant for regarding Daniel's usage as indicative of a later age.

(iii) It is further said that Daniel, a Jew, would not have permitted himself to become initiated into the class of 'wise men', nor would such a group have allowed Daniel to be admitted. But the book of Daniel does not say that Daniel was admitted to any order. He was given political authority *over* all the wise men of Babylon (2:48, 49). That is all. 'If the book of Daniel really teaches that Daniel became a heathen priest, as apparently some critics think it does, would not such teaching be one of the strongest arguments against a post-exilic origin for the book? In the third century BC, when Jewish nationalism was being emphasized, how can we conceive of a "legendary" Jewish hero becoming a heathen priest? And if this narrative is from Maccabean times, how can such a representation possibly be accounted for?'[8]

(iv) Objection has been taken to the account of Nebuchadnezzar's madness given in chapter 4. Thus, recently Cartledge states, 'History knows nothing of the madness of Nebuchadnezzar reported in Daniel.'[9] But is such a statement accurate? In his *Praeparatio Evangelica* (ix.41) Eusebius gives a quotation from Abydenus, which describes the last days of Nebuchadnezzar. It relates that, 'being possessed by some god or other', the king went up to his palace and announced the coming of a Persian mule (*i.e.*, Cyrus), who would bring the people into slavery. Then says Abydenus, 'He, when he had uttered this prediction, immediately disappeared.' These last words seem to have reference to the king's madness, which is covered up under the form of a prediction. Thus, in Abydenus' time there was in existence a tradition about something peculiar and extraordinary having occurred towards the close of Nebuchadnezzar's life. It should be noted that the king is thought to have been seized by some divinity; he was in his palace, as Daniel also states; and this event occurred after the king's conquest and shortly before his death.

Berossus also (*Contra Apionem* i.20) remarks that after a reign of forty-three years, Nebuchadnezzar, after beginning the construction of a certain wall, fell sick and died. The Greek text conveys the idea that the king was *suddenly invaded by sickness*. Now sickness before death is so common that there would be no point in mentioning it, were it not of an unusual kind. Hence, here also we probably have a garbled reflection upon the tragedy which overcame the king. But it should be remembered that, even if history (apart from the Bible) was silent upon the subject of the king's madness, that in itself is not a sufficient reason for denying the historicity of the account in Daniel.

(v) In chapter 5 and elsewhere Belshazzar is called king, but as a matter of fact the last king of the neo-Babylonian empire was Nabonidus, the father of Belshazzar. Did the author of Daniel make a historical mistake in calling Belshazzar king?

It is perfectly true that all of the available cuneiform evidence speaks of Belshazzar as son of the king (*mar sharri*) *i.e.*, crown-prince. But it is stated on one text (the so-called Persian Verse Account of Nabonidus)[10] that Nabonidus entrusted the kingship to his son Belshazzar, and that he

[8] *CD*, p. 273.
[9] *Op. cit.*, p. 221.
[10] See Smith, *Babylonian Historical Texts* (1924).

himself established his dwelling at Tema (in Arabia). Furthermore, Belshazzar is spoken of in such a way as to show that he did exercise regal functions. Thus, in praying for length of days, Nabonidus associates Belshazzar with him in a unique way. Oaths are taken in the name of both men. Thus we read, 'The decrees (*a-di-e*) of Nabonidus king of Babylon and Belshazzar, son of the king.' Belshazzar grants leases, issues commands, performs an administrative act concerning the temple at Erech, possesses subordinate officials who are equal to those of the king. In the delivery of royal tribute, the two names are closely associated. In addition, it must be remembered that the Aramaic word translated 'king' (*malka*') need not have the connotation of absolute monarch.

Belshazzar, then, technically occupied a position subordinate to that of Nabonidus. Nevertheless, since he was the man *in regal status* with whom the Jews had to do, Daniel calls him king. This cannot justly be charged as an inaccuracy.[11]

(vi) Nebuchadnezzar is spoken of in Daniel 5 as the father of Belshazzar, whereas Nabonidus was his father. But this objection is hardly worthy of serious consideration, since, in oriental languages, the word 'father' may have many connotations. Doubtless it is here used merely in the sense of ancestor. It must be remembered that the author of Daniel knew Jeremiah, where Evil-Merodach is said to reign after Nebuchadnezzar (Je. 52:28–31). In the light of this fact, it seems that we are to understand the word here simply in the sense of ancestor.

(vii) The mention of Darius the Mede is said to be evidence of confusion upon the part of the writer. As yet no mention of Darius has appeared upon the inscriptions, and it is impossible to identify Darius with any known historical character. Attempts have been made to identify him with various known individuals, such as Gobryas, Cambyses, Astyages, and others. However, as Rowley has pointed out, these attempted identifications do not carry conviction. But this does not prove that there never was a Darius. It is quite possible that he was placed in charge of the kingdom as Daniel says. Driver wisely remarks, 'A cautious criticism will not build too much on the silence of the inscriptions, where many certainly remain yet to be brought to light.'[12]

(viii) Darius the Mede is said by some critics to have organized the kingdom into 120 satrapies, which is thought to be historically improbable. But the text of Daniel does not say that the kingdom was organized into 120 satrapies, only that Darius appointed 120 satraps

[11] See Special Literature at the end of this chapter.
[12] *LOT*, p. 469.

(kingdom protectors) throughout his kingdom. These may have been given the special mission of caring for the newly conquered country, because of the hostility of the land to the conquerors. It may have been, in other words, merely a temporary arrangement and not a formal organization of the country into 120 satrapies. And the satraps may have had responsibilities over districts that were smaller in size than actual satrapies. Some of them may merely have been appointed to special missions, as, *e.g.*, Darius Hystaspis says in one of his inscriptions, 'There was a man, Dadrsis by name, a Persian, my subject, satrap in Bactria, him did I send.' There simply is not extant any objective evidence which will justify one in denying the statements of 6:1. For that matter, even if the text did say that the kingdom was divided into 120 satrapies, such a statement could not be shown to be in error.

(ix) The Persian title 'satrap' is said to be used in Daniel (*e.g.*, 3:3) as though it were a Babylonian title. But in reply it may be said that this is not necessarily an anachronism. For one thing, it is quite possible that such a term, because of Persian influence, might have been employed in Babylon even during the reign of Nebuchadnezzar. But it is not necessary to make such an assumption. If Daniel wrote after the fall of Babylon, say in the third year of Cyrus, he might very well have employed Persian terms in certain cases as substitutes for the older Babylonian terms. Thus his writing would become understandable to readers who lived during the Persian age. If this were the case the use of the term 'satrap' is in no sense an anachronism.

(x) In Daniel 9:2 it is stated that Daniel 'understood by the books' the length of the exile. It is thought by many critics that this expression refers to a collection of sacred books, which would not have been formed as early as the close of the exile. But to deduce from this that the Canon was already formed is to be guilty of a *non sequitur*. The expression 'by the books' (*bassefarim*) simply refers to a group of writings among which were also the prophecies of Jeremiah. The term is probably a broad designation of the Scriptures.

(xi) It is claimed that the position of Daniel in the Hagiographa rather than in the Prophets is evidence that it was not written until after the close of the 'Canon of the Prophets'. But this argument is inconclusive. For it appears that there were those who at an early date did place Daniel among the Prophets. Melito, bishop of Sardis about AD 175, gives in his *Eclogues* a catalogue of the Old Testament books, in which the following sentence occurs: 'Of Prophets, Isaiah, Jeremiah, of the Twelve Prophets, one book, Daniel, Ezekiel, Ezra'. In the Syriac fragments in which this list also occurs, the same order is followed. Further, in many of the Greek manuscripts of the Old Testament, Daniel is placed among the Prophets.

But to my mind, this argument is not conclusive. The reason why Daniel came finally to be placed among the Hagiographa is that he did not occupy the technical óffice of prophet (*munus propheticum*). He was trained to be a statesman and as such he served. A prophet was a mediator between God and the theocratic nation (Dt. 18:18), and this Daniel was not. In speaking of Daniel as a prophet, the New Testament and other witnesses evidently have reference to the prophetic gift which Daniel possessed (*donum propheticum*). The same is true of the reference to Balaam (2 Pet. 3:16). The position of Daniel in the Canon therefore in reality has no bearing upon the date of the composition of the book.

(xii) The book of Ecclesiasticus (*c.* 176 BC), although it mentions Isaiah, Jeremiah and Ezekiel, is nevertheless silent as to Daniel. But this does not prove that Daniel had not yet been written. For Ecclesiasticus does not mention Asa, Jehoshaphat, Ezra, Mordecai, and others. But even if the existence of the book of Daniel were unknown to the author of Ecclesiasticus, which is very unlikely, this does not prove that the book had not yet been written.

(xiii) It is said that the unknown author of Daniel erroneously thought that after the downfall of Babylon there was an independently existing Median empire. Hence, critics of the negative school assert that Daniel's four kingdoms are: Babylonia, Media, Persia, Greece. In support of this erroneous charge three arguments are generally adduced.

a. A Median king is said to have ruled after Belshazzar. True, the king who ruled after Belshazzar was of Median ancestry. That is all Daniel says about him. To deduce from this that a Median empire was in control is to read into Daniel what is not found there.[13]

b. A racial distinction between Cyrus and Darius is said to be repeatedly emphasized. But only once (6:28) is Cyrus called a Persian, twice Darius is called a Mede (5:31; 11:1) and once he is said to be of the seed of the Medes (9:1). These passages simply show that the two men were of different racial ancestry. How does it follow from this that there was an independent Median empire just preceding the Persian empire?

c. It is claimed that 5:28 means that Belshazzar's kingdom is to

---

[13] Wilson (*Studies in the Book of Daniel*, II, 1938, p. 261) well remarks, 'The statement that Darius was a Mede no more proves that he was king of Media than does the statement that Napoleon was a Corsican prove that he was king of Corsica. Besides he may have been a king of Media and still have been a subordinate to Cyrus king of Persia. Murat was a Frenchman who was made king of Naples and was subordinate to a Corsican Italian who had become emperor of the French.'

fall partly to the Medes and partly to the Persians. But this interpretation is absolutely precluded by the fact that in the immediately succeeding context, when Darius *the Mede* is on the throne, he is subject to the laws of Media and Persia. Thus, in this very context, Medo-Persia is regarded as a unit. The mention of Darius the Mede, therefore, is not evidence of confusion or inaccuracy upon the part of the author of Daniel.

(xiv) It is also claimed that the language of Daniel proves that the book must have been written long after the sixth century BC. We have already considered this argument in part in connection with the Persian word 'satrap'. There are also present other Persian words in the section of Daniel which deals with the neo-Babylonian empire. Driver finds at least fifteen such words. But if Daniel wrote his book after the Persian conquest of Babylon, it is to be expected that he might have used such words, particularly to designate offices, institutions and the like. Nor does the presence of Greek words in Daniel 3 necessarily militate against Daniel's authorship.[14] For it is becoming increasingly clear that evidences of Greek culture penetrated into the Near East at a much earlier date than has hitherto been supposed.

As to the nature of the Hebrew and Aramaic languages, it may be said that there is nothing in them which in itself necessarily precludes authorship by Daniel in the sixth century BC. But it is quite possible that the Hebrew portions of Daniel were modernized, possibly by Ezra and the scribes, and this also may have been the case with the Aramaic portions. On the other hand, as Baumgartner and others have shown, the grammatical forms (*Formenbildung*) of the Aramaic portions of Daniel do contain much that is old. The recently discovered (1929) texts from Ras Shamra also contain Aramaic elements, which in some respects have relation to the Aramaic of Daniel. Thus, Daniel in certain instances spells words with d instead of z (*e.g.*, *dehav* for *zehav*). This peculiarity in the orthography has been regarded as an evidence for a late date for Daniel. But precisely this same phenomenon appears upon the texts from Ras Shamra (fifteenth century BC). Hence, our judgments with respect to the Aramaic of Daniel may have to be revised. At least it is becoming more and more clear that the languages cannot be employed as arguments against the antiquity of the book. The defender of the genuineness of Daniel is not required to prove that the Aramaic was that spoken in the sixth century in Babylon. It is not necessary to make such a claim, nor would such a claim be justified.

(xv) The theology of the book is also said to point to an age after the

---

[14] These words may have come into the book by way of Persia. See Hans Heinrich Schalder, *Iranische Beiträge*, I (1930).

exile, particularly with respect to the doctrines of the Messiah, angels, resurrection, and judgment. These, says Driver, 'are taught with greater distinctness, and in a more developed form than elsewhere in the Old Testament, and with features approximating to (though not identical with) those met with in early parts of the Book of Enoch, *c.* 100 BC.'[15] But this objection is by no means sufficient to overthrow the early date of Daniel.

The doctrine of the Messiah appears in germ form from the very beginning (Gn. 3:15) and permeates the entire Old Testament. This is true, even though the designation Messiah appears outside of Daniel only in Psalm 2. The Book of Enoch apparently speaks of the Messiah under the symbolism of a white bull with large horns (90:37). This is utterly unlike the representation in Daniel. In the doctrine of angels Daniel is similar to Enoch only in that he mentions Gabriel and Michael by name. Enoch says much more than does Daniel. Further, the doctrine of angels also appears throughout the Old Testament. The doctrine of the resurrection is found in several passages of the Old Testament (*e.g.*, Is. 26:19; 53:10; Ezk. 37; Jb. 19:25; 1 Ki. 17; 2 Ki. 4). Only in 12:2 does Daniel mention the resurrection, and this is not similar to the mention of Enoch 25; 90:33. The book of Enoch, like Daniel, states that there will be a judgment, but so also do certain other books of the Old Testament (*e.g.*, Is. 42:1–4; Joel 3:9–17; Ps. 1:5; 9:7, 8; 68:14; 76:9). The argument from the theology of Daniel, therefore, cannot be used to prove a late post-exilic date for the book.

By way of conclusion it may be said that whereas there are difficulties in holding that the book of Daniel was written in the sixth century BC by Daniel himself, nevertheless, the arguments generally adduced against this position are not of sufficient weight to overthrow it.

PURPOSE

The book of Daniel seeks to show the superiority of the God of Israel over the idols of the heathen nations. Although these nations had been God's instruments in punishing Israel, nevertheless they themselves will in time pass from the scene. In the latter days the God of heaven will erect a kingdom that will never be destroyed. Although the end of the indignation will be a time of persecution for God's people, the Messiah will come, and the eternal kingdom will be established. Daniel, then, may be said clearly to teach the sovereignty of God in His dealing with human kingdoms.

[15] *LOT*, p. 477.

ANALYSIS

1. Chapter 1. Introduction to the entire book. Nebuchadnezzar besieges Jerusalem and among the captives whom he brings to Babylon are four youths who are trained for service at the court. By refusing to partake of the appointed food of the king they show the triumph of God's grace, and make remarkable progress in their training.

2. Chapter 2. Nebuchadnezzar is troubled by a dream in which he has seen a colossus. The wise men cannot interpret his dream, but the interpretation is revealed to Daniel. The king is told that the colossus represents four kingdoms, human in origin, and temporal and limited in scope. While they exist, the God of heaven will set up an eternal and universal kingdom.

There are three principal interpretations of these kingdoms.

I	II	III
1. Babylon	Babylon	Babylon
2. Medo-Persia	Media	Medo-Persia
3. Greece	Persia	Greece
4. The successors of Alexander	Greece	Rome

Of these, III alone can be correct. I is held principally by Stuart and Zoeckler. II is held by critics of the negative school. III is really supported by the New Testament.[16]

3. Chapter 3. Nebuchadnezzar erects a golden image in the plain of Dura and requires that his subjects, upon penalty of death, shall worship it. Certain Chaldeans inform the king that Shadrach, Meshach, and Abednego have not worshipped the golden image. Nebuchadnezzar commands the accused men to be brought before him and asks if the accusation is true. He repeats his edict, whereupon they reply that their confidence is in God. In rage the king commands that the furnace be heated seven times hotter than is customary and that the three be cast into its midst. These commands are carried out. But in the furnace the king sees the men unharmed and accompanied by a Fourth. He thereupon commands them to come forth and blesses their God.

4. Chapter 4. Nebuchadnezzar, being troubled by a dream, summons his wise men who are unable to tell the dream. Daniel is brought in and relates the dream, which is to the king's disadvantage. The dream is

[16] For the arguments in defence of this view see my article 'The Identity of the Fourth Empire'* in *CD*, pp. 275-294.

then fulfilled upon the king who, for a season, is bereft of his sanity. Upon his recovery he praises the God of Daniel.

5. Chapter 5. Belshazzar the king makes a great feast, during which a miraculous writing appears upon the wall of the palace. Daniel interprets the writing as a warning of doom to Belshazzar. The warning is fufilled, and Belshazzar is slain.

6. Chapter 6. Darius the Mede follows upon the throne after Belshazzar. Aroused by jealousy certain rivals of Daniel devise a plot to destroy him. Daniel is accused of violating the law of the Medes and Persians and is cast into a den of lions from which he is miraculously delivered.

7. Chapter 7. In the first year of Belshazzar Daniel has a vision in which he sees four great beasts. These beasts represent the same kingdoms as the image of chapter 2. However, an enlargement is made upon the revelation of chapter 2. It is here revealed that the fourth empire has a threefold history. On the head of the fourth beast are ten horns which symbolize ten kings or kingdoms. These represent the second stage in the beast's history. There comes up a little horn which uproots three of the ten horns and utters great things against God, making war with the saints. However, as in chapter 2, God also erects a kingdom, eternal and universal, which is given to the heavenly Figure who is 'like unto a son of man'. When finally the little horn seems to have overcome the saints of the Most High, God intervenes, and the fourth beast (in its entirety) is destroyed, the saints receiving the kingdom.

8. Chapter 8. Under the symbolism of a ram and a he-goat, Daniel in a vision sees the Medo-Persian empire destroyed by Greece under Alexander the Great. When Alexander perishes, the kingdom is divided, which fact is represented by the four horns. From one of these four comes forth a little horn. This horn (Antiochus Epiphanes) becomes great and opposes the people of God. At last he is cut off 'without hand'.

9. Chapter 9. Daniel has studied Jeremiah's prophecy concerning the seventy years of exile. He prays to God, making confession of the sins of his people. Chapter 9:4–20 is regarded by Eissfeldt and others as a late addition. But his prayer is earlier than Nehemiah 9, which is more expanded.

Gabriel answers Daniel's prayer with the famous prophecy of the 'Seventy Weeks'. A period of sevens – the exact length of the seven is not stated – in fact, seventy of them, has been decreed for the purpose of accomplishing the Messianic work. This Messianic work is described in both negative and positive terms; negative – restraining the transgression, completing sin, and covering iniquity; positive – bringing in everlasting righteousness, sealing vision and prophet, and anointing a holy of holies. Daniel, therefore, is to know and understand that from the going forth of a word to restore and build Jerusalem to an anointed one who is also a prince (*i.e.*, a royal priest) is seven sevens and sixty and two sevens. We are not told when this word went forth from the Lord but the effects of its being issued first appear in the return from bondage during the first year of Cyrus. This period is divided into two. The first period of seven sevens is evidently intended to include the time from the first year of Cyrus to the completion of the work of Ezra and Nehemiah, and the second that from the completion of the work of Ezra and Nehemiah to the first advent of Christ who alone can be described as an Anointed One, a Prince. During this entire period the city will be completely rebuilt, although this will be accomplished during times of distress and affliction.

After the expiration of these two periods, two events are to occur. Whether or not these two events fall within the seventieth seven is not immediately stated. One of them is the death of the Messiah and the other follows as a consequence, the destruction of Jerusalem, and the Temple by the Roman armies of Titus.

For the period of the seventieth seven the Messiah causes a covenant to prevail for many, and in the half of this seven by His death He causes the Jewish sacrifices and oblation to cease. His death is thus seen to belong within the seventieth seven. Consequent upon this causing of the sacrifices and oblation to cease is the appearance of a desolator over the pinnacle of the Temple, which has now become an abomination. Upon the ruins a determined full end pours out. This event, the destruction of the city, does not, therefore, take place within the seventy sevens, but follows as a consequence upon the cutting off of the Messiah in the seventieth seven.[17]

10. Chapter 10. A divine message is revealed to Daniel, which serves as an introduction to the revelation given in chapters 11 and 12.

11. Chapters 11 and 12. The wars between the kings of Egypt (Ptolemies) and those of Syria (Seleucids) are depicted. Emphasis is then placed upon the rise of Antiochus Epiphanes to power, his campaigns against Egypt and his severe persecution of the people of God. The rise of Antichrist and his warfare is then described. Daniel is commanded to seal up the book and the prophecy is concluded.

THE TWO LANGUAGES OF THE BOOK

2:4b–7:28 is composed in Aramaic, whereas the remainder of the book is

---

[17] The foregoing explanation of the 'Seventy Weeks' is taken from my *Prophecy of Daniel* (Grand Rapids, 1949), p. 220.

Hebrew. What is the reason for this use of two languages? Various attempts have been made to answer this question. Bevan, for example, maintained that the entire book was originally written in Hebrew, a part of which had become lost and was replaced by an Aramaic translation. Others have held that the original was Aramaic and that the Hebrew portion is a translation. Rowley believes that chapters 2–6 were written in Aramaic during the Maccabean age. At a somewhat later time the same author also composed chapter 7 in Aramaic. He found, however, that the Hebrew language was more suitable for the visions, and so for the visions of chapters 8–12 he used Hebrew. Since he wished the book to appear as a unit he wrote the introduction over again in Hebrew. Some scholars who do not hold to the unity of authorship of the book believe that the first six chapters appeared as an older book of sagas written in Aramaic. It must then be assumed that the author of the visions began his work in Aramaic and then changed to Hebrew. For some reason he also wrote 1:1–2:4a in Hebrew.

Of these theories Rowley's is by far the most satisfactory, but even it fails because it posits the late date for composition of Daniel. There does not appear to be any truly satisfactory explanation of the two languages. The explanation which seems to be freest from difficulty is that the use of two languages was deliberate and intentional upon the part of the author. Aramaic was used for those parts which dealt primarily with the world nations, and Hebrew for those which treated principally the future of the kingdom of God. This view is surely not free from difficulty, but on the whole it appears to be the most satisfactory.

SPECIAL LITERATURE ON DANIEL

G. Ch. Aalders, *Het Herstel van Israel Volgens het Oude Testament** (Kampen, n.d.); Oswald T. Allis, *Prophecy and the Church** (Philadelphia, 1945), pp. 111–128; Sir Robert Anderson, *The Coming Prince, the Last Great Monarch of Christendom** (London, 1881); *Daniel in the Critic's Den** (New York, n.d.); K. A. Auberlen, *The Prophet Daniel and the Revelation of John** (ET by Adolph Saphir; Edinburgh, 1856); W. Baumgartner, 'Ein Vierteljahrhundert Danielforschung', in *ThR*, pp. 59–83, 125–144, 210–228; G. Boutflower, *In and Around the Book of Daniel** (1939, London, 1923); *Dadda'dri, or The Aramaic of the Book of Daniel** (London, 1931); E. W. Hengstenberg, *Die Authentie des Daniel und die Integrität Sacharjah** (1831; ET, 1848); *Christology of the Old Testament,*[2]* III (1858), pp. 77-264; Hertlein, *Der Daniel der Römerzeit* (1908); Junker, *Untersuchungen über literärische und exegetische Probleme des Buches Daniel* (1932); J. Kennedy, *The Book of Daniel from the Christian Standpoint** (London, 1898); Philip Mauro, *The Seventy Weeks and the Great Tribulation,** revised edn. (Swengel, Pa., 1944); E. B. Pusey, *Daniel the Prophet** (New York, 1891); H. H. Rowley, *Darius the Mede and the Four World Empires in the Book of Daniel* (Cardiff, 1935); 'The Bilingual Problem of Daniel', in *ZAW*, 50, 1932, pp. 256–268; M. Thilo, *Die Chronologie des Danielbuches* (1926); Adam C. Welch, *Visons of the*

End (London, 1923); J. C. Whitcomb, *Darius the Mede** (Grand Rapids, 1959); Robert Dick Wilson, *Studies in the Book of Daniel** (New York, Series I, 1917, Series II, 1938 – these two volumes constitute by far the best recent defence of the authority, genuineness and trustworthiness of the book of Daniel. They will serve as an admirable introduction to the study of the book); C. H. H. Wright, *Daniel and His Prophecies** (London, 1906).

ON THE THIRD YEAR OF JEHOIAKIM

Albertus Pieters, 'The Third Year of Jehoiakim',* in *From the Pyramids to Paul* (Grand Rapids, 1935).

ON THE WORD 'KING'

The available cuneiform is presented in R. Dougherty, *Nabonidus and Belshazzar* (New Haven, 1929). The best criticism of the historicity of Daniel's usage of the word 'king' is by H. H. Rowley, 'The Historicity of the Fifth Chapter of Daniel', in *JTS*, XXIII, pp. 12–31. For the opposite position see Edward J. Young, *The Prophecy of Daniel* (Grand Rapids, 1949).

ON THE ARAMAIC OF DANIEL

H. H. Rowley, *The Aramaic of the Old Testament* (Oxford, 1929); G. R. Driver, 'The Aramaic of the Book of Daniel', in *JBL*, 45, 1926, pp. 110–119, 323–325; W. Baumgartner, 'Das Aramaische im Buche Daniel', in *ZAW*, 1927, pp. 81–133; R. D. Wilson, 'The Aramaic of Daniel',* in *BTS*.

ON THE THEOLOGY IN DANIEL

R. D. Wilson, 'The Origin of the Ideas of Daniel',* in *Studies in the Book of Daniel*, II (New York, 1938), pp. 117–156.

CHAPTER TWENTY-EIGHT

EZRA AND NEHEMIAH

POSITION IN THE CANON

IN *Baba Bathra* 15a, Ezra and Nehemiah are regarded as one book; 'Ezra wrote his book'. But this does not mean that Ezra was also regarded as the author of Nehemiah, for in the *Gemara* we read, 'And who finished it?' To which question the answer is given, 'Nehemiah the son of Hachaliah'. This remark evidently would have us understand that Nehemiah completed the work by adding his own. The two books were also considered as one by Josephus (*Contra Apionem* i.8), Melito of Sardis (in Eusebius' *Ecclesiastical History* iv.26) and Jerome (*Prologus Galeatus*). The Vulgate calls Nehemiah the second book of Ezra (*liber secundus Esdrae*).

In a Hebrew manuscript of 1448 the division into two books was introduced, and this has been retained in modern Hebrew Bibles. However, even in modern Hebrew Bibles the Massoretic notes which give the number of verses in each book are placed after Nehemiah, and the middle verse is said to be Nehemiah 3:32.

In the LXX the two were united and given the title Esdras B to distinguish them from Esdras A, which is an Apocryphal book. Origen is the first to attest this division in the LXX.

The two books are indeed closely related, but the repetition of Ezra 2 in Nehemiah 7:6–70 shows that they were not one originally. One can only conjecture as to why the two came to be regarded as one. It may have been because Nehemiah continues the history of Ezra, or it may have been to make the total number of canonical books agree with the number of letters in the Hebrew alphabet.

THE RELATION BETWEEN EZRA AND NEHEMIAH

There are some scholars who deny the historicity of the exile and consequently also the restoration. Chief of these is C. C. Torrey, who thinks that the story of Ezra has no basis in fact. Gustav Hoelscher holds essentially the same position.

Largely through the influence of the Roman Catholic scholar A. Van

Hoonacker, who has written extensively upon the subject, some scholars, notably Batten and Père Lagrange, believe that the work of Nehemiah preceded that of Ezra. They would assign Nehemiah to the reign of Artaxerxes I (465–424) and Ezra to that of Artaxerxes II (404–359).

Van Hoonacker found it necessary to rearrange the biblical text as follows: Ezra 1:1–4:3; 4:24b–6:22; 4:4–24a; Nehemiah 1:1–7:5; 11:1–13:31; Ezra 7–10; Nehemiah 8–10. However, while the ministry of Nehemiah may be assigned to the reign of Artaxerxes I, as we believe it should be, it by no means follows that the work of Ezra is to be placed after this time. We shall therefore discuss the books in agreement with the traditional arrangement.

EZRA

NAME

The book is named in the Hebrew Bible after its principal character Ezra. In the LXX it bears the designation *Esdras deuteron*, and the Vulgate calls it the first book of Ezra (*liber primus Esdrae*).

AUTHOR

Although the book itself does not in its entirety claim to be the work of Ezra, nevertheless tradition seems to be justified in making such an assumption. For one thing, some of the book (chapters 7ff.) is written in the first person singular. It is quite possible that Ezra used these passages as a basis and added to them information obtained from other sources. The book bears the marks of unity, and if the 'I' sections are the work of Ezra, it would seem to follow that the remainder is his also.

Appeal cannot be made to the Aramaic portions in support of a date later than Ezra's time. For while the present Aramaic of Ezra may be later than that of Elephantine, this may simply be due to orthographical modification. However, this Aramaic may belong to the fifth century BC, and, even as it stands, may be the work of Ezra.

This view of authorship is not accepted by scholars of the negative critical school. Many of them maintain that the book is a compilation, which was made by the so-called 'Chronicler' long subsequent to the events which it records. The arguments against the authorship of the book by a contemporary are the following.

1. The title 'king of Persia' (Ezr. 1:1, *etc.*) is thought to be unnecessary

at a time when Persia was in the supremacy. The official title of the Persian kings, it is maintained, was not 'King of Persia', but 'the King', 'the great King', 'the King of kings', 'the King of the land', *etc.* This objection seems to have been first raised by Heinrich Ewald. When Ezra and Nehemiah speak in their own person or in passages which, according to negative criticism, go back to Persian times, they speak merely of 'the king'. In answer to this we cannot do better than to quote from the late Robert Dick Wilson, who made an exhaustive study of the subject. Dr. Wilson says, 'It is a sufficient answer to this assertion to say that eighteen different authors in nineteen different documents from Persian times use this title altogether thirty-eight different times, and of at least six different Persian kings; that it is used of Cyrus seven years before the conquest of Babylon in 539 BC and of Artaxerxes II about 365 BC; that it is used in Persian, Susian, Babylonian, Greek, Aramaic, and Hebrew; that it was used in Media, Babylonia, Asia Minor, Greece, and Palestine, according to Herodotus in Ethiopia; and that it is used in letters, dates, and other like documents of the Scriptures just as it is used in the extra-biblical documents. Further, it has been shown that it was not common for authors of the Greek period to use the title.'[1] The objection has been made that instances of the usage 'King of Persia' before the conquest of Babylon are irrelevant since at that time Persia was only a province of Iran. This objection is without validity, since the principle of the usage is the same, no matter what the size of Persia itself may have been.[2]

2. It is argued that the Hebrew (Ezr. 1:1–4) and the Aramaic (Ezr. 6:3–5) transmissions of the edict of Cyrus contain important differences, and hence both cannot be authentic. The authenticity of the second decree is generally maintained, but many deny the authenticity of the first because of its supposed Jewish colouring. Some regard the first edict as merely a Jewish forgery, whereas others have maintained that if Cyrus did issue such a decree, it passed unnoticed.

But no objection can be taken to the supposed Jewish colouring, for in proclaiming religious freedom to the Babylonians, Cyrus had also used the name of their god Marduk. 'The entirety of all the lands he [*i.e.*, Marduk] surveyed and examined. He sought out a righteous prince, the desire of his heart, who would grasp his hand. Cyrus, the king of Anshan, whose name he uttered, he called for kingship over all.'[3] Furthermore, it

---

[1] *A Scientific Investigation of the Old Testament* (1926), pp. 202–203.

[2] For a full discussion of this problem the reader should consult R. D. Wilson, 'The Title "King of Persia" in the Scriptures',* *PTR*, 15, 1917, pp. 90–145, and 'Royal Titles in Antiquity: An Essay in Criticism',* *PTR*, 2, 1904, pp. 257–282, 465–497, 618–664; 3, 1905, pp. 55–80, 238–267, 422–440, 558–572.

[3] R. Dougherty, *Nabonidus and Belshazzar* (1929), pp. 175–179.

appears that Cyrus was influenced by the prophecy of Isaiah 40ff.
Moeller calls attention to Isaiah 45:13, *ha'irothihu*, and also to Isaiah
41:15; 44:28; 45:1ff. Kittel[4] maintained that Isaiah knew the Persian
court style, but there is also the possibility, as Moeller points out, that he
helped to form this style.[5]

The question must now be raised whether the two edicts are the same.
The edict of Ezra 6 was found not in Babylon but in Persia (Ecbatana).
However, it does agree essentially with the policy of the earlier edict. The
earlier edict is designated in Aramaic as *qol* (1:2), the latter as *te'em* (6:3).
The first is addressed to all the people; the second seems to be without
such address, being apparently intended rather to serve as an official
record to be preserved and to which appeal might be made. In 6:14 a
distinction is made between the decree of God and the decree of Cyrus,
Darius, and Artaxerxes. This appears to show that the two are different
decrees. In Ezra 1:1,2 Cyrus is called the king of Persia, but in 5:13 king
of Babylon.

The earlier proclamation was evidently made when Cyrus had first
conquered Babylon. Since it had to do with Jews, it had a Jewish
colouring, just as the edict quoted above, since it has to do with Babylonia,
has a Babylonian colouring. The second edict was evidently the formally
drawn-up record of the decree, to be deposited in the official house of
records in Ecbatana. Hence, both are to be regarded as historical and
authentic.

3. The section 4:6–23 is said to be out of place. These verses refer to
the time of Ahasuerus (Xerxes, 485–465 BC) and Artaxerxes I. It is said
to be confusing that such an account should occur before events in the
time of Darius (verse 24). A table will make clear the nature of the
problem.

> 4:1–5 – time of Cyrus the Great
> 4:6 – Xerxes
> 4:7–23 – Artaxerxes
> 4:24 – Darius the Great
> 5:1–17 – Darius the Great

Before discussing the merits of this arrangement, we would remark that
it does not follow from this disposition of the material that the writer
thought that the Samaritan schism occurred in 536. The purpose of
Ezra is to trace the history of opposition to the building in its entirety.

[4] 'Cyrus und Deuterojesaja', *ZAW*, 1898, pp. 149ff.

[5] For an introduction to this subject see Jacob William Behr, *The Writings of Deutero-
Isaiah and the Neo-Babylonian Royal Inscriptions* (1937). See also Elias J. Bickerman, 'The
Edict of Cyrus in Ezra I', in *JBL*, 1946, pp. 249–275.

Hence, we are told (4:1–5) that this opposition appeared throughout the reigns of Cyrus and Darius. The writer then continues by saying that this opposition was found even during the days of Xerxes. More than that, it reached its culmination in the time of Artaxerxes I, when a letter of complaint was sent to the king, and Artaxerxes commanded that the work of building should cease. This was the whole history of the controversy. The writer then reverts to the time of Cyrus and states that the work ceased until the time of Darius. Chapter 5 continues with the subject. When the purpose of the writer is taken into account, namely, to finish one subject before going on to the next, even at the expense of chronological sequence, how can objection be legitimately raised? When the text is carefully read, the alleged confusion disappears.

4. The statement (Ezr. 3:3) that the people offered the daily sacrifices upon the altar *before* the Temple was built is thought to be unhistorical. But why? Haggai 2:14 presupposes just this action. Also, in itself the action is very likely. If it were such an utterly foolish thought, would not the 'Chronicler', assuming that he had any sense at all, have refrained from mentioning it?

5. In Ezra 3:8 it is stated that the Levites began service at the age of 20, whereas the Pentateuch specified that they should not serve before the twenty-fifth or thirtieth year (Nu. 4:3; 8:24). But if there is a contradiction here (which there is not) it surely is strange that the 'Chronicler' would thus dare to deviate from the 'Priestly writing' which is supposed to have influenced him so greatly. The passages in Numbers refer to the age of those Levites who served in the Tabernacle. 1 Chronicles 23:24 and 31:17, and Ezra 3:8 refer to service in the Temple.

6. The book is said to be in confusion as to the time when the building of the Temple commenced. According to 4:24 and 5:1ff. it began in the second year of Darius, but according to 3:8–13 and 5:16 in the reign of Cyrus. However, it is not the book of Ezra that is in confusion, but modern critics of the destructive school who think that there is an inconsistency or contradiction between these two sets of passages. The building of the Temple did begin in the days of Cyrus (3:8–13; 5:16). However, as related in 4:1–5, opposition to this project appeared almost immediately, and counsellors were hired to frustrate the purpose. The result was that work on the house of God ceased until the days of Darius (4:24). Since it had ceased, God sent the prophets Haggai and Zechariah to arouse the people to renewed interest, with the result that the work began again (4:24; 5:1ff.).

7. The statement in Ezra 5:13–17 that the Temple had been in building since the time of Sheshbazzar (verse 16) is said in the light of Haggai

2:15 to be false. But Haggai does not deny that there had been work upon the Temple before his time. In 1:4 he speaks of the Temple in such a way as to imply that whereas the people were dwelling comfortably, the Temple was lying waste (1:9, 'mine house that is waste'). And the phrase 'did work in the house' (*wayya'asu mela'ka beveth yehowah*, 1:14) seems to imply that there was something there already when they began to work. Furthermore, Ezra 5:16 does not state that the building was carried on without interruption, but that it was not completed (*wela shelim*). (The participle *mithbene'* does not imply that there was no interruption.)

8. The genealogy of Ezra (7:1-10) is said by Pfeiffer to be a 'worthless concoction of the Chronicler'.[6] The genealogy is said to be in error in making Zadok a son of Ahitub, and also in making Ezra a son of Seraiah, since Seraiah is said to have died at the capture of Jerusalem (2 Ki. 25:18-21), hence Ezra would be about 127 years old when he went to Jerusalem.

But in answer to this it may be pointed out that where Ezra and Chronicles (1 Ch. 6:3-14, 50-53) make Zadok a son of Ahitub, so also does 2 Samuel 8:17. That Ahiah or Ahimelech was also a son of Ahitub is perfectly possible (*cf.* 1 Sa. 14:3; 22:9, 11, 20). And in calling Ezra the son of Seraiah, the writer obviously uses the word 'son' in the sense of descendant (as, *e.g.*, in Mt. 1:1).

9. The phrase 'after these things' in Ezra 7:1 is said to be strange, if the entire book were the work of one writer, since immediately preceding this there is an interval of over sixty years. The phrase 'after these things', it is thought, suggest events that were nearer the time of that which is related in 7:1. But this does not follow at all. The phrase 'after these things', taken in itself, does not imply how long a time had elapsed since 'these things' had occurred. Furthermore, 7:1 dates the next recorded event as in the reign of Artaxerxes.

10. Verses 1 and 13 of Ezra 10 shows that there was a large population in Palestine. From this it is argued that such would only have been the case in the days of Nehemiah, hence Nehemiah must have preceded Ezra. Otherwise, it is claimed, we must assume that from Ezra's time onwards the population was dwindling. But this by no means follows. At the time of Ezra the people were poor and needed help from the royal treasury (Ezr. 7:20), whereas in Nehemiah's time the Jews were able themselves to support the Temple worship (Ne. 10:32ff.). Furthermore, the language of verses 1 and 13 need not be pressed to conflict with other statements of the book. It is certainly applicable to those who were in Palestine during Ezra's ministry.

[6] *IOT*, p. 825.

DATE OF EZRA'S MINISTRY

It now seems clear that the ministry of Ezra is to be placed during the reign of Artaxerxes I (465-424 BC). The evidence for this is briefly as follows. The Elephantine papyri (c. 408 BC) makes mention both of the high priest Johanan and of Sanballat the governor of Samaria. This Johanan was a grandson of the Eliashib mentioned in Nehemiah 3:1, 20, and Nehemiah was a contemporary of Eliashib. Now it is said that Nehemiah went to Jerusalem in the twentieth year (445) and in the thirty-second year of Artaxerxes. In the light of the Elephantine papyri this can only have been Artaxerxes I. Since Ezra preceded Nehemiah, and since he went to Jerusalem in the seventh year of Artaxerxes, it would follow that his journey is to be dated in 458 BC.

Against this it is not to be argued (as do Oesterley and Robinson) that Ezra lived at the time of Johanan the grandson of Eliashib (Ezr. 10:6), and hence somewhat later than Nehemiah. For it should be noted that the Johanan of 10:6 is said to be the son of Eliashib. This is evidently not Johanan the high priest of later time, but probably the son of Eliashib, mentioned in Nehemiah 13:4, 7. If, however, he is the later high priest, he is here mentioned merely in private character, since he was not yet high priest. If he were the later high priest, why may he not be mentioned here as a youth, heir to the office, and so having a chamber by the Temple?

PURPOSE

This work serves the purpose of giving an account, from the religious or priestly points of view, of the restoration of the nation to its land. It lays its emphasis upon the establishment of the people in the land as a kingdom of priests and a holy nation which is to walk in the light of the law.

ANALYSIS

a. *Ezra 1:1–2:70. The first return of the exiles*

   1. 1:1–4. Cyrus makes his proclamation.

   2. 1:5–11. The people respond to Cyrus' edict. Offerings are made for the project, and Cyrus restores the vessels of the Temple.

   3. 2:1–70. The first exiles return, under Zerubbabel and Joshua. If this chapter be compared with the list given in Nehemiah 11:1–13:3, it will be observed that there are some numerical differences. These, however, are to be explained as due to copyists' errors in the course of the transmission of the text.

b. Ezra 3:1–6:22. The restoration of the worship of Jehovah

1. 3:1–3. In the seventh month the people gather at Jerusalem and the altar of burnt offering is erected. The people then offered their offerings to the Lord.

2. 3:4–7. The offerings are renewed, and the Feast of Tabernacles observed.

3. 3:8–23. In the second month of the second year of the return, work is begun upon the Temple itself. This work is accompanied with praise and thanksgiving, but many of those who had seen the Temple of Solomon weep.

4. 4:1–5. The adversaries of Judah and Benjamin first seek to help in the building of the Temple. But Zerubbabel rejects their aid, whereupon they hire counsellors to frustrate the purpose of the returned exiles. This continues until the reign of Darius the Persian.

5. 4:6–24. Opposition comes during the reigns of Xerxes and Artaxerxes I. A letter is sent to Artaxerxes, with the result that the work is brought to a stop. A similar effect had been produced even during the days of Zerubbabel, for in verse 24 we read that the work on the Temple ceased even until the second year of Darius.

6. 5:1–17. Haggai and Zechariah stir up the people to work upon the Temple. Opposition appears, and the matter is referred to Darius. Verses 6–17 contain a copy of the letter which is sent to Darius.

7. 6:1–12. Darius searches for Cyrus' decree, and himself decrees that the work on the Temple is to continue.

8. 6:13–16. The edict of Darius is obeyed, and on the third day of Adar, in the sixth year of the reign of Darius, i.e., 515 BC, the Temple is finished.

9. 6:17–22. The Temple is dedicated, and on the fourteenth day of the first month the Passover is observed, and this is followed by the Feast of Unleavened Bread.

c. Ezra 7:1–10:44. The return under Ezra

1. 7:1–10. The book now skips over many years in order to introduce the reader to the events which are connected with Ezra in the reign of Artaxerxes. Ezra's lineage is given and he is described as a ready scribe in the Law of Moses. In the fifth month of the seventh year of Artaxerxes he comes to Jerusalem.

2. 7:11–26. Artaxerxes gives Ezra a commission.

3. 7:27–28. Ezra blesses God for the king's commission.

4. 8:1–14. A list of those who went up to Jerusalem with Ezra in the seventh year of Artaxerxes is given.

N

5. 8:15–20. Ezra gathers the chiefs together at the river by Ahava and there the people remain for three days.

6. 8:21–36. At the river of Ahava Ezra proclaims a fast. On the twelfth day of the first month the people leave Ahava to go to Jerusalem

7. 9:1–14. Ezra mourns when he learns that the people have not separated themselves from the world, but have intermarried with the inhabitants of the land.

8. 9:5–15. Ezra prays.

9. 10:1–17. Ezra undertakes reform.

10. 10:18–44. A list of those among the priests who had taken strange wives is given.

NEHEMIAH

NAME

In modern Hebrew Bibles the book is named after its principal character, *Nehemyah*. In the LXX the name appears as *Neemias*, and in the Vulgate as *Liber Nehemiae* or *Liber secundus Esdrae*.

AUTHOR

The author of the book was Nehemiah himself as appears from the usage of the first person pronoun. The book records Nehemiah's mission to Jerusalem and the reforms which he instituted there. Unlike Ezra, Nehemiah was a layman. Yet his work served to complement that of Ezra, and the two were used of God in the establishing of the post-exilic Jewish nation.

By many critics of the negative school Nehemiah is regarded as the last portion of the great historical work of the so-called Chronicler. However, high regard is usually paid to the 'memoirs' of Nehemiah, although critics differ as to their extent. They are thought to have been worked over by the final compiler of the book. The reasons why it is thought that Nehemiah himself cannot have been the author of the entire book are the following:

1. In Nehemiah 12:11, 22 mention is made of Jaddua who was high priest from 351–331 BC when Alexander the Great entered the city. But it should be noted that these references occur in a list of the priests and Levites which may have been a later addition. It is not necessary to assume this, however, since Jaddua is not here mentioned as the high

priest. It is perfectly possible that Nehemiah may have lived to see the youthful Jaddua, a great-grandson of Eliashib, since he does mention a grandson of Eliashib as married, the son-in-law of Sanballat (Ne. 13:28).

2. In Nehemiah 12:22 Darius the Persian is mentioned, and since he is thus connected with Jaddua, he is said to be Darius Codomannus (336–332 BC). But if the reference is merely to Jaddua as a youth and not as high priest, the king in question may be Darius Nothus (424–395 BC).

3. Nehemiah 12:26, 47 is said to mention 'the days of Nehemiah' as a period that has long been past. But in reply we may note that the phrase is in each instance used in conjunction with the day of someone else: Jehoiakim (verse 26), Zerubbabel (verse 47). Hence, it would seem natural for Nehemiah to employ a similar phrase with reference to his own time.

ANALYSIS

a. Nehemiah 1:1–7:73. Nehemiah restores the city walls of Jerusalem

1. 1:1–2:20. Introduction. Nehemiah begins speaking in the first person: 'And it came to pass in the month Chislev, in the twentieth year, as I was in Shushan the palace', *etc.* Thus the date and setting are given. Word is brought to Nehemiah that the Jews in Palestine are in great affliction and reproach, and that the walls have been broken down and the gates burned with fire. Nehemiah grieves over this news, and prays to God to show mercy to him. He then introduces himself as the king's cup-bearer. The prayer is answered. In His mysterious providence God brings it about that the king should ask why Nehemiah's countenance is sad. Nehemiah explains the situation, and the king permits him to go to Jerusalem. After his arrival in the holy city Nehemiah waits three days, and then by night makes a tour of the walls of the city.

2. 3:1–6:19. The rebuilding of the city walls. The high priest Eliashib takes the initiative, and with the other priests begins to build the Sheep Gate. Chapter 3 contains a list of those who worked upon the various gates of the city and the places where they worked.

Opposition soon appears, however, for Sanballat mocks the Jews. Tobiah the Ammonite also ridicules them by saying that the wall is so weak that if a fox should go upon it, he would break it down. These men conspire to stop the work upon the walls. Nevertheless, Nehemiah cries to God and fortifies the men for the work. Some build and some guard, and thus they continue. But the stratagem and opposition of Sanballat continues. The wall, however, is finally completed after fifty-two days. This entire account is told by Nehemiah in the first person.

3. 7:1–73. Nehemiah now gives to his brother Hanani and to Hananiah the charge over the city of Jerusalem. There follows a list of the people who had returned from Babylon.

b. Nehemiah 8:1–13:31. The reforms of Ezra and Nehemiah

1. 8:1–10:39. The covenant is renewed. Ezra reads the Law of Moses to the assembled people, and they confess their sins and ratify the covenant. Julius Wellhausen and others have taught that this section contains in reality an account of how the Law of Moses was canonized. But a careful reading of the passages shows that such an interpretation is incorrect.

2. 11:1–36. This chapter contains a list of those who dwelt in Jerusalem. The rulers of the people are to dwell there and also one out of every ten.

3. 12:1–26. A list of the priests and Levites is given.

4. 12:27–43. The walls are dedicated.

5. 12:44–47. The people support the priests.

6. 13:1–31. Nehemiah visits Jerusalem a second time.

SPECIAL LITERATURE ON EZRA AND NEHEMIAH

James Oscar Boyd, 'The Composition of the Book of Ezra',* *PRR*, XI, 1900, pp. 261–297; 'The Documents of the Book of Ezra',* *ibid.*, pp. 414–437; 'The Historicity of Ezra',* *ibid.*, pp. 568–607; Millar Burrows, 'Nehemiah's Tour of Inspection', *BASOR*, LX, 1936, pp. 11–21; A. Fernandez, 'Epoca de la actividad de Esras', *Biblica*, II, 1921, pp. 424–427; 'La voz gader en Esd. 9:9', *ibid.*, XVI, 1935, pp. 82–84; 'Esd. 9, 9 y un texto de Josefo', *ibid.*, XVIII, 1937, pp. 207ff.; W. H. Kosters, *Het Herstel van Israel in het Perzische Tijdvak* (Leiden, 1893); Edward Meyer, *Die Entstehung des Judentums* (Halle, 1896); Sigmund Mowinckel, *Ezra den Skriftlarde und Statholderen Nehemia* (Kristiana, 1916); H. H. Schaeder, *Ezra der Schreiber* (1930); Charles Cutler Torrey, *The Composition and Historical Value of Ezra-Nehemiah* (1896); *Ezra Studies* (Chicago, 1910); A. Van Hoonacker, 'Notes sur l' histoire de la restauration juive après l'exil de Babylone', *RB*, 1901, pp. 5–26, 175–199; 'La succession chronologique Nehemie-Esdras', *ibid.*, 1923, pp. 481–494; 1924, pp. 33–64; Adam C. Welch, *Post-Exilic Judaism* (Edinburgh, 1935); J. Stafford Wright, *The Date of Ezra's Coming to Jerusalem** (London, 1946); and *The Building of the Second Temple** (London, 1958).

CHAPTER TWENTY-NINE

THE BOOKS OF CHRONICLES

NAME

IN the Hebrew Bible the two books of Chronicles form a single work and bear the title 'the words of the days' (*divere hayyamim*). As is seen from Chronicles 27:24, the term is used in the sense of annals. The LXX divided the book into two and called them *Paraleipomena, i.e.,* things omitted or passed over. Jerome interpreted the Hebrew title as *verba dierum* ('words of the days'), and suggested that the books might be more significantly called a chronicle of the entire divine history (*chronicon totius divinae historiae*). He says that they were commonly designated *Paralipomenon primus* and *secundus*.[1]

AUTHOR

According to *Baba Bathra* 15a, 'Ezra wrote the genealogy of Chronicles unto himself' (*adh lo*). This Jewish tradition thus attributes the authorship of Chronicles to Ezra and by the words 'unto himself' possibly intends us to understand that Ezra continued the history down to his own time.

What may be said of the value of this opinion? It must be remarked that in the light of passages such as 1 Chronicles 3:19–21 and 2 Chronicles 36:22, 23, the books cannot have been composed before Ezra's time.

When, however, one compares the conclusion of 2 Chronicles with the opening verses of Ezra, it appears that the opening verses of Ezra are taken from Chronicles (not *vice versa*). The edict is expanded or given in fuller form in Ezra, and one or two minor changes are made. Now, if an editor had added this edict to Chronicles, why did not he make the wording in both instances identical?

A comparison of the two edicts, therefore (2 Ch. 36:22, 23 with Ezr. 1:1–4), seems to show that Chronicles is earlier than Ezra. But this, of course, is not decisive. The language of Chronicles shows that it comes from the general period of Ezra, and we may date the book in the latter half of the fifth century BC, probably between 450 and 425. It is quite possible that Ezra was the author.

[1] *Prologus Galeatus, PL,* xxviii, col. 554.

It appears to be rather generally accepted among scholars today that, together with Ezra and Nehemiah, the books of Chronicles originally formed a single work. The reasons usually adduced in support of this view are that (1) the same religious standpoint, centring about the Temple and priesthood, is found in all these works; (2) the same predilection for statistical records and genealogies appears in all these works; (3) the language and style of the books are similar. (4) The similarity between the conclusion in Chronicles and the beginning of Ezra is thought to show that the books were originally one. It is suggested by Oesterley and Robinson that at first only Ezra and Nehemiah were admitted into the Canon. This left Chronicles without a proper conclusion. Later when Chronicles was admitted it was deemed fitting to provide the book (which was not placed immediately preceding Ezra and Nehemiah) with a conclusion, and, in so far as they ended upon a note of triumph, the opening verses of Ezra served as such a conclusion.

With respect to the above, we may say that these arguments do support the view that all these books were written from the same standpoint, and they also strengthen the view that Chronicles was written by Ezra. But they do not prove by any means that all the books were originally one. And it is difficult to see how, if these books were originally one, only a part was at first recognized as canonical and then later the other part came to be so recognized but was placed, not in its original position *before* Ezra and Nehemiah, but *after* them. This is fanciful and most improbable, and without any foundation in fact. Further, why did the editor or final redactor insert Ezra 1:1–4 in an *altered* form? Why did he not merely insert it word for word?

Here appears the great problem which faces those who think that the books were originally one. How did these books come to be separated and placed in their present order, and how did it happen that the conclusion of Chronicles and the beginning of Ezra are so similar? Up to this time no satisfactory answer to these questions has been given.

Not only are Chronicles and Ezra and Nehemiah generally regarded as originally having formed one work, but the date of this work is often placed in the latter half of the fourth century or even later. Pfeiffer would date it at about 250 BC. Many of these arguments have to do with Ezra and Nehemiah, and these we shall consider in the proper place. It is often argued that Ezra and Nehemiah are late, and since Chronicles was originally part of them, it also must be placed late. But this is to beg the question. Are there in Chronicles itself indications which prove that it comes from the fourth century or later? This, and this alone, is the question which is relevant to the present discussion. Two arguments are generally adduced to show that Chronicles belongs, at least, later than 350 BC.

1. Chronicles 3:19–24 is said to carry on the genealogy of David down to the sixth generation after Zerubbabel (to the eleventh generation in the LXX). If Zerubbabel be dated at about 520 BC, and if we allow twenty years to a generation, it would carry us down at least to 400 BC, and hence, so the argument runs, the book cannot have been written before that time. But to argue thus, as so many have done, is to be guilty of reading into the passage what is not found there. A careful reading of the verses in question shows that the genealogy of Zerubbabel is carried on for only two generations after him.

The genealogy is carried on to Pelatiah and Jesaiah, grandsons of Zerubbabel. Then (in verse 21b) follows the mention of four families which were probably contemporaries of Pelatiah and Jesaiah and were somehow related to the Davidic line. But, what in this connection is of importance to observe, *they do not carry on the line of Zerubbabel for four generations.*

2. In 1 Chronicles 29:7 mention is made of the daric, a Persian coin. It is said that this coin was named after Darius I (died in 486), and that the presence of this coin in Palestine points to a time well on into the Persian period. But it is by no means certain that this coin (*adarkonim*) was named after Darius I. Apparently it appeared also during the time of Nabonidus. At any rate, even if it had been named after Darius, it certainly would have been in circulation during the latter part of the fifth century BC. This appeal to the daric really proves nothing with respect to the disputed dates for Chronicles.

William F. Albright has argued that the author of Chronicles was Ezra and that he composed the book sometime between 400 and 350 BC.[2] Although this view has not yet found a wide acceptance, nevertheless Albright has presented it so capably that his arguments must be taken into account in any serious discussion of the question.

In 1939 Adam C. Welch published a series of lectures on Chronicles which calls for particular mention. Welch thinks that the books are not homogeneous, but reveal the presence of more than one hand. He professes to find two strands, each revealing a different viewpoint. One is a self-consistent narrative, containing the history of Judah from the accession of David, and omitting all mention of the northern kingdom. It parallels Samuel and Kings, and although containing new material,

2 'The Date and Personality of the Chronicles', *JBL*, 40, 1921, pp. 104–124. This article contains a particularly valuable discussion of the genealogy in 1 Ch. 3:19–21.

nevertheless has unity and outward cohesion. The second strand, however, does not form a continuous narrative, but contains mere fragments,
which, when separated from their context, present no coherent meaning.
Their cohesion consists in their attitude and viewpoint. Thus, Chronicles
consists of an original narrative which at a later date had been subjected
to careful annotation and revision.

The annotation belonged to the generation which followed the return
from captivity, and hence the original work was earlier and must be
regarded as one of the programmes put forth for the settlement of the
difficult questions which faced the post-exilic nation. Like all Welch's
work, this book is stimulating and helpful, and we rejoice in the emphasis
upon an early date. But we cannot accept any view which denies the
unity of the books, since the evidence does not favour such a procedure.

THE SOURCES OF CHRONICLES[3]

For the information contained in the early genealogies, 1 Chronicles
1–9, the writer made use of old statistical lists which had survived the
downfall of Jerusalem and the exile. Only the patriarchal genealogies
could have been taken from the canonical scriptural books, for elsewhere
the deviation in order and arrangement is so great that the lists were
obviously taken from the sources that are not now preserved for us. Very
few of these genealogies find parallels elsewhere in the Scriptures.

In regard to the historical narratives which are also found in Samuel
and Kings, these latter books are not to be regarded as the source. This is
seen from the fact that the passages in Chronicles contain many details
which are not found in Samuel and Kings and they also often differ in
arrangement of the material. In fact, it may justly be said that they
follow a course of their own. Hence, since each historical narrative
exhibits a peculiar point of view, it seems best to regard them as each
having been taken from a common source.

Compare, *e.g.*, 1 Chronicles 10 with 1 Samuel 31. These seem to agree
almost word for word, yet note the difference in verses 9 and 10:

Chronicles	*Samuel*
9. And when they had stripped him, they took his head, and his armour, and sent into the land of the Philistines round about, to carry tidings unto their idols, and to the people.	9. And they cut off his head, and stripped off his armour, and sent into the land of the Philistines round about, to publish it in the house of their idols, and among the people.
10. And they put his armour in the house of their gods, and fastened his head in the temple of Dagon.	10. And they put his armour in the house of Ashtaroth: and they fastened his body to the wall of Beth-shan.

[3] In discussing this subject I have followed Keil very closely.

Is it not obvious that each of these is written from a certain standpoint? Chronicles stresses what was done with the head, whereas Samuel emphasizes what happened to the body. Compare also in this connection 2 Chronicles 2 with 1 Kings 5; 2 Chronicles 8 with 1 Kings 9:10–28; 2 Chronicles 32 with 2 Kings 18 and Isaiah 36–38; 2 Chronicles 3, 4 with 1 Kings 6 and 7.

For his treatment of the history of David the author mentions the following source: 'The words of Samuel the seer, of Nathan the prophet, and of Gad the seer' (1 Ch. 29:29).

The source mentioned for the history of Solomon is: 'The words of Nathan the prophet, the prophecy of Ahijah the Shilonite, and the visions of Iddo the seer against Jeroboam the son of Nebat' (2 Ch. 9:29).

For the kingdom of Judah, mention is made of: 'The book of the kingdoms of Judah and Israel' (16:11); 'The book of the kings of Judah and Israel' (25:26; 28:26; 32:32); 'The book of the kings of Israel and Judah' (27:7; 35:27; 36:8); 'The book of the kings of Israel' (20:34); 'The words of the kings of Israel' (33:18); 'The story [midrash] of the book of the kings' (24:27).

There seems good reason to believe that the first five of the foregoing titles are but variant designations of the same work. Evidently this history contained essentially the same material as did the chronicles of the kings of Judah and Israel which are mentioned in the canonical books of Kings, since the extracts in both cases are in such great agreement. The last title (midrash) is also to be regarded as a designation of the same work. The author of Kings quotes the annals of the kingdoms as two separate works, but evidently the history had been worked up into one volume or book which lay before the Chronicler and which he could designate Midrash. Keil points out that the history of Joash in Chronicles, compared with 2 Kings 11 and 12, shows that the works were the same.

Other sources mentioned for the history of Judah are: 'And the remainder of the words [deeds] of Uzziah, the first and the last did Isaiah, the son of Amoz, the prophet, write' (26:22); 'The words of Shemaiah the prophet and of Iddo the seer' (12:15); 'The midrash of the prophet Iddo' (13:22); 'The words of Jehu the son of Hanani' (20:34); 'The words of Hozai' (33:19).

Of the above it should be noted that 'the words of Jehu' is said to have been 'inserted [ho'alah] upon the book of the kings of Israel'. Apparently, therefore, the other works still remained distinct from this history. Also, this historical work from which the author of Chronicles drew was compiled not only from historical but also from prophetical writings.

According to adherents of the Wellhausen school, the books of Chronicles have little historical value. The reason for this depreciatory estimate is basically philosophical. Since these books present a picture of Israel's history which is at variance with the Wellhausen conception of what that history was, they are rejected as trustworthy sources of history.

Robert H. Pfeiffer,[4] one of the most recent and competent advocates of this viewpoint, argues that Chronicles is both a sequel and a supplement to the so-called priestly code. It carries on the history from where P ends to the time of Nehemiah. It also describes the levitical institutions in such a manner as to bring them into accord with the actual practices of the Chronicler's day. In Pfeiffer's opinion the Chronicler is an epigonous imitator who cannot be compared with the Priestly author as a creative thinker. As a historian he is, in fact, a disciple of this Priestly author, but his history is limited to the Jewish kingdom in the late period. He deliberately adopted the methods and principles which he found in the P history, and in his work exhibited a similarity which extends even to details. Like this Priestly author, the Chronicler is thought to have lived during a time of peace since he is said to have no knowledge of real battle. The stories of battle were manufactured by the Chronicler to show how God controlled history. Pfeiffer regards these books, therefore, as apologetical and polemical utterances, written in defence of the Levites and designed to enhance the prestige of the Levites.

Similarly, after their discussion of the religious standpoint of the author of Chronicles, Oesterley and Robinson remark, 'From what has been said it will be clear that not much importance can be attached to the history as presented in Chronicles' (p. 118). And Cornill has even gone so far as to say that 'the picture drawn by the Chronicler is in no respect historical' (p. 239), and he also alludes to 'what, in modern language, would be called the falsification of history in Chronicles' (p. 239). Eissfeldt is more moderate. He thinks that the books have considerable value as sources of information about the time in which the Chronicler himself lived, namely, the third and fourth centuries BC. The narratives may even have some value for a study of previous history, as, for example, the account of Manasseh's visit to the Assyrian king (2 Ch. 33:11-13), which may be a trustworthy account.

These estimates of the value of Chronicles must all be rejected because they are based upon a theory of the history of Israel which is at variance

4 *IOT*, pp. 785-801.

with the Christian religion. It will be necessary, however, to consider in more detailed fashion the principal objections which are generally raised against the trustworthiness of Chronicles.

a. Objections which have been raised against the sections of Chronicles that parallel the books of Samuel and Kings
The following is a list of parallel passages (based upon Keil):

1 Ch.	10:1–2	1 Sa.	31
	11:1–9	2 Sa.	5:1–3, 6–10
	11:10–47		23:8–39
	13:1–14		6:1–11
	14:1–7, 8–17		5:11–16, 17–25
	15, 16		6:12–23
	17		7
	18		8
	19		10
	20:1–3		11:1; 12:26–31
	20:4–8		21:18–22
	21		24
2 Ch.	1:2–13	1 Ki.	3:4–15
	1:14–17		10:26–29
	2		5:15–32
	3:1–5:1		6; 7:13–51
	5:2–7:10		8
	7:11–22		9:1–9
	8		9:10–28
	9:1–12, 13–28		10:1–13, 14–29
	9:29–31		11:41–43
	10:1–11:4		12:1–24
	12:2, 3, 9–16		14:21–31
	13:1, 2, 22, 23		15:1, 2, 6–8
	14:1, 2; 15:16–19		15:11–16
	16:1–6, 11–14		15:17–22, 23, 24
	18:2–34		22:2–35
	20:31–21:1		22:41–51
	21:5–10, 20	2 Ki.	8:7–24
	22:1–6, 7–9		8:25–29; 9:16–28;
	22:10–23:21		10:12–14
	24:1–14, 23–27		11
	25:1–4, 11, 17–28		12:1–17, 18–22

26:1–4, 21–23	14:1–14, 17–20
27:1–3, 7–9	14:21, 22; 15:2–7
28:1–4, 26, 27	15:33–36, 38
29:1, 2	16:2–4, 19, 20
32:1–21	18:2, 3
32:24, 25, 32, 33	18:13–19:37
33:1–10, 20–25	20:1, 2, 20, 21
34:1, 2, 8–28, 29–32	21:1–9, 18–24
35:1, 18–24, 26, 27	22; 23:1–3
36:1–4	23:21–23, 28, 29–34
36:5, 6, 8–12	23:36, 37; 24:1, 5, 6, 8–19
36:22, 23 Ezr.	1:1–3

1. Particular exception is taken to the use of numbers in Chronicles. Cornill compares the Chronicler with a 'seven-figure champion [*Messer millone*], he flings about his hundred thousands and millions in this way wherever the bare attempt to give concrete representation to the things described is sufficient to demonstrate their utter impossibility'. Driver's judgment is more moderate. He speaks of the figures as 'incredibly high'. What may we say about the usage of numbers in Chronicles?

In 2 Chronicles 13:3 Judah has 400,000 chosen men, and Israel 800,000. Of these latter 500,000 (verse 17) were slain. Asa had an army of 580,000 (2 Ch. 14:8), and Zerah the Ethiopian a thousand thousand and 300 chariots (verse 9). In 1 Chronicles 21:5 we read that Israel had 1,100,000 men and Judah 470,000, whereas in 2 Samuel 24:9 Israel had but 800,000 and Judah 500,000.

These examples will suffice. In approaching the problem, we must insist that the writer would not deliberately have sought to make his work appear ridiculous. And this would be so, particularly if this writer were the 'Chronicler' of destructive criticism. If he were writing a propaganda work, would he not have tried to make his history appear as genuine as possible? If it were true that he was without knowledge of real warfare, would he not have sought to learn something about it before writing? Otherwise, what would be accomplished by thus writing? Would he not have defeated his own purpose? We may, there-fore, approach this subject with the conviction that the Chronicler did not deliberately or through ignorance (the work is too superb for that) make his writing appear ridiculous.

(i) It should be noted that the numbers given are round numbers, apparently representing only approximate estimates. Only thousands are taken into account, and the intention, apparently, is merely to indicate the greatness of the armies. Thus, when Zerah's great host (2 Ch. 14:8) is said to consist of thousand thousands (*'eleph 'alaphim*), the text does not mean that he had precisely a million men in his army. This would surely be strange in comparison with only 300 chariots. Rather, the text means that Zerah had a vast army. The LXX interprets correctly 'in thousand thousands'.

(ii) While the numbers in Chronicles are usually larger than those in Samuel or Kings, sometimes they are smaller. Thus, 1 Kings 4:26 mentions 40,000 stalls for Solomon's horses, whereas 2 Chronicles 9:25 has 4,000. 1 Chronicles 11:11 has 300 instead of 800 as in 2 Samuel 23:8. 1 Chronicles 21:12 has three years for the seven years of 2 Samuel 24:13.

(iii) Most of these differences in numbers as well as the size of the numbers in Chronicles are found also in the LXX. Hence, they were in existence before the settlement of the text by the Massoretes. In early times numbers were sometimes represented by letters of the alphabet. It is quite probable, therefore, that somewhere along the line these letters were misunderstood, and the numbers written out in full. This may account for some of the difficulties as far as the numerals are concerned. In such a case textual errors may very easily have been introduced. The following, for example, are probably to be explained upon such a basis: 1 Chronicles 18:4 with 2 Samuel 8:4; 2 Chronicles 3:15; 4:5 with 1 Kings 7:15, 26; 2 Chronicles 13:3, 17 and 17:4ff., in which the numbers in the passages of Chronicles are obviously too large. Corruptions in the transmission of the text have doubtless had a great deal to do with the situation.

(iv) Even though we, today, are not in a position to explain satisfactorily precisely how the textual errors in the numerals may have arisen, it must be remembered that these numerals, since they are so isolated, cannot shake the general historical credibility of Chronicles. There are so many passages which are in accordance with historical fact that these few numbers are not sufficient to bring against the Chronicler the charge of 'unhistorical' or 'not trustworthy'.

2. The charge is frequently made that, out of apologetical interest, statements derogatory to David and Solomon have been omitted by the Chronicler. Thus, as the most notable example, the account of David's adultery (2 Sa. 11:2–12:26) is omitted in Chronicles, as is also the account of Solomon's idolatry (1 Ki. 11). It may be that we, today, cannot explain why these things, and other derogatory acts also, were omitted from the parallel accounts of Chronicles. But it certainly is not likely that this was done out of any apologetical interest. It would have

been pointless to attempt to conceal such blemishes in the characters and actions of the kings, since the Chronicler names the sources from which he derived his information. Now, if these sources were in part the canonical books of Samuel and Kings, as negative criticism (wrongly, I believe) holds, could not any devout Jew turn to these canonical books to discover the truth? Further, it should be noted that the author sometimes alludes to events which he does not narrate (*e.g.*, 1 Ch. 19:19; 29:22 – the *second* time). 2 Chronicles 11:2-4 implies that the reader knows of the sin of Solomon. 2 Chronicles 17:3 ('The *first ways* of his father David') shows that the later fall of David was perfectly well known. Nehemiah 13:26 (which, according to negative criticism, is the work of the Chronicler) states that outlandish women caused Solomon to sin.

Again it should be noted that almost everything which bears on the private lives of David and Solomon is omitted. This refers even to praiseworthy deeds, such as David's anger at those who murdered Abner and Ishbosheth (2 Sa. 3:22-4:12), and his magnanimity towards the house of Saul (2 Sa. 9). David says that because he has been a man of war and had shed much blood he is not permitted to build the Temple (1 Ch. 22:8; 28:3). And the picture of Solomon's wisdom and magnificence, given in 1 Kings 3, 4, is omitted in Chronicles.

In the light of the above considerations we may say that, whatever the reason for the omission of certain events or derogatory actions of David and Solomon may have been, it was not because of apologetical interests.

3. It is sometimes maintained that Chronicles is the 'first apology of Judaism'. The reason for passing over the history of Israel in almost complete silence is that this latter is thought to be irrelevant to the history of the sacred nation, or else the omission is said to be due to the Chronicler's hatred of Israel. But the reason why the Chronicler omitted the history of the northern kingdom is not that he hated that kingdom nor that the history of that people was irrelevant for the history of the sacred nation. The reason is that the Chronicler (under divine inspiration) did not regard as essential to his purpose such a treatment of Israel's history (see under Purpose below).

b. Objections which have been raised against the sections of Chronicles which do not parallel Samuel and Kings[5]

The levitical genealogy of 1 Chronicles 6 has been criticized very severely. Thus Pfeiffer remarks, 'Although the Levitical genealogies

[5] This section deals with objections raised against the historicity of the levitical genealogies in 1 Ch. 6. Although some of the material contained in this list appears also in Samuel and Kings, nevertheless a parallel list as such does not occur there, and for that reason I have dealt with it under this heading.

may include some historical characters, they are concocted on the basis of the artificial genealogies in the Priestly Code for two purposes: to provide a mutual blood relationship for the various classes of Temple functionaries, and secondly, to prove that the ecclesiastical organizations of the middle third century can trace their origin to David if not to Moses himself, and are therefore valid.'[6]

1. It is said that the Chronicler transforms the Ephraimite Samuel and the Gittite Obed-edom into genuine Levites. But is this true? Samuel is nowhere pictured as an Ephraimite, in the sense of being a lineal descendant of Ephraim. In 1 Samuel 1:1 Elkanah (Samuel's father) is said to be from Ephraim, *i.e.* Ramathaim-zophim. But this is not to say that he was descended from Ephraim. Hence, the Chronicler does not, as charged, turn an Ephraimite into a Levite.

As for Obed-edom, he was called a Gittite because he belonged to the levitical city Gath-rimmon (Jos. 21:24). Hence, in this case also there is no evidence of the Chronicler turning anyone into a Levite.

2. Obed-edom is said to be 'at the same time a Philistine captain of David hailing from Gath (I 13:13), a gatekeeper (I 15:18, 24), the eponym of a guild of gatekeepers (26:4–8, 15), a member of a guild of harp players (15:21; *cf.* 16:5), and, in the same verse (16:38 patently annotated), both musician and gatekeeper'.[7] All of this is urged to show that the levitical genealogies are fictitious. But neither in 1 Chronicles 13:13 nor anywhere else in the Bible is Obed-Edom said to be 'a Philistine captain of David hailing from Gath'. He is merely said to be a Gittite, and there seems to be no doubt that this refers to the levitical Gath-rimmon. In 1 Chronicles 15:18, 24 Obed-edom simply serves as a gatekeeper (*shoarim*) for the ark while it was being brought into Jerusalem. This Obed-edom is obviously to be distinguished from the man of the same name in verse 21, since it is clear that one man could not perform the two tasks at the same time. In 1 Chronicles 16:38 the two appear to be distinguished. The text of this latter passage, however, is apparently defective as it stands, a fact for which the Chronicler is not to be blamed. In summation, then, we may say that the statements made about Obed-edom do not prove the levitical genealogies fictitious.

3. The case of Ethan is also supposed to show these genealogies to be fictitious. He is said to have been an Edomite sage (1 Ki. 4:31). He is thought to be the author of Psalm 89 and, finally, to have become a Levite (1 Ch. 6:42, 44). But there is not sufficient evidence to show that Ethan was changed into a Levite by the Chronicler. I do not know what the designation 'the Ezrahite' means. It is by no means clear that Ethan

[6] *IOT*, p. 799.   [7] Pfeiffer, *op. cit.*, p. 800.

the Ezrahite is to be identified with the Ethans of 1 Chronicles 6, Ethan the son of Zimmah (verse 42), or Ethan the son of Kishi (verse 44; cf. 15:17, the son of Kushaiah).

4. Pfeiffer further argues that the lineage of the high priests from Levi to the fall of Jerusalem in 586 is twenty-six generations (1 Ch. 6:1–15). In the lineage of a singers' guild, however, twenty-two generations are listed from Levi to Heman (a contemporary of David) and only four generations for the entire time between David and the downfall of Jerusalem (1 Ch. 6:33–38). This again is supposed to show the un-historical character of the genealogies.

However, instead of being an argument against the genuineness and historical character of the levitical genealogies, these lists are strong arguments for the very opposite. Had some mere editor composed these lists for the most part out of his imagination, he would have taken care of any supposed discrepancies. It is obvious that the genealogy of the singers is given in the greatest detail. Since it stops with Heman, we have no idea how many generations the writer thought should be included between the time of Heman and the downfall of Jerusalem. In giving the list of priests for the period between Levi and David the writer saw fit to include only fourteen names. It may be that he intentionally passed over some generations (if, as some critics think, the Chronicler was the author of Ezra, he certainly passed over some generations in Ezr. 8:1–5). Lastly, it should be noted that the genealogy of Heman traces his ancestry back, not to Levi, but to Israel. Hence, these lists which the Chronicler has left are not to be regarded as valueless concoctions of the imagination, but as accurate records of sober history.

PURPOSE

By stating the view of the purpose of Chronicles which is advocated by the school of negative criticism, and thus seeing what the purpose is not, we can perhaps come to see more clearly what the purpose really is. In the first place, we are told that the Chronicler is not a historian and his work is not history. The Chronicler's purpose was, we are told, to defend Judaism against the claims of the Samaritans and the pretensions of the Gentiles. He sought to prove that the Judaism of the third century BC was the only true one, and to accomplish this he appealed both to its antiquity and to its wonderful achievements. But to prove his case he had in part to fabricate the evidence. Hence he attributes the origin of the sacred institutions to men such as Moses or David.

With this statement of the purpose of Chronicles we find ourselves in hearty disagreement, for this statement is based upon the assumption that the books are not historically trustworthy, and this assumption, we have endeavoured to show, is not justifiable. It is perfectly true that the writer had a religious aim. The exiles had now returned from Babylon, and through his work the writer sought to show them the true glory of their nation as the theocracy and to show them the rights and importance of the Davidic dynasty.

It is because of this purpose that the writer uses his materials in the manner that he does. He therefore passes over the history of the northern kingdom practically in silence, and in the life of David he treats principally those events which have to do with the nation's worship on Zion and which are preparatory to the erection of the Temple. For this reason also, in the life of Solomon, it is the Temple and its dedication, rather than personal events in Solomon's life, which receive the central emphasis. For this same reason also he stresses the work of those kings who opposed idolatry, as Asa, Jehoshaphat, Hezekiah and Josiah, and he brings into prominence the formal worship of the theocracy, the Temple singers, the Levites and their functions, and all that had to do with such worship. He stresses the importance of the Davidic dynasty because of its value for the well-being of the theocracy. By reminding the people of the glory of that which God has given them, he hopes to convince them that true weal and blessing will come only by obedience to the theocratic principles which God has established.

This does not mean that the books are valueless as history. Nor does it mean that facts have been distorted to accomplish an apologetical aim. The books were written for a specific purpose, one that was noble and praiseworthy. And they were designed to accomplish that purpose, not by foul, but by fair means. They are true history.

ANALYSIS

a. *1 Chronicles 1:1–9:44. Genealogical material*

 1. 1:1–54. Generations of patriarchal times.
 2. 2:1–3:24. The twelve sons of Israel.
 3. 4:1–23. The family of Judah.
 4. 4:24–43. The sons of Simeon.
 5. 5:1–26. The sons of Reuben, Gad and Manasseh.
 6. 5:27–6:66. The families of Levi.
 7. 7:1–40. The families of Issachar, Benjamin, Naphtali, half Manasseh, Ephraim, Asher.
 8. 8:1–40. Benjamin; genealogy of Saul's house.
 9. 9:1–44. Family of Saul.

b. *1 Chronicles 10:1–29:30. The reign of David*

    1. 10:1–14. The last days and death of Saul.

    2. 11:1–12:40. The capture of Jerusalem. David's heroes.

    3. 13:1–16:43. The ark brought from Kirjath-jearim to Zion. David's psalm of gratitude to God.

    4. 17:1–27. David forbidden to build the Temple. His throne to be established.

    5. 18:1–20:7. The account of David's conquests.

    6. 21:1–22:1. The numbering of the people.

    7. 22:2–19. Preparations for building the Temple.

    8. 23:1–26:32. Arrangement of the Levites.

    9. 27:1–34. Organization of the government.

    10. 28:1–29:30. David's last instructions and his death.

c. *2. Chronicles 1:1–9:31. The reign of Solomon*

    1. 1:17. The theophany at Gibeon. Wisdom and wealth of Solomon.

    2. 2:1–18. Solomon's preparations for building the Temple.

    3. 3:1–5:1. The building of the Temple.

    4. 5:2–7:22. The dedication of the Temple.

    5. 8:1–9:28. Various activities of Solomon.

d. *2 Chronicles 10:1–36:23. The history of Judah to its fall*

    1. 10:1–12:16. The revolt of the tribes and the reign of Rehoboam.

    2. 13:1–22. The reign of Abijah.

    3. 14:1–16:14. The reign of Asa.

    4. 17:1–20:37. The reign of Jehoshaphat.

    5. 21:1–20. Joram's reign.

    6. 22:1–12. Ahaziah and Athaliah.

    7. 23:1–24:27. The reign of Joash.

    8. 25:1–28. Amaziah.

    9. 26:1–23. The reign of Uzziah (Azariah).

    10. 27:1–9. The reign of Jotham.

    11. 28:1–27. The reign of Ahaz.

    12. 29:1–32:33. The reign of Hezekiah.

    13. 33:1–25. Manasseh and Amon.

    14. 34:1–35:27. The reign of Josiah.

    15. 36:1–23. The destruction of Judah and the captivity.

SPECIAL LITERATURE ON CHRONICLES

Kerr, D. Macmillan, 'Concerning the Date of Chronicles',* in *PRR*, XI, pp. 507–511;
Adam C. Welch, *The Work of the Chronicler: Its Purpose and Its Date* (London, 1939).

BIBLIOGRAPHY

Periodicals

Bulletin of the American Schools of Oriental Research
Biblica
The Expository Times
The Journal of Biblical Literature
The Journal of Theological Studies
Theologische Literaturzeitung
Theologische Rundschau
The Westminster Theological Journal*
Zeitschrift für die alttestamentliche Wissenschaft
Book List of The Society for Old Testament Study
Internationale Zeitschriftenschau für Bibelwissenschaft und Grenzgebiete
Svensk Exegetisk Arsbok
Hebrew Union College Annual

Works and General Commentaries

The Commentaries of John Calvin on the Old Testament* (Grand Rapids).
These are exegetical and reveal a profound understanding of the meaning of the biblical books.
(KD) Keil and Delitzsch* (ET, Grand Rapids). These commentaries represent the best of conservative Protestant thought.
(ICC) The International Critical Commentary (New York). Philological and thorough.
(WC) The Westminster Commentary Series (London).
(SL) The Schaff-Lange Series.* An English translation of Lange's *Bibelwerk*.
The Interpreter's Bible (Nashville and New York). Good material in the introductions, but the exegetical treatment is not satisfactory.
(OTL) Old Testament Library (London).
(TC) Tyndale Old Testament Commentaries* (London).
The New Bible Dictionary* (London).
The Biblical Expositor* (Glasgow).
Albrecht Alt, *Kleine Schriften zur Geschichte des Volkes Israel* (I, München, 1953; II, München, 1953; III, München, 1959).
Otto Eissfeldt, *Kleine Schriften* (I, Tübingen, 1962; II, Tübingen, 1963).

IN GERMAN

(KHAT) Kurzgefasstes exegetisches Handbuch zum alten Testament (Leipzig).
(KKHS) Kurzgefasster Kommentar zu den heiligen Schriften des Alten (und Neuen) Testaments (Munich).
(HKAT) Handkommentar zum Alten Testament (Göttingen).

(*KHC*) *Kurzer Hand-commentar zum Alten Testament*, edited by Karl Marti.
(*KAT*) *Kommentar zum Alten Testament* (Leipzig).
(*HAT*) *Handbuch zum Alten Testament* (Tübingen).
(*SAT*) *Die Schriften des Alten Testaments in Auswahl* (Göttingen).
(*EHAT*) *Exegetisches Handbuch zum Alten Testament* (Münster) (Roman Catholic).
(*HSAT*) *Die Heilige Schrift des Alten Testaments* (Bonn) (Roman Catholic).
(*BKAT*) *Biblischer Kommentar Altes Testaments* (Neukirchen).
(*ATD*) *Alte Testament Deutsch* (Göttingen).

IN DUTCH

(*KV*) *Korte Verklaring der Heilige Schrift** (Kampen).
(*COT*) *Commentaar op het Oude Testament** (Kampen).
De boeken van het Oude Testament (Roermond en Masseik).

IN ITALIAN

(*SB*) *La sacra Bibbia* (Turin) (Roman Catholic).

IN FRENCH

La Sainte Bible (Jerusalem) (Roman Catholic).

IN NORWEGIAN

Det gamle testamente (Oslo).

Commentaries on Individual Books

The abbreviations refer to the above series. I have mentioned books from these series only when they seem to be particularly noteworthy.

GENESIS

Calvin*; Delitzsch, 1899; Dillmann (*KHAT*, 1892, ET, 1897); Driver (*WC*, 1931); Gunkel (*HKAT*,[5] 1892); Heinisch (*HSAT*, 1930); B. Jacob, *Das Erste Buch der Torah* (Berlin, 1936); Keil* (*KD*); E. Koenig (Guetersloh, 1925); H. Leupold* (Columbus, 1942); J. Murphy* (Andover); O. Procksch (*KAT*, 1923); J. Sikkel* (Amsterdam, 1906); Skinner (*ICC*, 1930); Von Rad (*BKAT*, 1953); Von Rad (*OTL*, 1961).

EXODUS

Dillman (Exodus–Leviticus, *KHAT*); Heinisch (*HSAT*, 1934); Keyser (Grand Rapids, 1940); McNeile (*WC*, 1908); Murphy* (Andover, 1881); Noth (*OTL*, 1962).

LEVITICUS

Baentsch (Exodus–Numbers, *HKAT*, 1903); Heinisch (*HSAT*, 1935); Murphy (Andover, 1874); Strack (Genesis–Numbers, *KKHS*, 1894).

NUMBERS

Binns (*WC*, 1927); Heinisch (*HSAT*, 1936); Gray (*ICC*, 1912); Greenstone (Philadelphia, 1939 – an excellent popular commentary).

DEUTERONOMY

Dillmann (Numbers, Deuteronomy, Joshua, *KHAT*, 1886); Driver (*ICC*, 1902); J. Reider (Philadelphia, 1937 – forms an excellent introduction to the book); Steuernagel (*HKAT*, 1923).

JOSHUA

Holzinger (*KHC*, 1901); Noth (*HAC*, 1938).

JUDGES

Bertheau (*KHAT*, 1883); Budde (*KHC*, 1897); Burney (London, 1930); Moore (*ICC*, 1895); Nowack (*HKAT*, 1900).

SAMUEL

Caspari (*KAT*, 1925); Goslinga* (*COT*, 2 Samuel, 1962); Keil* (*KD*); Thenius (*KHAT*,3 by Loehr, 1898).

KINGS

Benzinger (*KHC*, 1899); Burney (Oxford, 1903); Eissfeldt (*HAT*); Keil* (*KD*); Kittel (*HKAT*, 1900); Landersdorfer (*HSAT*, 1927); Sanda (EHAT, 1911); Schloegl (Vienna, 1911); Thenius (*KHAT*, 1873).

ISAIAH

Alexander* (1846–7 – one of the finest commentaries on any biblical book); Delitzsch (*KD*); Dillmann-Kittel (*KHAT*, 1898); Duhm (*HKAT*, 1923); Feldmann (*EHAT*, 1925–6); Fischer (*HSAT*, 1937–39); Gray (*ICC*, 1912, on Isaiah 1–27); Kissane (Dublin, 1941–43); Koenig (Guetersloh, 1926); Orelli (*KKHS*, 1904); Volz (*KAT*, 1932); Wade (*WC*, 1912). In *SIJAA* I have listed the principal commentaries which have appeared between 1846 and 1946; Herntrich (*BKAT*, 1950).

JEREMIAH

A. Condamin (1936); Cornill (1905); Duhm (*KHC*, 1901); Keil* (*KD*); Orelli (*KKHS*, 1905); Rudolph (*HAT*, 1947); Volz (*KAT*, 1928).

EZEKIEL

G. Ch. Aalders (*COT*, I, 1955, II, 1957); Bertholet (*KHC*, 1897); Cooke (*ICC*, 1937); Ellison* (London, 1956); P. Fairbairn* (Edinburgh, 1863); Heinisch (*HSAT*, 1923); Hengstenberg* (*ET*, 1896); Herrmann (*KAT*, 1924); Keil* (*KD*); Kraetzschmar (*HKAT*, 1900).

THE TWELVE

Van Gelderen and Gispen* (*COT*, 1953, Hosea); Harper (*ICC*, 1905, Amos-Hosea); Keil* (*KD*); Nowack (*HKAT*, 1922); Orelli (*KKHS*, 1896); Pusey*; Robinson (*HAT*, 1936, Hosea-Micah); Sellin (*KAT*, 1930); Steiner (*KHAT*, 1881).

PSALMS

Alexander* (New York, 1861); Briggs (*ICC*, 1906–1907); Cales (Paris, 1936); Calvin*; Delitzsch* (*KD*); Gunkel (*KHAT*, 1926); Hengstenberg* (Edinburgh, 1857); Herkenne (*HSAT*, 1936); Koenig (Guetersloh, 1927); Oesterley; *The Psalms, Translated with Textcritical and Exegetical Notes* (London, 1939); J. Ridderbos* (*COT*, I, 1955, II, 1958); Weiser (*ATD*, 1955); Weiser (*OTL*, 1962).

PROVERBS

Delitzsch* (*KD*); Malan (London, 1889–1893); Miller (New York, 1872); Toy (*ICC*, 1899).

JOB

Delitzsch* (*KD*); Dillmann (*KHAT*, 1891); Dhorme, 1926; Driver-Gray (*ICC*, 1921); Hoelscher (*HAT*, 1937); Szczygiel (*HSAT*, 1931); Thilo (Bonn, 1925).

ECCLESIASTES

Aalders* (Kampen, 1948); Allgeier (*HSAT*, 1925); Hengstenberg* (ET, 1860); Hertzberg (*KAT*, 1932); Nowack (*KHAT*, 1883).

ESTHER

Paton (*ICC*, 1908).

SONG OF SOLOMON

Ginsburg, 1857; Zoeckler (tr. by W. H. Green in the Schaff-Lange series).

RUTH

Lattey (London, 1935); Rudolph (*KAT*, 1939, Ruth and Lamentations).

LAMENTATIONS

Loehr (*HKAT*, 1907); Paffrath (*HSAT*, 1932).

DANIEL

G. Ch. Aalders* (*COT*, 1962); Behrmann (*HKAT*, 1894); Bentzen (*HAT*, 1937); Beven (Cambridge, 1892); Charles (Oxford, 1929); Goettsberger (*HSAT*, 1928); Hitzig (*KHAT*, 1850); Keil* (*KD*); Leupold* (1949); Marti (*KHC*, 1901); Meinhold (*KKHS*, 1899); Montgomery (*ICC*, 1927); Prince (New York, 1899); Young* (Grand Rapids, 1949).

EZRA–NEHEMIAH

Batten (*ICC*, 1913); Keil* (*KD*).

CHRONICLES

Bertheau (*KHAT*, 1874); Curtis (*ICC*, 1910); Goettsberger (*HSAT*, 1939); Keil* (*KD*); Rothstein-Haenel (*KAT*, 1927); Schoegl (Vienna, 1911).

In addition to the above, attention may be called to a series of commentaries which is very valuable for the elementary student of Hebrew. These are issued by the Soncino Press, Surrey, England. These works contain the Hebrew text and English translation in parallel columns, together with useful comments from the Jewish point of view.

INDEX OF SCRIPTURE

NOTE: *The chapter on a given book or books of the Bible has not been indexed with reference to that book or books. For example, all references to Genesis in the chapter devoted to Genesis (Chap. 3) have not been included in this index. Similarly, all references to the minor prophets in the chapter on these prophets (Chap. 17) have not been here given.*

INDEX OF PERSONS AND PLACES

(including biblical names)

416

DATE DUE

12/9/74 NOV 2 1 1989	JAN 2 6 1990	
APR 8 '75 FEB 2 7 1990		
MAY 13 '75		
NOV 1 5 NOV 1 6 1990		
OCT 31 '78 DEC 1 3 1991		
DEC 5 7 MAR 2 3 1992		
JAN 3 MAY 2 3 1994		
JAN 1 5 '85 NOV 2 8 1995		
OCT 1 DEC 1 2 1995		
SEP 2 9 DEC 2 4 2005		
FEB 2 1988		
MAY 3 1988		